M.A.D.
Make A Decision

James "Bonecrusher" Smith

ISBN: 148208810X
ISBN-13: 978-1482088106

DEDICATION

This book is dedicated to my Momma and Daddy, Bertha and Jessie Smith. Without them I would not have a story. They were simple people who made sure that I respected others. They made sure I went to school and got an education. Momma and Daddy taught me the value of an education. To their credit, I graduated as the first Heavyweight Champion of the World with a college degree. I am their legacy and they have always been my inspiration.
Special thanks to my brothers and sisters who tolerated my eccentricities growing up in Magnolia:
Jesse Smith, Jr.,
Anthony Craig Smith,
Geraldine Bryant,
Cathy Gilliard, and Goldie Byrd.
Thank you to Reba Smith
who was married to me for 25 years.
Thank you my daughters,
Jamie Smith and Rachel Smith.
And my stepson, Raymond Dobson.

CONTENTS

ACKNOWLEDGMENTS

I would like thank James Sprunt Community College for being there for me when I started my college education. Special thanks to Shaw University for allowing me to continue my college education. There is not enough good things that can be said about these great institutions of higher learning.

1 FAMILY

This is the story of how I started from humble beginnings and with only a **seven day notice**, I fought for the WBA Heavyweight Boxing Championship of the World... and won.

My life began in April of 1953. I was born to Bertha and Jessie Smith on a sharecropper's farm in Magnolia, North Carolina. I was the third child among eight children. Bertha and Jessie did their best to raise and love all of us. Two of my sisters died at an early age which left me with five siblings.

I learned how to work on the farm doing simple chores like chopping firewood. Firewood was our main source of heat and it was my job to make sure the firewood was always chopped and stacked, so we would never be cold.

"Chopping and splitting logs during a snowstorm was not my idea of fun. I learned that a person could work up a sweat during a blizzard...and feel the sweat freezing on my collar at the same time."

The axe taught me some tough lessons. It was very hard work and that heavy axe would some days get the best of me. Everybody was counting on me to keep the house warm. Many nights, I went to bed tired with sore muscles.

Little did I know that the hard labor of chopping wood was building muscles and stamina that would later serve me in over 60 professional boxing matches.

The hard work on that little farm honed a champion's body that would later become known famously around the World as

"The Bonecrusher".

It was one thing to knock a man down in a boxing match. It was entirely another thing to break bones with rapid punches. It demoralizes the opponent and steals his will to fight.

Chopping wood with that heavy maul axe made both my hands powerful. There were other jobs around the farm that shaped my mindset from a very young age.

Dad had a produce business. That was his main income source. We grew potatoes, peanuts, collards and a myriad of other vegetables. All of the children would participate in growing the vegetables; tilling the land; and then harvesting the vegetables.

All of us helped in cleaning and preparing vegetables for our Dad to sell. We did not know that we were being trained to have a good work ethic. To us, it was a way of life. We were all hard workers around the farm and we knew what needed to be done in each season of the year.

That is important because there is a season for everything. There was a lot of heavy lifting which continued to make me stronger. There were bales of hay which I lifted out of the field and onto the back of a truck. Then the bales of hay needed to be stacked again at the barn. The hay was important to feed the farm animals throughout the year.
There were always bags of fertilizer that needed to be lifted and stacked. Don't even get me started talking about the sacks of peanuts, potatoes, corn, tobacco, beans...you get the picture.

I ate my share of those vegetables and meat that was raised on the farm. Chasing chickens for dinner was fun. Killing hogs in Winter was easier. Those were big, old hogs that weighed what seemed like 300 pounds at times. I had to give them a bang right between the eyes and they would fall.

It always amazed me that a behemoth as monstrous as those hogs would drop right down on their front knees when hit with a .22 shot between the eyes.

In my boxing career, sometimes the image of those giant hogs would come back to me when I faced giants in the ring. I would remember to hit them between the eyes and let the referee count them out.

In business I met those giants of adversity head-on with the same passion. Winning meant everything to me. If I was under pressure to perform in business, then I would stay focused and keep chopping away at the problem.

2 EDUCATION

My first introduction to education came at P.E. Williams Elementary School in Magnolia, NC.

When I was about six years old, I was a big cry baby. In school I was a little scrawny kid who was scared of everything. All I wanted to do was stay home with my Momma and Daddy.

One day, my parents instructed my older sister, Geraldine and my older brother, Jessie to drop me off at my first grade teacher's class. It was the **first day of school** and nobody told me. They picked me up and that was the first I knew about it. The first grade teacher was a no-nonsense kind of woman. She heard me crying and said I was annoying the class. That teacher had an old fan belt that she used to whip the children. The fan belt had come off of an old car and she had seen another use for that belt, right away.

The teacher told me to turn my butt around...so she could put the fan belt on it. I was already crying, "Please don't beat me!"

She whipped me anyway. She felt like I was disrupting the class . Then to add insult to injury, she sent me home with a note, saying that I got a beating in school.

The rule in our house was...if you got a beating in school...you got one more at home. My Momma said, "Odell, Go get me a switch." I am going to whup you because you got a whupping in school." Momma always called me by my middle name, Odell.

I went to get a switch and returned for my whupping.

When Daddy came home I got *another* whupping. Daddy whupped me with his belt. It was more than I could stand and I did not deserve it. After the third beating I stopped crying.

I got mad.

I made a decision. I made two decisions:

One: **I was going to school**.
Two: **I was going to whup me somebody if I ever got grown.**

Those unfair beatings caused me to decide that one day I was going to whip somebody.

I got mad. I was angry and someday, somebody was going to pay for it.

When you get mad, you feel like you've been violated and you want to strike out at anybody.

That was the first time I ever got mad. That anger marked me for life. I wasn't taking any more beatings from anybody. If they could not hit me harder than my Daddy, they were going to be in big trouble.

I guess you could say the rest is history.
I whupped a lot of people in 18 years of boxing from 1981-1999. I had over 60 professional fights.

So, my first day of school consisted of a whupping on my backside with that fan belt, followed by more whuppings when I got home from school. My first grade teacher was a holy terror as far as I was concerned. I had just discovered a weapon of mass destruction.

"The first day of school was the worst day of my life."

Nobody had prepared me for that day. Somebody should have warned me. I had to get tough if every day was going to be like this one. What did I know? I was six years old. My education had just begun. Ouch!

At the time, I was a little guy who was afraid of everything. Momma talked about the importance of education, so it looked like there was no turning back. At first, I tried to run away from school and they would run me down and catch me.

"I got mad and decided to whup this education and whup anybody else who hit me."

I finally settled into school and realized it was going to be a part of my life. My decision was to make it a big part of my life.
Those things that I learned in school back then are

still part of the way I do things today.

Through my experiences early on in school, I learned how to make friends. Making friends instead of enemies can go a long way to advance your career choices.

My early formative years from First Grade to Eighth Grade were all spent at this same school.

In the Ninth Grade I went to E.E. Smith in Kenansville, N.C.
Tenth Grade through my Senior year I went to James Kenan High School in Warsaw, N.C.

I was a basketball standout in high school and made All-Conference in basketball. That was a big decision not to play football.
The other coaches wanted me to play football because of my size but I chose basketball instead. It is likely that I could have done well as a football player, because of my great size. My Momma and Daddy did not want me to play football because as they used to say, "You might get hurt."

I had to wait until I was grown and had left home to make the decision to be a prize fighter. I became a boxer in the US Army and at the age of 23.

Before that time, I went to James Sprunt Community College in Kenansville, N.C. In 1972, I met my bride, Reba Dodson at the college and we dated for many years before marrying. We both transferred to Shaw University in Raleigh, N.C. where I played basketball. In my senior year, I made a decision to make the football team at Shaw

University.

Understand, I had never played football before, but I made a decision to walk onto that field and play the game. It was a big decision for me and I gave it my all and was invited as a walk-on to join the college team. Much of my life had been directly inspired by my decisions to try something new.

Boxing came after I graduated from Shaw University. I remember sitting on the steps of Shaw University and imagining that one day I would be a boxer. At that time it was just a dream but every success starts with a dream.

~My First Amateur Fight~

I joined the U.S. Army and made the decision to try out for the boxing team. It all happened one day when I walked into the basketball gymnasium at the US Military post in Leighton Barracks, Wurzburg, Germany.

Sgt. Herbert Ruffin approached me in the gym and asked me if I had ever boxed. He told me that I was perfectly built for boxing and I should try out for the US Army Boxing Team. He suggested that I participate in a **smoker** which was an amateur boxing match.

I had a few weeks to get ready for the fight. There was another guy there named Joe Lee. We always played racquetball which I believed gave me good hand-and-eye coordination.
On the day of the fight, I had butterflies in my stomach and was supremely confident at the same time.

9

I thought that to be a little bit odd but wrote it off as adrenalin. I was not scared. I was excited.

At the smoker, my goal was to hit him between the eyes and see him go down. If I could not hit him between the eyes, I would hit him in the right ear...but I would go *through his left ear* to get there.

I knew from Physics class in college that, **"Two bodies of mass could not occupy the same space at the same time."** So, either my fist was going to be stuck through his head, or his head was going flying fast. That was a solid plan. I was going to keep it simple.

When the bell rang I got to work right away. The fight did not last very long. I knocked the guy out of his shoes.

Looking back, I learned that keeping a simple strategy yields better success. People often over complicate things and fail miserably. I will talk about this again later and how it relates to building a business.

That first fight set my internal compass for Madison Square Garden. There was no doubt in my heart. One day I was going to fight for a World Heavyweight Boxing Title.

I could see Madison Square Garden. I could hear the crowds cheering. I was already there...in my mind. If I believed it, I knew I would someday see it.

3 MAGNOLIA TO MADISON SQUARE GARDEN

Magnolia is a small town with only one caution light. It was too small to have a red and green traffic light. That is where I grew up. There were only about 500 to 1,000 people living in the town. It was a good place to grow up. Everybody knew each other.

This is my story about going from Magnolia, NC to Madison Square Garden. . This begins my story about how I started working my way into the boxing ring.

Boxing in the US Army was where it all started....
As I kept on amateur boxing in the Army, I got better at it. I was on special duty in Germany and I travelled from city to city like a European army champion.

I won the army base heavyweight championship. That lead to the touring of other military bases and cities. My special assignment was to promote boxing throughout the European army bases. The boxing matches were always against US Army fighters from those other bases. Stuttgart Germany was a regular stop on the journey. They had their champions and we had ours.

I used to rush in on an opponent and break his jaw or a rib, sometimes a nose and someone shouted the name **"Bonecrusher"** across the room. Soon the name stuck and I kept it.

After getting out of the US Army, I began fighting as an amateur boxer in civilian life. I knew the only way to make a living at it was to become a real prizefighter. That meant turning pro.

First Pro Fight

My pro-debut fight was May 11, 1981 against James Broad, the Olympic Trials Champion. He had beaten everybody in the trials leading up to the Olympics. It was 1980 and the United States boycotted the Moscow Olympic Games, so James Broad did not get to fight as the Heavyweight in the Olympics. The USA did not go to Russia and support their Olympics because Russia had invaded Afghanistan the year before in 1979. So Broad lost the opportunity to win the gold medals at Moscow. He probably could have won it all. He was that good.

Now for you young people out there I want to explain what happened next. Your first time trying a new idea is usually important for shaping your attitude toward success and failure.

You know, your first professional fight is a big deal. You want to be impressive and show the world that you deserve to be fighting with the pro's. You know what I mean? I was prepared physically for the fight, but I got a surprise when I got to the ring.

There were television cameras everywhere and what looked like 20 million people watching me. It was like **stage fright** all of a sudden. This was not amateur hour anymore. This was the big times with bright lights. The fight was being broadcasted on ESPN.

There was a real paycheck on the line for $300. Having a burning desire to do it made me sign for the fight. All of that was running through my head.

I did not know what I was doing. It was too much for me. I was overwhelmed by all of the distractions of being in my first pro fight with the added pressure of the ESPN TV cameras. I had not really anticipated the television cameras and being on national tv. I could not stop thinking about them. James Broad stopped me in that fight. I was overmatched from the start. He capitalized on my bewilderment and inexperience. It was going to be a long night for the Bonecrusher. Every round seemed to go on forever. He stopped me in the fourth round.

> **"Sometimes life will throw you a
> curve ball. But it is what you do after you
> have been struck out that determines a man's
> character."**

Anybody can lose in the beginning of a new venture, but that does not mean you are a failure. Remember that. After the setback, you need to make a decision! Think about what shall I do next?

Your decision about what to do next following a setback is key to your success. Getting knocked down your first time out, is decision making time.

"A setback is a setup for a comeback."

With the first pro fight ***nervous jitters*** behind me, it was time to go back to the gym. Go back to the drawing board and start over. The one good thing that came out of the fight was that I could watch the playback and see every mistake that I made.

I dropped my right hand too often. My timing was way off. It was all clear to me. The body shots were coming in and I was seeing it in slow motion. Why didn't I block those shots? It was like I was watching a nightmare. Was that really me? Did I go to sleep in front of the cameras? Why didn't I let my hands go? Why didn't I do this...and why didn't I do that? I was rough on myself, more than anybody could be. I would have given anything for a chance to redeem myself. I was determined not to be a failure.

That lesson would not go wasted on the Bonecrusher. I may have come from a small country town but the World was going to hear from me again.

I made a decision.

I decided it was better to give a whupping than to receive a whupping. I came back out and fought every man they could put in front of me.

"I won the next 14 fights in a row!"

12 of those wins came by way of Knock Out.

Not bad for a beginner who got knocked down in my first fight. If I had quit after the first failure, I would not have won 14 victories in a row.

Now I was showing up on everybody's radar.
I received a phone call from Don King who asked me if I wanted to fight.

Don King informed me on short notice that Tony Tubbs who was supposed to fight Tim Witherspoon for the WBA World Heavyweight Title had just dropped out for unexpected reasons.

What people don 't know is that I only had *seven days notice* to fight for the World Championship Heavyweight Title.

I was not supposed to win. Witherspoon had beaten me before.

"This was a setup and it made me mad."

Oh, they thought that I would lose that fight for sure because one and a half years earlier, Tim Witherspoon had beaten me in a 12 round fight. I accepted the fight and headed to New York City with one week to get ready.

Welcome to Madison Square Garden
12/12/1986

"This was my big chance. This was what I was waiting for."

The Garden was jam packed on that night. This time I was focused. We walked to our corner and I got ready to come out for Round One. I did not see the bright lights and the TV cameras this time...I was mad. They really thought this was going to be a repeat of the first fight with Witherspoon. Boy, I had a surprise for them.

In the moments before the fight began, my trainer, Emile Griffith said to me, " I have a sharp needle here...and if you come back to me after round one, I am going to stick you with this thing."

He showed me the pin. I could tell by the look in his eye that he was dead serious. He **motivated** me to knock Witherspoon out in the first round. He said, "I want you to jump on him immediately and knock him out. Then we go home."

The training and preparation leading up to this fight was in New York city. I was exposed to a lot of boxers who were World Champions in that gym. They were from different weight classes and from different parts of the World. Some were flyweights. Some were welterweights.

One thing that most people don't know is that Emile, my trainer was much smaller than me. Here I was, this big heavyweight being trained by a smaller man. To his credit, he was a former 6 time World Champion in different weight classes. He was known as a middleweight champion. I learned respect as a very young boy. I did my best to show as much respect to him and I did exactly as he instructed me to do in the fights. I knew his experience and wisdom was valuable no matter what his size was.

The point is that it does not matter if you are so much more impressive than your mentor; you need to remember to humble yourself and be coachable.

At the sound of the bell, I rushed out there and made my move on Witherspoon. **I got mad.** I started throwing heavy leather upside his head and he was in trouble immediately. I could feel power surging through my whole body.
For a brief second, I remembered when at a low moment in my life, God had spoken into my spirit,..."***There is a champion in you, blessed and highly favored.***"

To me it was a sign that victory was at hand. I stepped to my opponent and let my hands go. Twice I knocked him down in the first round.
Then I heard the referee say, ***"The three knockdown rule is in effect."*** That was the last thing I heard before knocking him to the canvas. That was the last thing Witherspoon heard as well.

I knocked out Witherspoon at 2:12 of the first round and I became the WBA Heavyweight Champion of the World!

I want to encourage you that there is a champion in YOU...who is blessed and highly favored in the eyes of God.

There was a fight previous to the championship fight with Witherspoon, where I knocked out another fighter in the first round. He was also a former heavyweight champion.

His name was Mike "Hercules" Weaver.

Mike Weaver's manager said at a press conference

on CBS that, "When Mike Weaver knocks out Bonecrusher Smith, he will take the winner of the upcoming Larry Holmes and Michael Spinks fight.

I got mad and I made a decision to knock Mike Weaver out in the first round. See what happens when you get mad. You go into an ACTION mode....not a thinking mode. Fear is nowhere to be found when you get mad. You feel like you have been violated and you want to strike out at someone. But you must make a good decision. Use that anger to do something constructive for your future. **Do not go out and hit someone.**

You must channel that energy to push yourself beyond normal performance and achieve new levels of success.

There is a time and a place for everything and there is a season. Wait for your season.

4 WIN BIG AT NETWORK MARKETING

People ask me all the time, "How do you do it? How are you able to reach the top pay plans in the network marketing companies? What makes you different?"

I tell them first of all you have to believe in yourself and *believe in the company*. Believe in the product. Believe in the compensation plan. Believe that what you are doing right now is what you are supposed to be doing.

That sounds really simple...but it is HUGE. I mentioned my strategy in the boxing ring. It was to keep it simple and work your plan.

A champion has the ability to believe 100 percent in the task at hand. He believes 100 percent in his abilities to win.

You must believe there is a place for you at the top. You must see the top before you can go there.
"You must see it and seize it."
A champion **sees** the opportunity and will **seize** the opportunity. He will go after it until he wins. There is no room for doubt in a champion's mind.

The character of a champion is tested in an economy like the one we are experiencing today. In today's economy it has never been more important for people to step out of their comfort zones and try something new.

Sometimes I ask a team member to do something and I can see the fear on his face. He lacks faith.

Fear is **F**alse **E**vidence **A**ppearing **R**eal. Have you heard that before?

Something must change if you want your fortune to change. Do something now.
Years ago network marketing was looked down upon. The recession has affected everything. Lawyers, doctors, professionals from every walk of life have become disappointed with their incomes. Through no fault of their own the incomes that they have enjoyed for years have now shrunk. They are just broke at a higher level. Their time freedom is gone. Time with their family is gone.
They miss the good-life and are motivated to get it back. They want their time back.

With network marketing and a great work ethic, they can invest a small amount of money to get started, when compared to a traditional business and see more profitable results.

I love to talk to people. If I introduce myself to people as a friend, they will engage me in conversation. That opens the door for me to talk to them about the **new project** that I am working on. My new project is the home based business that I am building.

"If you talk to a few people, you make a few dollars. If you talk to many people; you make many dollars."

Massive action equals massive income.
I ask people if they are willing to commit an hour a day to their new project.

Soon they fall in love with the new venture and they forget all about the time. They end up working their home based businesses with great energy and it begins to be fun.

If I can show folks how to spend more time with their family, and how they can make more money, and have more fun...they will join my business wholeheartedly.

There is a secret ingredient in network marketing.

It is called **LEVERAGE!**

Anyone who has ever experienced leverage can tell you how it works. When I was growing up on the farm, my daddy would tell me and my brother to move a heavy tree trunk. He would tell us to go get a pole to *pry* up that giant log. Daddy said, "Go get that prize pole. We felt like we could pick up anything with that "prize" pole as he called it.

He would say to us, *"Get that prize pole and win the prize."*

It was the lever action of that skinny pole that could move a much larger tree. That is called **leverage.**

When we put a small log under that skinny pry pole and stepped on the other end of the pole, we could move anything. We could pick up that huge oak. We picked up a car to change a tire using our "prize" pole once when we did not have a car jack. Anything is possible if you have leverage. A skinny oak sapling could indeed move a giant oak if we used leverage in the right place.

Likewise, when you sign up 2 people to join your company you are now leveraging the work of 2 people. When they do the same thing, you begin to leverage the efforts of 6 people.

Those 6 people introduce 2 each to the business and your sales force has grown to 18 sales people. You don't know those people but their sales will count toward your own sales volume. Now you can have the "prize pole" working for you too. You get paid on the volume of a huge sales team. That is the power of leverage.

Now I know this sounds like a simple concept and it is creative. Thinking outside of the box has helped me in situations today. Creative thinking always sees an answer to solve a problem.

If you join a network marketing company and begin building a sales team, you can leverage the efforts of a large group of people.

Imagine how you will feel when you are leveraging the efforts of 10,000 people? Can you imagine how many hours those 10,000 people combined together would total? You could not possibly find that many hours to do the same amount of work during the same period of time. That is the magic of leverage. It is a lot of people doing a little bit of work which yields BIG RESULTS.

"I love network marketing!"

There is one more benefit of joining a network marketing business.

The biggest benefit is called RESIDUAL INCOME.

That is when you work hard in the beginning and the work you do pays you more in the end. You put forth more time and energy when you first get started and it will continue to pay you for the rest of your life....if you don't quit. Quitters never win.

When I worked on the farm we used to try and get water from an old well. We had a pump and had to hand crank it to get any water out of that well. We had to pour water down that pump and pump, pump, pump it manually and strenuously. Then I pumped it some more. It took a lot of cranking and pumping to make even a tiny bit of water come out, but once the water began to flow it got easier. The pipes below got filled with the water pressure and soon you could pump it with one finger and water came gushing out of that spout like it was never going to end. We had a gusher!

It is the same way with building a network marketing business. You are working to build a team of salespeople who are actually working for themselves.

Those people may be referred to as your downline or your team. Each one of them starts at the same level as yourself. Some will work slowly and methodically to build their residual incomes. Because you joined before they did you may receive some beneficial income even though they did the work. In most companies that income stream is rewarded to you each month. That is an example of residual income. Do not be sad at the beginning when your overriding residual check is only a few dollars. That is how it always starts.

I have seen people lose their minds over ten dollars.
It was not the ten dollars that turned them on. It was the mere fact that somebody else did the work and they got paid. They got paid off someone else's efforts.

That person had discovered **leverage**.
That person had discovered the principle of **residual income**.

Now that person was positioned in front of an **income stream**.

Do you see how it all works? You go out and begin inviting people to try your products or services. Some people will buy your products and use them every month, personally.

Some others will want to save money by becoming

a distributor. Now they can buy your products wholesale and actually make some extra income themselves.

It all begins by telling others about the benefits of the products and services. Think about it for a moment. Have you ever referred someone to a local restaurant that you really enjoy? It is the same thing except now you are getting a cash reward for referring someone to try it out.

It is the company's way of saying, "Thank you for sending us a customer."

"The more you tell the more you sell."

That's how you build a huge team. It starts out by you telling two people and they tell two people; and they also tell two people.

It is like the story of Noah in the Bible. He brought everybody in two-by-two until the Ark was filled. Hah!

In today's marketplace there are 10,000 people retiring daily...with not enough money. They need a retirement income and must find an investment coach to make sure they can afford their lifestyles.

If they want to retire prosperously, then they must find someone who has experience in that area. Most people have waited too late to get on the good side of compound interest. They feel they are too old and wonder how they are going to retire.

My advice is to get an **income stream**.

For most people that will mean getting a part-time job after they retire from their full-time job. If you ask me, there is an easier way to accomplish a second income stream. That would be to join a home based business and get to work. Your home based business has the best chance of succeeding because your overhead expenses are kept at a minimum.

Are You Coachable?

Once you have decided which company to join, the best advice this champion can give you is to find a coach.

That's right. You can follow the person who invited you to join the business, or go up-line to find the most motivated leader in the team. Choose someone to mentor you. Go to their meetings and listen every chance you get. It does not matter so much if you have direct contact with that leader, but you must learn as much as you can from her...or him.

I recommend that you record the meetings and listen to the playbacks repeatedly. Repetition is the mother of all learning. Everybody knows that. Listen intently for the benefits of the product and learn to recite the benefits **exactly** as you heard it.

A coach can answer your questions and shorten the learning curve dramatically. You will make money faster with a coach.

If you depend on reading everything to learn about all aspects of your company's products, you will be a loner. Your business will not go anywhere.

Ask me how I know this?

It takes the synergy of a big group of people to make the magic begin.

People use different language to describe the benefits of your products. In a group you will hear their stories. Later on, you will find yourself repeating those stories to other people. That creates excitement. If you have no success stories of your own to tell, because you just started out...then tell other peoples' stories of success.

This is how it all begins in network marketing. Talk about your products and tell what they will do for the customer. Talk about the benefits.

Then **invite** those people to hear more about it at a local meeting. That is the *fastest* way to build your own company. **You must become a master inviter**. Become really good at this *one* thing and you will see thousands of people join your business. Allow the group to help you grow your business.

It is easy and it is the one strategy that will keep you motivated.

Become a master of the ***invitation*** if you want the group energy working in your favor all the time.

believe that your finances will get better. You believe your health will get better. No matter what others may say...you always believe that you are better than what they are describing. Your past does not equal your future. You have greatness inside of you and it is waiting for you to believe in yourself.

A champion may fall down 7 times and he gets back up again.

Some folks can't even see opportunity. Everybody gets the opportunity to win big. But, when the opportunity comes, they are not focused.

They are easily persuaded to do something else. They fail to take action when the opportunity shows up.

I get offers all the time from people, but inside of me my spirit knows which opportunity has promise.

For example. Throughout my boxing career, I would have people come to me and tell me how to throw my right hand. I have one of the best right hands in the history of boxing, but people who had no experience would tell me how to throw a right punch.

That always disturbed me. How in the world could you expect to instruct me about boxing when you have no real knowledge.

The moral of the story is that you need to know who is coaching you....or trying to coach you.

Don't listen to your co-worker for marriage advice.

It is much wiser to go to a marriage counselor.

Everybody that gives advice is not a good coach. So it is important to know that your coach has experience and knowledge. Even the great professional athletes have coaches. Tiger Woods has a coach! Michael Jordan had a coach. Muhammad Ali had a coach. The list goes on forever.

We all need a good coach to keep our
Championship Mindset.

You need to listen to your inner voice, so you can discern when the right coach shows up. Your inner voice is God inspired.

Before I fought every boxing match, I would pray and ask God to protect me and help me win.

A Championship Mindset believes in a Spirit bigger than your own.

A champion can hear words of encouragement coming from the inside. That is where it all begins. You must believe in yourself. You must believe you are worthy to win at whatever you do.

You must believe that you can win even though you are retired. Retired champions are always excited to learn something fresh.

And another thing about a Championship Mindset..."A champion will always perform better under pressure."

How does that translate to you and your financial predicament? Simple. You will always perform better under pressure to come up with money to pay bills....when your back is against the wall.

You must make a decision. Fight or flight? Which is it going to be? I meet people all the time who used to live in a big house and go on vacation to Florida in a camper trailer. Now they tell me that their main home *is* the camper trailer. In today's economy many of you are suffering. I am here to tell you that your best days are still yet to come. Did you hear me?

The bad news is too many people are **mad**.
The good news is they are one decision away from a major breakthrough.

Circumstances change. Houses will come and go. The nice cars will come and go. One thing that is certain. This too shall pass!

Now, I have told you my own secrets of how I always succeed in network marketing and home based businesses. The plan is simple enough and it works.

If you follow step-by-step the suggestions laid out before you, then you can enjoy success, too.

Let me encourage you by saying, " It only works if you take action. Become a **master inviter** to local meetings. Tap into the group energy and put them to work for you.

Find a coach and go faster toward victory."

You are a champion waiting for an opportunity to grow again. Your faith will attract resources and people to come to you with the right opportunity.

So remember once again...

"There is a champion inside of you that is *ready* to be revealed. That champion, is blessed and highly favored."

ABOUT THE AUTHOR

He was born a sharecropper's son and rose to fame by winning the World Heavyweight Boxing Championship with only seven days notice. James Bonecrusher Smith was ordained in 1996. He was the first Heavyweight Champion of the World to graduate with a college degree. He has won boxing titles but the title of "Reverend James Bonecrusher Smith" is special to him. He will carry it with him for the rest of his life.

He tours the World, speaking at network marketing conferences and home based business conventions where he shares his branded message of **"The Championship Mindset"**.

The Champ is available for speaking engagements and may be reached at www.championforkids.org

Made in the USA
Charleston, SC
01 March 2014

The Market for Force

The legitimate use of force is generally presumed to be the realm of the state. However, the flourishing role of the private sector in security over the last twenty years has brought this into question. In this book Deborah Avant examines the privatization of security and its impact on the control of force. She describes the growth of private security companies, explains how the industry works, and describes its range of customers – including states, NGOs, and commercial transnational corporations. She charts the inevitable trade-offs that the market for force imposes on the states, firms, and people wishing to control it, suggests a new way to think about the control of force, and offers a model of institutional analysis that draws on both economic and sociological reasoning. The book contains case studies drawn from the US and Europe as well as Africa and the Middle East.

DEBORAH D. AVANT is Associate Professor of Political Science and Director of the Institute for Global and International Studies at the Elliott School of International Affairs, George Washington University. She is the author of *Political Institutions and Military Change: Lessons From Peripheral Wars* (1994) and of numerous articles.

The Market for Force

The Consequences of Privatizing Security

Deborah D. Avant

CAMBRIDGE
UNIVERSITY PRESS

CAMBRIDGE UNIVERSITY PRESS
Cambridge, New York, Melbourne, Madrid, Cape Town, Singapore, São Paulo

Cambridge University Press
The Edinburgh Building, Cambridge, CB2 8RU, UK

Published in the United States of America by Cambridge University Press, New York

www.cambridge.org
Information on this title: www.cambridge.org/9780521615358

First published 2005
Reprinted with corrections 2006
Third printing 2007

Printed in the United Kingdom at the University Press, Cambridge

A catalogue record for this book is available from the British Library

Library of Congress Cataloguing in Publication data

ISBN-13 978-0-521-85026-1 hardback
ISBN-13 978-0-521-61535-8 paperback

For my boys

Contents

viii   Contents

Figure and tables

Acronyms

ACCS	African Center for Strategic Studies
ACOTA	African Contingency Operations Training Assistance
ACRI	African Crisis Response Initiative
ANC	African National Congress
BP	British Petroleum
CARTS	Army Readiness Training Program
CDF	Civil Defense Forces
CONDO	Contractors on Deployed Operations
CPA	Coalition Provisional Authority
DFARS	Federal Acquisitions Regulations for Defense
DFID	Department for International Development
DOD	Department of Defense
DPKO	Department of Peacekeeping Operations
DRC	Democratic Republic of Congo
DSB	Defense Science Board
DSL	Defense Systems Limited (aka ArmorGroup)
DTAP	Democracy Transition Assistance Program
EAST	Eagle Aviation Services and Technology
ECOMOG	Monitoring Group set up by ECOWAS
ECOWAS	Economic Community of West African States
EO	Executive Outcomes
EU	European Union
FAR	Forces Armées Rwandaises
FARC	Revolutionary Armed Forces of Colombia
FARS	Federal Acquisition Regulations
FCO	Foreign and Commonwealth Office
FDI	Foreign Direct Investment
FMF	Foreign Military Financing
FMS	Foreign Military Sales
FND	Frederick, Nicholas, and Duncan
FY	financial year

FZS	Frankfurt Zoological Society
GDP	Gross Domestic Product
GSG	Gurkha Security Guards
GWP	Gross World Product
HDZ	Croatian Democratic Community
HV	Croatian Armed Forces
ICCN	Institut Congolese pour le Conservation de la Nature
ICG	International Crisis Group
IMATT	British International Military Training Team
IMET	International Military Education and Training
IMF	International Monetary Fund
INGO	International Non-Governmental Organization
IO	International Organization
IRF	International Rhino Foundation
ITAR	International Transfer of Arms Regulation
IUCN	World Conservation Union
IZCN	Institut Zaïrois pour le Conservation de la Nature
JCET	Joint Combined Exchange Training
KBR	Kellogg, Brown, and Root
LOGCAP	Logistics Civil Augmentation Program
MAP	Military Assistance Program
MEJA	Military Extraterritorial Jurisdiction Act
MOD	Ministry of Defence
MOU	Memoranduma of Understanding
MPRI	Military Professional Resources Incorporated
MTT	Mobile Training Team
NATO	North Atlantic Treaty Organization
NGO	Non-Governmental Organization
NIS	Newly Independent State
NP	National Party
OAU	Organization for African Unity
OMB	Office of Management and Budget
OSCE	Organization for Security and Cooperation in Europe
PA&E	Pacific Architects and Engineers
PFI	Private Finance Initiative
PfP	Partnership for Peace
PME	Professional Military Education
PSC	Private Security Company
ROTC	Reserve Officer Training Program
RPF	Rwandan Patriotic Front

RSLMF	Republic of Sierra Leone Military Forces
RUF	Revolutionary United Front
SADF	South African Defense Force (pre-apartheid)
SAIC	Science Applications International Corporation
SANDF	South African National Defense Force (post-apartheid)
SAS	British Special Air Services
SCS	Southern Cross Security
SLPP	Sierra Leone People's Party
SPLA	Sudanese People's Liberation Army
TNC	Transnational Corporation
TRADOC	Training and Doctrine Command
UN	United Nations
UNAMSIL	UN Peacekeeping Mission in Sierra Leone
UNESCO	United Nations Education, Scientific and Cultural Organization
UNHCR	United Nations High Commissioner for Refugees
WHINSEC	Western Hemispheric Institute for Security and Cooperation
WWF	World Wildlife Fund
YPA	Yugoslavia People's Army
ZCSO	Zairean Camp Security Operation
ZNG	Croatian National Guard

Acknowledgments

While researching and writing this book I incurred debts to countless people. I initially took note of the privatization of security services at a conference Vince Davis held at University of Kentucky in 1995. Vince was the first to encourage me to pursue this research, even shipping me his box of clippings, and though I did not work quite fast enough for him to see the result (Vince passed away last year) I would like to thank him first for his support. As my initial ideas for this project took shape, I am grateful to those whose immediate encouragement and enthusiasm led me to forge ahead – particularly, Sam Popkin, Harry Harding, Peter Katzenstein, Judith Reppy, Ann Markusen, and Jeff Henig. The John D. and Catherine T. MacArthur Foundation's research and writing fellowship provided not only financial support but also validation of the worthiness of this project early on and I am grateful for both.

Conducting research on current events relies on participants willing to share their stories and I am beholden to all of those who took time out of their busy schedules to talk with me. Doug Brooks did me – and everyone studying this subject – a great service with his PMC list serve and discussion group and was a great help as I arranged my research trip to South Africa. This research would not have been possible without cooperation from people working for MPRI, DSL, Sandline, Brown and Root, ICI Oregon, Booz Allen, SAIC, FND, Gray Security, SCS, CusterBattles, Blackwater, and others – particular thanks to those who shared frustrations and worries as well as success stories. Thanks also to those at the US State Department and Department of Defence, the UK Foreign and Commonwealth Office and Ministry of Defence, and the South African Department of Defence who were willing to explain their procedures. INGOs such as International Alert, Human Rights Watch, Amnesty International, and others were helpful in sharing information and perspectives and those at the World Wildlife Fund and the International Rhino Foundation are to be especially commended for openly sharing their frustrations with the Garamba project even as they endorsed its goals.

Many people commented on portions of this manuscript – and it is much better for it. Thanks to Andrew Abbott, Peter Andreas, Doug Brooks, Risa Brooks, Alex Cooley, Martha Finnemore, Jim Goldgeier, Virginia Haufler, Herb Howe, Meyer Kessenbaum, Elizabeth Kier, Jim Lebovic, Kimberly Zisk Marten, Tom McNaugher, Kate Newman, Steve Osafsky, Chantal de Jonge Oudraat, Scott Pegg, Sam Popkin, Will Reno, David Segal, Susan Sell, David Shearer, Pete Singer, Deborah Snelson, Don Snider, Jo Spear, Hendrik Spruyt, Elizabeth Stanley-Mitchell, and Gayle Watkins. I am not sure that Ingrid Creppell and Lee Sigelman ever read any of the manuscript, but they deserve thanks for listening to me chatter endlessly about the subject and helping me use (sometimes critical) comments wisely. I thank Johanna Ayers, Jeffrey Becker, Shana Heflin, Michael MacLeod, and Katherine Tobin for research assistance. The reviewers and editors for Cambridge University Press, particularly John Haslam, gave me excellent comments and advice. I also benefited from presenting various parts of this research in seminars at the Council on Foreign Relations, the University of Maryland, the College of William and Mary, the University of Washington, Princeton University, and the University of Virginia. Throughout the entire process my colleagues and students in the Elliott School and the Political Science Department at George Washington University have provided a smart and friendly atmosphere – the very best of working environments.

Special thanks to my family and friends. My kids, Dan, Brandon, and particularly Noah (whom I left for long stretches to go tromping around Africa and Europe when he was only two) put up cheerfully with their absentee mother. Susan Holloway went well beyond the call of friendship when she designed the cover and many other friends and family members were sources of support, encouragement, and many glasses of wine throughout the process. Finally, Tim helps me balance our crazy mix of careers and family with a grace and good humor that makes it all fun.

1   Introduction

. . . a state is a human community that (successfully) claims the monopoly of the legitimate use of physical force within a given territory

Weber[1]

. . .the extent to which the state has a monopoly of physical force and the extent to which the use of physical force is legitimate are variables, not elements of a definition.

Levi[2]

It is common sense that the control, sanctioning, and use of violence fall to states. Weber's definition of the state is the obvious starting point in most investigations and even those who argue that globalization and the rise of non-state actors have affected vast portions of the world's political arena generally assume that coercive power still resides with the state. Private security activity in the last two decades, though, should lay waste to this conventional wisdom. When the US won a resounding victory against the Iraqi Army in 2003, one out of every ten people it deployed to the theater during the conflict were employed by private security companies (PSCs) performing the work (logistics, operational support of weapons systems, and training) that used to be done by military personnel.[3] As lawlessness followed the fall of the Iraqi government and

---

[1] H. H. Gerth and C. Wright Mills, *From Max Weber: Essays in Sociology* (New York: Oxford University Press, 1946), pp. 77–78.

[2] Margaret Levi, "The State of the Study of the State," in Ira Katznelson and Helen Milner, *Political Science: the State of the Discipline* (New York: W. W. Norton, 2002), p. 40.

[3] There is a debate over how to identify companies that provide violent services. David Shearer coined the term private military company and the acronym, PMC, which has become a common descriptor of these firms. Some argue that there is a clear distinction between PMCs and private security companies (PSCs) – PMCs do military tasks, PSCs do policing tasks. The distinction between PMCs and PSCs is hard to maintain, though, given the variety of services that any given company may provide and the increasing blur between traditional military and other security tasks in today's wars. Most recently, Peter Singer has introduced "privatized military firm," PMF. See Peter Singer, "Corporate Warriors: the Rise of the Privatized Military Industry and its Ramifications for International Security," *International Security* Vol. 26, No. 3 (winter

coalition forces were stretched thin, an "army" of private security personnel flooded into the country. Some were hired by the Coalition Provisional Authority (CPA) to train the Iraqi police force, the Iraqi army, and a private Iraqi force to guard government facilities and oil fields. Other PSCs worked for the US Army translating and interrogating prisoners, or for Parsons providing security for employees rebuilding oil fields, or for ABC News or the Research Triangle Institute or any of a number of international non-governmental organizations (INGOs) working in the country. By spring 2004, it was estimated that in excess of 20,000 private security personnel, mostly retired military or police from countries as varied as Chile, Fiji, Israel, Nepal, South Africa, the United Kingdom, and the United States, employed by some sixty different PSCs worked for the US government, the British government, the CPA, private firms and INGOs in that country.[4] The role of PSCs in the Iraqi occupation was thrust into the public eye when four private security personnel working for the US PSC, Blackwater, were killed and mutilated on 31 March 2004 and when contracted interrogators working for CACI and Titan were among those implicated in the abuses at Abu Ghraib prison.[5]

The role of private security in Iraq is simply the latest chapter in the private security boom. While the state's monopoly Weber wrote about was exaggerated from the start and there has been a role for the private sector in security for some time, in the last two decades that role has grown and is larger and different now than it has been since the foundation of the modern state. Private security companies now provide

2001/02): 186–220 and *Corporate Warriors: the Rise of the Privatized Military Industry* (Ithaca: Cornell University Press, 2003). I use PSC to denote the whole range of for-profit security companies because it both more aptly describes the range of services these companies provide and avoids adding a new acronym to the list.

[4] "Privatizing Peace and Security: a Hobbesian Dilemma," *Daily Star*, 28 February 2004; Thomas Catan and Stephen Fiddler, "With Post-War Instability Still a Pressing Concern, Western Companies and Government Agencies are Awarding Big Contracts to Ex-Military Personnel with Expertise in Providing Security," *Financial Times*, 30 September 2003. 4 May 2004 letter to Ike Skelton, ranking Minority Member, Committee on Armed Services, US House of Representatives from Donald Rumsfeld, Secretary of Defense, attachment "Discussion Paper on Private Security Companies Operating in Iraq." This discussion paper estimates 20,000 employees to PSC in Iraq working for 60 companies. The list of companies that accompanies the paper, however, does not include several prominent PSCs known to be working in Iraq (it is missing such companies as Vinnell, MPRI, CACI, and Titan, among others). One former member of the CPA claims that no one really knows how many private security personnel are in the country. Interview with former CPA official, March 2004.

[5] Press coverage of these events abound, but see for instance, James Dao, "Private US Guards Take Big Risks for Right Price," *New York Times*, 2 April 2004; Joel Brinkley and James Glanz, "Contract Workers Implicated in February Army Report on Prison Abuse," *New York Times*, 4 May 2004.

more services and more kinds of services including some that have been considered core military capabilities in the modern era. Also, changes in the nature of conflicts have led tasks less central to the core of modern militaries (such as operating complex weapons systems and policing) to be closer to the front and center of maintaining security, and private security companies provide these services readily. Furthermore, states are not the only organizations that hire security providers. Increasingly transnational non-state actors (INGOs, multi-national corporations, and others) are financing security services to accomplish their goals. A burgeoning transnational market for force now exists alongside the system of states and state forces.

Private security and the control of force: the question

Why should we worry – or even care – about this market? The answer is simple, private security may affect how and whether people can control violence. The effort to contain violence within collective structures – rules, laws, norms, and institutions – has been an ongoing struggle throughout human history. "War," John Keegan writes, "is not the continuation of politics by other means," we only wish that were so. He argues that Clausewitz's dictum was part of a theory of what war *ought* to be.[6] Clausewitz's conception reflected the emerging view in the west that the state – or the "public" sphere – was the institution through which the use of violence could be most effectively linked to endeavors endorsed by a collective. The endurance of references to Clausewitz indicates the degree to which state control of force (though often imperfect) has provided the best (even if highly uneven) mechanism human kind has known for linking the use of violence to political processes and social norms within a territory. How privatization affects this control, then, is a critical question. Does the privatization of security undermine state control of violence? Can the privatization of security enhance state control of violence? Does the privatization of security chart new ways by which violence might be collectively controlled? How does private security affect the ability to contain the use of force within political process and social norms?

---

[6] John Keegan, *A History of Warfare* (New York: Knopf, 1993), quote from p. 1, see also discussion pp. 1–6. Keegan is using "politics" in the more benign sense of the term as the practice of political government.

The contracting out of sovereign transactions poses grave difficulties.

Williamson[7]

Preying on the vulnerability of kleptocratic regimes, corporate armies are repackaging violence in pseudo-market frills, with their eyes firmly set on creating safe havens around enclaves that are rich in natural resources.

Musah and Fayemi[8]

My division . . . employs expatriates with military skills . . . all moral and professional people with a mission to protect the personnel and assets of our clients . . . To do this we inject millions of dollars into the local economy each year, employ and provide training and opportunities to nearly two thousand local people on equitable salaries . . . [and] contribute considerably to economic efficiency and the ability of the diplomatic, humanitarian and formal business community to safely fulfill their tasks.

Fennell[9]

As these statements attest, the implications of privatizing security for the control of force are debated. Pessimists claim that the turn to private security threatens to undermine state control and democratic processes.[10] Ken Silverstein characterizes this process as one "by which the responsibilities of government are transferred to corporate hands."[11] In the US this allows for foreign policy by proxy – where corporate entities do what the government cannot. The implication of Silverstein's argument is that the institutions that contain violence in the US are undermined by privatization. Violence becomes a private commodity rather than a public good – and the result, Silverstein argues, is a defense policy that ignores the real issues and threats only to be shaped by "the profit motives and egos of a small group of hardliners."[12] In Africa, according to Musah and Fayemi, the consequences are even more severe. Though contemporary mercenaries attempt to distinguish themselves from the lawless "guns for hire" that ran riot over Africa during the Cold War, their consortium with arms manufacturers, mineral exploiters, and Africa's authoritarian governments and warlords sustains the militarization of Africa.[13] This poses "a mortal danger to

---

[7] Oliver Williamson, "Public and Private Bureaucracies: a Transaction Cost Economic Perspective," *Journal of Law, Economics, and Organization* Vol. 15, No. 1 (1999), p. 320.

[8] Abdel-Fatau Musah and J. Kayode Fayemi, "Introduction," in *Mercenaries: an African Security Dilemma* (London: Pluto, 2000) p. 4.

[9] Communication from James Fennell, head of the Africa division of DSL, 29 November 2000.

[10] Ken Silverstein, "Privatizing War: How Affairs of State are Outsourced to Corporations Beyond Public Control," *The Nation*, 28 July 1997; Musah and Fayemi, *Mercenaries*.

[11] Ken Silverstein, *Private Warriors* (New York: Verso, 2000), p. 143.

[12] Ibid., p. xvii.

[13] Musah and Fayemi, "Africa: In Search of Security," in *Mercenaries*, pp. 23–25.

democracy in the region."[14] Unregulated private armies linked to international business interests threaten to undermine democracy and development in Africa.

Optimists, however, declare that private options offer solutions to intractable security problems that can operate within national interests and/or the values shared by the international community.[15] In the US, Eliot Cohen argues, privatizing security services can help governments make the most of advances in information technology in the civilian economy and manage in a complex world with fewer troops.[16] David Shearer argues that in Africa and elsewhere PSCs willing to take on messy intervention tasks that western militaries are eager to avoid can help end civil conflicts that would otherwise be intractable.[17] He argues that rather than outlawing PSCs, the international community should engage them, give them a legitimate role, and expect them to operate as professionals, according to the values held by the international social system.[18] Doug Brooks proposes that a consortium of PSCs could bring years of peacekeeping experience and North Atlantic Treaty Organization (NATO) level professionalism to protect vulnerable populations in places like the Democratic Republic of Congo (DRC); they could also train local gendarmes in policing and human rights so as to build a more professional local force.[19]

Who is right?

Private security and the control of force: the answer

I began research on this book intending to bring data to this dispute – to see whether optimists or pessimists provided the best guide to private security's implications. I found evidence, though, that supported both arguments. I soon realized that both arguments could be "right" because their arguments hinge on different conceptions of "control" and often hold private security alternatives to different comparative standards. Ken Silverstein is worried about *political* control – who gets

---

[14] Ibid., p. 26.

[15] See David Shearer, *Private Armies and Military Intervention* (Adelphi Paper 316, Oxford University Press, 1998); Doug Brooks, "Write a Cheque, End a War," *Conflict Trends* No. 6 (July 2000).

[16] Eliot Cohen, "Defending America in the Twenty-First Century," *Foreign Affairs* Vol. 79, No. 6 (November/December 2000): 40–56.

[17] Shearer, *Private Armies and Military Intervention*. See also Holly Burkhalter quoted in Sebastian Mallaby, "Think Again: Renouncing Use of Mercenaries Can Be Lethal," *Washington Post*, 5 June 2001.

[18] Shearer, *Private Armies and Military Intervention*, pp. 69–72.

[19] Doug Brooks, "Help for Beleaguered Peacekeepers," *Washington Post*, 2 June 2003, p. A17.

to decide about the deployment of arms and services. Eliot Cohen, though, is worried about *functional* control, or what kinds of capabilities will be present in American arms and services. Musah and Fayemi are also worried about political control, who calls the shots about the use of force – but unlike Silverstein, they are comparing privatization with a democratic ideal, not current African "public" forces. Finally, Shearer is worried about functional control – are forces capable for meeting current challenges that the international community (not just the US) sees and *social* control – the degree to which the use of force is integrated with prevailing international values.

Each of these definitions is problematic because they all ignore the fact that ultimately all three dimensions of control (and how they fit together) hold the key to controlling violence. Indeed, the control of force has been most stable, effective, and legitimate when all three aspects have reinforced one another – when capable forces have been governed by accepted political processes and operated according to shared values. Furthermore, any serious evaluation of privatization's impact must compare private alternatives against a common standard – most suitably the other available alternatives rather than an unachievable ideal.

To find a common framework with which to examine these different dimensions of control, I draw on the "new institutionalism," a diverse set of theory pulling from distinct "logics" in economics and sociology, but united by an interest in institutional mechanisms and how they affect collective outcomes. Juxtaposing economic and sociological institutionalist arguments, I argue that privatization's effect on the capability of forces and the values they serve should vary. Privatization sometimes leads to greater capabilities, other times to lesser capabilities, and sometimes leads to more, sometimes less integration of violence with prevailing international values. Inevitably, however, privatization should redistribute power over the control of violence, both within states and between state and non-state actors. In effect, the shift to private guardians changes who guards the guardians.

The key question, though, is how privatization affects the way these dimensions of control fit together. Do the political changes introduced by privatization engender needed capabilities governed by acceptable political processes that operate according to shared values? I argue that this is most likely when the consequential mechanisms economists pay attention to: screening and selection, monitoring, and sanctioning, work together with the mechanisms for transmitting appropriateness sociologists pay attention to: norms, standards, education, and practices among security professionals, creating something like an equilibrium outcome. When they work against one another, they present individuals with multidirectional imperatives and opportunities, portending friction, instability, and change.

A fundamental intervening variable in my analysis is the varying capacities of states. Strong states that are coherent, capable, and legitimate to begin with are best able to manage the risks of privatization and harness the PSCs to produce new public goods, but they also have the most to lose if privatization tips the ledger and undermines the capacities of public forces or legitimacy of foreign policy. Weak states with ineffective and corrupt forces potentially have the most to gain (or the least to lose) from privatization, but also are the least able to manage private forces for the public good – efforts to harness the private sector for state building in weak states are often desperate gambles.

I illustrate this argument and demonstrate its usefulness by looking at three ways in which private security has changed political control. I begin by looking at state contracts for the delivery of security services. How do these contracts compare with the execution of policy with regular security forces? I then explore states' attempts to control the export of private security services. Can states control the security services that emanate from their territories? Finally, I examine non-state actors' financing security. Does non-state financing of security enhance or erode the control of violence?

I find that changes in political control frequently introduce new dynamics that destabilize the "fit" between functional, political, and social control of force. Thus even as it enhances the capacities of individual states and responds to new social demands, the market for force has often led to less stable control over force. The institutional model I put forth, though, suggests a strategy of action for those interested in generating more stable control – working toward continuity between norms, standards, monitoring, and sanctions.

In the rest of this chapter, I describe the current market for force, define some key terms, compare this market to previous ones, and look briefly at its origins.

A transnational market for military and security services

Private security companies provide military and security services to states, international organizations, INGOs, global corporations, and wealthy individuals. Every multi-lateral peace operation conducted by the UN since 1990 included the presence of PSCs. States that contracted for military services ranged from highly capable states like the US to failing states like Sierra Leone. Meanwhile, global corporations hired PSCs to provide site security and planning, and INGOs working in conflict zones or unstable territories did the same. Since the 11 September terrorist attacks on the United States, the war on terrorism has offered even greater opportunities for the private security industry. This is evident not only in Iraq – where PSCs are the second largest member of the "coalition of the willing" – but also in the growing presence of PSCs in the new jobs that accompany the war on terrorism, interrogators and interpreters, for instance.[20]

The number of private security providers burgeoned during the 1990s. Trade in military and security services is not a category tracked by military or trade databases, so the data for this growth are rather piecemeal, but nonetheless compelling. Private industry projections suggested in 1997 that revenues from the global international security market (military and policing services in international and domestic markets) would rise from $55.6 billion in 1990 to $202 billion in 2010.[21] Recent estimates suggest that the 2003 global revenue for this industry was over $100 billion.[22] Private security companies with publicly traded stocks grew at twice the rate of the Dow Jones Industrial Average in the 1990s.[23] Between 1994 and 2002 US-based PSCs received more than 3,000 contracts worth over $300 billion from the US Department of Defense.[24]

News reports of mercenary and/or private security activity have mushroomed. Some document the activities of individual soldiers of fortune, frequently linked with international criminal networks that profit from shady deals in the extractive sectors (diamonds, oil, timber, coltan, and other minerals) or in the market for illicit drugs and sex. During the Democratic Republic of Congo/Zaire civil war, the white legions (composed of Serbian and other European individuals) made the press frequently and in Chechnya, similar reports

---

[20] Singer, *Corporate Warriors*; John Crewdson, "Contractor Tries to Avert Repeat of Bosnia Woes," *Chicago Tribune*, 19 April 2003; "US Firm to Rebuild Iraqi Army," *BBC News*, 26 June 2003. CSC's DynCorp is rebuilding the Iraqi police force, Northrop Grumman's Vinnell won the $48 million contract to create a new Iraqi army.

[21] Equitable Securites Corporation, *Equitable Securities Research* 27 August 1997. Cited in Alex Vines, "Mercenaries and the Privatization of Security in Africa in the 1990s," in Greg Mills and John Stremlau, eds., *The Privatization of Security in Africa* (Johannesburg: SAIIA Press, 1999), p. 47.

[22] Peter W. Singer, "Peacekeepers, Inc.," *Policy Review*, June 2003: 60.

[23] Jack Kelly, "Safety at a Price: Security is a Booming, Sophisticated, Global Business," *Pittsburgh Post Gazette*, 13 February 2000.

[24] International Consortium of Investigative Journalists, "The Business of War: Privatizing Combat, the New World Order" (Washington, DC: The Center for Public Integrity, 2002), p. 2, hereafter referred to as the ICIJ Report.

abound.[25] More frequently, however, reported "mercenary" activity is the activity of firms that offer security and military services. Well over two hundred such companies made the news between 1995 and 2004. Private firms trained militaries in more than forty-two countries during the 1990s. Some claim that several hundred companies globally operate in over one hundred countries on six continents.[26] While older companies such as Vinnell, Booz Allen Hamilton, Defense Systems Limited (DSL), DynCorp, and Cubic are still active, many of the highest profile firms (including MPRI – now part of L-3 Communications and Blackwater) have been established since 1985. Table 1.1 lists these firms organized by the services they provide and the countries from which their employees are generally drawn.[27]

Though the table catalogues PSCs by country, as with global corporations more generally, many PSCs defy easy national classification. Take DSL as an example. It began as a British firm (founded in 1981 during Margaret Thatcher's rule) but was purchased by a publicly held American conglomerate called Armor Holdings in 1997 and became ArmorGroup.[28] Most of its employees that operate out of its London office are former British Special Air Services (SAS), but the company also draws on retired US military personnel and local personnel in its offices all over the world. In 2000 ArmorGroup had offices in the US, the UK, South Africa, Democratic Republic of Congo/Zaire, Mozambique, Kenya, West Africa, North Africa, Zimbabwe, Uganda, Hong Kong, Nepal, Asia, the Philippines, France, Bosnia-Herzegovina, Russia, Kazakhstan, Ukraine, Colombia, Ecuador, Venezuela, and Brazil, and regional managers in Europe and the CIS, Russia, Latin American, Southern Africa, Central Africa, North Africa, the Far East, and the Middle East.[29] In most of the regional offices, a small expatriate core with mostly British military background employs predominantly local personnel. DSL works according to local laws and with local personnel, but its behavior in one area affects its reputation worldwide. The company's leadership claims to be keenly aware of the need to have

---

[25] See, for instance, "FSB Says British NGO Trained Chechens as Terrorists," *Radio Free Europe/Radio Liberty*, 11 August 2000; "Chechens Falling Prey to Russian Soldiers of Fortune," *Los Angeles Times*, 25 October 2000; Vladislav Dorofeyev and Yelena Artemkina, "Chechnya Opens Trade in Mercenaries," *Moscow Kommersant-Vlast*, No. 9, 17 March 1998: 34–36.

[26] Singer, "Peacekeepers, Inc.," p. 60.

[27] For a similar strategy of national attribution for global corporations, see Michael Porter, *The Competitive Advantage of Nations* (New York: Free Press, 1990), p. 25.

[28] Kevin O'Brien, "Freelance Forces: Exploiters of Old or New-Age Peacebrokers?" *Jane's Intelligence Review*, August 1998: 44.

[29] ArmorGroup company literature.

Table 1.1. *Military and security companies operational between 1990 and 2004*

Military advice and training			
Angola: Alpha 5 Saracen, International **Australia:** International Port Services Total Response Solutions International **Belgium:** International Defense and Security (IDAS) **Canada:** Black Bear Consulting CAE Global Risk Holdings Procon	**France:** COFRAS Eric SA Geolink Secrets Service and Security **Israel:** Beni Tal Golan Group Levdan Spearhead Limited **Philippines:** Grayworks Security	**South Africa:** Erinys Executive Outcomes Frederick, Nicholas, and Duncan (FND) Lanseria Meteoric Tactical Solutions Ronin Protective Services Saracen, International **UK:** AKE, Ltd. Blue Sky Chilport, Ltd. DSL Flagship Training, Ltd. Global Impact Gurkha Security Guards KAS Enterprises	**UK (cont.):** Northbridge Presidium Rubicon International Sakina Security Services Sandline Strategic Consulting Task International THULE Global Security Watch Guard Intn'l **US:** Akal Security Blackwater Booz Allen COMTek Cubic DynCorp Eagle Group Executive Defense Tactics	**US (cont.):** Global Options HSS, Intn'l Ibis Tek ICI, Oregon Logicon MPRI – L-3 Operation Corporate Training Raytheon Ronco SAIC Samson Intn'l Steele Foundation Total Security Services Trojan Securities Intn'l Vinnell Corp. Worldwide Security

Table 1.1. (cont.)

Operational support

Angola:	***Israel (cont.):***	***UK:***	***US:***	***US (cont.):***
Alpha 5	International Security and Defense Systems	Aims Limited	AAI	Eagle Aviation services and Technology (EAST)
Simportex	Levdan	Avient	Abunda	Flour Intercontinental
Saracen, International	Silver Shadow	DSL	ACS	Ibis Tek
		Gurkha Security Guards	AirScan	ICI, Oregon
Canada:	***Italy:***	Hart Group	Aviation Development	Logicon
CAE	Alenia Marconi	Northbridge	Bechtel	Omega Air
ATCO Frontec Corp.		Rubicon International Services	Bell Helicopter	Pacific Architects and Engineers
	Philippines:	Sandline	Betac	Parsons
France:	Grayworks	Securicor	Bird Air	Raytheon
COFRAS		Strategic Consulting International	Blackwater	Ronco
Eric SA	***South Africa:***	THULE Global Security International	Booz Allen	SAIC
EuroCorps	Executive Outcomes	Watch Guard International	Braddock, Dunn and McDonald (BDM) International	Titan Corp.
Geolink	FND		CACI	Vinnell Corp.
Secrets	Ibis Air		California Microwave Systems	
Service and Security	Lanseria		Cubic Diligence	
	Omega Support Ltd.		DynCorp	
Israel:	SA Bias Group			
Beni Tal	Southern Cross Security			
Golan Group				

Table 1.1. (cont.)

Logistics support				

Angola:
KK Group
Simportex
Saracen, International
	Italy:
	Alenia Marconi
	
	Russia:
	Alpha A
		UK:
		Avient
		Blue Sky
		CADA
		Crown Agents
		DSL
		Global Development
		  Four (GD4)
		Global Risk Strategies
		GSG
		Hart Group
		Logo Logistics
		Northbridge
		Rubicon International
		  Services
		Sandline
		Securicor
			US:
			Abunda
			AirScan
			AMEG
			BDM
			Bechtel
			Betac
			Booz-Allen & Hamilton
			Brown & Root Services
			Custer Battles
			Dalcorp
			Diligence
			DynCorp
			EAST
			Fluor
			ICI, Oregon
			International Resources
				US (cont.):
				Group
				Minetech
				Pacific Architects and
				  Engineers
				Parsons
				Ronco
				SCS
				US Defense Systems
				Vinnell

Canada:
Global Risk Holdings
ATCO Frontec Corp.
 	
France:
COFRAS
Eric SA
EuroCorps
Geolink
Service and Security
Setrico
Sofremi
 	
Israel:
Beni Tal
Golan Group
International Security
  and Defense Systems
Levdan
Silver Shadow
	South Africa:
	Erinys
	Falconeer
	FND
	Ibis Air
	Meteoric Tactical
	  Solutions
	Omega Support Ltd.
	SA Bias Group
	Strategic Resources
	  Corporation (SRC)			

Table 1.1. (*cont.*)

Site/personal security

Angola:	***Israel:***	***South Africa (cont.):***	***US (cont.):***
Alpha 5	Beni Tal	Omega Risk	GSGI
Guardesegura	Golan Group	Parasec Corporate	Guardesmark
KK Group	Hashmira	Dynamics	Hill and Associates
Saracen, International	International Security	Ronin Protective	Ibis Tek
	and Defence Systems	Services	ICI, Oregon
Australia:	Silver Shadow	Shield Security	ISI
Fynwest	Spearhead Ltd	Stabilico	KBR
Global Risk Awareness		Safenet	Kroll Associates
Global Support Agency	***Kuwait:***	Saracen International	Meyer and Associates
Optimal Solutions	Diligence, ME	Shibata Security	MVM
Total Response Solutions		Shield Security	New Bridge Strategies
International Unity	***Netherlands:***	Southern Cross Security	Nour
Resources Group	AON	Stabilico	O'Gara Protective
	Group 4/Falck		Operation Corporate
Belgium:		***Sweden:***	Training
IDAS	***New Zealand:***	Securitas	Orion Management
	Burrows and Associates		Overseas Security and
Canada:		***Turkey:***	Strategic Management
Global Risk Holdings	***Romania:***	Ultra Services	Parsons
PROCON	Bidepa		Potomac Group Security
		UK:	RamOPS
France:	***Russia:***	AD Consultancy	Samson International
Eric SA	Alpha-A	Aegis	SCG Int'l Risk
EHC		Aims Limited	SeaSecure
Geos		AKE	Source Incorporated
Secrets			

	UK (cont.):	
	Global Contingency	
	Projects Group	
	Global Impact	
	Gurkha Security Guards	
	Hart Group	
	Henderson Risk	
	ICP Group	
	Janusian Security	
	Logo Logistics	
	Olive Security	
	Peak	
	Presidium	
	Risk Advisory Group	
	Rapport Research	
	Rubicon	
	Sapelli SARL	
	Securicor	
	SSSI	
	Universal Guardian	
	Vance International	
	US:	
	Akal	
	Babylon	
	Bechtel	

Table 1.1. (cont.)

Site/personal security

Hong Kong:	**South Africa:**	**UK (cont.):**	**US (cont.):**	**US (cont.):**
Hill and Associates	Coin Security	Blue Sky	BH Defence	Secure Source
Hungary:	Empower Loss	BritAm Defense	Blackheart International	Steele Foundation
CNS Europe Kft	Erinys	Carnelian	Blackwater	Total Security Services
Iraq:	Executive Outcomes	Castleforce Consultancy	CTU Asia	Triple Canopy
Badr Reconstruction Org.	Gray Security	Centurion	Custer Battles	Trojan Securities
ISI	KWZ	Chilport, Ltd.	Diligence	US Defence Systems
Near East Security	Lanseria	Control Risk Group	DS Vance	Vance International
Sumer International	Lifeguard Security	DSL – Armor	DTS Security	Wackenhut
	Meteoric Tactical Solutions	Genric	DynCorp	Wade–Boyd
			EODT	WarRoom Research
			Executive Defense Tactics	Worldwide Security

Crime prevention/intelligence

Angola:	**Hungary:**	**South Africa:**	**UK:**	**US (cont.):**
Alpha 5	CNS Europe Kft	Bridge Resouces Ltd.	AD Consultancy	Custer Battles
Guardesegura	**Iraq:**	Corporate Trading International	Aegis	Diligence
KK Group	ISI	Coin Security	Aims Limited	DS Vance
Saracen, International	Near East Security	Executive Research Associates	AKE	DTS Security
Australia:	Sumer International	Gray Security	Blue Sky	DynCorp
Fynwest	**Israel:**	Lanseria	BritAm Defense	EODT
Global Risk Awareness	Beni Tal	Lifeguard Security	Carnelian	GSI
Global Support Agency	Golan Group	Omega Risk	Castleforce Consultancy	Hill and Associates
Optimal Solutions			Centurion	Ibis Tek
			Chilport, Ltd	ICI, Oregon

Table 1.1. (cont.)

Crime prevention/intelligence				
Australia (cont.): Total Response Solutions International Unity Resources Group **Belgium:** IDAS **Canada:** Global Risk Holdings PROCON **France:** Atlantic Intelligence Eric SA EHC Geos Secrets **Hong Kong:** Hill and Associates	**Israel (cont.):** Hashmira International Security and Defence Systems Silver Shadow Spearhead Ltd **Kuwait:** Diligence, ME **Netherlands:** AON Group 4/Falck **New Zealand:** Burrows and Associates **Romania:** Bidepa **Russia:** Alpha-A	**South Africa (cont.):** Parasec Corporate Dynamics Ronin Protective Services Safenet Saracen International Shibata Security Shield Security Southern Cross Security Stabilico **Sweden:** Securitas **Turkey:** Ultra Services	**UK (cont.):** DSL – Armor Global Impact Global Contingency Projects Group Hart Group Henderson Risk, Ltd. ICP Group Olive Security Peak Rubicon Sapelli SARL Securicor SSSI Universal Guardian Vance International **US:** Babylon BH Defence Blackheart International CACI CTU Asia	**US (cont.):** ISI Kroll Associates MVM New Bridge Strategies O'Gara Orion Management Overseas Security and Strategic Information Parsons Protective Operation Corporate Training Potomac Group RONCO SCG Intn'l Risk Sea Secure Secure Source Trojan Securities US Defence Systems Wackenhut Worldwide Security Service

professional standards for behavior and monitor them closely.[30] DSL works for a variety of customers including private businesses, INGOs, and states. It provided security and logistics personnel to the UN mission in the former Yugoslavia from 1992 to 1995, protects British Petroleum (BP) oil property against attacks in Colombia, provides security for Bechtel in Iraq, and has also worked for such clients as De Beers, Shell, Mobil, Amoco, Chevron, CARE and GOAL.[31]

DSL was privately held until 1997, but was publicly traded as part of ArmorGroup from 1997 to 2004. In January 2004, US based ArmorGroup informed the Securities and Exchange Commission that it intended to sell off its London-based affiliate DSL to a group of its own staff.[32] With that sale complete, DSL (now ArmorGroup, International) was again a privately held company. Like all PSCs DSL fills contracts from its database, supplemented by advertisements. That is, it has a small contingent of full-time employees and a large database of individuals from which to fill specific contracts. These databases are not exclusive – persons may appear on the databases of several different firms. This means that someone could be working for DSL one week and Control Risk Group, Erinys, or one of a dozen others the next.

The array of private security services

What kinds of services do these firms provide? A wide range, including tasks associated with external (protecting borders) and internal (keeping order within borders) security. Though few contracts promise participation in ground combat, PSCs offer three broad categories of external security support: operational support, military advice and training, and logistical support. PSCs also offer internal security services ranging from site security (armed and unarmed), crime prevention, and intelligence. Peter Singer has disaggregated these firms by the relationship of their primary services to "the tip of the spear" in "battlespace."[33] Services closest to the tip of the spear are those on the front lines of battle, typically the most deadly and dangerous. According to Singer, this leads to distinctions between type-one firms that provide implementation and command, type-two firms that provide advice and training, and

---

[30] Interview with Noel Philp, managing director, ArmorGroup's DSL, 2 June 2000.
[31] O'Brien, "Freelance Forces," p. 44.
[32] See http://www.intelligenceonline.com/ps/AN/Arch/ INT/INT_448.asp?rub=archives. Granville Baird Capital Partners invested 70% of the cost with the remaining 30% split among the managers. See http://www.armorgroup.com/news.asp. Many PSCs have gone back and forth between private and public holdings.
[33] Singer, "Corporate Warriors."

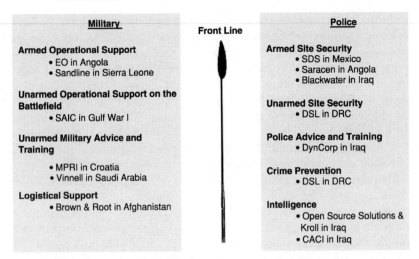

Figure 1.1. Contracts in battlespace.

type-three firms that provide military support. While the distinction between service type makes sense, the same PSC may provide type-one services in one contract and type-three in another. Indeed, given the way service firms fill contracts from databases and advertising, it is easy for them to move from one service type to another. Thus I use contracts rather than firms as the unit of analysis. Figure 1.1 draws on Singer's battlespace analogy, substituting contracts for firms and extending the categorization to internal as well as external security services.

A small number of contracts have stipulated services at the very tip of the spear that most closely resemble "core" military competencies – armed operational support on the battlefield. Executive Outcomes (EO) and Sandline (both now defunct) became famous for missions that included the deployment of armed personnel on the battlefield, EO in Angola and Sierra Leone and Sandline in Sierra Leone and Papua New Guinea.[34] Eric SA (a French company) was also involved in raising the "white legion" for Mobutu during the 1997 civil war in Zaire/ Democratic Republic of Congo and the French government purportedly received a proposal from Geolink to raise Serbian mercenaries for

[34] EO closed its doors for business after the South African government passed legislation ostensibly designed to regulate the export of military services but believed by many to try to outlaw this kind of activity. Though EO employees now operate or work for a variety of firms – some new, some outside of South Africa – the firms are less public about their dealings. A more detailed discussion follows in chapter four.

Mobutu.[35] EO's webpage boasted strategic and tactical military advisory services, sophisticated military training packages in land, sea, and air warfare, peacekeeping or "persuasion" services, advice on selections of weapons systems and acquisition, and paramilitary services.[36] Its most prominent contracts were with Angola and Sierra Leone, but it also worked in Zambia, Ghana, Algeria, Indonesia, and Papua New Guinea and was rumored to have worked in Colombia, Namibia, Uganda, and Burundi.[37] EO's affiliation with Ibis Air gave it significant capabilities in deployment and combat. Ibis Air equipment included a number of transport and surveillance planes and a force of helicopters.[38]

Many more contracts do not raise troops or deploy personnel on the battlefield, but offer advice and training to military forces. The training programs vary widely from the high end where PSCs are reorganizing the force structure and training officers in battlefield scenarios to more mundane troop training, simulations, and peacekeeping training. MPRI has played a large role in advice and training. As part of their contract with the Bosnian military, they created a mini replica of the US's renowned National Training Center and built another sophisticated training facility in Kuwait in the lead up to Operation Iraqi Freedom.[39] Other US firms that offer training include Booz Allen and Hamilton, Cubic, DynCorp, Global Options, Logicon, O'Gara Protective Services, Science Applications International Corporation (SAIC), Trojan Securities International, and Vinnell. Vinnell was initially in charge of the umbrella contract under which to train a new Iraqi army in the wake of US operation Iraqi Freedom.[40] From the UK, Aims Limited, DSL, Global Impact, Gurkha Security Guards, KAS Enterprises, Watchguard International, and Sandline have all offered military training. A Canadian firm, Black Bear Consulting, provides training in peacekeeping. Secrets, a French firm, had a contract with Cameroon to train a special force to guard the president. Two Israeli firms (Beni Tal and

---

[35] O'Brien, "Freelance Forces"; Raymond Bonner, "France Linked to Defense of Mobutu," *New York Times*, 2 May 1997: 6.

[36] http://www.eo.com, accessed January 1999. The terminology of the services EO offered, including "persuasion," are all from the EO site.

[37] Yves Goulet "Mixing Business with Bullets," *Jane's Intelligence Review* (September 1997); Singer, *Corporate Warriors*.

[38] Al J. Venter, "Gunships for Hire," *Flight International*, 21 August 1996; Al J. Venter, "Sierra Leone's Mercenary War," *Jane's International Defense Review* Vol. 28, No. 11, November 1995.

[39] Interview with Ed Soyster, 12 April 1999.

[40] BBC News, "US Firm to Rebuild Iraqi Army," 26 June 2003 available at http://news.bbc.co.uk/2/hi/business/3021794.stm. For reports of the difficulties Vinnell experiences, see Ariana Eunjung Cha, "Recruits Abandon Iraqi Army," *Washington Post* 13 December 2003.

Levden), two Australian firms (International Port Services Training Group Party, Ltd. and Fynwest Party, Ltd.), and a Belgian firm (International Defense and Security, IDAS) also offer training services for militaries.[41] Israeli firms are well known for covering the whole realm of weapons and services – one-stop shopping. The demand for training services is great in Africa and, in EO's wake, there are several firms located in and around South Africa (Saracen, Southern Cross Security, Frederick, Nicholas, and Duncan, and Erinys, to name a few) that offer these services as well.[42]

There are also firms that offer operational support in the form of command and control, transport, and weapons systems. Both Sandline and MPRI suggested they could offer command and control support to UN peace missions. More common are contractors that provide support for or operate weapons and information systems on the battlefield. As the technological sophistication of weapons systems and platforms have grown, more and more contractors have been hired to work with troops to maintain and support these systems. The United States Army's Task Force XXI Army Warfare Experiment (AWE) in March 1997 relied upon 1,200 civilian contractors from forty-eight different vendors. All of these people were in the field at the National Training Center providing advice, maintenance, and technical support.[43] During the first Gulf War, contractors provided operational support for TOW missiles, M1A1 tanks, Bradley fighting vehicles, and the Patriot missiles. During the 2003 war with Iraq, PSCs also provided operational support for the B-2 stealth bomber, the F-117 stealth fighter, Global Hawk UAV, U-2 reconnaissance aircraft, the M-1 tank, the Apache helicopter, and many navy ships. DynCorp's contracts to do aerial reconnaissance and crop spraying for the US in its support for Colombia's anti-drug war would also be included in the operational support category. AirScan, Eagle Aviation Services and Technology (EAST), ICI Oregon, Pacific Architects and Engineers (PA&E), and Sumairco are all US firms that provide operational support in the way of air services to the US or other militaries. Silver Shadow, an Israeli firm, and Ibis Air, a South African firm, both deliver these kinds of services as well.

---

[41] François Misser and Anver Versi, "Soldier of Fortune," *African Business* (December 1997): 3; http://www.beni-tal.co.il/.

[42] South Africa's attempt to regulate these companies, however, has caused them to operate less openly and it is thus harder to document the number and location of firms that actually sell services to other militaries. See chapter four for a more detailed discussion.

[43] See Mark Hanna, "Task Force XXI: the Army's Digital Experiment," *Strategic Forum* No. 119, July 1997.

Logistics support for militaries in the field is another significant market for the private sector that has many providers. A wide variety of PSCs offer transport, telecom, food, laundry, and other administrative services as well as setting up and taking down temporary bases and camps. Haliburton subsidiary, Kellogg, Brown and Root, KBR (a US company), has a huge presence in this market.[44] It supported American troops in Somalia, Haiti, Bosnia, Afghanistan, and the 2003 war with Iraq. Many others provide this kind of service: Bectel, ICI Oregon, PA&E, US Defense Systems, and Vinnell, are prominent in the US, ATCO Frontec Corp. and Global Risk Holdings are Canadian firms, Falconeer is a South African firm, Crown Agents, DSL, Global Development Four (GD4), and THULE Global Security International are all examples of British firms that do this kind of work.[45]

PSCs also offer internal security services, closer to what police routinely do, such as site security, international civilian police, police training, crime prevention, and intelligence. They include decades old private security companies such as Pinkertons and Wackenhut as well as new firms in South Africa, the UK, the US, and all over Europe. For instance, the US hires DSL to guard some of it embassies abroad. DSL frequently provides site security and crime prevention services for the UN and many INGOs as well as to transnational corporations (TNCs) working in the world's hot spots. Global Risk Holdings specializes in security and crime prevention and works mostly for mining and petroleum companies. Gray Security provides site security to oil and diamond companies in Angola and Lifeguard Security offers similar services to diamond mines in Sierra Leone.[46] Virtually all US contributions to international civilian police units in the 1990s were Dyncorp employees. DynCorp was also responsible for protecting Afghan president, Hamid Karzai.[47]

[44] Rachelle Cohen, "Potato Peeling Out, Peacekeeping In," *The Boston Herald*, 20 October 1999: 31. Also see Colonel Donald T. Wynn, "Managing the Logistics-Support in the Balkans Theater," *Engineer*, July 2000; Jane Nelson, *The Business of Peace* (London: Prince of Wales Business Leaders' Forum, 2000), p. 91; "Peacekeeping Helped Cheney Company," *Associated Press*, 28 August 2000; US General Accounting Office, "Contingency Operations: Army Should Do More to Control Costs in the Balkans," September 2000.
[45] http://www.icioregon.com/; http://www.thuleglobalsecurity.com/ (accessed 15 August 2001); Nelson, *Business of Peace*, p. 91; Yves Goulet, "DSL: Serving States and Multi-nationals," *Jane's Intelligence Review* Vol. 12, No. 6 (June 2000); Dean Andromidas, "Defense Systems Limited: Crown Jewel," *The Executive Intelligence Review* Vol. 22 (22 August 1997).
[46] "South African Security Consultant in Angola Murdered for Food", *Reuters*, 10 August 2000.
[47] David Isenberg, "Security for Sale in Afghanistan," *Asia Times Online*, 3 January 2003 http://www.atimes.com/atimes/Central Asia/EAO4AGO1.html.

Some companies provide advice and training to police. MPRI has recently acquired such a capability.[48] DynCorp won a contract with the US government to provide the initial training for the Iraqi police after the 2003 US war with Iraq, in addition to building a justice and prison system. London based TASK International has trained police in Malaysia, holds a contract to train police in Jamaica and has also trained the Nigerian Presidential Guard and the special forces of the United Arab Emirates.[49] Trojan Securities International offers similar services and draws from both British military personnel and US law enforcement.[50] Erinys, a new British and South African firm, is training a private Iraqi force to guard oil fields under contract with the US government.[51]

Harder to categorize are the contracts that offer operational capacity in counter-insurgency, anti-terrorism, and other special operations. These services, offered to states as well as multi-national corporations and other non-governmental entities, work in the nebulous area that connects external and internal security. Beni Tal is an Israeli firm that advertises a capacity to carry out special operations and Control Risk Group, of the UK, specializes in crisis response and has a large presence working in post-war Iraq.[52] US-based Blackwater also falls into this category. These companies promise to respond to crises offensively with armed personnel, but it is hard to know whether to call this a police/ SWAT-type action or a military special operations action. As their aim is combating not troops, but international criminal elements, they might be better characterized as internal security tasks. The demand for these kinds of services undoubtedly reflects the increasing concern with international criminal threats and the blurring of internal and external security.[53]

The role of PSCs in Iraq has yielded insights into the blurring of lines between policing and combat and the general blending of roles that accompany operating in a combat zone. Blackwater employees, under contract to the CPA to provide security to US administrator Paul Bremer and five outposts, carried weapons, had their own helicopters and fought off insurgents in ways that were hard to distinguish from

---

[48] See http://www.mpri.com.
[49] "Privatizing Combat: the New World Order," ICIJ Report, *The Business of War*, p. 6 available at http://www.icij.org/dtaweb/icij_bow.asp.
[50] Ibid.; see also http://www.trojansecurities.com/ (accessed 15 August 2001).
[51] Borzou Daragahi, "In Iraq, Private Contractors Lighten Load on U.S. Troops," *Special to the Post-Gazette*, 28 September 2003 available at http://www.post-gazette.com/pg/ 03271/226368.stm; Catan and Fidler, "With Post-war Instability."
[52] Ibid.
[53] Peter Andreas, "Redrawing Borders and Security in the Twenty-First Century," *International Security* Vol. 28, No. 2 (fall 2003): 78–111.

combat.[54] Also many jobs not technically considered core military tasks nonetheless have taken on greater danger or ability to inflict harm when performed in the midst of the insurgency. Truck driving may not sound like a core military responsibility, but KBR employees have died transporting fuel to troops when they have had to pass through combat zones to get there. Similarly, the four Blackwater employees who were killed and mutilated in Fallujah were simply guarding a convoy. Finally, interpreting may sound like a mundane job far from the core of military operations, but it may not be when interpreters are working at a military prison – indeed, two of the four contractors implicated in the abuses at Abu Ghraib prison were hired as interpreters or translators.[55] Indeed, though most were hired in operational support or internal security roles, contractors have played a central role in combating the Iraqi insurgency.

Mercenaries, privatization, and other slippery terms

While some have suggested that this market is the unleashing of another round of mercenaries, others claim that it is simply the extension of privatization further into the sphere of national security. But what is a mercenary? What is privatization? It turns out that everyday terms like "mercenary," "public," "private," "privatization," and "the state," have a variety of meanings that do not always travel well – across time or space. Thus a few definitions are in order.

The term "mercenary" has been used to describe everything from individuals killing for hire, to troops raised by one country working for another, to PSCs providing military services to their own country. Yet the organizational setup of German "mercenaries" fighting for the British during the American Revolution was quite different from the purely entrepreneurial French "mercenaries" active in Africa during the Cold War. In the American Revolution, the Germans sent organized units and the British paid the German rulers.[56] In the 1960s, guns for hire, such as the infamous Bob Denard, sold their individual skills for

---

[54] Dana Priest, "Private Guards Repel Attack on US Headquarters," *Washington Post*, 6 April 2004, p. A1; "Private Commandos Shoot Back on the Iraq Firing Line," *Associated Press*, 19 April 2004.

[55] Major General Antonio M. Taguba, "Article 15–6 Investigation of the 800th Military Police Brigade," report to US Central Command, March 2004.

[56] George III contracted with the Landgrave of Hesse-Cassel, who supplied 12,000 troops and the Duke of Brunswick and other petty German states provided another 5,000. An annual subsidy was paid to the dukes with extra payment for killed or wounded. Some have claimed that German contracts with other states paid rulers to build the foundations of what became the model military in Europe. See Gordon Craig, *The Politics of the*

their own personal profit. The fact that what "mercenary" refers to has changed over time is interesting for what it tells analysts about the shifts in what are considered legitimate uses of force, but makes the word less useful as an analytical term. Because efforts to catalogue activity as "mercenary" often refer to quite different phenomena with different implications for the institutions of violence, I will avoid it altogether.

What is private (and by association, public) offers up a different set of confusions. The public/private divide, as we generally understand it, is a modern phenomenon and one that has taken on a variety of meanings even within the modern era. It is commonly argued that the public/private divide only made sense with the consolidation of sovereignty, which allocated a public sphere over which the state had exclusive authority.[57] The terms "public" and "private" go back to the Greeks, though, and were used in the era before sovereignty as well.[58] The public sphere has been associated most clearly (in both the modern era and before) with the political: rule and government. In the modern era it has been specifically linked with the state, and, as democratic norms grew in parts of the world, with accountability.[59] The private sphere is taken to hold the market, the family, and the variety of activities that are deemed to take place outside the purview of the state – such as religion.

And yet, the distinctions do not always add up. When juxtaposing the private family with the public sphere, public may include the market-place. And, as Martha Minow points out, in modern times the very definition of what is private – from charity to marriage – is currently established by government policy. "What is a family, who is a parent, who can marry are each decisions made by governments with important

Prussian Army (London: Oxford University Press, 1955, 1979); Janice Thomson, Mercenaries, Pirates and Sovereigns: State Building and Extraterritorial Violence in Early Modern Europe (Princeton: Princeton University Press, 1994).

[57] See Thomson, Mercenaries, Pirates and Sovereigns; Hendrik Spruyt, The Sovereign State and its Competitors (Princeton: Princeton University Press, 1994).

[58] Jean Elshtain, Public Man, Private Woman (Princeton: Princeton University Press, 1981); in the pre-modern era, the words were used to distinguish between types of war – each subject to different rules. Public or open war (bellum hostile) referred to war between two sovereign Christian princes, in which spoils could be taken but prisoners had the right to expect to be ransomed. Feudal, covered war, or what came to be known as private war, referred to other conflicts where warring parties had license to wound or kill, but not to burn or take spoils. See Richard W. Kaeuper, War, Justice and the Public Order (Oxford: Clarendon Press, 1988), pp. 227–29.

[59] See John G. Ruggie, "Territoriality and Beyond: Problematizing Modernity in International Relations," International Organization Vol. 47, No. 1 (1993); Elshtain, Public Man, Private Woman; Claire Cutler, Virginia Haufler, and Tony Porter, "Private Authority and International Affairs," in Claire Cutler, Virginia Haufler, and Tony Porter, eds., Private Authority and International Affairs (Albany: SUNY Press, 1999), p. 18.

Table 1.2. *Dimensions of the public/private choice*

	Collective payment	Individual payment
Public Sector Delivery		
Private Sector Delivery		

Source: Donahue, *The Privatization Decision*, p. 7.

financial, reputational and moral consequences."[60] And then all of this refers to the world of advanced, industrialized countries where the state, government, and public revolve around some notion of collective good. In parts of the developing world, state institutions and international recognition of them function mainly as mechanisms for rulers to achieve personal (private) gain.[61]

In keeping with the most common usage, I will use "private" to refer to non-governmental actors. Commercial entities and NGOs fall into this category – however, so do vigilantes, paramilitaries, and organized crime bosses. Though I will use public to denote governmental institutions of whatever sort, because the meaning of public is associated with the pursuit of collective ends, my analysis will distinguish between governments that have the capacity and legitimacy to claim to work toward collective ends and those that do not.[62]

Privatization also refers to a range of phenomena.[63] In many parts of the world, privatization signified the sale of portions of state-owned industry to the private sector in the late twentieth century. During the same time in the US, privatization often indicated the private provision of public services – or private contracting. It also, however, can denote devolving control over the payment for services to the private sector. The US Postal Service is largely financed through private transactions and the British government has experimented with encouraging private investment in defense facilities. As John Donahue presents it, the Public/Private Choice has two dimensions – financing and performance (see Table 1.2).

---

[60] Martha Minow, *Partners, not Rivals: Privatization and the Public Good* (Boston: Beacon Press, 2002), p. 30.

[61] William Reno, *Warlord Politics and African States* (Boulder: Lynne Rienner, 1998).

[62] See chapter two for the development of this idea.

[63] John Donahue, *The Privatization Decision: Public Ends, Private Means* (New York: Basic, 1989); William Gormley, ed., *Privatization and its Alternatives* (Madison: University of Wisconsin Press, 1991); John Vickers and George Yarrow, "Economic Perspectives on Privatization," *Journal of Economic Perspectives* Vol. 5, No. 2 (spring 1991): 111–32.

Table 1.3. *The variety of arrangements for allocating violence*

	Financing for security services				
Delivery of security services	**NATIONAL FINANCING**	**FOREIGN NATIONAL FINANCING**	**MULTI-NATIONAL FINANCING**	**PRIVATE FINANCING (FOR-PROFIT)**	**PRIVATE (NOT-FOR-PROFIT) FINANCING**
NATIONAL DELIVERY	1. • US in WWII	2. • German troops in the American Revolution	3. • The first Gulf War	4. • Shell financing Nigerian Forces	5. • WWF financing park guards in Democratic Republic of Congo
FOREIGN NATIONAL DELIVERY	6. • German troops in the American Revolution	7. • Korean troops fighting for the US in Vietnam	8. • The first Gulf War	9. • Branch group contributing to Nigerian forces in Sierra Leone	10.
MULTI-NATIONAL DELIVERY	11. • NATO in Kosovo	12. • Muslim states' contribution to western military aid in Bosnia	13. • UN Peace-keeping	14.	15.
PRIVATE (FOR-PROFIT) DELIVERY	16. • MPRI's provision of ROTC trainers to the US	17. • MPRI's work for Croatia	18. • MPRI's work for Bosnia	19. • DSL working for Lonhro in Mozambique	20. • DSL working for ICRC around the world
PRIVATE (NOT-FOR-PROFIT) DELIVERY	21.	22.	23. • "Green Cross"	24. • BP financing Colombian paramilitaries	25. • Wildaid in Asia

In thinking about institutions for the management of violence, however, a variety of very different arrangements can end up in the top left-hand box: from traditional military arrangements, to foreign troops working for another state as the German forces worked for the British during the Revolutionary War, to UN troops. Also, deciding that governments should not pay for services does not necessarily mean individuals must pay. Private, but not individual, instruments exist such as commercial firms and NGOs. Table 1.3 parses out some of these arrangements and defines my key areas of focus.

As the shaded boxes in table 1.3 indicate, I will use the term privatization to refer to decisions to devolve *delivery or financing* of services to private entities – the two outermost rows and columns of table 1.3. The comparison then, is between private financing and/or delivery of security and the financing and/or delivery of security by states – either directly or through state-based consortiums such as international organizations. When states are trading tools of violence among themselves or allocating violence though international organizations made up of states, the monopoly over force remains (however imperfectly) with states.[64] The growth in the two outermost columns, however, potentially opens the way for markets, populated by non-governmental associations as well as states, to influence the control of violence. The privatization of finance gives private entities budgetary control over the use of forces. The privatization of delivery devolves control over the institutional setup of forces to private entities. The privatization of both moves the state out of a direct consequential role altogether. Furthermore, there are a variety of hybrid situations between private monies and foreign forces and foreign money and private forces that introduce new options for interface between actors on the world stage in the planning, execution, and management of violence. Though the market has not eclipsed other forms of allocating violence, it opens different avenues for interaction, different tools for intervention, and new possibilities for the participation of non-state actors in the use of violence.

The current market compared

This is not the first market for force. Markets for allocating violence were common before the systems of states came to dominate world politics. Feudal lords supplemented their forces with contracted labor

---

[64] A promising line of research would be to focus on the differences between these relationships. For a start down this path, see Kimberly Marten, *Enforcing the Peace: Learning from the Imperial Past* (New York: Columbia University Press, 2004).

from the beginning of the twelfth century, and from the end of the thirteenth century through the Peace of Westphalia in 1648 virtually all force was allocated through the market. Furthermore, the rise of the state did not immediately preclude the market allocation of violence. Early modern states both delegated control over force to commercial entities and participated in the market as both suppliers and purchasers.

In the era before the rise of the state, market allocation of force prevailed and virtually all force was contracted.[65] Stretching from the twelfth century through the Peace of Westphalia, military contractors employed forces that had been trained within feudal structures (and were frequently licensed by feudal lords) and then contracted with whomever could pay – Italian city states, the pope, emerging states, other feudal lords, and more.[66] In many cases, the contractor would earn the revenue for these forces, but sometimes the money went into government hands. For example, the Swiss cantons of the post-Renaissance period hired out their armies to rulers in France or Italy, with the payments coming directly into the coffers of the canton.[67] In this period, military enterprisers would put together forces to meet the diverse needs of a variety of different political forms including war-fighting, maintaining order and even providing taxation and administration services.[68]

Chartered companies, prominent in the seventeenth and eighteenth centuries, were an instance of state-delegated commercial control over

[65] For examinations of pre-modern contractors, see Fritz Redlich, *The German Military Enterpriser and his Workforce: a Study in European Economic and Social History*, Vols. 1 and 2 (Wiesbaden: Franz Steiner Verlag, 1964); Geoffrey Trease, *The Condottieri* (New York: Holt, Rinehart, and Winston, 1971); Charles Oman, *History of the Art of War in the Middle Ages*, 2nd edition (London, 1924); Geoffrey Parker, *The Thirty Years War* (London: Routledge, 1984); B. Guenee, *States and Rulers in Later Medieval Europe* (Oxford: Oxford University Press, 1985); Frederick H. Russell, *The Just War in the Middle Ages* (London: Cambridge University Press, 1975); Johan Huizinga, "The Political and Military Significance of Chivalric Ideas in the Late Middle Ages," in Johan Huizinga, *Men and Ideas: History, the Middle Ages, the Renaissance; Essays*. Trans. James S. Holmes and Hans van Marle (New York: Meridian, 1959); Richard Barber, *The Knight and Chivalry*, revised edition (Woodbridge: Boydell Press, 1995); Kaeuper, *War, Justice and the Public Order*; and, of course, Machiavelli, *The Prince*, ch. XII.

[66] Redlich, *German Military Enterpriser*, Anthony Mockler, *Mercenaries* (London: Macdonald, 1969), Oman, *History of the Art of War*.

[67] Anthony Mockler, *The New Mercenaries* (London: Sidgwick & Jackson, 1985), p. 8. There were actually two classes of Swiss mercenary. Competing with the "official" Swiss troops were privately contracted Swiss mercenaries. See Redlich, *German Military Enterpriser*, Vol. 1, p. 44.

[68] Martin Van Creveld, *The Transformation of War* (New York: Free Press, 1991).

violence.[69] Chartered companies were state-designated entities for engaging in long-distance trade and establishing colonies. The Dutch, English, French, and Portuguese all chartered companies during this time. French companies were state enterprises forged by the king and designed to increase state power later in the game.[70] Dutch companies were private wealth-seeking enterprises that were organized in a charter so as to enhance the Dutch profit relative to the English or (particularly) the Portuguese.[71] The crown chartered the English Companies for similar reasons.[72] These forces were both an army and a police force for establishing order and then protecting both trade routes and new territory.

Also during the early period of the state, states rented out their forces to other friendly states. German states supplied troops to a number of other countries including the Netherlands, Venice, and France, in addition to Britain.[73] The Dutch provided regiments to German princelings during the Seven Years War and to Britain in both the 1701 war with France and the 1745 Jacobite Rebellion within Britain.[74]

---

[69] S. P. Sen, *The French in India, 1763–1816* (Calcutta: Frima K. L. Mukhopadhyay, 1958); Holden Furber, *Rival Empires of Trade in the Orient, 1600–1800* (Minnesota: University of Minnesota Press, 1976); R. Mukherjee, *The Rise and Fall of the East India Company* (New York: Monthly Review Press, 1974); Bernard H. M. Velkke, *Evolution of the Dutch Nation* (New York: Roy Publishers, 1945); Gary Anderson and Robert Tollison, "Apologiae for Chartered Monopolies in Foreign Trade, 1600–1800," *History of Political Economy* Vol. 14, No. 4 (1983): 549–66; C. R. Boxer, *Jan Compagnie in War and Peace, 1602–1799* (Hong Kong: Heinemann Asia, 1979).

[70] Sen, *French in India*.

[71] The idea of a charter was proposed by a commission recommended by Johan van Oldenbarnevelt, the most prominent political figure of the time in Holland in the wake of news of dramatic profits had by Admiral Jacob Corneliszoon van Neck's ship in July 1599 (the haul of spices yielded a 400 percent profit) and similar English efforts. The United Netherlands Chartered East India Company was established in 1602. See Furber, *Rival Empires of Trade*, pp. 31–33.

[72] The English East India Company (incorporating the English Levant Company) was established in December 1600. The charter was renewed and altered in 1661. See Furber, *Rival Empires of Trade*, p. 32. See also the discussion in Thomson, *Mercenaries, Pirates, and Sovereigns*, pp. 33–35; Sen, *French in India*; Mukherjee, *Rise and Fall of the East India Company*; Velkke, *Evolution of the Dutch Nation*.

[73] German rulers who supplied troops to Britain in the American Revolution included His Most Sincere Highness of the Hereditary Court of Hanau (a few hundred infantry), His Most Sincere Highness the Duke of Brunswick (4,000 foot and 300 dragoons), and His Most Sincere Highness the Landgrave of Hesse Cassel (12,000 foot, 400 Jaegers armed with rifles, 300 dismounted dragoons, 3 corps of artillery, and 4 major-generals). See Mockler, *New Mercenaries*, p. 3.

[74] Thomson, *Mercenaries, Pirates, and Sovereigns*, pp. 28–29; Charles C. Bayley, *Mercenaries for the Crimea: the German, Swiss, and Italian Legions in British Service, 1854–1856* (Montreal: McGill-Queen's University Press, 1977), p. 4.

These troops would arrive equipped and ready to fight under the command of the contracting government.

Even in the modern system, some states have relied on the private sector, for weapons particularly, but also for logistics support, and for a variety of services idiosyncratic to a particular conflict. The US government, for instance, has a long history of looking to the market for military services.[75] Up until the beginning of World War II, most of these services were in the area of logistics support and weapons procurement. During the Cold War, however the US hired firms to perform military training missions as well.[76] Also, states still do "rent out" their forces – to UN peacekeeping units or to other states. In the first Gulf War, for instance, US forces were subsidized by Japan. In the 2003 war with Iraq, the US paid forces from other countries to participate in the coalition.

The extent of recent private security activity is a shift away from the practices common in the nation-state system since the French Revolution where citizen armies have been touted as the most appropriate (and effective) vehicles for generating security.[77] While market allocation of security was never completely eliminated in the modern era, it was frowned upon. This led private security to be informally organized, secretive, and directed to a specific customer base. Soldiers of fortune operated in the shadows – as did the covert private military services provided to individual governments. In the current system, though, PSCs have a corporate structure and operate openly, posting job listings on their web sites and writing papers and articles

---

[75] Though the first official statement on contracting did not come out until 1954 (the Budget Bureau Bulletin 55–4, revised in 1959 and 1966 and eventually renamed OMB Circular A-76), it is still in effect. The thrust of this directive is that government agencies should seek to obtain products and services through the private sector except in cases of national interest. See James Althouse, "Contractors on the Battlefield," *Army Logistician* (November/December 1998).

[76] The British government hired from the market for military services less frequently in the modern period than the US, but allowed its citizens to sell their services abroad. The commercial sale of security services by British citizens abroad can be traced back through the centuries. See Thomson, *Mercenaries, Pirates, and Sovereigns*, p. 22. More recently UK Special Air Services (SAS) personnel formed firms to sell military and security services during the Cold War. For instance, in 1967 Colonel Sir David Stirling founded WatchGuard International. See Kevin O'Brien, "PSCs, Myths, and Mercenaries," *Royal United Service Institute Journal*, February 2000. And, of course, individuals acting on their own sold a variety of services in Africa during the Cold War. See S. J. G. Clarke, *The Congo Mercenary* (Johannesburg: SAIIA Press, 1968); Mockler, *New Mercenaries*.

[77] Eliot Cohen, *Citizens and Soldiers: the Dilemmas of Military Service* (Ithaca: Cornell University Press, 1985); Thomson, *Mercenaries, Pirates, and Sovereigns*; Deborah Avant, "From Mercenary to Citizen Armies: Explaining Change in the Practice of War," *International Organization* Vol. 54, No. 1 (winter 2000): 41–72.

mulling over the costs and benefits of the private sector in security. They have sought, and received, some degree of international acceptance. Also, PSCs operate in a global market – not only does the US hire its PSCs, but so do foreign governments and private sector actors. While PSCs certainly operate with an eye toward their home government, they also attend to the character of demand from the wider consumer base outside their borders.

The corporate form, relative openness, acceptance, and transnational spread of today's security industry bear many similarities to the late Middle Ages and early modern period. There are some features of today's market, though, that are unique. First, unlike the military enterprisers of the late Middle Ages, today's PSCs do not so much provide the foot soldiers, but more often act as supporters, trainers, and force multipliers for local forces. PSCs, then, are different from private armies – when they leave, they leave behind whatever expertise they have imparted – subject to whatever local political controls (or lack thereof) exist. Second, unlike the period of the chartered companies, states do not authorize private take-over of other territories, even though TNCs and INGOs finance security on their own – either by subsidizing weak states or by hiring PSCs. Thus chartered companies provided a more specific administrative and legal framework for the private use of force than is the case with private financiers today.

Why the current market?

Though my aim is to describe the current market and explore its implications rather than explain its rise, some explanation is in order.[78] In 1994, Janice Thomson claimed that the twentieth century ushered in a stage where the practice of non-state violence became unthinkable.[79] Barely a decade later, it is apparent that the development of a market was already well under way even as her book was in publication. How did the unthinkable become commonplace?

As would be the case in the development of any market, the increase in private security can be tied to supply and demand. In the 1990s, the supply factors came from both local (the end of apartheid in South Africa) and international (the end of the Cold War) phenomena that caused militaries to be downsized in the late '80s and early '90s. Military downsizing led to a flood of experienced personnel available for

---

[78] For a model of military change that informs the discussion that follows, see Avant, "From Mercenaries to Citizen Armies."

[79] Thomson, *Mercenaries, Pirates, and Sovereigns.*

contracting.[80] Concomitant with the increase in supply was an increase in the demand for military skills on the private market – from western states that had downsized their militaries, from countries seeking to upgrade and westernize their militaries as a way of demonstrating credentials for entry into western institutions, from rulers of weak or failed states no longer propped up by superpower patrons, and from non-state actors such as private firms, INGOs, and groups of citizens in the territories of weak or failed states.

There are those who assume that the turn to PSCs was *the* obvious, natural, and functional response to the material changes technology brought to warfare and the shift in the balance of power after the Cold War.[81] Arguments about the future of defense in the US illustrate this thinking. The United States, as the sole remaining superpower, must accomplish a variety of international ends. It must leap ahead technologically, search for the next peer competitor, and maintain the capacity to keep some modicum of order in a variety of important, but less than vital, arenas.[82] Maintaining stability includes combating illicit by-products of globalization such as organized crime, drugs, and terrorism as well as enforcing emerging global norms about human rights and encouraging the democratic institutions that are seen as supporting such norms.[83] In response to these imperatives, Eliot Cohen

[80] Looking to history, it is often the case that the downsizing of militaries (for whatever reason) leads to a rise in private military activity as skilled military personnel look for places to sell their talents. See Peter Lock, "Africa, Military Downsizing and the Growth in the Security Industry," in Jakkie Cilliers and Peggy Mason, eds., *Peace, Profit, or Plunder?* (Pretoria: Institute for International Studies). He mentions the increase of European officers in Latin American states in the wake of the Congress of Vienna agreement and the influx of German military personnel to advise Chiang Kai-Shek following the Treaty of Versailles. Though exact comparisons are probably weak, it is useful to remember that the general phenomenon is not new.

[81] Joseph Nye and William Owens, "America's Information Edge," *Foreign Affairs* (March/April 1996): 20–36; Andrew Krepinevich, "Cavalry to Computer," *The National Interest* (fall 1994): 30–42; Eliot Cohen, "A Revolution in Warfare," *Foreign Affairs* (March/April 1996): 37–54; Cohen, "Defending America's Interest"; Thomas P. M. Barnett, "The Pentagon's New Map of the World," *Esquire* (March 2003); Robert Kaplan, "The Coming Anarchy," *The Atlantic Monthly* (February 1994).

[82] It is assumed that those countries most able to leap ahead in the technology necessary to integrate complex information systems will be advantaged in the next conflict. See Nye and Owens, "America's Information Edge," Krepinevich, "Cavalry to Computer," Cohen, "A Revolution in Warfare," Cohen, "Defending America."

[83] Barnett, "The Pentagon's New Map of the World," Kaplan, "The Coming Anarchy." For the illicit side of globalization, see H. Richard Friman and Peter Andreas, *The Illicit Global Economy and State Power* (New York: Roman and Littlefield, 1999). For the trend toward enforcing norms of human rights, see Anthony Clarke Arend and Robert J. Beck, *International Law and the Use of Force: Beyond the UN Charter Paradigm* (New York: Routledge, 1993); Martha Finnemore, "Constructing Norms of Humanitarian Intervention," in Peter Katzenstein, ed., *The Culture of National Security: Norms and*

has argued that it makes good sense to privatize. This way the US can make the most of information "spin on," take advantage of capitalist economies, and manage in a complex world with fewer troops.[84] Privatization will connect the military with the civilian sector, which is driving technological change in the information age and will produce the most cost-efficient solutions.

But this kind of argument begs important questions that indicate alternative paths. Why must the US leap ahead if it has no peer challenger? Why must the US rely on fewer troops (could downsizing not be reversed as military requirements grow)? And why were military requirements growing – particularly in the 1990s? Why must the US enforce *global* order and *global* norms?[85] Finally, why do non-state actors not simply leave areas where the state will not provide security? Why do they opt to pay for their own protection? While it is true that changes in the distribution of power and nature of technology unsettled Cold War patterns, neither necessitated that states turn toward private military services or that non-state actors assume responsibility for their own protection.

Scholars of globalization provide part of the rationale for the turn toward private security. In a globalizing world, market pressures, technology, and social change create new demands for goods that states have difficulty supplying or fostering because the scale of the goods people demand is different from the scale of the nation-state. As Philip Cerny puts it, "the more that the scale of goods and assets produced, exchanged, and/or used in a particular economic sector or activity diverges from the structural scale of the national state – both from above (the global scale) and from below (the local scale) – and the more these divergences feed back into each other in complex ways, then the more that the authority, legitimacy, policy making capacity, and

---

Identity in World Politics (New York: Columbia University Press, 1996); Laura Reed and Carl Kayson, *Emerging Norms of Justified Intervention* (Cambridge, MA: Committee on International Security Studies, American Academy of Arts and Sciences, 1993); Fernando Teson, *Humanitarian Intervention: an Inquiry into Law and Morality* (Dobbs Ferry, NY: Transaction Publishers, 1988).

[84] Cohen, "Defending America's Interest in the Twenty-First Century." Van Creveld builds this notion when he argues that the nature of war as we have known it since the Peace of Westphalia is changing. Unless the state can muster its capacity to confront low intensity conflict, it will destroy the basis of state authority and break down the divisions between public and private, crime and war, etc. Pretending that war against other states is the only real war and that past conventions will dictate the future, fallacies he attributes to Clausewitz, will cause the demise of the state. Van Creveld, *Transformation of War.*

[85] Waltz asked the same question. Kenneth Waltz, "The Emerging Structure of International Politics," *International Security* Vol. 18, No. 2 (fall, 1993).

policy-implementing effectiveness of states will be challenged from both without and within."[86] Though much analysis of globalization's effects has focused on the economy, as interests and values are directed toward global or transnational goals, security concerns are not far behind.[87]

Global security concerns are partly a result of the variety of ways people have come to see security – including environmental and economic well being – that cannot be guaranteed by one state alone.[88] More concretely, however, as disorder in one part of the world has combined with information technology and the speed of travel to feed insecurity in another, security has become increasingly diffuse and borders more complicated to defend.[89] The new threat environment has been heralded (from the right and the left) as bringing with it new forms of warfare and the merging of security with a variety of other economic and political forms.[90] Thus, "national" security has become difficult to distinguish from international or global security and the lines between internal and external security have blurred. This is true for moralists who feel responsible to intervene in order to help quell violence, pragmatists who worry about economic disruptions, and hard-headed

[86] Philip Cerny, "Globalization and the Changing Nature of Collective Action," *International Organization* Vol. 49, No. 4 (autumn 1995): 597. See also Susan Strange, *Retreat of the State: the Diffusion of Power in the World Economy* (Cambridge: Cambridge University Press, 1996); David Held, Anthony McGrew, David Goldblatt, and Jonathan Perraton, *Global Transformations: Politics, Economics, and Culture* (Stanford: Stanford University Press, 1999), pp. 137–43; Elizabeth Sköns and Herbert Wulf, "The Internationalization of the Arms Industry," *Annals of the American Academy of Political and Social Sciences*, Vol. 636, September 1994; David Silverberg, "Global Trends in Military Production and Conversion," *Annals of the American Academy of Political and Social Sciences*, Vol. 636, 1994.

[87] Held et al., *Global Transformations*, "Introduction," Ch. 2; Jean-Marie Guehenno, "The Impact of Globalization on Strategy," *Survival* Vol. 40, No. 4 (winter 1998–99): 5–19.

[88] For the debate about how to define security, see Joseph Nye and Sean Lynn Jones, "International Security Studies: Report of a Conference on the State of the Field," *International Security* Vol. 12, No. 4 (spring 1988); Jessica Tuchman Mathews, "Redefining Security," *Foreign Affairs* Vol. 68, No. 2 (spring 1989): 162–77; Barry Buzan, "New Patterns of Global Security in the Twenty-First Century," *International Affairs* Vol. 67, No. 3 (1991); Stephen Walt, "The Renaissance of Security Studies," *International Studies Quarterly* Vol. 35, No. 2 (June 1991): 211–40; Edward Kolodziej, "Renaissance of Security Studies? Caveat Lector!" *International Studies Quarterly* Vol. 36 (December 1992): 421–38; David Baldwin, "Security Studies and the End of the Cold War," *World Politics* Vol. 48, No. 1 (October 1995): 117–41; Roland Paris, "Human Security: Paradigm Shift or Hot Air?" *International Security* Vol. 26, No. 2 (fall 2001): 87–102.

[89] Andreas, "Redrawing Borders."

[90] See Van Creveld, *Transformation of War*; Mary Kaldor, *Old and New Wars: Organized Violence in a Global Era* (Stanford: Stanford University Press, 1999); Mark Duffield, *Global Governance and the New Wars: the Merging of Security and Development* (New York: Zed, 2002).

realists who worry about breeding grounds for terrorists. When illicit criminal networks produce not only social "bads" such as drugs and prostitution, but also funding for terror, the internal governance of far-flung territories are (arguably) crucial national security issues.[91] Indeed, the degree to which realists like Cohen and Kaplan openly acknowledge American interests in global order demonstrates the extent of interconnectedness between peoples.[92] The 11 September attacks intensified fears about order in distant parts of the world, and were a dramatic demonstration of the disjuncture between the scale of national military organizations and the security needs persons, groups, and countries feel.

The fact that global trends demonstrated a mismatch between security concerns and national military institutions, however, did not necessitate privatization. In fact, the pursuit of goals associated with public goods on a "greater than national scale" had been increasingly facilitated by multi-lateral institutions. In the immediate wake of the Cold War, some argued that reaching new security goals required greater capacity for multi-lateral security organs[93] and many predicted the growth and strengthening of multi-lateral institutions to meet new security concerns.[94] The possibility that the UN should be arranged to provide security tools (such as peace enforcement) for this new world was debated – as was the possibility that NATO or other regional security organizations might be strengthened to do the same. Funding, activism, and research on multi-lateral organizations like the UN, NATO, the European Union (EU), and the Organization for Security and Cooperation in Europe (OSCE) took off in the 1990s.[95] Even financial institutions like the World Bank and International Monetary fund (IMF) began to think about the security consequences of their actions.

[91] Barnett, "The Pentagon's New Map of the World"; John J. Hamre and Gordon R. Sullivan, "Toward Post-conflict Reconstruction," *Washington Quaterly* Vol. 25, No. 4 (autumn 2002); Robert Orr, "Governing When Chaos Rules: Enhancing Governance and Participation," *Washington Quaterly* Vol. 25, No. 4 (autumn 2002).
[92] Cohen, "Defending America"; Kaplan, "The Coming Anarchy."
[93] See, for instance, John G. Ruggie, *Constructing the World Polity* (London: Routledge, 1998).
[94] See Held et al., *Global Transformations*, p. 44; John G. Ruggie, ed., *Multilateralism Matters* (New York: Columbia University Press, 1993); James Goldgeier and Michael McFaul, "A Tale of Two Worlds: Core and Periphery in the Post-Cold War Era," *International Organization* Vol. 46, No. 2 (spring 1992).
[95] See for instance, Ruggie, *Constructing the World Polity*; Celeste Wallender, "NATO after the Cold War," *International Organization* 54:4 (autumn 2000): 705–36; Walter Mattli and Anne-Marie Slaughter, "Law and Politics in the European Union," *International Organization* Vol. 49, No. 1 (winter 1995): 183–90; John Duffield, "NATO's Functions after the Cold War," *Political Science Quarterly* Vol. 109, No. 5 (winter 1994–95): 763–87.

Prevailing ideas about the benefits of privatization, however, suggested an alternative response to this scale mismatch. In the US and Britain, the privatization movement began with the arguments of British academics and Conservative Party officials who articulated a sweeping privatization agenda as Margaret Thatcher took office in 1979.[96] Arguing that social programs generated massive inefficiencies and financing them required incentive-sapping levels of taxation and inflationary budget deficits, Conservatives "viewed retrenchment not as a necessary evil but as a necessary good."[97] Initially, these ideas were associated with the powerful conservative coalitions in the US and the UK in the 1980s, but the collapse of the Soviet block, the ensuing privatization of state-owned industries across Europe, and the endorsement of these principles by international financial institutions like the IMF and the World Bank led privatization to be endorsed much more widely. Privatization has been associated with comparative advantage and competition, leading to efficient and effective market responses and contrasted with staid, expensive, and backward-looking bureaucratic response.[98]

The appeal of privatization ideas both led people to see private alternatives as obvious and affected the growth of private supply. For instance, in the US the strength of privatization ideas was articulated administratively by revisions to the Office of Management and Budget (OMB) circular A-76, which required competition from the private sector for non-core governmental services.[99] The increasing enforcement of this requirement encouraged the development of new companies. The retired American military officers who founded MPRI report thinking of this trend as a chance to capitalize on their skills and connections to profit by supplying non-core services to the US military.[100]

The end of the Cold War moved these two trends together in western defense and foreign policy. Government bureaucracies, designed around what had been the forty-year Cold War reality, looked like especially poor tools to meet the challenges of a new and uncertain world. Also, western politicians promised a "peace dividend" to be had by shrinking the military in the face of a less dangerous world. Just two years into the "New World Order," though, a rash of smaller-scale conflicts unleashed

---

[96] See Madsen Pirie, *Dismantling the State* (Dallas: National Center for Policy Analysis, 1985); Donahue, *Privatization Decision*.

[97] Paul Pierson, *Dismantling the Welfare State? Reagan, Thatcher and the Politics of Retrenchment* (Cambridge: Cambridge University Press, 1994), p. 1.

[98] Harvey Feigenbaum, Jeffrey Henig, and Chris Hamnett, *Shrinking the State: the Political Underpinnings of Privatization* (Cambridge: Cambridge University Press, 1998), ch. 1.

[99] http://www.whitehouse.gov/omb/circulars/a076.pdf (accessed April 2003). See chapter four (this volume), footnote 20 for more detail on contracting and the A-76 process.

[100] Interview with Ed Soyster, 12 April 1999.

disorder and demands for intervention. As the clamor for a western response grew just as western militaries were shrinking, nascent PSCs provided a stop-gap tool for meeting greater demands with smaller forces.[101]

The Cold War's end had a different impact in the former eastern bloc (where it led to defunct governance structures and forces, new opportunities, and a sudden opening to global flows) and in the developing world (where it abruptly ended superpower patronage – revealing the enduring difficulties of these governments and their militaries: corruption, poor standards, poor management, ethnic rivalries, etc.). In each instance, the potential for violence increased.[102] Weak governments paved the way for ethnic mobilization, transnational criminal activity, warlords, rebels, and paramilitaries, and the result ravaged civilians, enslaved children, destroyed the environment, and otherwise disrupted order and violated global norms.[103] In some cases PSCs provided tools for weak governments in the eastern bloc and the developing world to shore up their capabilities.[104]

The utter incapacity of states in many areas also complicated the strategies of non-state actors. INGOs were eager to maintain a presence in conflicted territories, to provide relief for civilians, to protect the environment, or to foster development. This was partly to pursue their purpose – once released from the restricted movement during the Cold War, they were eager to do their work where it was needed most.[105]

---

[101] According to Robert Perito, who served as the Deputy Director of the International Criminal Investigative Training Assistance Program at the US Department of Justice during the 1990s, this was the logic for the initial use of DynCorp to mobilize a small group of international civilian police to send to Haiti. The US had no such force and DynCorp could provide one. Interview June 2004. See also, Robert Perito, *The American Experience with Police in Peacekeeping Operations* (Clementsport: Canadian Peacekeeping Press, 2002).

[102] Though the level of internal conflict grew steadily from the 1950s, it peaked in 1992. The particular nature of violence post Cold War was tied frequently to incompetent governments. See Ted Robert Gurr, Mony G. Marshall, and Deepa Khosla, *Peace and Conflict 2001* (College Park: Center for International Development and Conflict, 2000); Michael Brown, "The Cause of Internal Conflict," in Michael Klare and Yogesh Chandrani, eds., *World Security: Challenges for a New Century* (New York: St. Martin's Press, 1998); Kaldor, *New and Old Wars*.

[103] For the connection between weak governments and internal war, see James Fearon and David Laitin, "Ethnicity, Insurgency, and Civil War," *American Political Science Review* Vol. 97, No. 1 (February 2003): 75–90.

[104] Vladim Volkov, *Violent Entrepreneurs: the Use of Force in the Making of Russian Capitalism* (Ithaca: Cornell University Press, 2002); Sinclair Dinnen, Anthony J. Regan, and Ron May, eds., *Challenging the State: the Sandline Affair in Papua New Guinea* (Canberra: Australian National University, 1997).

[105] Margaret Keck and Katherine Sikkink, *Activists Beyond Borders: Advocacy Networks in International Politics* (Ithaca: Cornell University Press, 1998).

Their actions were also motivated, though, by a need to maintain
funding in order to carry out their purpose, which frequently required
them to be present in the most visible emergencies.[106] Commercial non-
state actors faced similar concerns about lack of order, which threatened
their property, personnel, and potential for generating profit.[107]
Transnational firms in the extractive industry, particularly, are often
likely to stay in dangerous areas if that is where the resources are.
Unable to rely on weak states for security and often unwilling to leave,
these actors have provided another pool of demand for non-state
protection that PSCs have exploited.

A key question, a decade and a half after the Cold War's end, is why
global security demands have enhanced the market rather than the
multi-lateral alternative. In part it is because multi-lateral institutions
have encountered operational difficulties. The UN experimented with
peace enforcement missions in Somalia, Bosnia, and Rwanda, but was
beset with problems.[108] Though the operational issues are potentially
overcome, the political issues that underlie them are more daunting. All
may agree that *something* should be done in a particular instance, but
generating agreement on what that something is has been difficult. In
this context, the UN has been increasingly seen in the same framework
as government bureaucracies – only worse, unresponsive, expensive, *and*
unaccountable.[109] The US, under President George W. Bush, has
specifically questioned the legitimacy of the UN by arguing that some of
the governments are poor representatives of their people because they
are illegitimate. Even within institutions such as NATO, where
countries are arguably held to greater standards of legitimacy than
among the UN General Assembly, agreement on intervention and
strategies for intervention have been hard to reach. This was an issue in
Bosnia and then in Kosovo.[110] Other regional organizations, particularly

---

[106] Alexander Cooley and James Ron, "The NGO Scramble: Organizational Insecurity and the Political Economy of Transnational Action," *International Security* Vol. 27, No. 1 (summer 2002): 5–39.
[107] Virginia Haufler, "Is there a Role for Business in Conflict Prevention?" in Chester Crocker, Fen Osler Hampson, and Pamela Aall, eds., *Turbulent Peace: the Challenges of Managing International Conflict* (Washington, DC: United States Institute of Peace, 2001).
[108] For an analysis of the difficulties, see Lakhdar Brahimi, "Report of the Panel on United Nations Peace Operations," A/55/305-S/2000/80 (21 August 2000).
[109] Ironically, some suggestions for improving UN missions involve the use of PSCs to train potential UN forces and perhaps provide some of the command and control that advocates of privatization believe would solve some UN problems.
[110] Ivo H. Daalder and Michael E. O'Hanlon, *Winning Ugly: NATO's War to Save Kosovo* (Washington, DC: Brookings, 2000); Wesley Clark, *Waging Modern War: Bosnia, Kosovo, and the Future of Conflict* (New York: Public Affairs, 2001).

in Africa, have manifested greater problems with operational capacity, legitimacy, and agreement.[111] When the political agreement necessary to field multi-lateral forces was hard to reach, PSCs provided an alternative tool.

Thus, while the growth of the current market was neither natural nor inevitable, changes (material and ideational) placed private security options on the agenda. The reluctance of states to take on the variety of missions that people have felt moved to respond to, and the poor performance of multi-lateral institutions have made the private alternative appear more workable, as have prevailing beliefs that private means cheaper and better. Though some countries have been less enthusiastic about PSCs than the US, the fact that the US (with defense expenditures greater than the next twenty-four countries combined and roughly 1 percent of Gross World Product, GWP) has embraced private security solutions guarantees strong state demand, demand that is increasingly joined by the UK and other western states.[112] The presence of PSCs has allowed transnational corporations and INGOs additional alternatives for maintaining a presence in those parts of the world where the state is weak or failing. As they have taken advantage of these alternatives, the demand for private security has become multi-faceted.

Plan of the book

In the following chapter, I detail the analytical claims I sketched above about the implications of this market for the control of force. I draw together insights from studies on privatization and studies on civil–military relations to bolster my claim that we need to examine all three dimensions of control (functional, political, and social) and how they fit together. I then review institutional theories inspired by economic and sociological reasoning, examine the mechanisms of control they posit, and generate hypotheses about the privatization of security for state contracts with PSCs, for state regulation of PSCs, and for non-state financing of violence.

Chapters three, four, and five illustrate my argument in the three different relationships, respectively. In chapter three, I examine how state contracts with PSCs affected the different dimensions of control

---

[111] Herbert Howe, *Ambiguous Order: Military Forces in African States* (Boulder: Lynne Rienner, 2001), ch. 4.

[112] *The World Factbook, 2001* (Washington, DC: CIA, 2001); Barry Posen, "Command of the Commons: the Military Foundations of US Hegemony," *International Security* Vol. 28, No. 1 (summer 2003), p. 10 gives the 1 percent of Gross World Product figure. See his footnote for his method of calculation.

and the fit between them in countries that have contracted for similar services: the United States, Croatia, and Sierra Leone. Chapter four examines the impact of state strategies to regulate the export of security services on control by considering experiences from the three largest exporters: the United States, Britain, and South Africa. In chapter five, I explore the impact of non-state financing of security on the control of force, looking at oil companies in Nigeria, relief INGOs in the Goma Camps, and conservation INGOs in Garamba National Park, Democratic Republic of Congo.

In chapter six, I elaborate on the challenges and opportunities surrounding both the use of market mechanisms to control force and the diffusion of control over force to a variety of different entities. I point out some dilemmas in current and historical examples and suggest relevant trade-offs to assess when thinking about strategies to manage the market for force. Chapter seven concludes and links the privatization of security to debates about international politics more generally.

2   Private security and the control of force

Optimists and pessimists disagree about the consequences of privatization for the control of force, but they also view control differently. This chapter begins by fleshing out these various conceptions of control and then describing how I will define, measure, and evaluate the control of force in this study. In the second section, I develop a synthetic institutional model to generate expectations about how privatization should affect the control of force. In keeping with the discussion in the previous chapter about the variety of ways privatization can occur, I develop the logic for both the private *provision* of security and the private *financing* of security. Do contracts with PSCs affect the ability of states to control force? Can states control the export of security services? How does private financing affect the control of force? In the third, fourth, and fifth sections, I deduce hypotheses from this institutional model for each relationship and explain the set of cases I will examine to probe their plausibility. The sixth section ends the chapter by explaining the claims I am making in the study and justifying my methodology.

Clarifying the control of force

The civil–military relations literature, which specifically examines the control of force, reflects attention to all three dimensions of control evident in the debate over private security: functional, political, and social. Those who emphasize the functionality of force use a military's ability to deploy coercion effectively to defend the state's interests as the standard by which to measure control.[1] Others claim that not only should forces defend the state's interest, they should do so within the bounds of received political structures.[2] Still others have judged control by the military's fidelity to the larger social context – the degree to which

---

[1] Samuel Huntington, *Soldier and the State: the Theory and Politics of Civil–Military Relations* (New York: Vintage 1957).
[2] S. E. Finer, *Man on Horseback: the Role of the Military in Politics* (New York: Praeger, 1962) was particularly concerned with this. See also Huntington, *Soldier and the State*.

the military has achieved a meaningful integration with social values.[3] Scholars of privatization refer to a similar range of meanings when evaluating privatization's merits in other issue areas.[4]

It is clear that control of the military varies by the polity's ability to generate the security function it requires – an effective military. This functional imperative, Huntington argued, is primary.[5] Does the military perform well or not? Troops with lax discipline, ill prepared to defend the nation's interests, reduce functional control, while crack troops ready to perform the tasks required for security enhance functional control. This assumes that the function a military should perform is clear (a big assumption in some cases) but in general, functional control varies according to how effective the military agent is at generating security.

The control of force, however, can also vary in its allegiance to the political structures in place. Even if they are highly effective, Finer argued, troops that seize power in a coup have evaded control. Many analysts have suggested that even more moderate changes in the political control of force that redistribute power within a polity count as losses in control.[6] This assumes, first and foremost, that civilian judgments should carry the day – civilians have a "right to be wrong" – but also that

---

[3] Morris Janowitz, *The Professional Soldier: a Social and Political Portrait* (New York: Free Press 1960), p. 420.

[4] John Donahue endorses the need to think of cost efficiency, political integrity, and fidelity to public values. He also speaks of the special burden of accountability in the public realm based on the importance of public functions, the need for public authorities to attend to the public's interest, and the vulnerability of individuals to the powers of government. See Donahue, *Privatization Decision*, pp. 172, 12, and 11. Jody Freeman similarly speaks of four objections to contracting out that reflect worries over how well contracts function, how they affect power and law, and whether they are ethical within the received public value system. See her discussion of consequentialist concerns, technocratic concerns, ethical concerns, and legal concerns. Jody Freeman, "The Contracting State," *Florida State University Law Review* Vol. 28 (2000): 169–76. Harvey Feigenbaum and Jeffrey Henig look at the various effects privatization can have – on the efficiency of government, on the interests of individual politicians, interest groups, or political parties, and on the structural reallocation of power, which enshrines the public value system. See Harvey Feigenbaum and Jeffrey Henig, "The Political Underpinnings of Privatization: a Typology," *World Politics* Vol. 46, No. 2 (January 1994): 185–208. They call the third dimension "systemic" and look particularly at the structural reallocation of power among classes or the diminished capacity, authority, and legitimacy of the state (p. 206). Both of these, however, can be seen as different manifestations of the underlying public value system.

[5] Huntington, *The Soldier and the State*, p. 3.

[6] For the classic concern, see Finer, *Man on Horseback*. For arguments that we should also look at more moderate effects, see Michael Desch, "War and State Strength," *International Organization* Vol. 50, No. 2 (spring 1996); Peter Feaver, *Armed Servants: Agency, Oversight, and Civil–Military Relations* (Harvard: Harvard University Press, 2002); Peter Feaver and Richard Kohn, *Soldiers and Civilians: the Civil–Military Gap and American National Security* (Cambridge: MIT Press, 2001).

the control of force should not advantage one group over another. The political control of force, then, varies by whether it reinforces or redistributes power among individuals, organizations, and institutions.[7] Analyses of civil–military relations generally assume a conservative bias calling changes in political control, control loss. This is an unfortunate by-product of applying models developed for the United States or other advanced industrial democracies to different kinds of polities.[8] It is not hard to imagine countries for which change in the political control of force could enhance the legitimacy of the political process and be viewed as an improvement.[9] Thus I do not assume an inherent benefit or cost associated with changes in political control. Political control varies according to whether there is a shift in the power of different actors over the control of force.

Finally, force can be more or less consistent with the larger values, culture, and expectations of people in society. As general societal views on democracy, international law, human rights, and the protection of civilians in warfare change, for instance, the tools of force may reflect these values to a greater or lesser degree. Janowitz argued in the 1960s that among western, industrialized countries societal values demanded something different from the military than they had in the past – a commitment to the minimum use of force and "viable international relations" rather than the maximum use of force and victory.[10] Over the course of the Cold War and in its aftermath, military professionalism within advanced industrial states has increasingly enshrined principles drawn from theories of democracy (civilian control of the military and abidance by the rule of law), liberalism (respect for human rights), and the laws of war.[11] The *social* control of force can be said to vary by the degree to which the tools that perform security tasks reflect these prevailing societal values.

---

[7] I am using power in its classic sense – the ability of A to get B to do what he would otherwise not do. See Herbert Simon, "Notes on the Observation and Measurement of Power," *Journal of Politics* Vol. 15 (November 1953). A political structure sets the terms by which people compete for power and change in that structure, or evasion of its terms, redistribute power among political actors.

[8] This, of course, is just what modernization theory was criticized for. See Leonard Binder, "The Natural History of Development Theory," *Comparative Study of Society and History* Vol. 28, No. 1 (1986). The study of civil–military relations has been faulted for the same problem. See Rebecca Shiff, "Civil–military Relations Reconsidered: A Theory of Concordance," *Armed Forces and Society* Vol. 22, No. 1 (fall 1995): 7–24.

[9] Huntington's theory of political development makes this point. See Samuel Huntington, *Political Order in Changing Societies* (New Haven: Yale University Press, 1968).

[10] Janowitz, *Professional Soldier*, p. 418.

[11] See Charles Moskos, John Allen Williams, and David Segal, *The Postmodern Military: Armed Forces after the Cold War* (New York: Oxford University Press, 2000).

How to measure privatization's effects on these variables requires comparing private options with the "public," or state-based, alternative. There is generally some loss of control, or slippage, associated with *any* delegation; the question should not be how private choices compare with an ideal relationship, but how they compare with other available options. In the case of functional control, I will assess the effects of privatization by comparing the capabilities of state versus private agents to perform security tasks, taking into account their relative cost.[12] To judge privatization's effect on political control, I will compare the political processes by which state and private entities finance or deploy force. If using private security providers changes the process in a way that privileges some institutions or actors more than others, adds new actors to the process, alters the resources (such as access to information) available to political actors, or most dramatically changes the regime, it has changed political control.

Ascertaining whether privatization leads to a greater or lesser integration of force with the referent values surrounding violence is more complicated. I will largely adopt the techniques prominent among other studies that examine values: looking at whether values are more or less likely to be referred to, comparing the behavior of actors to assess their (implied) attendance to values, and comparing the values represented in the decision-making process to assess the difference between the financing and delivery of security by private entities and their alternative. There may be tensions, however, in the way the "basket" of international norms is interpreted in different contexts. This is particularly likely in weak states. Widely recognized international values have developed in western advanced industrial democracies and cannot be assumed to represent predominant values in less developed or less western areas. In the US, meaningful integration with societal values is often taken as a good thing (even though it may not mean the same thing to everyone) and assumed to be consistent with other international norms like the sovereignty of the state.[13] In a country like Sierra Leone,

---

[12] Some will quibble with including the cost in a judgment of functional control – arguing that it is military effectiveness, not efficiency, that we should be measuring. Many definitions of military effectiveness, however, do refer to the capacity to convert a given set of resources into fighting power. See Allan Millet, Williamson Murray, and Kenneth Watman, "The Effectiveness of Military Organizations," in Millet and Murray, eds., *The Postmodern Military, Vol. I: the First World War* (Boston, MA: Houghton Mifflin, 1988), pp. 1–30.

[13] For an example of the different interpretations, Feigenbaum and Henig, "The Political Underpinnings of Privatization," write about the way in which the private provision can change the underlying meaning of the state. Because the state is the sphere within which public is defined, moving from public to private provision can shift people's

however, respect for human rights, democracy, civilian control of the military, and the rule of law may require change in the values society holds as well as the orientation of security forces. So, the introduction of *international* values to the control of force may lead away from meaningful integration with societal values in the local context but (arguably) toward values more broadly endorsed within the international community.[14] The standard I will use for evaluating whether control over force is moving toward or away from meaningful integration with social values in the cases to follow will rely on those values endorsed, at least in principle, by the international community – respect for human rights, the laws of war, democracy, civilian control of the military, and the rule of law.[15]

Breaking control into its various elements is useful because it helps make sense of those instances when the privatization of security affects the dimensions of control differently. Privatization may increase functional control and yet change political control in ways that some view as distasteful. Similarly maintaining political control may cause losses in functional or social control in some instances. Understanding

expectations of the proper size and responsibilities of the public sphere and thus the value attached to the public delivery of services. They therefore talk about "systemic privatization" (privatization that changes values and expectations) as shrinking the state. The implication of their analysis is that this moves away from a meaningful integration with societal values. Others claim, though, that privatization fits well with – and is even the culmination of – the liberal revolution begun in the eighteenth century. See Shearer, *Private Armies and Military Intervention*.

[14] See William Reno, "How Sovereignty Matters; International Economics and Local Politics," in Thomas Callaghy, Ronald Kassimir, and Robert Latham, *Intervention and Transnationalism in Africa* (Cambridge: Cambridge University Press, 2001).

[15] I do this with some reservation because this implies a normative bias that I do not always share and a bias toward intervention that is problematic in many cases. However, any other treatment would either require a greater understanding of local values than I am able to undertake or treat changes in social control as artificially objective and devoid of substantive content. Furthermore, even though these values are realized differently in different settings, the language of human rights, democracy, rule of law, and even civilian control of the military is increasingly used by actors in many parts of the world. For criticisms of this normative bias, see Stephen Hopgood, "Reading the Small Print in Global Civil Society: the Inexorable Hegemony of the Liberal Self," *Millennium* Vol. 29, No. 1 (2000):1–25; David Campbell, "Why Fight? Humanitarianism, Principles, and Post-Structuralism," *Millennium* Vol. 27, No. 3 (1998): 497–521. For argument about the worldwide spread of these values, see W. Richard Scott, John Meyer, and Associates, eds., *Institutional Environment and Organizations: Structural Complexity and Individualism* (Thousand Oaks, CA: Sage, 1994); George Thomas, John Meyer, Francisco O. Ramirez, and John Boli, eds., *Institutional Structure: Constituting State, Society, and the Individual* (Newbury Park, CA: Sage, 1987). See also, Finnemore, "Constructing Norms of Humanitarian Intervention"; Hedley Bull, *The Anarchical Society* (New York: Columbia University Press, 1977); Barry Buzan, "From International System to International Society: Structural Realism and Regime Theory Meet in the English School," *International Organization* Vol. 47 (1992): 327–52.

these dimensions separately can inform political judgments about the trade-off involved in selecting state versus private security options in a given situation. Though different people may judge the value of these differently, knowing the trade-offs is important for them in making an informed evaluation.

Most fundamentally, however, the control of violence varies by whether these dimensions fit together or not. While different analysts have privileged one or another of these dimensions in their arguments about the proper route to civilian control of the military, a rational legal body's authority depends on delivering a function a collective wants according to political processes and undergirded by values the group views as legitimate.[16] The logic of rational legal authority that underlies the idea of the state (and these studies), therefore, implies that all these elements, and how they fit together, hold the key to stable, legitimate, and effective civil–military relations – the situation that we recognize as effective control. Privatization could lead to changes that not only affect these dimensions differently, but also lead to increased or decreased integration between the three dimensions. In addition to assessing privatization's impact on each individual dimension of control, then, I will also evaluate its effect on the fit between them as an indicator of the longer term prospect for either the stability often associated with effective control or the instability and change associated with its absence.

How should privatization affect the control of force?

Will privatization matter for any or all of these dimensions of control? How? "New institutional" theories from economics and sociology suggest answers to different variations on these questions.[17]

Economic institutionalism

Economic institutionalism focuses on privatization's effect on functional and political control and analysts argue that violence can be best

---

[16] For discussion of rational legal authority, see Gerth and Mills, *From Max Weber*, p. 299. See also the discussion in Michael Barnett and Martha Finnemore, "The Politics, Power, and Pathologies of International Organizations," *International Organization* Vol. 53, No. 4 (autumn 1999): 699–732; Michael Barnett, "Authority, Intervention and the Outer Limits of International Relations Theory," in Thomas Callaghy, Ronald Kassimir, and Robert Latham, eds., *Intervention and Transnationalism in Africa* (Cambridge: Cambridge University Press, 2001), p. 59.

[17] James March and Johan Olsen, "The New Institutionalism: Organizational Factors in Political Life," *American Political Science Review* Vol. 78, No. 3 (September 1984); Paul DiMaggio and Walter Powell, eds., *The New Institutionalism in Organizational Analysis* (Chicago: University of Chicago Press, 1991).

controlled through state bureaucracies. The privatization of sovereign tasks should be a less efficient means to collective ends, reducing functional control and/or changing political control.

Building on the Hobbesian supposition that life is "nasty, brutish, and short" in anarchy, economic institutionalists focus on the importance of the state for the control of violence. North, Levi, Olson and others suggest that state monopoly over violence is necessary to move out of anarchy and into a situation where productive activity can take place.[18] Transaction cost economics further develops this logic, suggesting that a state can best control violence if it organizes internally to create public bureaucracies.[19] Williamson argues that just as hierarchies are some-times preferable to markets there are conditions under which public bureaucracies are preferable to private firms. In general, contracts are problematic when uncertainty and bounded rationality occur together, because they make it costly or impossible to identify future contingen-cies and specify how to handle them in a contract.[20] Also, when there are few competitors and they are opportunistic, contracts become risky and expensive.[21]

States, on the other hand, have mechanisms for aggregating interests via procedures people have agreed to and thus promote convergent expectations.[22] States also contain mechanisms by which authority to

[18] See Douglass North, *Structure and Change in Economic History* (New York: W.W. Norton, 1981); Margaret Levi, *Of Rule and Revenue* (University of California Press, 1989); Mancur Olson, "Dictatorship, Democracy, and Development," *American Polit-ical Science Review* Vol. 87, No. 3 (September 1993): 567–76. Recent game theoretic work by Greif, Bates, and Singh reinforces the necessity of the state, and its control of violence, for productive societies. They argue that societies cannot be both peaceful and prosperous without a state. Stateless societies can be peaceful, but only if they are poor. As economic prosperity grows, so do the incentives for raiding and predation. Only by contracting with a "specialist in violence" can people can move beyond the trade-off between peace and prosperity. If the specialists in violence become governments, coercion can be used in productive ways. Robert Bates, Avner Greif, and Smita Singh, "Organizing Violence," *Journal of Conflict Resolution* Vol. 46, No. 5 (October 2002): 599–629.

[19] Oliver Williamson, "Public and Private Bureaucracies: A Transaction Cost Economics Perspective," *Journal of Law, Economics and Organization*, Vol. 15, No. 1 (1999).

[20] See Oliver Williamson, *Markets and Hierarchies: Analysis and Anti-Trust Implications* (New York: Free Press, 1975). See also, R. H. Coase, "The Nature of the Firm," *Economica* Vol. 4, No. 16 (November 1937); H. A. Simon, *Administrative Behavior* (New York: Macmillan 1961); A. A. Alchian and H. Demsetz, "Production, In-formation Costs, and Economic Organization," *American Economic Review* Vol. 62 (December 1972).

[21] Williamson, *Markets and Hierarchies*, pp. 8–10.

[22] In such a complex market, bureaucracies facilitate adaptive decision making that can respond to change. Also, because bureaucrats are less able to appropriate subgroup or personal gains and organizations can be more effectively audited, the incentives for opportunistic behavior decrease. Furthermore, being part of an organization can

use and oversee force is delegated, which mediate problems of common agency.[23] Williamson adds that internal organizations are more likely to make allowances for quasi-moral involvement.[24] He builds on this quasi-moral involvement in his analysis of public versus private provision of sovereign transactions.[25] Sovereign transactions (foreign affairs, the military, foreign intelligence, managing the money supply and, possibly, the judiciary) are characterized by particular "contractual hazards" – asset specificity and probity.[26] Transactions that are long term, highly incomplete, and require loyalty (to leadership and mission) and integrity are best provided by public bureaucracies.[27]

Like all relationships of delegation, public bureaucracies are subject to agency slippage, and many have documented the loss of flexibility and bureaucratic disabilities that sometimes arise.[28] Market-based solutions may ameliorate these but, so long as the environmental conditions favor hierarchies, at a cost – either opportunistic incentives will increase, convergent expectations will erode, adaptations will not be appropriate, or cost will rise.

Studies on privatization in the US have yielded a large body of literature consistent with Williamson's claims.[29] In a widely acclaimed

---

promote convergent expectations, mediate information asymmetry (and the strategic use of it), and has advantages for settling disputes. Ibid., pp. 29, 40.

[23] Common agency refers to the situation where principals must solve collective action problems among themselves even as they try to minimize agency slippage. This problem can take the form of multiple principles – where two or more organizationally distinct principals delegate to an agent – or common agency – where a principal is made up of more than one actor. See discussion in Mona Lyne and Michael Tierney, "Variation in the Structure of Principals: Conceptual Clarifications," paper presented at the Conference on Delegation to International Organizations, Park City, Utah, May 2002. See also Daniel Nielson and Michael Tierney, "Delegation to International Organizations: Agency Theory and World Bank Environmental Reform," *International Organization*, Vol. 57, No. 2 (spring 2003): 241–76.

[24] Williamson, *Markets and Hierarchies*, p. 38.

[25] See Williamson, "Public and Private Bureaucracies." See also discussion in Freeman, "The Contracting State."

[26] Williamson, "Private and Public Bureaucracies," pp. 321–22.

[27] Ibid., p. 324.

[28] See Jonathan Bendor, Serge Taylor, and Roland van Gaalen, "Stacking the Deck: Bureaucratic Missions and Policy Design," *American Political Science Review* Vol. 81, No. 3 (September 1987); Gary Miller, *Managerial Dilemmas: the Political Economy of Hierarchy* (Cambridge: Cambridge University Press, 1992); Deborah Avant, *Political Institutions and Military Change: Lessons from Peripheral Wars* (Ithaca: Cornell University Press, 1994).

[29] For ringing endorsements of privatization, see E. S. Savas, *Privatizing the Public Sector* (Chatham, NJ: Chatham Publishing, 1982); James T. Bennett and Manuel H. Johnson, *Better Government at Half the Price* (Ottawa, IL: Caroline House Publishing, 1981); Stuart M. Butler, *Privatizing Federal Spending: a Strategy to Eliminate the Deficit* (New York: Universe Books, 1985). More guarded endorsements include Terry Peters,

synthesis of the diverse research on privatization John Donahue lays out a framework to weigh the relative costs and benefits of private delivery of public services in different situations.[30] Donahue argues that there are basic differences between profit-seeking contractors and civil servants: profit seekers, in exchange for a price, deliver a product; while civil servants, in exchange for a wage, agree to accept instructions. The nature of the task determines whether private contractors or civil servants will be most effective. Contracting makes sense if a government knows exactly what it wants and cares more about the ends than the means. Sometimes, contracting can even force discipline on the government, leading to a better specification of its goals. On the other hand, if the government cares about means and wants its agents to follow a set of guidelines for how to go about providing a service, civil servants – geared to follow instructions – are superior. Furthermore, the effect of privatization is "highly dependent upon the wider market, regulatory, and institutional environment in which it is implemented."[31]

Looking back at the range of security services PSCs provide, there are tasks within logistics support, such as laundry and food services, that may yield contracts for which private provision is efficient.[32] Many other services, however, such as the provision of troops, advice and training, operational support near combat areas, and security or crime prevention services, prompt significant concerns about means and loyalty.[33]

"Public Services and the Private Sector," in *Privatization: the Provision of Public Services by the Private Sector* (Jefferson, NC: McFarland & Company, Inc., 1991); John Miller and Christopher Tufts, "A Means to Achieve More with Less," in *Privatization: the Provision of Public Services by the Private Sector* (Jefferson, NC: McFarland & Company, Inc., 1991); Robert W. Bailey, "Uses and Misuses," in *Privatization: the Provision of Public Services by the Private Sector* (Jefferson, NC: McFarland & Company, Inc., 1991); Harry P. Hatry, "Problems," in *Privatization: the Provision of Public Services by the Private Sector* (Jefferson, NC: McFarland & Company, Inc., 1991).

    For arguments with an eye to comparisons with other governments as well see William T. Gormley, Jr., "The Privatization Controversy," in William T. Gormley, Jr., ed., *Privatization and its Alternatives* (Madison: University of Wisconsin Press, 1991); Paul Starr, "The Case for Skepticism," in Gormley, *Privatization and its Alternatives*. See also essays in Sheila B. Kamerman and Alfred J. Kahn, *Privatization and the Welfare State* (Princeton: Princeton University Press, 1989).

[30] Donahue, *Privatization Decision*.
[31] Vickers and Yarrow, "Economic Perspectives on Privatization," 130.
[32] Even in these cases, however, some have argued that the fact that these services are provided in war-like situations make private firms unsuitable. See Lou Marano, "The Perils of Privatization," *Washington Post*, 27 May 1997. These concerns have been amplified by the experience with PSCs in Iraq.
[33] See J. Q. Wilson, *Bureaucracy* (New York: Basic Books, 1989); Williamson, "Public and Private Bureaucracies," p. 321. Indeed, Donahue argues that many of the problems with defense procurement might be solved if we moved more of the process back within the public realm. Donahue, *Privatization Decision*.

Privatization of these services should lead to decreased functional control (such as rising costs and inappropriate adaptations) or change in political control (redistributions of power that lead to imbalance and opportunism). As Williamson puts it, "replication of a public bureau by a private firm, with or without the support of regulation, is impossible."[34]

Thus, economic institutionalists expect the private delivery of sovereign services to erode functional control and change political control, they are skeptical about the ability of states to regulate the export of sovereign services, and they are worried about the private financing of sovereign services, which moves the state out of a direct consequential role altogether. Many arguments about the consequences of privatizing force have relied (implicitly) on this logic – assuming that the state is the appropriate mechanism for holding violence in check and expecting the privatization of violence to lead to decreased functional control (more expensive or inappropriate services) and/or changed political control.[35]

Sociological institutionalism

Sociological institutionalism expects that privatization either will have little effect on functional and social control, or (given the right conditions) may have a positive effect. Focusing not on the importance of the state, per se, but on the prevailing structure of social norms and practices, these analysts see privatization either as unimportant to the control of violence or as having the potential to enhance what forces can do and draw more actors into the prevailing system of social norms.

Sociological approaches concentrate on the social institutions that define a collectivity.[36] They argue that people often pursue purpose rather than interests and look for rules rather than expecting consequences.[37] Social institutions provide insight into the internal life of a collectivity and define the "logic of appropriateness" (and thus the

---

[34] Williamson, "Public and Private Bureaucracies," p. 311.

[35] Silverstein, *Private Warriors*; Musah and Fayemi, *Mercenaries*.

[36] James March and Johan P. Olsen, "The Institutional Dynamics of International Political Orders," *International Organization* Vol. 52, No. 4 (autumn, 1998). See also, Friedrich V. Kratochwil, *Rules, Norms, and Decisions: on the Conditions of Practical and Legal Reasoning in International Relations and Domestic Affairs* (Cambridge: Cambridge University Press, 1989); John G. Ruggie, "What Makes the World Hang Together? Neo-Utilitarianism and the Social Constructivist Challenge," *International Organization* Vol. 52, No. 4 (autumn 1998): 855–85.

[37] David Dessler has called such behavior "value-rational." See David Dessler, "Constructivism within a Positivist Social Science," *Review of International Studies* Vol. 25 (1999): 123–37. See especially pp. 131–35.

values that control the provision of a function).[38] It is not the state structure, per se, but the values that underlie a collective that are important for determining the appropriate bounds of behavior – and thus what being "in control" means.

Values need not be held by state institutions, but among any group of people who share connections in a social structure. Indeed, different concepts of "us" may lead to different kinds of states – leading some constructivist scholars to argue that not all states are alike. Some have examined differences over time, looking at the variation in the practice of sovereignty when states justify their behavior through "territorial" as opposed to "national" norms.[39] Others have examined how cultural differences even within the advanced, industrialized world lead to alternate patterns of state behavior.[40] In the developing world, the differences are often even greater as the relationship between internal and external authority is more tenuous.[41] Finally, a variety of actors such as international organizations (IOs) and NGOs influence both the interests of states and the degree to which actions are seen as legitimate.[42] So, the relationship between a social structure and a state is variable and it is the social structure, rather than the state, per se, that is important for eliciting functional and social control.

In this social structure values are communicated and reinforced through day-to-day practices. It is possible to influence behavior by

[38] March and Olsen, "Institutional Dynamics," pp. 943–44; As Gianfranco Poggi argues, "how can a collectivity discriminate between friend and foe if not by referring to a conception of what makes Us into Us; and how can such a conception be generated except by ordering in some distinctive fashion the internal life of the collectivity?" Gianfranco Poggi, *The Development of the Modern State: a Sociological Introduction* (Stanford: Stanford University Press, 1978), p. 12.
[39] Samuel Barkin and Bruce Cronin, "The State and the Nation: Changing Norms and the Rules of Sovereignty in International Relations," *International Organization* Vol. 48, No. 1 (winter 1994); Rodney Bruce Hall, *National Collective Identity* (New York: Columbia University Press, 1999).
[40] See Robert Herman, "Identity, Norms, and National Security"; Thomas Berger, "Norms, Identity, and National Security in Germany and Japan"; Thomas Risse-Kappen, "Collective Identities in a Democratic Community," and Michael Barnett, "Identity and Alliances in the Middle East," all in Peter Katzenstein, ed., *The Culture of National Security* (New York: Columbia University Press 1996).
[41] See Robert Jackson and Carl Rosberg, "Why Africa's Weak States Persist," *World Politics* Vol. 35, No. 1 (October 1982): 1–24; Christopher Clapham, "African Security Systems: Privatization and the Scope for Mercenary Activity," in *The Privatization of Security in Africa* (Johannesburg: SAIIA Press, 1999); Joel Migdal, *Weak States and Strong Societies* (Princeton: Princeton University Press, 1988).
[42] Martha Finnemore, "International Organizations as Teachers of Norms," *International Organization* Vol. 47, No. 4 (autumn 1993); Barnett and Finnemore, "Politics, Power, and Pathologies of International Organizations."

presenting conceptions of the self and the situation.[43] This can be conservative, reminding actors of their proper role in the social system – professional militaries abide by the law of war[44] – or it can aim at better behavior by presenting alternate conceptions of the self – for instance, the recent efforts to get businesses to abide by the principles of "corporate social responsibility." Janowitz's argument about military professionalism anticipates just this kind of logic. "He [the military officer] is subject to civilian control, not only because of rule or law and tradition, but also because of self-imposed professional standards and meaningful integration with civilian values."[45] Janowitz claimed that social, political, and technological changes so altered the use of force in international relations that it provided the basis for a radical alteration of the military profession – the constabulatory concept. Janowitz noted a commonality among military professionals in disparate states and implied that control worked through the appropriate professional standard that dictated a particular role for the military in society.[46]

The current practice of military professionalism reveals two strands of values that have become enshrined in norms regulating proper behavior, one based on liberalism and the inherent rights of individuals and the other on democratic processes and primacy of civilian control and the rule of law.[47] Though the practice of these is subject to variation,

---

[43] March and Olsen, "Institutional Dynamics"; Jeff Checkel, "The Constructivist Turn in International Relations Theorizing," *World Politics* Vol. 50 (January 1998): 324–48; Martha Finnemore and Kathyrn Sikkink, "International Norm Dynamics and Political Change," *International Organization* Vol. 52, No. 4 (autumn 1998): 909–15.

[44] As James Burk points out, the use of the term profession implies a positive value orientation. Professionalism, then, does not simply describe what the military does, but prescribes a standard of how the military ought to behave. See James Burk, "Expertise, Jurisdiction, and Legitimacy of the Military Profession," in Don Snider and Gayle Watkins, eds., *The Future of the Army Profession* (Boston: McGraw Hill, 2002), p. 19.

[45] Janowitz, *Professional Soldier*, p. 420.

[46] Ibid., p. 418.

[47] See Michael Walzer, *Just and Unjust Wars* (New York: Basic Books, 1977), part III, for an overview of duties based on human rights. The law of war is taught widely in the curriculum of US military schools. See Don Snider, Robert Priest, and Felisa Lewis, "The Civilian–Military Gap and Professional Military Education at the Precommissioning Level," *Armed Forces and Society* Vol. 27, No. 2 (winter 2001): 249–72; Judith Hicks Stiehm, "Civil–Military Relations in War College Curricula," *Armed Forces and Society* Vol. 27, No. 2 (winter 2001): 273–94.

The literature on civilian control and the rule of law is extensive. See Janowitz, *Professional Soldier*; Sir Michael Howard, *Soldiers and Governments: Nine Studies in Civil–Military Relations* (London: Eyre & Spottiswoode, 1957). More recent treatments include: K. W. Kemp and Charles Hudlin, "Civil Supremacy Over the Military: its Nature and its Limits," *Armed Forces and Society* Vol. 19, No. 1 (1992): 7–26; Peter Feaver, "The Civil–Military Problematique: Huntington, Janowitz, and the Problem of Civilian Control," *Armed Forces and Society* Vol. 23, No. 2 (1996): 149–78; Richard Kohn, "How Democracies Control the Military," *Journal of Democracy* Vol. 8, No. 4

western military personnel see it as obvious that they should abide by the obligations of international law with respect to the conduct of war and domestic law with respect to civilian authorities.[48] These requirements are embedded in professional military education not only as moral obligations but also as integral to effective military operations. In other words, in the eyes of military professionals, military organizations that respect the rights of non-combatants and abide by the hierarchy of domestic law are more likely to accomplish their military missions effectively.[49]

Although these values operate more or less consistently (with each other and with the norm of sovereignty) in many western states, there is potential tension between them. As liberal values have become codified in international agreements, they have, in principle, circumscribed the sovereign authority over violence. Most clearly this is seen in the results of the International Tribunal at Nuremburg, which found that when international rules protecting humanitarian values come in conflict with state laws, individuals are obligated to transgress the laws of their government (except when there is no room for "moral choice"). Individual military personnel cannot escape criminal responsibility for actions that violate international law by citing civilian orders. This can be cited as a budding *international* standard for military professionals.[50]

In an argument building on this logic (though ignoring the tensions with sovereignty), David Shearer claimed that states in the international community might influence the behavior of private military companies

(1997): 140–53; Douglas Bland, "Patterns in Liberal Democratic Civil–Military Relations," *Armed Forces and Society* Vol. 27, No. 4 (summer 2001): 525–40; James Burk, "Theories of Democratic Civil–Military Relations," *Armed Forces and Society* Vol. 29, No. 1 (fall 2002): 7–30.

[48] The obligations under international law enshrine liberal principles of human rights found in the Geneva Convention of 1864 (revised in 1906), the Hague Convention of 1899, the Hague Convention of 1907, the Geneva Conventions of 1929, the London Protocol of 1936 and the Geneva Convention of 1949. See Held et al., *Global Transformations*, p. 71. See also Geoffrey Best, *Humanity in Warfare: the Modern History of the Law of Armed Conflict* (London: Weidenfeld and Nicolson, 1980).

[49] A colonel from the United States Southern Command explained this to me quite eloquently during a meeting of the Board of Visitors at the Western Hemispheric Center for Security and Cooperation. He argued that the fact that these principles were key to effective military operations made the human rights training the US military gives to other militaries more effective. This connection is reinforced in curriculum and training exercises. For some empirical support for this proposition, see Dan Reiter and Al Stam, *Democracies at War* (Princeton: Princeton University Press, 2002).

[50] See the discussion in Held et al., *Global Transformations*, pp. 71–73. See also Y. Dinstein, "Rules of War," in J. Krieger, ed., *The Oxford Companion to the Politics of the World* (Oxford: Oxford University Press, 1993); J Vincent, "Modernity and Universal Human Rights," in A. G. McGrew and P. G. Lewis, eds., *Global Politics* (Cambridge: Polity Press, 1992).

by treating them as legitimate military professionals. He pointed out that PSCs became popular precisely because they were able to take on the messy tasks of intervention that western militaries were eager to avoid. He suggested that instead of outlawing military companies, states and the international community should "engage" them. Within the right structure of international norms, organizations, and law these companies could provide an important social good – an end to civil conflict that would otherwise be intractable – without undermining the norms that motivate the international community.[51] Though Shearer hardly recognized himself as a constructivist, he was making just that kind of argument. He noted that western states were unwilling to provide important intervention functions and argued that PSCs made up of retired professional soldiers were likely to provide a function that the international community demands. By shifting the categorization of PSCs, he argued that the international community could both capitalize on their usefulness and, by giving PSCs a legitimate role as military professionals, insure that they operated according to international values.

This kind of logic has also been aired in studies on privatization more generally, which have made reference to the way contracts can provide mechanisms through which to communicate professional norms and practices that reinforce societal values. For instance, Jody Freeman, in a study of health care, suggests "public–private contracts could function not only as mechanisms for delivering social services or effective regulatory purposes, but as vehicles for achieving public law values, such as fairness, openness, and accountability."[52] She goes on to suggest that contracts for Managed Care Organizations can require accreditation, community group and patient advocate involvement, and compliance with standards set by a variety of professional organizations.[53] Martha Minow applauds such efforts as "committed to public values, notably democracy and anti-discrimination, while drawing on successful practices in market settings that tackle hard problems by using information rather than command-and-control management."[54]

Thus, these sociological analyses offer a more agnostic view of private security's implications, suggesting the potential for privatization without a loss – and perhaps with a gain – in functional and social control.

---

[51] Shearer, *Private Armies and Military Intervention*, discusses these issues on pp. 69–72. He also mentions international norms for transparency.
[52] Freeman, "The Contracting State," pp. 201–02.
[53] Ibid., pp. 202–05.
[54] Minow, *Partners Not Rivals*, p. 171.

Rather than establishing with categories of tasks that should be provided only by states, they tend to see the potential for private actors to provide security within the context of prevailing social values. If PSCs are accorded a place in the global social system, they may operate within accepted social values. For sociologists, the key issue in each of the relationships above should not be state control, per se, but the availability of the kinds of force needed to pursue international social demands within the bounds of international norms. More concerned with functional and social control, these analyses would underscore the continuities likely as states contract with PSCs, the potential for international regulation based on a legitimate role for PSCs, and the proliferation of non-state actor financing as an additional tool by which force might be educated, and, thus, controlled.

A new institutionalist synthesis

These arguments emphasize different elements of control, focus on different parts of the control process, and come to different conclusions about the consequences of privatization. Economists generally assume actors follow the "logic of consequences" and look at functional and political control changes elicited by a reduction of state control over consequences. Sociologists assume actors follow the "logic of appropriateness," and look at the functional and social control changes elicited by the expansion of appropriateness claims into the private sphere and conflicted political arenas.

Neither analysis ignores the other's logic altogether. Indeed, Williamson admits that appropriateness matters in his analysis of sovereign transactions, acknowledging that he *assumes* existing institutions are appropriate. A public institution, he explains, cannot be assumed to be the most efficient solution for sovereign transactions if it is "(1) the product of an unacceptable political regime, or otherwise has unacceptable political origins, (2) has been continued through recourse to unacceptable strategic ploys, (3) is wrongly classified as efficient because of a defective calculus, or (4) has undergone a series of unforeseen and convoluted changes that defy rational interpretation."[55] Williamson also argues that hierarchies, and particularly public bureaucracies, are more effective for sovereign transactions not only because of consequential mechanisms but because they more easily allow for quasi-moral

---

[55] Williamson, "Public and Private Bureaucracies," pp. 319–20.

involvement by parties, promote convergent expectations, and enshrine integrity.

Likewise, sociological theorizing recognizes that not all values have equal "hold" on behavior – and generally argues that values matter most when they are institutionalized.[56] Institutionalization is a complex process, depending on both the acceptance of values as good (which strengthens with the degree to which they are commonsensical or obviously the right way to do things) and their embeddedness in daily practice (the degree to which they are reinforced by social and material benefits).[57] Being embedded in daily practice includes *consequential* incentives. Jody Freeman's analysis of privatization's implications for Medicaid hinges on incentives that lead practices consistent with public values to be carried out by the private sphere. She claims that carefully drawn contracts that stipulate education and allow for third party involvement can lead to the institutionalization of a process by which what we recognize as good, professional medical treatment may be provided by a wider range of medical providers. Similarly, David Shearer's hope for the beneficial use of PSCs relies not only on a

[56] Ann Swidler, while arguing that strategies of action are more important than values, still acknowledges that values are more likely to determine behavior in settled rather than unsettled lives. See Ann Swidler, "Culture in Action: Symbols and Strategies," *American Sociological Review* Vol. 51 (1986): 282. Elizabeth Kier uses this analysis to examine the way in which civil-military culture affects the choice of offensive or defensive doctrine and argues that when culture is settled, political elites are free to attend to the strategic demands of the international system but constrained in what they can imagine because some options appear silly or do not appear at all. See Elizabeth Kier, *Imagining War* (Princeton: Princeton University Press, 1997). Finnemore and Sikkink, "International Norms Dynamics," allow a much greater role for values but agree that norms are most likely to affect behavior when they appear natural and may not be noticed at all. They call this stage "internalization."

[57] As Ann Swidler puts it, "values are important pieces of cultural equipment for established strategies of action, since part of what it means to have a strategy of action is to have a way of making the choices that ordinarily confront one within it." Swidler, "Culture in Action," p. 282. See also Theodore R. Schatzki, Karin Knorr Cetina, and Eike von Savigny, *The Practice Turn in Contemporary Theory* (New York: Routledge 2001). Some have argued that international norms exert more hold on behavior in local normative frameworks that are reflective of the same values. Cortell and Davis talk about the domestic salience of international norms as a key condition for their effect on particular actors. Andrew Cortell and James Davis, Jr., "How Do International Institutions Matter? The Domestic Impact of International Rules and Norms," *International Studies Quarterly* Vol. 40, No. 4 (December 1996). Others have shown how domestic actors are receptive to international norms as a way of gaining legitimation from the international community that enhances their domestic standing and how norms among states seen as successful and desirable models are those most likely to spread. Finnemore and Sikkink, "International Norm Dynamics." See also Ann Florini, "The Evolution of International Norms," *International Studies Quarterly* Vol. 40, No. 3 (September 1996): 363–89.

legitimate role for them as military professionals, but on an international system of regulation by which professional practices can be reinforced with incentives that tie PSC behavior to international norms and values.

Furthermore, both arguments focus on the mechanisms important to elicit appropriate behavior – through either suggesting roles or promising consequences. Economists focus on the effect of privatization on screening and selection, monitoring, and sanctioning. Sociologists focus on privatization's effect on promoting standards, educating, and socializing. In the real world, of course, actors use both kinds of mechanisms all the time. Indeed, principals often screen and select agents in order to attain a particular standard and use sanctions to reinforce education and socialization. Furthermore, sanctions (intentional or not) are often key to the development of common values and practices.[58]

Can these two logics be additive and complementary? Might a model building on both indicate more clearly the range of privatization's effects across all three dimensions of control? I join a variety of scholars who question the gulf between economists (rationalists) and sociologists (constructivist) to argue that this is the case.[59] To begin, I simply juxtapose these two arguments to generate hypotheses that look separately at the three different dimensions of control. As I said above, this is useful in and of itself for understanding the trade-off among the different dimensions of control entailed in choosing private security in particular settings.

Looking at the interaction between the mechanisms these models point out, though, may have a greater payoff than their juxtaposition. If what we recognize as effective control is the situation where the functional, political, and social dimensions of control fit together,

---

[58] Pierre Bourdieu, *Outline of a Theory of Practice* (Cambridge: Cambridge University Press, 1977); Robert Sugden, *The Economics of Rights, Cooperation, and Welfare* (New York: Blackwell, 1986).

[59] Avant, "From Mercenary to Citizen Armies"; James Fearon and Alexander Wendt, "Rationalism v. Constructivism: a Skeptical View," in Walter Carlsnaes, Thomas Risse, and Beth Simmons, eds., *Handbook of International Relations* (London: Sage, 2002); Michael Brecher and Frank Harvey, "Evaluating Methodology in International Studies," in Michael Brecher and Frank Harvey, eds., *Millennial Reflections on International Studies* (Ann Arbor: University of Michigan Press, 2002); Harvey Starr, "Cumulation, Synthesis, and Research Design for the Post-Fourth Wave," in Michael Brecher and Frank Harvey, eds., *Millennial Reflections on International Studies* (Ann Arbor: University of Michigan Press, 2002); Gerald Schneider and Mark Aspinwall, *Rules of Integration: Institutionalist Approaches to the Study of Europe* (Manchester: Manchester University Press, 2001); Joseph Jupille, James Caporaso, and Jeffrey Checkel, "Integrating Institutions: Rationalism, Constructivism, and the Study of the European Union," *Comparative Political Studies* Vol. 36, No. 1 (2003): 7–40.

whether privatization leads toward or away from what we recognize as effective control should depend on whether the control mechanisms sociologists attend to – such as norms, standards, and education – and those economists attend to – such as screening and selection, monitoring and sanctions – reinforce one another or not. When the variety of control mechanisms points actors in a similar direction it is most likely that a "reinforcing process" of control will develop that will facilitate a "fit" between the functional, political, and social dimension of control. When mechanisms point in different directions, however, they will "collide and chafe," presenting actors with imperatives and opportunities that pull them in different directions, portending friction, instability, and change – situations we recognize as less effective control.[60]

In the next three sections, I develop this argument for how privatization should matter for the control of force in three different situations: (1) when states contract for private delivery of security services, (2) when states regulate security services exports, and (3) when non-state actors finance security services.

State contracts for private force

How should state contracts with PSCs affect the control over force? A key variable will be the quality of the state and state forces to begin with. As indicated in the previous discussion, economic analyses *assume* appropriate institutions and focus on expected difficulties with monitoring and information asymmetry that should make the private delivery of sovereign tasks problematic.[61] Not all states, though, have such institutions in the first place. Williamson's description of the necessary circumstances for assuming that states best provide sovereign services corresponds to the environment in what Joel Migdal has called "strong" states – states that are coherent, capable and legitimate.[62]

---

[60] See, for instance, Paul Pierson, "When Effect Becomes Cause: Policy Feedback and Political Change," *World Politics* 45 (July 1993): 595–628; Paul Pierson, "Increasing Returns, Path Dependence, and the Study of Politics," *American Political Science Review* Vol. 94, No. 2 (June 2000): 251–67; Douglass North, *Institutions, Institutional Change and Economic Performance* (Cambridge: Cambridge University Press, 1990); Robert L. Lierberman, "Ideas, Institutions, and Political Order: Explaining Political Change," *American Political Science Review* Vol. 96, No. 4 (December 2002): 697–712.

[61] See Jurgen Brauer, "An Economic Perspective on Mercenaries, Military Companies, and the Privatization of Force," *Cambridge Review of International Studies*, Vol. 13, No. 1 (autumn/winter 1999): 130–45; Singer, *Corporate Warriors*, pp. 151–68.

[62] Though the difference between strong states and weak states has a long and rather disputed pedigree in political science, the most sophisticated of these analyses capture the essence of what would be important in the economic model. Joel Migdal, for

States that contract with PSCs, though, span the whole range of strength. Indeed, some of the most prominent examples of privatization involve states that look more like Weber's notion of patrimonial authority than the rational legal authority that underlies Williamson's analysis.[63] Institutionalist analysis suggests that privatization entails different promise and risk for strong and weak states.

Strong states are the focus of Williamson's analysis of the difficulties associated with outsourcing sovereign services. Given the trade-off between their ability to direct the bureaucracy to respond and their ability to only select from contractors, strong states risk paying more for private military services or losing some of their capacity to monitor and oversee the provision of these services. Depending on the level of competition and the degree to which the government specifies the details of security services, states may pay more for contractors to supply sovereign services than they would for their militaries, or be more likely to suffer problems in monitoring and information asymmetry that should increase the slippage between government goals and policy on the ground – in other words, privatizing sovereign services in strong states is likely to lead to some functional loss.[64] When new threats arise and/or PSCs offer services that the state's military is not set up to deliver, PSCs may offer short run benefits. Over the long term, though, functional control in strong states would be better served by encouraging bureaucratic change than by relying on PSCs.

Strong states nonetheless have superior monitoring and sanctioning capacity that should lead them to be in a better position to control PSCs than weaker states. Strong states have mechanisms to extract revenue in a central tax system, an established system of contracting, and a variety of mechanisms to inhibit rent seeking by either the state or private agents. Though contracting for security services may be less ideal than

instance, argues for a distinction between strong and weak states on the bases of the state's capacity, coherence, and legitimacy. Varying degrees of "stateness" are tied to the state's ability to maintain firm control over the military and police; to influence members of society; to generate functionally complex organizations; and to have those agencies work together in a coherent fashion. Migdal, *Strong Societies and Weak States*, pp. 18–19.

[63] See Max Weber, *The Theory of Social and Economic Organizations* edited and with an introduction by Talcott Parsons (New York: Free Press, 1964), pp. 346–58. I thank an anonymous reviewer for suggesting this point.

[64] Functional loss should affect, but not be equated with, the balance of power between states. All things being equal functional loss should reduce a state's effectiveness in deploying military power. Things are often not equal, however, and some states can afford much more expensive militaries than others. Furthermore, the political changes introduced by privatization if unchecked may enhance the "political will" for foreign defense expenditures.

reforming military institutions, the capabilities of strong states mitigate some risks of privatization and allow PSCs to provide short-term functional benefits when state institutions are stretched thin or required to produce new functions.

Weak states, in contrast, both have more to gain from privatization and run the highest risks from it. Whether because sovereignty rests on international acclaim more than capability[65] or the culture of power in the country discourages leaders from building strong institutions,[66] many weak state militaries, based on patrimonial authority systems, are incapable to the point that contracts with outside PSCs may provide functions not available from the state. In these cases, contracting with PSCs may buy the state the means to defend its territory in the short run. In some cases the functions provided by a PSC could bolster a state-building strategy by defeating opponents and centralizing power over coercion so as to perform a more state-like function – potentially laying the functional foundation for a rational legal authority claim. Also, in the execution of contracts, PSCs could educate the state's forces in ways that enhance their long-term ability to carry out operations.[67]

The very weakness of state institutions, however, decreases the chance that privatization will lead to the provision of public security or long-term military effectiveness. In some cases, contracts become just another tool for maintaining a corrupt leader's rule or protecting private interests.[68] Also, the participation of private actors often creates or enhances the capacity of parallel security structures that inhibit state building. Though privatization may promise greater functional gains to weak states, it is a rather desperate state-building gambit.

Contracting should cause changes in political control in both strong and weak states – though the degree of change should vary. In general contracting reduces the range of consequential control mechanisms by removing direct state authority over the setup of violent institutions. Though states retain budgetary control and can select between contractors, screening and selection of individuals and the organizational incentives for individuals are left in the hands of firms. In and of itself, this is a political change because the control over individuals authorized to use violence slips into the hands of a firm rather than being in the hands of the state. In addition, however, the contracting process

---

[65] Jackson and Rosberg, "Why Africa's Weak States Persist."
[66] Migdal, *Strong Societies and Weak States*.
[67] Shearer, *Private Armies and Military Intervention*.
[68] See Weber's discussion of decentralized patrimonial authority, Weber, *Theory of Social and Economic Organization*, pp. 352–54.

often operates differently from the process of deploying a state's military forces. Contracting avoids the need to mobilize state machinery and centralizes influence with those in charge of dispersing funds to and overseeing the contractor. The redistribution of power generally favors executives relative to legislators, reduces transparency in a way that advantages the government relative to the electorate, and opens the way (through the provision of information) for private interests to affect policy implementation and goals.

In strong states, this change should be milder, opening new avenues for private influence on policy and new possibilities for more adventurous executive decisions. In weak states, the paucity of state capabilities may lead the redistribution of power to be more extreme. This can work to a weak ruler's advantage if he can use centralization to decimate his opposition and consolidate control. It can also work against a ruler if he cannot control the contractor and the contractor takes actions that undermine his control or bolster his opponent's, perhaps leading to regime change or a coup. Furthermore, in weak states contracts tend to be with foreign PSCs and financing for contracts, even if it flows through state institutions, often involves foreign governments or TNCs, both of which spread political control outside the state's borders and allow external actors to influence the political process.[69] In both weak and strong states, however, state contracts with PSCs change the process by which security policy is made, redistribute power and influence, and thus change the political control of force.

The effect of private contracts on social control should also vary according to the institutional starting point. Among strong states (which overlap heavily with advanced industrial democracies), two features should lead the control of violence to be integrated with international values whether carried out by public or private entities. First, strong states often hire PSCs made up of retired personnel from their militaries. Partly because "international" values are often drawn from just these societies, international values are likely to be accepted as commonsense in strong states and the PSCs that grow out of their retired security personnel. In other words, international values should be highly salient in these societies making it more likely that these values will be seen as legitimate – and obviously so.[70] Second, in these societies, there should also be many ways in which international values are reinforced in day-to-day practices of military professionals. On the

---

[69] William Reno argues that this is precisely the point and the reason weak leaders often choose private options. See Reno, *Warlord Politics and African States*.
[70] Cortell and Davis, "How Do International Institutions Matter?"

basis of their socialization in the military profession, retired service personnel from western militaries should see proper military behavior as most effective and exercise that behavior in their execution of contracts. This effect should be enhanced to the degree that PSCs and their personnel are entrenched in networks that reward their attendance to the values underlying military professionalism on a daily basis. The institutionalization of international values in strong states – the obvious "good" attached to these values (for both functional and ethical reasons) and their reinforcement in day-to-day practice – should lead PSCs that contract with strong states to proclaim their commitment to international values and to be more likely to act in accordance with them. Under these conditions, strong state contracts with PSCs, even for sovereign services, need not change the social control of force. Though these conditions are variable, the more PSCs recruit from strong state militaries and are involved in professional networks that reinforce professional military values, the more likely social control will remain strong.

In weak states, contracts for sovereign services may result in an improvement in the social control of violence. Weak states are likely to hire PSCs that hail from capable, strong (or at least stronger) states and bring with them international values. Even if the state is not concerned with international values, the firm, not the state, exercises control over the personnel it deploys. The firm is more likely to be concerned with international norms and the professional behavior of its personnel, particularly if acquiescence to these is important to its reputation (and future contracts). Furthermore, if PSCs believe that functional effectiveness is enhanced by practices that ascribe to these norms, they have additional incentives to act appropriately. As professional PSCs advise, train, or provide operational support to less professional local forces, they may simultaneously "educate" these forces about proper behavior and the benefits (in military effectiveness) attached with it. Though this hardly guarantees that local forces will be professionalized, the presence of professional PSCs should enhance the chance that violence in weak states will be influenced by international norms that govern military professionals (respect for human rights, democracy, and attention to the rule of law). Again, these features are variable, the more PSCs are recruited from strong state military, are involved in professional networks, and specifically target professional development in their contracts, the more likely social control is to improve.

The weak state/strong state distinction can also generate expectations about the effect of privatization on the "fit" between these dimensions of control. Public institutions in strong states have within them designs that allow executives the information and tools with which to respond to foreign threats but also mediate these according to prevailing norms and/or situations where the executive's near-term political interests conflict with the long-term public interest.[71] Private contracts do not have the same safeguards and offer avenues for leaders to pursue policies that would be forbidden by agreed upon governmental processes. Private contracting changes established systems of government.[72] From one perspective this can be seen as eroding an existing "fit." With more executive control and less transparency, the government may be drawn into more adventurous foreign policy. Furthermore, private contractors with commercial interests in policy may be providing information necessary for policy formation – enhancing the private interests of the corporation rather than the public good. The political change in strong states, then, may encourage policies that cater to individual interests of executives and commercial interests in ways that lead away from rather than toward the effective control of force.

Some of the motivation behind the turn to contracting in the first place, though, may be change in the larger social milieu (technological change, change in the nature of threats, and change in the scale of security demands – as discussed in chapter one) to which the military has been slow to adapt. If contractors are providing a new service or one that the military is reluctant to provide, contracts with PSCs may provide flexible new avenues for the provision of different functions. So long as the government exercises effective oversight and the social control of force remains strong (i.e., professional networks extend into the private sector and military effectiveness is tied to respect for international values) these services could be delivered within the bounds of international norms. In this situation, contracting for some services may yield additional military capacities within social bounds.[73]

It is possible that social control will mediate political changes and that PSCs may provide a flexible alternative to strong states as they face a new and complex world. However, contracts with PSCs also generate feedback effects on the state's coercive forces and the political arena in general that may alter the institutional environment in which future articulation of values unfolds. For example, when the government hires

---

[71] Williamson, "Public and Private Bureaucracies," pp. 323–24.

[72] Feigenbaum, Henig, and Hamnett, *Shrinking the State*, argue that privatization efforts are sometimes designed precisely in order to augment political and/or social change. I agree that this is sometimes the case, but note that what they call "pragmatic" privatization also has political effects when it is associated with sovereign services.

[73] Even though this may be more expensive, some may argue that it is also more effective in some areas.

contractors to perform a security task, it signals to military professionals that this task is less important, perhaps leading to less focus on these tasks within military organizations – both eroding the state's capacity to do some missions and also projecting a smaller pool of retired professionals with experience in these areas. Future PSC employees in these arenas may be less integrated into professional military networks and their associated international values. The current structure of military professionalism and the values it reflects has developed in a particular institutional environment: national militaries and interaction between them. Changes in that environment may result in changes in future values, norms, and practices.

In general, then, private contracts often provide flexibility in strong states and their use is, itself, an indicator of some erosion of the fit between the three dimensions of control in the normal policy process – i.e., military organizations short on some functions or lack of political agreement around the pursuit of some goals. In the best circumstances these contracts can enhance military effectiveness with only minor functional losses (such as increased cost) and political changes within the bounds of what is considered legitimate. Because contracting also shifts the sand on which existing institutions were built, though, it may also hasten the erosion of fit.

In weak states without the same degree of control to begin with, change may lead toward more effective control or even further away. Writing contracts with profit-seeking agents used to working in a rational, legal environment could impose discipline on state officials, increase their attention to functional capacities, and enhance their oversight abilities in the future.[74] If combined with international diplomatic and financial pressures, one could imagine the political change beginning a process of state building.

The chances that political change will move toward effective control may nonetheless be impeded by several circumstances. Rulers in weak states may benefit from the status quo and use contracts to maintain their rule and privilege rather than increase governance.[75] Even if rulers want to improve governance, the very fact that the state does not have solid control tools suggests that it may have difficulty controlling PSCs. Left on their own, PSCs acting on commercial interests or even worried about the short-run effectiveness of their operations may make decisions that further weaken state institutions. Furthermore, privatization in weak states frequently redistributes power to external actors, which may

[74] Donahue, *Privatization Decision*, p. 85.
[75] Reno, *Warlord Politics and African States.*

lead these states further away from strategies that enlist the support of their populations.[76]

In weak states, then, the specifics of the contract, its effect on political processes, and how both interact with other political changes in the country are important to predict the likelihood of a fit between functional, political, and social control. Contracts with PSCs that educate rulers as to functional outputs, enhance a ruler's control vis-à-vis domestic opponents, and enhance the influence of external actors with an interest in strengthening the state will be the most likely to translate change in political control into increases in functional control that may feed back into more stable and (eventually) legitimate political processes. Contracts that do less to educate the ruler, that erode a ruler's control vis-à-vis domestic opponents, or that enhance the influence of external actors with an interest in a continued weak state should lead away from enhanced functional control.

Furthermore, while contracts with PSCs often introduce international values, the endurance of these values should not be automatic, but depend on whether they are viewed as legitimate and salient in the local context, and whether they are reinforced by day-to-day practices.[77] The perceived effectiveness of PSC operations will obviously affect the legitimacy with which any associated values are viewed. Beyond that, the longer the contract, the more it specifically references professional values and the more PSC personnel are embedded in professional networks that reinforce their attendance to international values, the more likely will be improvement in the social control of force. Also important is the reaction of local actors, those within the state as well as other important social groups. Moreover, just as political changes in strong states have feedback effects on the future basis for values, so may the changes in weak states. Thus, if the redistribution of influence favors actors (inside and outside the country) that are persuaded by international norms surrounding the use of force and reference these values in their decisions, change in the social control of force should be more likely – and the reverse.

---

[76] Olle Tornquist, "Rent Capitalism, State, and Democracy: a Theoretical Proposition," in Arief Budiman, ed., *State and Civil Society in Indonesia* (Monash Papers on Southeast Asia, No. 22, 1990); Terry Lynn Karl, *The Paradox of Plenty: Oil Booms and Petro States*, (Berkeley: University of California Press, 1997); John Clark, "Petro-Politics in Congo," *Journal of Democracy* Vol. 8, No. 3 (July 1997); Theda Skocpol, "Rentier State and Shi'a Islam in the Iranian Revolution," *Theory and Society* Vol. 11 (April 1982).

[77] Cortell and David, "How do Institutions Matter?"; Migdal, *Strong Societies and Weak States*.

In weak states, the use of PSCs is a more extreme indicator of a lack of fit between the dimensions of control. To the extent that contracts encourage consolidation of power to actors persuaded by international norms and practices, they may enhance the emergence of a fit between the dimensions of control and thus a reinforcing process of control over force. When all these factors do not come together, PSCs may yield no change or even worsen already weak control.

State regulation of private security

The private security market also holds implications for states' control of the violence that emanates from their territories. The growing market for military services has bolstered and added a new dimension to the defense industry. Industries that produce the tools of war have long presented dilemmas for states.[78] Because the industries can sell goods and services that affect the power projection capabilities of potential rivals, states often want to control the dissemination of their products. PSCs, for instance, draw on the skills learned in their state's military and, in the execution of contracts, share these skills along with information about military organization and operations that could affect the future power of their home state. Also, a company's behavior might affect the reputation of the state from which it hails or implicate the state in conflicts to which it is not a party. To the degree that a PSC's activities are at odds with government policy or implicate the government in conflicts, they risk eroding functional control.[79]

These industries, though, also provide mechanisms by which governments can garner additional wealth, power, and influence. Governments can tax sales of weapons or services. The profits from foreign sales can provide the state's defense industry with resources to push ahead new technologies or capitalize on economies of scale. Also, trade in arms and services can enhance a state's influence abroad: rewarding security-enhancing behavior by other states without tapping state funds. Furthermore, commercial sales can provide a means for influencing security relationships abroad without necessarily implicating the state – opening the way for foreign policy by proxy. To the degree

---

[78] Keith Krause, *Arms and the State: Patterns of Military Production and Trade* (Cambridge: Cambridge University Press, 1992); William Keller, *Arm in Arm: the Political Economy of the Global Arms Trade* (New York: Basic Books, 1995); Kevin O'Prey, *The Arms Export Challenge* (Washington, DC: Brookings, 1995).

[79] In the seventeenth and eighteenth centuries states were implicated in conflicts and even fired upon by non-state purveyors of force. Thomson, *Mercenaries, Pirates, and Sovereigns*, pp. 43–68.

that PSCs further their government's policy abroad, bring income home, or advantage other industries abroad, they can improve functional control.

In the modern era, states have generally shied away from exporting violent services by de-legitimating non-state venues for allocating these services and harnessing citizen soldiers for state use or exchange with allies through state-based institutions.[80] In effect, states acted to produce something like a collective good – the state monopoly over legitimate international violent services.[81] This action was made possible by the prevailing belief among states that citizen armies were most effective, which reduced demand for foreign soldiers just as some states sought to regulate the behavior of their citizens abroad.[82] As long as states raised armies from their own citizens and only exchanged violent services with other states, the demand for non-state services was small, as was the resulting dilemma states faced. As the demand for non-state services has increased, the collective monopoly has broken down. How do increasing exports of military services affect a state's control of force? Do exports erode state control? Or can states regulate the sale of these services to enhance their control?

Characteristics of the current market and industry increase the costs of the authoritative controls generally associated with states in ways that should decrease regulatory effectiveness. Transnational markets usually make oversight and sanctioning more challenging.[83] If the state is no longer the container of socio-economic activity, but merely a site through which transnational flows of goods and services pass, national governments have more difficulty keeping track of the flow of goods and services that pass through their borders and have to pay more to deny those flows.[84] The particular character of some service industries – those with low capitalization and little attachment to territory – are even more awkward for states to manage (states have greater leverage over the behavior of firms that are capitalized and have sunk costs in particular territory that the state controls).[85] Also, a glut can make it more costly

[80] See ibid. See Krause, *Arms and the State*, chs. 2–3 for the pattern of state decisions regarding the export of weaponry during this period.

[81] Thomson, *Mercenaries, Pirates, and Sovereigns.*

[82] Avant, "From Mercenary to Citizen Armies."

[83] Robert Keohane and Joseph Nye, *Power and Interdependence* (Boston: Little, Brown, 1977).

[84] Held et al., *Global Transformations*, p. 4.

[85] Jeffrey Herbst, "The Regulation of Private Security Forces," in Greg Mills and John Stremlau, eds., *The Privatization of Security in Africa* (Johannesburg: SAIIA Press, 1999); Porter, *Competitive Advantage of Nations*, pp. 239–76; Peter Drucker, "Trade Lessons from the World Economy," *Foreign Affairs* (January/February 1994): 99–108.

for suppliers to control the industry in general – if a customer cannot buy something from one state, it simply goes to another supplier, rewarding the industry and enhancing the influence of another state.[86]

Today's private security market exhibits all of these characteristics. It is transnational with PSCs recruiting from and selling to a variety of state and non-state entities. Also, PSCs incur few costs from moving. Most firms operate with a small full-time contingent and a large database from which to draw teams to carry out contracts. Though many are more than "a retired military guy sitting in a spare bedroom with a fax machine and a Rolodex,"[87] firms offering private security services generally have little capital and are not attached to a particular location. Indeed, PSCs have a fluid structure and can rapidly dissolve and recreate themselves as need be.[88] This has been most visible in South Africa, but also in the UK. Furthermore, PSCs often set up counterparts in many different regions – British based DSL has some twenty subsidiaries or counterparts. These characteristics allow PSCs that want to avoid state regulation to simply move elsewhere. Since the end of the Cold War, there has also been a glut of supply in both arms and services – though the recent US war in Iraq has tightened up both.[89]

The market does issue consequential control mechanisms, however, that can be used by states as well as private actors. For instance, states that purchase services can influence the behavior of firms through consumer demand. Furthermore, states that are consumers of security services can employ their market power to reinforce and strengthen their regulatory efforts. In other words, governments that buy services from PSCs both affect the behavior of PSCs with their procurement decisions and give firms incentives to abide by authoritative controls in order to secure future contracts. States can gain functional control over the behavior of PSCs and the private security industry, then, on the

---

General analyses of services include: Geza Feketekuty, *International Trade in Services: an Overview and Blueprint for Negotiations* (Cambridge: Ballinger, 1988); Michel Kostecki, *Marketing Strategies for Services* (Oxford: Pergamon Press, 1994).

[86] Krause, *Arms and the State*; Herbert Wulf, ed., *Arms Industry Limited* (Oxford: Oxford University Press, 1993); Paul Cornish, *Controlling the Arms Trade: the West versus the Rest* (London: Bowerdean, 1996); Ann Markusen and Sean Costigan, eds., *Arming the Future: a Defense Industry for the Twenty-First Century* (New York: Council on Foreign Relations, 1999).

[87] Ken Silverstein quotes James Woods. See "Privatizing War," p. 11.

[88] Singer, *Corporate Warriors*, p. 75.

[89] Jeffrey Boutwell, Michael Klare, and Laura Reed, eds., *Lethal Commerce: The Global Trade in Small Arms and Light Weapons* (Cambridge, MA: American Academy of Arts and Sciences, 1995); Richard Bitzinger, *The Globalization of Arms Production* (Washington, DC: Defense Budget Project, 1993). See also the ACDA annual publication, *World Military Expenditures and Arms Transfers* (Washington, DC: ACDA).

coat-tails of their purchasing share in the market as well as their regulatory capacity. When a state is confident that PSCs will act in accordance with its interests, it may be able to pursue its interests abroad simply by licensing the sale of security services. This opens the way for foreign policy by proxy where state leaders can affect conditions abroad without sending troops or even money – increasing functional control.

As the previous section suggested, however, government consumption of private security services also alters the political process, redistributing power among government institutions and creating new pathways for private interests to affect foreign policy.[90] Furthermore, some of the very functional gains that private security exports deliver such as the potential for foreign policy by proxy reinforce this redistribution of power. Through proxies, state leaders can affect conditions abroad without mobilizing broad support for troops or (sometimes) even money. Policy changes can be instituted with the input of a very few actors, circumventing the domestic institutional processes. Furthermore, the private actors that gain influence over policy decisions by providing information about implementation success or creating standards by which regulation is judged sometimes have a financial stake in the policy – leading away from foreign policy restraint in democratic systems.[91] Thus, the conditions favorable to functional control of private security exports in a transnational market also redistribute power over the control of force – changing political control.

State leaders also can use markets to generate social control.[92] Many analyses have focused on state efforts within international organizations or regimes to set agendas, influence standards, link issues, and exercise leadership to enhance the chance that policy results will reflect their values.[93] States can also gain social control of private force, though, with their consumption patterns. Not only do state purchases of security services affect the incentives for PSCs to reflect that state's interests abroad, they also communicate the state's values and standards for

---

[90] Donahue, *Privatization Decision*; Feigenbaum and Henig, "Political Underpinnings of Privatization"; Feigenbaum, Henig, and Hamnett, *Shrinking the State*; Freeman, "The Contracting State."

[91] See Immanuel Kant, "Perpetual Peace" (1795) in Carl J. Friederick, ed., *The Philosophy of Kant* (New York: Modern Library, 1949); Michael Doyle, "Kant, Liberal Legacies, and Foreign Affairs," *Philosophy and Public Affairs* Vol. 12 (summer 1983); David Lake, "Powerful Pacifists: Democratic States and War," *American Political Science Review* Vol. 86, No. 1 (March 1992).

[92] Keohane and Nye, *Power and Interdependence*; Louis Pauly, *Who Elected the Bankers?* (Ithaca: Cornell University Press, 1997).

[93] Ibid.

proper behavior by a PSC. Through procurement and other efforts to set and communicate standards and educate the private sector as to the proper modes of security service provision, then, states can also influence the ecology of the global market for security services.[94] States that choose not to participate in these efforts essentially give up this influence – allowing other states, IOs, INGOs and corporations to play a greater role in shaping the ecology of the global market.

Ironically, however, the most effective use of markets to "engage" PSCs as legitimate purveyors of military services and thus influence their behavior flies in the face of the international norm that security should be the exclusive realm of states. Many have held that states' collective monopoly of the legitimate use of force is a fundamental feature of the modern state system.[95] Indeed, international law bans "mercenaries" and many of the UN's actions on this subject have focused on upholding that standard.[96] Though efforts to participate in the market and otherwise engage PSCs may enhance an individual state's role in encouraging PSCs to work within international values that uphold human rights, international laws, and democratic control of the military, such action simultaneously communicates disregard for the norm that states have primary responsibility for and monopoly over legitimate security services.

In effect, the opportunities for state regulation in the private security market present two trade-offs. First, between influencing the behavior of PSCs abroad and maintaining the integrity of political processes of foreign policy making and second, between influencing the professional values PSCs attend to and reinforcing the overarching value that the

---

[94] See Neil Fligstein, "Theoretical and Comparative Perspectives on Corporate Organization," *Annual Review of Sociology* Vol. 21 (1995): 21–43.
[95] See Thomson, *Mercenaries, Pirates, and Sovereigns*, pp. 7–18. See also Weber, "Politics as a Vocation," in Gerth and Mills, *From Max Weber*. Thomson is careful to note that soldiers of fortune nonetheless persisted as did state use of "proxy" forces. In this sense, PSCs are just another tool to add to this list. What is distinctive, though, is that PSCs are increasingly accepted as open (and legitimate) forces on the world stage making their use a powerful challenge to the norm that Thomson observed.
[96] Ballesteros, "International Convention Against the Recruitment, Use, Financing and Training of Mercenaries, A/Res/44/34, 72nd plenary meeting, 4 December 1989; Enrique Bernales, "Report on the Question of the Use of Mercenaries as a Means of Violating Human Rights and Impeding the Exercise of the Right of Peoples to Self Determination," submitted to the United Nations Commission on Human Rights 53rd Session, Item 7, 20 February 1997; UNHCR, "Protocol Additional to the Geneva Conventions of 12 August 1949, and Relating to the Protection of Victims of International Armed Conflicts," Adopted on 8 June 1977 by the Diplomatic Conference of International Humanitarian Law applicable in Armed Conflicts, *Entry into Force* 7 December 1979, in accordance with Article 95. Available at http://www.unhchr.ch/html/menu3/b/93.htm.

state should provide security. States may respond to these in different ways.[97] Their responses, though, should generate predictable variation in the quality of governmental influence of security exports, the degree of political change, and the role of individual states in influencing the standards of military professionalism. The best strategy for garnering functional control and enhancing the state's influence over professionalism in PSCs should simultaneously change political control and erode the norm that the state should provide military services. Though states may choose different strategies to manage the trade-offs in state control, they should not be able to avoid them altogether.

Non-state financing and the control of force

States are not the only actors exerting control over violence in the current market. As chapter one suggests, non-state actors also participate in the market as consumers, giving them consequential mechanisms by which to exert control (through their purchasing decisions) over both the behavior of PSCs in contract with them as well as the emerging ecology of the market. Transnational non-state actors finance security in a variety of ways: subsidizing state forces (for instance, corporations subsidize state protection of their property), paying for protection by non-corporate forces such as paramilitaries or rebel groups that offer protection, or hiring private forces (either to provide security themselves or to train elements of state or other local forces).

The financing of security by non-state actors issues some particular challenges to states. First, non-state financing of security is most likely to occur when the state has failed to provide the desired protection and is thus, in itself, an indication of state weakness. Non-state financing could further weaken the state both in terms of its control of consequential incentives (when non-state entities pay for state forces, they potentially erode the state's control of budgetary influence over its

---

[97] Porter, *Competitive Advantage of Nations*, pp. 657–82. See also Peter Katzenstein, ed., *Between Power and Plenty* (Madison: University of Wisconsin Press, 1978); Peter A. Gourevitch, "The Macropolitics of Microinstitutional Differences in the Analysis of Comparative Capitalism," in Suzanne Berger and Ronald Dore, eds., *National Diversity and Global Capitalism* (Ithaca: Cornell University Press, 1996): 239–59; John Goodman, Deborah Spar, and David Yoffie, "Foreign Direct Investment and the Demand for Protection in the United States," *International Organization* Vol. 40, No. 4 (autumn 1996); Louis Pauly and Simon Reich, "National Structures and International Corporate Behavior: Enduring Differences in an Age of Globalization," *International Organization* Vol. 51, No. 1 (winter 1997); Ronan Palan and Jason Abbott, *State Strategies in the Global Political Economy* (London: Pinter, 1996).

forces – when non-state entities hire private security, whether corporate or other, they evade state institutions altogether) and in terms of its coherence and legitimacy. On the other hand, by providing a weak state with additional resources with which it can govern, non-state entities could help a weak state consolidate control. When accompanied with education about rational legal forms of governance and appropriate military behavior, non-state financing could aid the development of control in weak states. Does transnational financing of security further erode the potential for state control of force or can it subsidize weak states and move the use of force closer to international standards?

Arguments from economic institutionalism are consistent with those most concerned about the challenge to a state's consequential controls – worrying that non-state financing of security services, subsidizing state forces, paying for protection by other non-corporate forces (paramilitaries or rebel groups), or hiring PSCs – could further erode a weak state's ability to control violence. The literature on transnational corporations (TNCs) reflects this logic, looking at transnational financing's corrupting effect on political practices in weak states.[98] Analyses of the impact of foreign direct investment on the creation of repressive state apparatuses that cater to foreign investors and their domestic allies look primarily at TNC effects on the trade-off between functional and political control of force.

Sociological analyses often look beyond the effects on the state, per se, to see the potential for non-state financing of security to enhance the encouragement or promotion of more appropriate state behavior. Indeed, studies of INGOs, in general, have examined their ability to set new standards for states, educate states about standards, and/or pressure states to abide by standards.[99] Those who have looked at the effect of INGOs on state control of violence have generally followed a

---

[98] Terry L. Karl, "The Perils of the Petro-State: Reflections on the Politics of Plenty," *Journal of International Affairs* Vol. 53, No. 1 (fall 1999): 34; Jedrzej George Frynas, "Political Instability and Business: Focus on Shell in Nigeria," *Third World Quarterly* Vol. 19, No. 3 (1998): 457–78; Global Witness, *A Crude Awakening: the Role of Oil and Banking Industries in Angolan Civil War* (London: Global Witness, 1999); Scott Pegg, "The Cost of Doing Business: Transnational Corporations and Violence in Nigeria," *Security Dialogue* Vol. 30, No. 4 (1999): 473–484.

[99] See Keck and Sikkink, *Activists Beyond Borders*; Thomas Risse, "The Power of Norms versus the Norms of Power: Transnational Civil Society and Human Rights," in Ann M. Florini, ed., *The Third Force: the Rise of Transnational Civil Society* (Washington, DC: Japan Center for International Exchange and Carnegie Endowment, 2000); Audie Klotz, *Norms in International Relations: the Struggle Against Apartheid* (Ithaca: Cornell University Press, 1995); John Boli and George Thomas, *Constructing World Culture: International Non-Governmental Organizations Since 1975* (Stanford: Stanford University Press, 1999).

similar pattern focusing on INGOs' effect on the social control of force.[100]

Extrapolating from this research, one could argue that transnational financing's effect on security will depend on what kind of transnational entity is doing the financing. The literature on transnational actors has largely studied different parts of the transnational community (distinguished by actor motivation) separately. Those who study INGOs often argue that these "value motivated" actors should provide positive effects on the standards of action. Those who study "interest motivated" transnational corporations often argue that these actors introduce negative effects on the distribution of power.

The synthesis of the institutionalist approaches I have suggested, though, redirects attention from the motivations of transnational actors to how their strategies affect the mechanisms for controlling violence. Furthermore, much of the existing literature looks at only part of what transnational actors affect. The literature on INGOs' effect on the control of force generally focuses on social control. The literature on TNCs' effect on the control of force mostly looks at functional and political control. The institutional approach I have introduced suggests we should examine the effects of transnational financing of security across all three dimensions of control. We should also examine the effect of transnational strategies on the fit between the three dimensions – something that has not yet been examined at all.

Institutional analysis should expect transnational financing of security to have its clearest effect on the political control of force. By definition, transitional financing for security redistributes political power over decisions about the use of force to actors outside the state.[101] It may also redistribute power within the territory as a result – INGOs and TNCs pursue the goals that brought them to the territory in the first place, and in so doing advantage local actors who share their goals or can use the

---

[100] Martha Finnemore, *National Interests in International Society* (Ithaca: Cornell University Press, 1996), ch. 3; Richard Price, "Transnational Society Targets Land Mines," *International Organization* Vol. 52, No. 3 (summer 1998); Rebecca Johnson, "Advocates and Activists: Conflicting Approaches on Nonproliferation and the Test Ban Treaty," in Ann Florini, ed., *The Third Force: the Rise of Transnational Civil Society* (Washington, DC: Japan Center for International Exchange and Carnegie Endowment, 2000); Motoko Mekata, "Building Partnerships Toward a Common Goal: Experiences of the International Campaign to Ban Landmines," in Ann Florini, ed., *The Third Force: the Rise of Transnational Civil Society* (Washington, DC: Japan Center for International Exchange and Carnegie Endowment, 2000); Risse, "Power of Norms versus the Norms of Power."

[101] Of course, this is not confined to transnational actors. When states finance security, they also cause a redistribution of political control over force – just to different actors and (potentially) for different purposes.

new resources to their advantage. This will not be surprising to analysts of foreign direct investment where links between the state and transnational corporations have been connected to a larger than normal security apparatus and one that works to secure the interests of foreign investors first.[102] Analyses of INGOs, though, have found similar effects in particular issue areas.[103] When transnational actors fund state forces, they also advantage or solidify the advantage of those actors that share their preferences on a narrow issue area – conservation, for instance, for conservation INGOs and the stabilization of property rights for commercial corporations.[104] Furthermore, savvy local actors may use transnational resources for their own ends, in opposition to what transnational financiers intended.[105] Funding PSCs, rebel or paramilitary forces promises more political change. Transnational financing of PSCs, in particular, undermines the state's consequential tools altogether and may focus resources on narrow issue areas.[106] Indeed, the transnational provision of security services may build constituencies loyal to a transnational community rather than any local governance framework.[107] If transnational financing redistributes power over who gets to decide about violence, political control has changed.

Transnational financing may also affect the social control of force. Analyses of INGOs have examined how these organizations use a variety

---

[102] Karl, "Perils of the Petro-State"; Frynas, "Political Instability and Business"; Global Witness, "A Crude Awakening"; Pegg, "Cost of Doing Business."

[103] See Nancy Peluso, "Coercing Conservation," in Ronnie D. Lipschutz and Ken Conca, eds., *The State and Social Power in Global Environmental Politics* (New York: Columbia University Press, 1993).

[104] The *means* state forces use may or may not reflect the preferences of transnational actors.

[105] Carrie A. Meyer, "Environmental NGOs in Ecuador: an Economic Analysis of Institutional Change," *Journal of Developing Areas* Vol. 27 (January 1993): 191–210; Ben Barber, "Feeding Refugees or War? The Dilemma of Humanitarian Aid," *Foreign Affairs* Vol. 76, No. 4 (July/August 1997); Ken Conca, "International Regimes, State Authority, and Environmental Transformation: the Case of National Parks and Protected Areas," University of Maryland, Harrison Program on the Future Global Agenda, Occasional Paper No. 15 (September 1996); Nancy Peluso, "Coercing Conservation."

[106] William Reno, "Shadow States and the Political Economy of Civil War," in Mats Berdal and David Malone, eds., *Greed and Grievance: Economic Agendas in Civil Wars* (Boulder: Lynne Rienner, 2000).

[107] As Will Reno notes, transnational financing of private security in Angola helps secure mines and pay off supporters, but in ways that erode both public capabilities and any expectation that the state is beholden to the local population. "Companies like Tricorn, which operates a foreign mining firm, are connected to the Angolan army's chief of staff. This man's brother heads Alpha 5, a mine protection service that reportedly worked for a Canadian firm . . . The director general of the state-run oil company bought into the (now defunct) private South African military firm Executive Outcomes, then established Teleservices with South Africa's Gray Security Services," ibid., p. 57.

of mechanisms (though generally not financing) to prompt improvements in social control. The provision of information about the activities of military forces, the creation of standards by which to judge states or military forces, and educating states and military forces about their proper role have all been tied to increased integration between prevailing international values and the use of force.[108] Tied to these other activities, the financing of security could underscore and enhance transnational efforts to encourage appropriate behavior.[109] Though it is much more common for studies of INGOs to focus on the social control of violence, there is nothing to preclude TNCs from having a similar effect. For instance, if foreign direct investment is predicated on or otherwise encourages due respect for human rights and international law in the exercise of violence, TNCs might enhance the integration of violence with international norms. Recent analyses have introduced the potential that transnational corporations could encourage behavior more in keeping with international values,[110] and some companies have endorsed this view.[111]

Though transnational financing, by definition, has some effect on social control of force (by reinforcing transnational financiers' *goals* and linking the goals of force to a transnational community of sorts), we should not expect transnational financiers to automatically enhance the integration of the practice of violence with international norms. The effect of transnational financing should vary with whether they appeal to international norms surrounding the use of force in their financing decisions, and also whether they tie their financing of security to efforts at educating organizations about the proper use of force and cultivating

[108] Florini, *Third Force*; Keck and Sikkink, *Activists Beyond Borders*; Ann Marie Clark, *Diplomacy of Conscience: Amnesty International and Changing Human Rights Norms* (Princeton: Princeton University Press, 2001); Paul Wapner, "Politics Beyond the State: Environmental Activism and World Civic Politics," *World Politics* Vol. 47, No. 3 (1995): 311–40.
[109] Social norms are frequently undergirded by material power and the expected material consequences of violations. Conversely, established social institutions affect what material people value. Finally, social norms do not simply inform actors of appropriate behavior, they can also promise consequences – social or material – for misbehavior. Ron Jepperson, Alexander Wendt, and Peter Katzenstein, "Norms, Identity, and National Security," in Peter Katzenstein, ed., *The Culture of National Security* (New York: Columbia University Press, 1996); Finnemore and Sikkink, "International Norm Dynamics"; Jack Snyder, "Anarchy and Culture," *International Organization* Vol. 56, No. 1 (winter 2002): 7–46.
[110] Haufler, "Is There a Role for Business in Conflict Prevention?"; Nelson, *Business of Peace*; Nick Butler, "Companies in International Relations," *Survival* Vol. 42, No. 1 (spring 2000): 149–65.
[111] "Voluntary Principles on Security and Human Rights," US Department of State, Democracy, Human Rights and Labor, January 2001.

changes in their day-to-day culture and practices.[112] If transnational financiers appeal to international norms about the proper use of force and tie financing decisions to education about (and social rewards for) proper behavior, they should enhance the integration of force with international values. Transnational encouragement of effective socialization processes also depends on a certain degree of expertise within the transnational community, which allows transnational actors to encourage social as well as material incentives for appropriate action and allows transnational actors to effectively judge the behavior of forces. In the absence of these appeals, ties, and expertise, however, transnational financing alone should not improve the social control of force.

How should transnational financing affect functional control? This should vary with whether it consolidates power in the state or diffuses power to other actors. When funneled through state institutions, solidifying central control over forces, transnational financing is more likely to enhance military capabilities in the weak states – at least in the short run.[113] The very fact that the state is weak, however, also increases the chances that rulers will divert resources to parallel forces or pay off local strongmen rather than build up a central security bureaucracy. The potential for diversion sometimes leads transnational financiers to pay a portion of the forces directly. This choice, however, can disperse control to different entities – or multiple principals – with separate and competing controls over violence.[114] If the state still controls personnel but transnational actors control budgetary incentives, and the two do not coordinate their direction of forces, the competition between these "principals" can result in less effective forces, in forces that become

---

[112] Finnemore and Sikkink, "International Norms Dynamics," p. 895; Paul DiMaggio and Walter Powell, "The Iron Cage Revisited: Institutional Isomorphism and Collective Rationality in Organizational Fields," in Paul DiMaggio and Walter Powell, eds., *The New Institutionalism in Organizational Analysis* (Chicago: University of Chicago Press, 1991).

[113] See Tornquist, "Rent Capitalism, State, and Democracy"; Karl, *Paradox of Plenty*; Clark, "Petro-Politics in Congo"; Skocpol, "Rentier State and Shi'a Islam in the Iranian Revolution."

[114] For analyses of both economic and sociological approaches to principal-agent problems, see John Pratt and Richard Zeckhauser, *Principals and Agents: the Structure of Business* (Harvard: Harvard Business School Press, 1985). For the consequences of multiple principles, see Bendor, Taylor, and van Gaalen, "Stacking the Deck"; Jonathan Bendor, J. Glazer, and T. Hammond, "Theories of Delegation," *Annual Review of Political Science* Vol. 4, No. 1 (2001): 235–69. For application to civil–military relations, see Avant, *Political Institutions and Military Change*. For application to NGOs see Andrew Natsios, "NGOs and the UN System in Complex Humanitarian Emergencies: Conflict or Cooperation?" *Third World Quarterly* Vol. 16, No. 3 (1995): 405–19; Cooley and Ron, "The NGO Scramble."

political powers unto themselves, or in forces that direct their energies toward functions that are not public at all.[115]

The interaction between these hypotheses suggests that while it is possible for non-state financing to lead toward a greater fit between the dimensions of control, it will be difficult. Transnational pressure to abide by international norms is most effective when it is directed toward an entity that can respond – like the state. The conditions that lead transnational financing to strengthen the state – funneling money into state coffers – though, frequently distributes power to actors interested in preserving or enhancing their benefits in a corrupt, patrimonial system. Though transnational financing does strengthen the influence of external actors, the ability of these actors to oversee the intricacies of state implementation may be limited. Both of these conditions decrease the potential that political change will reinforce international norms for proper military behavior so long as a weak state is involved. Transnational action to go around corrupt state institutions, however, may simultaneously introduce a new principal, essentially weakening the state and making it less capable of doing anything – including responding to external pressure.

One could imagine a situation where transnational actors might enhance the potential for functional gains not only by financing security, but by essentially taking over for the state with regard to security tasks in a particular area. With help from professional military forces such as PSCs, this could lead to more capable forces that operate in closer integration with international norms, potentially even laying the foundation for localized state-building efforts. This possibility, though, challenges basic features of "non-state" identity, pushing INGOs and even TNCs to assume roles more like governments. Because concerns over reputation, fundraising, and potential future claims to accountability lead many non-state actors to reject this possibility, the potential for transnational financing to enhance the fit between the different dimensions of control and thus what we judge as effective control is small.

---

[115] Paul Collier, "Doing Well out of War: an Economic Perspective," in Mats Berdal and David Malone, eds., *Greed and Grievance* (Boulder: Lynne Rienner, 2000); Frynas, "Political Instability and Business"; Reno, "Shadow States and the Political Economy of Civil Wars"; Reno, "How Sovereignty Matters"; William Reno, "Foreign Firms, Natural Resources, and Violent Political Economies," *Social Science Forum* (21 March 2000) available at www.social-science-forum.org.

Methods and claims

The discussion above has generated a series of hypotheses about how privatization will affect the control of violence in these different privatization relationships. In the following three chapters, I illustrate these hypotheses and probe their plausibility by looking at specific instances of private security within these general relationships.

To illustrate how state contracts with PSCs affect the control of force, I examine the experiences of the US, Croatia, and Sierra Leone in contracting for a similar type of sovereign service – military advice and training. All three states contracted with PSCs during the 1990s for military advice and training services. The states vary from strong (the US), through weak (Croatia and Sierra Leone) and thus should experience different effects on functional and social control. Also, the two weak states' contracts with PSCs vary on many of the counts important for predicting the direction of political and social change (length, source of funding, effect on consolidation of power, strength of professional network), which should influence the potential for a reinforcing process of control. In each country, I look at many different contracts over a several year period. By tracing the processes in these cases and linking the process to the outcomes, I both illustrate the hypotheses in action and demonstrate their plausibility.

To illustrate how exports of private security services affect states' ability to control the force that emanates from their territory, I examine the way the three largest exporters of military services, the US, the UK, and South Africa, have approached the regulation of military service exports. These countries provide a reasonable plausibility probe of the institutionalist hypotheses because each of these countries exported similar kinds of services (again military advice and training) during the 1990s. These countries also chose different strategies of control and thus should experience accompanying differences in control gains and losses. The experiences of these countries also ratify the institutionalist hypotheses, demonstrating both that the governments experienced a trade-off in control as expected, and also that, in some cases, state leaders were aware of the trade-offs as they made their choices.

To demonstrate how the private financing of security affects the control of force and to probe the plausibility of the institutionalist hypotheses in this relationship, I examine three cases of transnational financing of security: oil companies (particularly Royal Dutch/Shell) in Nigeria, relief organizations in the camps of Goma, Zaire/Democratic Republic of Congo and conservation organizations in Garamba National Park, Zaire/Democratic Republic of Congo. In each of these cases, transnational private actors financed forces in a territory. These cases were selected to cast a broad net in terms of motivations (commercial versus larger purpose) and issue focus (oil extraction, relief, conservation) to see if there are the kinds of similarities among private financiers that the institutionalist model suggests. What I find supports the hypotheses above. Both INGOs and TNCs that finance security introduce changes in political and social control over violence, but these changes were rarely, in these cases, joined by improved functional control. In all these cases transnational actors appear to have effects on the different dimensions of control over violence that work against one another – in some instances, spreading international norms even as they undermine functional control and/or lead to a redistribution of power that may be inconsistent with these norms. Finally, in each of these cases, I also found something I was not looking for. The non-state financing of security led to a contentious debate within the non-state community, suggesting that the political changes introduced by privatization are not only found among states, but also echo among non-state actors – a point I return to when discussing the more general implications of this research in chapter six.

Though this study was originally devised to test what appeared to be competing claims about the consequences of privatizing security, its ultimate argument is that the claims of optimists and pessimists do not compete – they focus on, and illuminate, different dimensions of privatization's effect on the control of force.[116] Realizing that these arguments were speaking past one another and reflecting on how similar arguments about the control of force were prominent among debates in the literature on civil–military relations led me to offer a new way to think about the control of force by examining the three dimensions of control and how they fit together. While this is vital for understanding privatization's effects on the control of force, it should also be helpful for thinking about civilian control of the military more generally. Debates about civilian control of the military are often muddled by different standards for control. Recognizing the three dimensions of control and their fit can both provide a common standard and illuminate the trade-offs involved in emphasizing one dimension over another.[117]

---

[116] King, Keohane, and Verba cite this kind of finding as an important contribution to knowledge. See Gary King, Robert Keohane, and Sidney Verba, *Designing Social Inquiry: Scientific Inference in Qualitative Research* (Princeton: Princeton University Press, 1994), pp. 14–17.

[117] Deborah Avant, "Conflicting Indicators of 'Crisis' in American Civil–Military Relations," *Armed Forces and Society* Vol. 24, No. 3 (spring 1998): 375–88.

Thinking of control this way also led me to search for a theoretical structure that could make sense of sociological and economic institutionalist arguments together. I began with a "domains of applicability" argument – juxtaposing hypotheses that explained different parts of the control problem.[118] As I began to add these up to assess the overall fit between functional, political, and social control in each case, I noticed a pattern – in many instances the demands placed on individual actors contradicted one another. This pattern was probably made more apparent by the fact that much of my research involved conducting interviews and interviewees repeatedly complained about contradictions they faced. My focus on mechanisms and whether they reinforce or contradict one another grew out of this discovery.[119]

In the end, then, I suggest not only that economic and sociological arguments have different domains, but that the two together hold the key to predicting stability or change. When control mechanisms work with one another, we should expect a stable process that is often viewed as effective control; when they do not we should expect instability and change – and generally see control as more problematic. This theoretical insight – whether the mechanisms economists and sociologists point to work together or not – adds a new twist to the growing literature on the complementary relationship between rationalist and constructivist approaches. It should travel easily to examine other governance and delegation problems.

The cases I examine are designed to illustrate and probe the plausibility of institutionalist hypotheses. In each case I both employ process tracing to see if the causality works the way I expect and consider the outcome for evidence about the plausibility of my arguments. I note cases where the outcome is uncertain, and rely more heavily on process indicators for my judgment in those circumstances. There are a variety of ways one might test these hypotheses – looking at

---

[118] This is identified as one strategy for bridging gaps between what appear to be competing theories. See Michael Tierney and Catherine Weaver, "Principles and Principals? The Possibilities for Theoretical Synthesis and Scientific Progress in the Study of International Organizations," paper prepared for the conference on Theoretical Synthesis in the study of International Organizations, Washington, DC, 6–7 February 2004, pp. 16–17. As they note, Charles Lipson suggested that security and economic issues areas in international relations were roughly consistent with the domains in which realist and liberal theory would apply respectively. See Charles Lipson, "International Cooperation in Economic and Security Affairs," *World Politics* Vol. 37 (1984): 31–63. A similar logic is suggested by other studies attempting to bridge the gap between rationalists and constructivists in the study of a variety of pheonomenon in international affairs. See Juptille, Caporaso, and Checkel, "Integrating Institutions."

[119] For a defense of the style of interaction between theory and data, see Charles Ragin, *Fuzzy Set Social Science* (Chicago: University of Chicago Press, 2000).

more cases and cases with clearer outcomes, sorting through other potential explanations for the variation in outcomes, conducting experiments to test their logic, etc. While I welcome this further research, for now I do not claim to have tested these hypotheses, but only to have proposed a new and plausible way to think about both variation in the control of force more generally and the specific consequences of privatizing security for this control.

3   State capacity and contracting for security

Can state contracts with PSCs enhance a state's control of force? Optimists and pessimists come to different conclusions about this important question. Much of their disagreement, however, can be explained by the fact that they emphasize different dimensions of control and compare PSCs to different state forces. The institutional synthesis proposed in chapter two suggests that privatization's effects should vary, first and foremost, with the capacities of existing state forces. Furthermore, privatization is likely to have different effects on functional, political, and social control.

Particularly, strong (capable, coherent, legitimate) states have more capacity with which to direct and oversee contracts, but also a better force to begin with. In general, strong states should experience some loss in efficiency (dollar cost) or effectiveness (responsiveness) related to functional control when they outsource "sovereign services" already provided by public security organizations. They may also gain new capabilities (either services not provided by the military or more services than are available from the current structure) but these should cost more or be less responsive than military forces. Weak states do not have the same kinds of capacities to begin with and thus may achieve short-run functional gains from contracting with PSCs. If state institutions are corrupt or otherwise debilitated they may be so ineffective and/or illegitimate that private alternatives offer capabilities simply not available via the state. However, the poor capacity of weak states also makes their use of PSCs risky. Specific predictions in each case will vary with functional needs, the type of service outsourced, and the specifics of the contract.

The social control effects should also differ for strong and weak states. To the degree that strong states hire PSCs staffed with retired military personnel, highly institutionalized professional norms should create an environment where outsourcing is less likely to change the meaningful integration of force with societal values. Because weak states frequently purchase services from the same PSCs, these firms should bring with them the potential for greater integration with international values. Thus, in general, contracts with PSCs should maintain social control in strong states and enhance social control in weak states. Specific predictions in each case will vary with the length of the contracting relationship, its references to military professionalism, and the integration of PSC personnel with professional networks.

The political control of force should change when states contract with PSCs regardless of the strength of the state – though the manifestations of change should be more extreme in weak states. The private delivery of sovereign services to strong states should alter the process through which force is controlled – generally reducing transparency and redistributing power among domestic institutions and groups. In weak states the political change may be much more dramatic, shifting power to those outside the state and sometimes leading to regime change. Specific predictions will depend on the task outsourced and the nature of the contracting arrangement – such as who controls the financing of services, how the PSC is monitored, and how the contract is implemented.

The resulting fit (or not) between these dimensions of control will depend on the degree to which the new mechanisms of control support one another. To probe the plausibility of these hypotheses, I examine how outsourcing a similar set of sovereign services – particularly advice and training – mattered for control in two weak states: Sierra Leone and Croatia, and one strong state: the United States of America.

Sierra Leone's contracts for military services

Sierra Leone was widely recognized as the paradigmatic weak state in the 1990s.[1] Its path from colonialism to weak state is well documented by Joel Migdal.[2] The British decision to obtain security and stability in the least costly manner led them to rely on local chiefs for governance. Once this pattern was established, it became hard to overturn – even for the British. By independence in 1961, Sierra Leone's people were organized in eighteen different ethnic groups.[3] Chiefs used tribal ties to associate themselves and their constituencies with coalitions or blocs large enough to preclude domination by others. Rulers bought loyalty from ethnic and political strongmen and then used state bureaucracies to manipulate resources and undercut challengers.[4] The state became

---

[1] Migdal, *Strong Societies and Weak States*; Reno, *Warlord Politics and African States*.
[2] Migdal, *Strong Societies and Weak States*, ch. 3.
[3] Ibid., p. 129.
[4] William Reno, "Privatizing War in Sierra Leone," *Current History* Vol. 96, No. 610 (May 1997).

quite prominent – with a large bureaucracy and authoritarian, coercive strategies – but social control remained with the chiefs and tied to localities. Rather than establishing authority in itself, then, the state became a prize through which payoffs could be generated that different local blocs fought to control. This proved a fertile environment for nepotism, cronyism, and corruption. Though large, state bureaucracies were neither strong nor effective.[5]

Sierra Leone's rulers bought loyalty in a variety of ways and the country's diamond deposits played an important role. President Siaka Stevens (who retained office from 1967 to 1985) used diamond mines both as a source of revenue for payoffs and then as a source for payoffs themselves. One of the benefits he bestowed upon his cronies before he left office was control of the diamond industry and its exemption from taxation.[6] Stevens' successor, Joseph Momoh, lacked independent support from which to challenge these gifts and (with reduced revenues from the mines) had only limited ability to supply either state services or patronage. Momoh faced a crisis when in 1991 the Revolutionary United Front (RUF) seized portions of territory along its border with Liberia.[7] He increased the army's strength, but, with few financial resources and mounting pressure from international institutions to reduce the country's deficits, many soldiers went unpaid. Capitalizing on soldiers' disgruntlement, a group of officers led by Valentine Strasser took matters into their own hands, marched on the capital, and overthrew Momoh in April 1992.[8]

Strasser was young and charismatic, but was no more able than Momoh to provide even basic services. By late 1994 and early 1995, the government was on the ropes. Its finance minister estimated that although 70 percent of state revenues was going to fight the rebels, the regime was still losing ground. In 1995 the rebels attacked (and ended production at) two diamond mines that were the last major source of state revenues. Rebel forces then drove toward the capital, Freetown.[9]

---

[5] Migdal, *Strong Societies and Weak States*, pp. 129–39; Christopher Allen, "Sierra Leone," in John Dunn, ed., *West African States: Failure and Promise* (Cambridge: Cambridge University Press, 1978); Reno, *Warlord Politics and African States*.

[6] Reno, *Warlord Politics and African States*, p. 228.

[7] John L. Hirsh, "War in Sierra Leone," *Survival* Vol. 43, No. 2 (autumn 2001): 145–62. The RUF had grown in the 1980s sponsored by Liberian warlord, Charles Taylor, and filled with young men who had few other options. See Ibrahim Abdullah, "Bush Path to Destruction: the Origin and Character of the Revolutionary United Front/Sierra Leone," *Journal of Modern African Studies* Vol. 36, No. 2 (1998): 203–35.

[8] Reno, "Privatizing War in Sierra Leone," p. 228.

[9] Reno, "Privatizing War in Sierra Leone"; Herbert Howe, "Private Security Forces and African Stability: the Case of Executive Outcomes," *Journal of Modern African Studies* Vol. 36, No. 2 (1998): 307–31.

Strasser's internal strategies to manage the escalating crisis included executing prison rioters and introducing conscription to shore up the Republic of Sierra Leone Military Forces (RSLMF). These strategies only worsened the situation, however; the former by aggravating international opinion against Strasser's regime and the latter by sending untrained and unprofessional youths to the battlefield.[10]

The RSLMF was a poor force before the conscription and even worse after. President Stevens had maintained his tenure in office through cooptation – first striking a deal with the opposition party, the Sierra Leone People's Party (SLPP), and essentially turning Sierra Leone into a one-party state, and then selectively courting top military brass while eviscerating the army and cultivating alternative forces loyal to him.[11] The army was largely ceremonial – part of the patronage system.[12] As the financial situation worsened, however, and wages were not forthcoming, its soldiers were not only untrained and poorly paid, they were also induced to serve with supplies of marijuana and rum.[13] This led to accidents, poor performance, poor behavior among the civilian population (particularly rape and looting), and a tendency to flee when they met the RUF on the battlefield.[14] The RUF fostered this behavior with its policy of torturing its captives. Furthermore, as more and more conscripts were sent to the field without pay, rumors of collusion with the rebels (at least in the pursuit of loot) surfaced. These "sobels" – soldier by day, rebel by night – undermined state control and security in Sierra Leone.[15] The functional bar with which to compare private security was rather low.

Private training: Gurkha Security Guards

In early 1995, Strasser turned to PSCs for help. The first on the scene was a British firm, Gurkha Security Guards (GSG).[16] Fifty-eight

---

[10] Reno, "Privatizing War in Sierra Leone," Venter, "Sierra Leone's Mercenary War."

[11] Musah, "A Country Under Siege," p. 81.

[12] Ian Douglass, "Fighting for Diamonds in Sierra Leone," in Jakkie Cilliers and Peggy Mason, eds. *Peace, Profit, or Plunder: the Privatization of Security in War-Torn African Societies* (Pretoria: Institute for Security Studies, 1999), p. 178.

[13] Venter, "Sierra Leone's Mercenary War."

[14] Musah, "A Country Under Siege," p. 86.

[15] Venter, "Sierra Leone's Mercenary War"; Douglass, "Fighting for Diamonds." Given that the rebel base was the same youth population and its conscription tactics even more barbarous, this is not surprising. Howe, "Private Security Forces and African Stability"; Howe, *Ambiguous Order*.

[16] Leaders in Sierra Leone had cultivated their own forces and relied on forces from other territories before and private forces had been engaged in a number of internal security tasks before this time, so this was not so much a new strategy as a new twist on old practices.

Gurkhas and three European managers arrived in January to train Sierra Leone Special Forces and officer cadets.[17] On 24 February, though, members of the company and a platoon of RSLMF came in contact with the RUF while on a reconnaissance mission to find a place for live fire exercises. At least twenty-one (including several GSG personnel) were killed.[18] GSG sent replacements but reportedly came under increased pressure from the government to not only train the RSLMF, but also engage in operations with them. GSG, however, stuck to the terms of its contract rather than adapting to the government's security needs and refused to perform this more active role. Ultimately the company pulled out in April 1995.[19]

GSG did not improve functional security. Though the company remained in the field in support of its contract – even in the wake of brutal casualties, they sent reinforcements – it would only follow the terms of its contract with Sierra Leone's government. These terms did not yield the security outcome the government was looking for. Indeed, the government refused to send its troops to be trained by GSG out of fear that the troops were targets for the RUF while they were training, because GSG did not provide effective security. The government also expressed dissatisfaction with GSG's refusal to accompany the Army on operations.[20] This is a common criticism of private contracts – they do not adjust easily to changes in (or poorly specified) government goals. The contract instrument is useful for delivering a product, not for taking instructions.[21] GSG had agreed to provide training – not to do whatever was necessary to ensure the safety of the Army either while it was training or in the field.

GSG's refusal to protect the Army also appears to have been a calculated strategy to preserve its commercial reputation, indicating where the company looked for information about its appropriate role. The company had significant experience in Africa doing some mine removal for the UN and working for the British based global corporation, Lonhro, to provide security services and training for local militias in Mozambique. Company officials claimed to have been worried that GSG would acquire a "mercenary" reputation that could undermine the

[17] Alex Vines, "Gurkhas and the Private Security Business in Africa," in Jakkie Cilliers and Peggy Mason, eds., *Peace, Profit, or Plunder: the Privatization of Security in War-Torn African Societies* (Pretoria: Institute for Security Studies, 1999).
[18] Vines, "Gurkhas and the Private Security Business"; Tim Ripley, *Mercenaries: Soldiers of Fortune* (London: Paragon Publishing, 1997).
[19] Venter, "Sierra Leone's Mercenary War"; Douglass, "Fighting for Diamonds," p. 179; Vines, "Gurkhas and the Private Security Business in Africa," p. 129.
[20] Vines, "Gurkhas and the Private Security Business in Africa," pp. 130–31.
[21] Donahue, *Privatization Decision*, p. 39.

potential for future contracts were it to engage in obviously offensive operations on behalf of Sierra Leone's government.[22] GSG was also attuned to the preferences of its other consumers. Some in the British government were worried that GSG's work would be interpreted as British intervention and lead the rebels to execute some British hostages they were holding.[23] GSG did not want to jeopardize future British contracts by working against British interests for the government of Sierra Leone.

Thus, GSG did not enhance functional control in Sierra Leone. The company saw its broader interests and reputation as connected to a variety of audiences beyond Sierra Leone's government and, when the direction of the government came in conflict with these, GSG used the terms of its contract to resist government direction. Though evidence of the contract is sketchy, it also appears as if it was expensive, or at least more expensive than the contract that would come with Executive Outcomes (EO).[24] The market, however, was at least moderately competitive. Strasser's dissatisfaction led him to fire GSG and turn to EO, which offered services closer to what the government wanted (at least initially) and at a lower cost.

Private training: Executive Outcomes

In March 1995, Strasser hired EO to begin an immediate training program.[25] The details of EO's contract with Strasser's government are also murky. Executives of Branch Energy, a mining company, introduced Strasser to EO. According to Branch Energy executive, Michael Grunberg, Branch Energy and Sierra Leone's government had a common problem that EO could solve.[26] Branch Energy negotiated the contract between EO and the government of Sierra Leone. The contract stipulated that EO would provide 150 to 200 soldiers (fully equipped with helicopter support) to support, train, and aid the RSLMF in their war against the RUF.[27] The bill was to be $2 million per month, but the company issued credit to the government, agreeing to be paid with 50 percent of the tax revenues from the Sierra Rutile mine once it was opened. EO's deputy

---

[22] Vines, "Gurkhas and the Private Security Business in Africa," pp. 128–30.
[23] Ibid., p. 131.
[24] A GSG representative claimed that EO won the contract because they agreed to take on offensive operations and also because their costs were less, "they didn't offer their employees comprehensive insurance cover or demand an upfront fee from the government," ibid., p. 132.
[25] Ibid.
[26] Douglass, "Fighting for Diamonds," p. 179.
[27] Ibid., p. 180.

commander, Colonel Andy Brown, was set up in an office directly below Sierra Leone's defense staff chief, Brigadier Maada-Bio, and the government delegated significant authority to EO over training, logistics, and command and control of Sierra Leone's forces.

EO arranged for an intensive three-week training cycle (for 120 soldiers at a time) at an RSLMF base just east of the capital emphasizing basic skills, tactics, discipline, and procedures.[28] They also established intelligence and effective radio communications. "EO intelligence operators identified possible informants, isolated them, trained them, and then supplied them with communications equipment."[29] EO handled logistics for the operations in which they participated, employed a doctor on board one of the MI-17 troop-carrying gunships on all ground operations, and had two casualty evacuation aircraft available.[30] Though they saw their prime mission as training the RSLMF, EO director Lafras Liutingh admitted that his forces reacted "with vigor" when under attack.[31]

Just a month after their arrival, EO led the RSLMF on a counter-offensive. They assumed operation control, provided intelligence information, and accompanied units on operations. Under EO's leadership, the RSLMF drove the rebels away from the capital and caused hundreds of rebel deaths (and over 1,000 desertions).[32] Two EO employees were killed while on convoy duty.[33]

EO then continued to work for the government with the goals of clearing the rebels from the diamond areas (in the Kono district) and destroying the RUF headquarters. The Kono district, near the town of Koidu, was in the east of the country, far from the capital on the coast. Even under EO's direction, the RSLMF looked weaker as it moved to the interior of the country; it failed to coordinate with EO and soldiers often fled when faced with RUF ambushes.[34]

---

[28] Venter, "Sierra Leone's Mercenary War." Three groups of 120 were trained in the first three months.

[29] Howe, "Private Security Forces and African Stability," p. 316.

[30] Venter, "Sierra Leone's Mercenary War."

[31] Ibid.

[32] There is some dispute over the exact timing of EO's arrival and this offensive. Venter claims that Colonel Andy Brown arrived in March and the offensive began in April; Ian Douglass, Herb Howe, and William Reno suggest it was a little later. There is general agreement on the chain of events, though. The rebels withdrew 100 kilometers from the capital within ten days of the beginning of the offensive. See Douglass, "Fighting for Diamonds," p. 182.

[33] Kevin Whitelaw, "Have Gun, Will Prop up Regime," *US News and World Report* (20 January 1997).

[34] EO's post mortem of an attack on 2 August suggested that the rebel band of only forty had few weapons and little ammunition. Even a token fight by the RSLMF could have driven the rebels off. Venter, "Sierra Leone's Mercenary War."

In the east, however, EO found a new resource. Local squads of forest hunters or rural militias knew the terrain, had an incentive to fight the RUF to protect their families, and became a good source of intelligence. The *Kamajoisia* or Kamajors, an ethnic Mende group from the southeast of the country, were particularly strong.[35] EO trained the Kamajors in counter-insurgency, supplied them with weapons, and gained much from their local knowledge.[36] The Kamajors both were useful in retaking the Kono district and remained as a force to be reckoned with (along with private forces at the actual mines – taken on by Lifeguard Security) as EO and the RSLMF moved on to destroy the RUF's base.[37]

Under EO's training and direction, the Kamajors became a significant regional defense force. In a sense, EO was following the path of British colonialism, relying on the local chiefs for power. In this case, they strengthened and legitimized a security institution beholden to local rather than national authority. As the Kamajors and other civil militia groups gained recognition for their success, a split widened between these groups and the RSLMF. According to some, the RUF looted the countryside, the RSLMF looted the areas surrounding its bases and only the civil militias protected civilian life and property.[38] Suspicions about Strasser and his plans for the Kamajors weakened his control over the RSLMF. When Strasser announced (in late 1995) that elections would be held in February the following year, rumors claimed that the RUF and the RSLMF were collaborating to stop the election.[39] Issues with the EO contract complicated matters further. As of November 1995, EO had not been paid and was threatening to leave if payment was not

---

[35] This was in part due to the efforts of a retired army officer, Captain Hinja Norman, who mobilized a local militia for defense of Tetu Bogor (a chiefdom south of Bo where he was the regent chief) in 1994. Douglass, "Fighting for Diamonds," p. 183 cites C. Dietrich, "Altered Conflict Resolution: EO in Sierra Leone," unpublished thesis, Princeton University, 1997.

[36] Howe, "Private Security Forces," pp. 316–17.

[37] The RUF headquarters was attacked in October 1996. Douglass, "Fighting for Diamonds," p. 184.

[38] This is disputed. International Crisis Group (ICG) claimed that the Kamajor Civil Defense Force was also responsible for the atrocities of war, though admit that they are not nearly as responsible as the RUF and the Sierra Leone Army. ICG, "Sierra Leone: Managing Uncertainty," International Crisis Group Africa Report, No. 35 (24 October 2001).

[39] Douglass, "Fighting for Diamonds," pp. 183–85. Strasser was under severe international and domestic pressure to hold elections. Internationally, peace talks pushed elections, but, perhaps more importantly, a civil society movement for elections had emerged and held a national consultative conference in Bintumani in August 1995 and again in January 1996. See Musah, "A Country Under Siege," p. 90.

forthcoming – awkward timing given the threat of a coup.[40] By the end of December, the government had agreed to pay a smaller bill and make an installment of $3 million in January and $1.6 million per month thereafter.[41]

In January, however, Strasser was overthrown by his defense chief, Bio, the RUF announced a ceasefire agreeing to talk with only Bio, and it was discovered that Bio's elder sister was working for the RUF. There was some speculation that EO aided Bio's coup because Bio's brother, Steven, was a partner in Soruss – a Belorussian company that leased aircraft to EO.[42] Whether this speculation is true or not, EO did not step aside as the coup was launched but continued to work. This decision aided the coup regardless of EO's intentions.

Despite efforts to frustrate them, elections were held in February 1996 and Ahmed Tejan Kabbah (a lawyer who had spent many years working at the UN) was elected from the Sierra Leone People's Party. The newly elected President Kabbah reportedly did not even learn of the contract with EO until April at which point he claimed that his government simply did not have the money to pay.[43] He renegotiated with EO to pay $1.2 million per month beginning in May (with April provided free of charge). In September, the government unilaterally reduced the amount to $900,000 and then again to $700,000.

In the ensuing months, Kabbah did manage to get a rebel cease-fire and open peace talks, but tensions between the RSLMF and the militias heightened and broke out into clashes on several occasions. When Kabbah (in response to rumors of coup planning within the RSLMF) purged the army and cut its budget in half in September these tensions increased. It was the Kamajors that struck "with devastating effect"[44] against renewed RUF attacks in the fall.[45] The RSLMF operated as virtually a force unto itself in large parts of the country. Nonetheless, the rebels did sign a peace accord on 30 November 1996. One of their conditions, though, was that all foreign military presence, including EO, should leave the country.[46] EO withdrew according to the terms of the

---

[40] Douglass, "Fighting for Diamonds," p. 184.
[41] Ibid.
[42] Musah, "A Country Under Siege," p. 89.
[43] Douglass, "Fighting for Diamons," p. 186.
[44] Ibid.
[45] The RUF believed that EO was the reason for the Kamajor success. Rebel leader Foday Sankoh reportedly offered a $25,000 reward for the destruction of an EO helicopter and an additional bounty (paid in diamonds) for the capture of an EO employee. Ibid., p. 185.
[46] The Adibjan Peace Accord 30 November 1996, United Nations.

peace accord in January 1997, having received $15.7 million from a $35.3 million contract.[47]

EO delivered on the Strasser government's functional needs for security. It helped the RSLMF push the rebels out of the capital, helped the Kamajors retake the diamond-mining areas, and destroyed RUF headquarters. Even though Kabbah inherited the contract and did not even know of its existence when he took office, EO continued to deliver short-term functional improvements as they aided the Kamajors in repelling RUF offensives. These were probably a large factor in the ensuing peace agreement.[48]

The contract with EO also changed the political control of force within the country in several ways. First, EO became a political player. EO's decision to rely more strongly on the Kamajors opened a rift that ultimately unseated Strasser in a coup.[49] Though EO did not participate in the coup, neither did they prevent it or even step aside as it occurred. Even though they claimed not to support the coup, their decision to stay in the country in its wake influenced the political stability of Strasser's successor, Bio.[50] The government did not have strong mechanisms with which to control EO's actions – indeed, given their inability to pay for the contract, they had very few control levers available. In this situation EO's decisions had significant political power.

Second, as others have noted, by financing the contract with EO (as well as other contracts for the local security of particular mines) international mining companies exerted greater political control over force.[51] Indeed, given the inability of the government to pay EO, we might expect that EO would attend more closely to those who did pay them – that is the mining companies.

Third, EO's decision to work with the Kamajors and other civil militias had longer lasting political effects. EO's actions enhanced the power of the local chiefs – essentially creating parallel forces in Sierra Leone that further diffused the control of force in the country. The infusion of arms and training enhanced the capacities of these forces, and their association with EO enhanced their status and prestige.

---

[47] Douglass, "Fighting for Diamonds," p. 187.

[48] Musah reports on a document prepared for President Kabbah by Soloman Berewa suggesting that EO was the key reason for success against the RUF and outlines an essential role for EO in the restructuring of the RSLMF. Musah, "A Country Under Siege," pp. 93–95.

[49] Ibid., p. 183.

[50] Reno, "Privatizing War in Sierra Leone."

[51] Ibid.; Musah, "A Country Under Siege"; Scott Pegg, "Corporate Armies for States and State Armies for Corporations," paper presented to the annual meeting of the American Political Science Association, Washington, DC, 2001.

Without control by a national political structure or a mechanism through which their behavior could be oriented toward national goals, the militia forces frustrated state building and prompted destabilization. In some instances, fighting between the militias and RSLMF led towns once under government control to fall back into the hands of the RUF.[52] Militia forces also contributed to the crimes against civilians, particularly through reprisals against suspected supporters of the RUF, and reportedly worked as spoilers in the period before the Lome peace accord in 1999.[53] The militias' presence and their association with entities that worked against the consolidation of state power also decreased the likelihood of generating broad societal agreement on security in the country.[54]

The degree to which the government's contract with EO led to a more meaningful integration of violence with international values is less clear. EO's behavior in the field did appear to bring with it elements of military professionalism and international values. Many reports indicate that citizens of Sierra Leone regarded EO behavior as professional and were happy with its ability to put an end to the violence.[55] EO claims to have operated on the assumption that winning the hearts and minds of the civilian population was the key to success and did manage to operate in the country for some time without accusations of looting, atrocities, harassment, or other misbehavior. "'We train our soldiers to behave with the locals,' states Barlow, 'and not [to] become their enemy . . . we build trust and acquire more intelligence.'"[56] Compared with the RSLMF, the RUF, and the militias, EO's record looks stellar. And, under EO's protection Sierra Leone did hold elections.

EO, however, did not undertake special training in military professionalism or human rights. Furthermore, some claim that EO's actions appear to have been integrated with commercial interest rather than values associated with human rights, democracy, and the rule of law. EO's efforts focused in the diamond areas. Though the government had obvious interest in the tax revenues from these areas, so did commercial mining companies. Some claim that EO was really Branch Energy and

---

[52] Christopher Spearin, "Executive Outcomes in Sierra Leone: a Human Security Assessment," paper prepared for the 2001 annual meeting of the American Political Science Association, San Francisco, 29 August–2 September.

[53] ICG, "Sierra Leone: Managing Uncertainty." See also, Spearin, "Executive Outcomes in Sierra Leone," p. 3.

[54] Comfort Ero, "Vigilantes, Civil Defense Forces, and Militia Groups: the Other side of the Privatization of Security in Africa," *Conflict Trends* No. 1 (2000), p. 4.

[55] Elizabeth Rubin, "An Army of One's Own," *Harper's Magazine* (February 1997).

[56] Howe quotes Eban Barlow, see Howe, "Private Security Forces," p. 316.

that it prompted commercial interests and values to trump all others.[57] Indeed, the original deal promising EO proceeds from the Sierra Ruptile mine put EO's financial interests squarely in line with Branch Energy's. Will Reno has argued that EO was operating at the intersection of foreign, global, and commercial interests. Elections, he points out, led to global good will, the stability required to generate tax revenues needed for debt payment and foreign aid. He argues that this harkens a new period of "minimal government and globalized commerce" rather than integration with international social values such as human rights, democracy, and the rule of law.[58]

Private training: Sandline

Kabbah took steps to solidify security in the wake of EO's departure. He had already begun to give new authority to the Kamajors and other civil militia groups, but he formalized these, making Chief Norman, a public advocate of the Kamajors, the Deputy Minister of Defense.[59] Chief Norman then reorganized and formalized several militias into the Civil Defense Force (CDF) of Sierra Leone.[60] Norman's public disrespect for the RSLMF heightened tensions between the government and the army. Kabbah also signed a "Status of Forces Agreement" with Nigeria in March 1997 arranging for Nigeria to provide military and security assistance for the Sierra Leone government.[61]

The steps were for naught, however, as army associates of the coup plotters from September (led by Major Johnny Paul Koroma) overthrew the Kabbah regime and Kabbah fled to Guinea in May 1997.[62] The

---

[57] David Francis, "Mercenary Intervention in Sierra Leone: Providing National Security or International Exploitation?" *Third World Quarterly* Vol. 20, No. 2 (April 1999), p. 333.

[58] Reno, "Privatizing War in Sierra Leone," p. 230.

[59] Norman had a long history in Sierra Leone – though initially as a part of the RSLMF. He was a participant in the first post-independence coup that unseated Siaka Stevens after his APC party had defeated the SLPP in the 1967 general elections. See Musah, "A Country Under Siege," p. 81.

[60] Douglass, "Fighting for Diamonds," p. 185; Musah, "A Country Under Siege," pp. 94–95; Spearin, "Private Security Companies and Humanitarians," p. 12. The CDF was to coordinate five different militia groups: the Kamajors in the south, the Gbethis in the center, the Donzos in the east, the Kapras in the west, and the Tamaboros in the North. The coordination effort was less than successful. Much of the training EO and, to a lesser degree, Sandline accomplished was with the Kamajors.

[61] The Status of Forces Agreement Between the Government of the Federal Republic of Nigeria and the Republic of Sierra Leone, Lagos, 7 March 1997, cited in Musah, "A Country Under Siege," p. 93.

[62] Douglass, "Fighting for Diamonds," pp. 188–89; Musah, "A Country Under Siege," pp. 95–96.

plotters justified their actions by referring to Kabbah's marginalization of the army.[63] The connection between Koroma and his cronies and the rebels, however, soon became clear. The RUF aligned itself with the new junta and senior members of the RUF were appointed to positions in the administration.[64]

As chaos again took hold in Sierra Leone, the Economic Community of West African States (ECOWAS) sent in Cease-fire Monitoring Group (ECOMOG) peacekeepers (primarily Nigerians) to maintain law and order and, eventually, reverse the coup.[65] Control of the country was then spilt between the new junta, which controlled the capital, the Nigerian force, which held the Lungi airport, the Kamajors and civil militia groups, which controlled most of the country's interior, and PSCs still protecting the mines. A ground operation to retake the capital by the Nigerians was unsuccessful and resulted in further destabilization – including the closing of some mines and increased clashes between civil militia groups and the junta/RUF forces in the interior. In July, Kabbah turned to another PSC (Sandline) for help.[66]

Sandline's role was to train and equip 40,000 Kamajor militia, plan a strategy for (and coordinate) the assault on Freetown, provide arms, ammunition, transportation, and food for the assault coalition, coordinate with the 20,000 ECOMOG troops in control of the Lungi airport, and provide air support and intelligence gathering.[67] The financing for Sandline's work was heavily reliant on the private sector. Jupiter Mining Company and its owner/representative Rakesh Saxena paid for a Sandline representative to travel to Sierra Leone in July and assess the Kamajors' needs and promised to underwrite the costs of personnel ($1.5 million) and equipment ($3.5 million) in return for concessions from the restored government.[68]

Planning for this contingency continued through the fall as Kabbah and his international supporters negotiated with Koroma's government.[69] During the fall, the Kamajors undertook some operations and Sandline acquired LifeGuard Security (the former EO-owned security company in charge of guarding mines in Sierra Ruptile and Kono).[70] In

[63] Ibid.
[64] Douglass, "Fighting for Diamonds," pp. 188–89.
[65] Ibid., p. 188; Hirsh, "War in Sierra Leone," p. 146.
[66] Purportedly at the suggestion of British High Commissioner Peter Penfold. Douglass, "Fighting for Diamonds," p. 189; Musah, "A Country Under Siege," p. 98.
[67] Musah, "A Country Under Siege," p. 98; Douglass, "Fighting for Diamonds," p. 190.
[68] Douglass, "Fighting for Diamonds," p. 190.
[69] It appeared as if agreement was reached in late October, but it fell apart over details in November. Ibid., p. 191.
[70] Ibid.

December 1997 and January 1998 the $1.5 million was delivered and the operation began in earnest.[71] Kabbah's forces quickly moved on initial areas in Bo and Kenema and then ECOMOG launched an offensive on Freetown.[72] As he was about to deliver the second ($3.5 million) installment, however, Rakesh Saxena was arrested in Canada on passport charges. Sandline went ahead and put up the money for the equipment, but the equipment was then impounded by ECOMOG at the Lungi airport.[73] Forces friendly to Kabbah continued to make progress, though, and by mid-February, Freetown was secured and Kabbah ordered a country-wide push for 27 February. The push was successful in securing Bo, Kenemo, and Zummi. Ultimately, the RUF fell back, but continued to occupy key mining areas in Koindu/ Kono and Kailahun.

President Kabbah returned to power in March 1998. By April, however, "a stalemate seemed to have developed, with the RUF and its allies settling in the alluvial diamond areas, their rear secured by the Liberian border and supported by Charles Taylor's government in Liberia."[74] Though Kabbah was restored to power, the civil war continued to drag on.

There are debates over how important the Sandline contract was to Kabbah's return and thus its impact on functional control. Sandline's effort to broker arms had little effect as the arms ended up impounded by the Nigerians at the airport. Moreover, the arms brokering led to scandal in the British government (something I will discuss in greater detail in chapter four). Some claim that Sandline's involvement was limited to a small number of people doing primarily advising and coordination, and credit the Nigerian force with a greater role in restoring Kabbah to power.[75] Others suggest that the capital was set free by "combined forces of Nigerian troops, the Kamajors and about 200 mercenaries of Sandline"[76] and claim that the Nigerians had failed when they tried an assault on their own and that without Sandline, Kabbah would not have returned to power.[77] Sandline's functional benefits, though, are not as clear as EO's were.

[71] Ibid.   [72] Ibid., p. 189.
[73] Just why these arms were impounded is unclear. Alex Vines suggests that Kabbah had changed his mind about purchasing the weapons. See Vines, "Mercenaries and the Privatization of Security," p. 65; Douglass suggests that they were impounded on the basis of questions about their legality, given the UN arms embargo. See Douglass, "Fighting for Diamonds," p. 192.
[74] Douglass, "Fighting for Diamonds," p. 193.
[75] Howe, *Ambiguous Order*, p. 220.
[76] Musah, "A Country Under Siege," p. 99.
[77] Douglass, "Fighting for Diamonds," p. 194.

There is less debate over the political effects of Sandline's contract. Like the EO contract, the Sandline contract was financed through international mining interests – and interests with criminal links, at that. Once financier, Saxena, was imprisoned, Sandline turned its attention to those who could pay. Reports suggest that EO, Sandline, or individuals affiliated with each remained in the country but working for those who could afford their services: allegedly, the Nigerians, INGOs (providing escort services), IOs, and foreign businesses. Individuals affiliated with these companies also reportedly had first dibs on lucrative mining and security deals.[78] Even while Sandline was working for the Kabbah government, it also had interests in these other areas. Like the EO contract, Sandline worked with the Nigerians and the CDF, further enhancing the power of the parallel forces and those outside the country over decisions about the use of force.[79] Sandline's training improved the capacities of forces beholden to local leaders.

Sandline boasts of its abidance by international laws and norms.[80] It is probably true that Sandline personnel operated according to international norms more than did other forces in Sierra Leone. The impact of Sandline on any integration with international values, however, was slight and short lived (in part due to its relatively short time in the country and small interactions with forces on the ground). Indeed, although the Kamajors were credited with good behavior among civilians in 1995 and 1996, as they have moved away from their villages and into the cities, they too have engaged in behavior that stands in sharp contrast to the dictates of international norms that govern military professionals.[81]

State contracts for security and the control of force in Sierra Leone

Sierra Leone's civil war did not end with Kabbah's return to power. In 1999 the rebels again occupied Freetown, and Nigeria, the UK and the US pressed for new negotiations, which resulted in the controversial Lome peace agreement in July 1999 and the deployment of a UN

[78] Musah, "A Country Under Siege," p. 105.
[79] ICG Report, "Sierra Leone: Time for a New Political and Military Strategy" (11 April 2001); ICG, "Sierra Leone: Managing Uncertainty," p. 20.
[80] Sandline, "Private Military Companies: Independent or Regulated," 28 March, 1998, available at http://www.sandline.com/site/index.html.
[81] Danny Hoffman, "The Brookfield Hotel Freetown, Sierra Leone," manuscript (2003). See also, Mark Malan, Sarah Meek, Thokozani Thusi, Jeremy Ginifer, and Patrick Coker, *Sierra Leone: Building the Road To Recovery*, ISS Monograph 80 (Pretoria: ISS, 2003), "Introduction," ch. 5.

peacekeeping mission (UNAMSIL).[82] The RUF did not abide by the agreement and even seized UN peacekeepers as hostages in May 2000.[83] A British intervention in June and enhancements to the UN mission stabilized the situation and made slow progress toward peace. In January 2002, President Kabbah declared the civil war over, elections were held the following May, and a process of truth and reconciliation began.[84] Worries about the army's loyalty (fueled by its overwhelming support for Johnny Paul Koroma's People's Liberation Party in the 2002 election) and its ability to secure the border with Liberia, however, remain. And though other civil defense forces have disbanded and the Kamajor's one-time leader Sam Hinga Norman faces a war crimes tribunal, the Kamajors remain an organized and potential third security force in the country.[85]

Overall the participation of PSCs under contract with the government of Sierra Leone enhanced the state's short-term functional control, though different PSCs performed differently. Strasser hired GSG to provide training for an army that was being defeated by rebel forces. The fact that GSG did not deliver the training protection Strasser wanted is linked to the competing controls that market forces respond to. GSG was worried about its reputation among its entire customer base – not just its one customer in Sierra Leone – and was concerned that providing the protection Strasser wanted would compromise its reputation as a legitimate security firm. The market for security suppliers, however, was competitive and Strasser could fire GSG and hire a firm that was more inclined to provide the services he wanted. EO delivered the services Strasser sought and enhanced the country's security in the short run, freeing the capital from rebel assault, freeing the diamond mines from rebel control, and attacking the RUF headquarters.

The contracts with PSCs also generally changed the political control of force, though again, different contracts to a greater or lesser extent. GSG had the least impact, partly because it was for a short time period and had limited functional effect. The contract with EO had a greater effect. Because EO was affiliated with diamond mining companies and saw its larger market to be one where these companies weighed heavily, some have argued that it served the government only as its interests

[82] See Hirsh, "War in Sierra Leone"; ICG Report, "Sierra Leone: Time for a New Political and Military Strategy."

[83] Hirsh, "War in Sierra Leone"; ICG Report, "Sierra Leone."

[84] See ICG Report, "Sierra Leone's Truth and Reconiliation Commission: a Fresh Start?" (20 December 2002), available at http://www.intl-crisis-group.org/projects/showreport.cfm?reportid=858.

[85] Ibid.; Malan et al., *Sierra Leone*. Stephanie Maupas, "War Crimes Trial Opens," *Le Monde*, 11–17 June 2004.

overlapped with mining interests.[86] Just hiring the PSC alone diffused the political control of force outside of the state and further enhanced the power of international commercial interests. In the execution of the contract, however, EO also relied on civil militias, which diffused control within Sierra Leone's territory (to the very social forces that had complicated the state's consolidation in the first place). Finally, EO's functional effect made it a political player in the country as well. In the lead up to the coup, EO in effect supported the plotters by refusing to tie its continued work in the country to Strasser's regime. The contract with Sandline also enhanced both international mining interests and the civil militias. Indeed, the fact that the payment for Sandline's services came directly from international mining interests undermined Kabbah's symbolic role as the ultimate boss.

Both EO and Sandline (and their advocates) have argued that these companies enhanced the integration of force with international social values. There are many who support their claims, in part, and provide evidence that the expatriate personnel each company fielded did behave appropriately in the field – much more in line with international social values governing human rights than the forces they operated with and against.[87] It is harder to make the case, though, that these values had much enduring effect on the forces in Sierra Leone. Contracts did not specify training in human rights and there were few mechanisms other than example by which international social values were communicated.

The key to the less than stellar outcome in Sierra Leone is that any improvement in functional and social control was undermined rather than solidified by the changes in political control. Particularly, the diffusion of political control both to commercial elements outside the country and to social forces outside state control within the country made it unlikely that the short-run functional gains would last. The diffusion of political control often caused functional problems by introducing multiple principals. Even within strong states, when different institutions have competing controls over military forces, disagreement between the institutions leads to lapses in functional control.[88] When multiple principles are not just institutions of the state, but foreign governments, commercial firms, and the like, the prospect for disagreement and functional loss increases. One effect of multiple principals in Sierra Leone was to create a parallel force without clear ties to the state. The subsequent tensions between the army and the civil

[86] Reno, "Privatizing War in Sierra Leone."
[87] See for instance, Daniel Bergner, *In the Land of Magic Soldiers* (New York: Farrar, Straus, and Giroux, 2003).
[88] Avant, *Political Institutions*; Feaver, *Armed Servants*.

militias that led territory to fall back into rebel hands can be traced to this effect. Also the fact PSCs play to their ultimate customer base, not just this one customer, led to problems in the execution of both the GSG and EO contracts (leading to GSG reluctance to embrace a new role and EO's refusal to stick by Strasser once a coup was threatened). Though it is not clear that Sierra Leone would be any closer to a capable force had it not contracted with PSCs, neither did hiring PSCs enhance the long-run functionality of the country's forces.

The redistribution of political control also hampered any long-run improvement in the social control of force. Lack of agreement about the long-term goals of the country – an enduring problem in weak states – and the lack of legitimacy accorded to the leadership put stress on the development of effective social controls on forces even before the government hired PSCs. The fact that the PSCs contracted by the government had large international commercial clients, though, made this more difficult. The legitimacy of PSCs and trust that they would train an army to meet Sierra Leone's national goals was questionable given this customer base.[89] The fact that both EO and Sandline's contracts were secured by private entities with the promise of mining proceeds deepened the questions about their ultimate purpose. Finally, the fact that the contracts were short-run and did not reference professional military values also suggests they would have a limited effect on the socialization of forces.[90]

To the degree that Sierra Leone is on the way to rehabilitation – still under dispute – few credit PSCs. Most credit for any improvements in the capacity of the RSLMF or its attention to international values is given to the British International Military Assistance Training Team (IMATT) rather than to PSCs.[91]

Croatia's contracts for military services

Croatia was a new state in the 1990s, born of Yugoslavia's disintegration. The breakdown of order in Yugoslavia began even before the Cold War's end with Tito's death in 1980, but the end of the Cold War and the fall of communist regimes across Eastern Europe exacerbated

---

[89] Interview with Raymond Gilpin, African Center for Strategic Studies, November 2003.
[90] A plethora of PSCs still operate in Sierra Leone, protecting private property and providing a range of services for expatriates working in a variety of capacities.
[91] ICG Report, "Sierra Leone After Elections: Politics as Usual?" (12 July 2002). Though Sierra Leone has undergone a reasonably successful demobilization, there are worries that neighboring conflicts in Côte d'Ivoire and Liberia will fuel the already anarchic situation surrounding many diamond mining areas. See Malan et al., *Sierra Leone*, ch. 5.

the instability. Yugoslavia physically fell apart in the 1990s with dramatic consequences for the people living in its territories.[92] The Yugoslav elections of 1990 brought the Croatian Democratic Community (HDZ) under Franjo Tudjman to power. Also in 1990 the constitutional changes made Croatia a *de jure* nation-state, with frightening implications for the Serbs living in Croatian territory. Fears were aggravated when Croatia took steps to develop military capacity, including setting up a National Guard, an action deemed unconstitutional by the federal government in Yugoslavia.[93] In April 1991, Croatia simultaneously formed the Assembly of the National Guard (ZNG) within the framework of the police forces and halted enlisting Croats in the Yugoslav Army (YPA). Thus the stage was set for a uniformed and armed military structure when a referendum in May 1991 resoundingly expressed a desire among Croatians for independence. The Republic of Croatia declared its independence from Yugoslavia in June 1991.

This declaration led to war.[94] Croatian political (party) militias and local militias, nominally coordinated by the ZNG structure, fought against (YPA) troops and Serb paramilitary forces, hastily organized among Serbs in the Srpska Krajina and Eastern Slavonia regions. Initially, the Croatians were handily defeated. The fragmented Croatian political structure had little concerted control over its loosely organized military units.[95] YPA troops and sympathetic Serbs inflicted destruction

[92] See Leonard Cohen, *Broken Bonds: the Disintegration of Yugoslavia* (Boulder: Westview, 1993); James Gow, *Legitimacy and the Military: the Yugoslav Crisis* (New York: St. Martin's Press, 1992); Susan Woodward, *Balkan Tragedy: Chaos and Dissolution after the Cold War* (Washington, DC: Brookings, 1995).

[93] See Ozren Zunec, "Civil–Military Relations in Croatia," in Constantine P. Danopoulos and Danile Zirker, *Civil–Military Relations in the Soviet and Yugoslav Successor States* (Boulder: Westview, 1996), p. 217. See also Sinisa Tatalovic, "Military and Political Aspects of the Croato-Serbian Conflict," *Politicka Misao* Vol. 33, No. 5 (1996) cited in Biljana Vankovska, "Privatization of Security and Security Sector Reform in Croatia," draft manuscript 2002, p. 5.

[94] For the international politics of Yugoslavia's disintegration and how it affected the extremism of each of the republics, see Woodward, *Balkan Tragedy*. She argues that with the Brioni Agreement of 7 July, the EC ignored the cause of the problems in Yugoslavia (economic decline, market reforms, and quarrels over how to reform politics to meet economic demands) and accepted the representation offered by the radical nationalisms in Slovenia, Croatia, and Serbia. It opened the door to war in Croatia and Bosnia-Herzegovina and deprived moderates, southerners, the federal government, and the majority of the population of a say in the problem. See p. 169.

[95] The Supreme State Council organized volunteer formations for national defense and created a Crisis Headquarters on 30 June. The president drew up the documents specifying the defense system in mid-August and the General Staff of the Croatian Armed Forces was formally instituted in September. Vankovska, "Privatization of Security," p. 6.

on the poorly organized Croatian forces in Vukovar and Dubrovnik, among others.[96] Though they performed poorly on the battlefield, Croatian forces were nonetheless able to exact revenge on the Serb population. Perhaps most infamous were Tomislav Mercek's paramilitaries in the Vukovar region – known as "Autumn Rains" – who allegedly committed crimes including mass executions of Serb civilian populations in 1991.[97] Though the Croatian government had begun to establish some control over its forces by the end of 1991 (unifying paramilitary groups and setting up a rudimentary system of state control), some argue that Tudjman was not so eager for an effective military force in the initial period of the conflict because he wanted Croatia to be seen as a victim of Serb abuses so that members of the international community would recognize the legitimacy of its claims to independence.[98]

By 1992, though, states in the international community had begun to recognize Croatian independence and it behooved Tudjman to enhance the effectiveness of his armed forces. He began this process with the creation of the Croatian Armed Forces (Hrvatska Vojska, HV).[99] The force was designed to reflect and reinforce the Croatia that Tudjman and his party envisioned. Thus party leaders from the dominant HDZ occupied prominent military positions to insure that the force would be under their control.[100] Given the party's ultra-nationalist perspective, its

[96] Ibid.
[97] Included among those fighting were sympathetic foreigners – whether there for profit or ideology – whom, some have argued, had an easier time committing atrocities given their lack of connection to the local population. Ibid.

The breakdown of order in the Croatian territory as it seceded also opened opportunities for purely profit-motivated violence. Operation Group "Rashic" would fire on the Serbs from a Croatian village, provoking a harsh Serb reaction that would cause the villagers to flee in panic. Profiteers would then loot and plunder the empty village. They operated in the Kupa River region. Ibid., p. 15. Mary Kaldor's analysis of Bosnia points to similar profiteering. See Kaldor, *New and Old Wars*, pp. 53–55. See also Peter Andreas, "The Clandestine Political Economy of War and Peace in Bosnia," *International Studies Quarterly* Vol. 48, No. 1 (March 2004): 29–52.
[98] According to Woodward, gaining international recognition was the key to Tudjman's strategy and it caused him to orchestrate the war in order to cast Croatia as the victim of Serb aggression. He even went so far as to halt the military preparations of General Martin Spegelj causing the youth drafted into the Croatian National Guard to be untrained and poorly armed, which led to higher casualties. It also led many to defect to the right-wing paramilitary forces, which purported to be doing the real fighting in Croatia. See Woodward, *Balkan Tragedy*, p. 171 and footnote 69, p. 463. See also Vankovska, "Privatization of Security," p. 6.
[99] Woodward, *Balkan Tragedy*, pp. 146–47; Vankovska, "Privatization of Security," p. 6.
[100] Zunec, "Civil–Military Relations in Croatia," p. 225. The 1991 defense act prohibited military officers from being members of political parties, but the provisions of the 1992 Service Code overrode this prohibition. See Vankovska, "Privatization of Security," p. 8.

infusion into the armed forces opened the way for extremist elements in the force.[101] Many argue that this encouraged the Army's participation in offensives to fan ethnic allegiance in advance of elections (the HDZ consolidated power in the Croatian Parliament in elections in 1992 and 1993).[102] The HV's participation in the war in Bosnia, which broke out in 1992, and its behavior there (inflicting the same kinds of violent abuses on the Muslim population there as the Serbs had inflicted on Croatians) lends support to those who argue that extremist elements and their hold on key positions in the military led to more ethnic violence.[103] Like in Croatia, the war in Bosnia had many private (paramilitary and profiteering) elements.[104]

In 1994, despite some efforts at consolidation, the HV still looked rather weak. It had poor leadership and an unprofessional organizational structure (where some forces reported directly to the President and the Minister of Defense). Morale was low, as were skill levels and professionalism was taught through a motley assortment of military education in the former Yugoslavia, the west, and the French Foreign Legion. Some officers were reportedly foreign soldiers of fortune.[105] Furthermore, troops were poorly disciplined and poorly supplied. A 1991 UN arms embargo made this hard to remedy as it prohibited the sale of weapons as well as military training to any of the warring parties. According to one analyst, "the HV would not be able to wage the offensive operations necessary to liberate its territory and crush the Serbian (Croatian Serbs) insurgency."[106] It was at this point that Croatia turned to MPRI for help.

MPRI and private training for the Croatian force

As the official story goes, in March the Minister of Defense, Gojko Susak, requested permission from the US government to negotiate with MPRI over the provision of civil–military relations and program and

---

[101] Jill Irvine, "Ultranationalist Ideology and State-Building in Croatia, 1990–1996," *Problems of Post-Communism* Vol. 44, No. 4 (July/August 1997).
[102] Zunec, "Civil–Military Relations in Croatia," p. 217, Vankovska, "Privatization of Security," pp. 8–9.
[103] The republican assembly of Bosnia-Herzegovina adopted a memorandum declaring the republic a sovereign and independent state within its existing borders on 15 October 1991. See Woodward, *Balkan Tragedy*, p. 181.
[104] Zunec, "Civil–Military Relations in Croatia"; Vankovska, "Privatization of Security"; Andreas, "Clandestine Political Economy of War."
[105] Zunec, "Civil–Military Relations in Croatia," p. 221.
[106] Ibid., p. 222.

budget services to the HV.[107] These services were ostensibly for the purpose of moving the Croatian forces closer to participation in NATO's Partnership for Peace Program (PfP).[108] In September MPRI President, Carl Vuono and Croatian Defense Minister Susak signed two contracts. The first, for long-range management, was begun in January 1995, headed by retired Major General John Sewell, and designed to help Croatia restructure its defense department for long-term strategic capabilities.[109] The second, for assistance in the democratic transition, provided for "military education and training of staff officers and uncommissioned [sic] officers of the Croatian army."[110] The Democracy Transition Assistance Program (DTAP) was meant to democratize the military and reorganize its troop structure so as to ensure Croatia would meet the standards for entry to the PfP program. MPRI sent a fifteen-man team headed by retired major general Richard Griffiths to run this program.

MPRI's official training in the DTAP consisted of fourteen weeks with sessions eight hours a day, five days a week. Eleven courses were offered in physical training, education management, instructor training, topography, logistics, military service (international military law), leadership, military management (including analyses of historical battles and lessons), and first aid. The materials used were translated textbooks identical to those used at US professional military education institutions such as West Point.[111] They graduated their first officers in April 1995.[112]

---

[107] This is disputed. According to Roger Cohen, Croatia asked the US for help and the US referred the Croats to MPRI. See Roger Cohen, "US Cooling Ties with Croatia after Winking at its Buildup," *New York Times* (28 October 1995), p. A1. See also Matt Gaul, "Regulating the New Privateers: Private Military Service Contracting and the Modern Marque and Reprisal Clause," *Loyola Law Review* (June 1998): p. 1.

[108] PfP was designed as a stepping stone to NATO. See NATO, "Partnership for Peace: Framework Document" (January 1994); available at http://www.nato.int/docu/comm/49-95/c940110b.htm.

[109] Shearer, *Private Armies*, p. 58, Singer, *Corporate Warriors*, p. 125.

[110] Igor Alborghetti, "MPRI, Croatia – an Example for B&H?" *Globas* No. 254 (October 1995) translated by Srecko Bartl and posted on BosNet 18 November 1995, downloaded 12 March 2002 from http://www.bosnet.org/archive/bosnet.w3archive/9511/msg00448.html. Carl Vuono, a US retired four-star general, served as Chief of Staff of the Army from 1987 to 1991.

[111] Yves Goulet, "MPRI: Washington's Freelance Advisors," *Jane's Intelligence Review* Vol. 10, No. 7 (July 1998).

[112] Ibid. Ed Soyster claims a six-person assessment team was sent in November 1994. Also in November Joe Kruzal made a trip to Croatia offering some, limited mil-mil contacts and a token IMET ($65,000) program. When Croatia (in January 1995) announced that it wanted the UN out by March 1995, the US withdrew the mil-mil contact and the IMET but, "someone in State with some vision decided that we needed to maintain contact with them and saw the long range benefits to DTAP." Email correspondence from Pentagon official, 23 March 2000.

The exact nature of MPRI's work for the Croatian government is disputed. Many have taken issue with the official story.[113] When MPRI began work for Tudjman, the Serbs occupied 30 percent of Croatian territory. Shortly thereafter, the HV undertook military operations "Lightning" (in the spring of 1995) and "Storm" (in the later summer of 1995).[114] The spring offensive retook the areas to the southwest of Zagreb and then recaptured parts of Western Slavonia. Operation Storm in the fall, though, drew particular attention. In a series of lightning quick movements that observers reported to be strikingly similar to NATO style, the HV retook the Krajina region (20 percent of Croatian land) without apparent difficulty.[115] This was a significant success for the Croatian forces that had been trounced by the Serbs just years earlier. By November 1995, Tudjman had retaken all but 4 percent of Croatian land and come to occupy 20 percent of Bosnia.[116] The HV's dramatic turnaround drew speculation that MPRI was, in fact, doing far more than training the Croatians in civil–military relations.[117]

During MPRI's initial training mission, Croatia spent an estimated $1 billion to arm itself with Eastern European weapons, and analysts have hypothesized about the advice MPRI might have given the Croatians on procurement and weapons acquisitions.[118] Speculation that MPRI played a role in upgrading the performance of the Croatian army was further bolstered by first-hand accounts that suggest MPRI's involvement in planning for the offensive. A Croatian liaison officer told the local press that "just weeks before the offensive General Vuono held a secret top level meeting at Briono Island, off the coast of Croatia, with General Varimar Cervenko, the architect of the Krajina campaign" and

[113] Some question the timing – suggesting that MPRI employees were in Croatia in 1994 or even 1993. Interview with former State Department official, January 1999.
[114] Rudovan Vukadinovic and Lidija Cehulic, "Development of Civil–Military Relations in Croatia," in *Civil–Military Relations in South Eastern Europe* edited by Plaman Panter (Zurich: Partnership for Peace, ISN, 2001) available at www.isn.ethz.ch/onlinepubli/ publihouse/ p. 66. See also Alan Cowell, "Conflict in the Balkans," *New York Times*, 1 August 1995, p. A6.
[115] Samantha Power, Robin Knight, Douglas Pasternak, and Alan Cooperman, "The Croatian Army's Friends", *US News and World Report*, 21 August 1995; Charlotte Eagar, "Invisible US Army Defeats Serbs," *The Observer*, 5 November 1995; Juan Carlos Zarate, "The Emergence of a New Dog of War: Private International Security Companies, International Law, and the New World Disorder," *Stanford Journal of International Law* Vol. 34 (1998), p. 107.
[116] Zarate, "Emergence of a New Dog of War," p. 108.
[117] Robert Fox, "Fresh War Clouds Threaten Ceasefire: Secret US Military Advice Helps 'Cocky' Croats Push toward Eastern Slavonia," *Sunday Telegraph*, 15 October 1995; Power et al., "The Croatian Army's Friends," p. 41; Eagar, "Invisible US Army Defeats Serbs"; Economist, "Croatia: Tudjman's New Model Army," *Economist*, 11 November 1995, p. 148; Cohen, "US Cooling Ties to Croatia," p. 1.
[118] Cohen, "US Cooling Ties to Croatia."

that Vuono went on to meet ten times with Croation officers in charge of the operation in the five days prior to its launch.[119]

On the basis of this evidence, some have surmised that MPRI's contract was the result of a deal between the US and Croatian government where the Croats agreed to a Croat–Muslim federation in Bosnia in exchange for US military assistance – aimed not just at democratizing the military, but also improving it so as to take back Croatian territory.[120] Given the awkward nature of sending US military assistance to Croatia during a UN arms embargo, a private contract between the Croatian government and MPRI allowed US expertise to flow to Croatia without direct US government involvement.[121] This view sees MPRI's role in Croatia as key to the HV's success in Operation Storm. At the least, proponents of this view argue, MPRI gave the Croatians doctrinal advice and maybe did some scenario planning. Some also claim that MPRI allowed the US government to share satellite information with the Croatians.[122] And a few have reported that MPRI helped the Croatians with logistical support or even accompanied them in the field.[123]

MPRI, however, has categorically denied that it rendered any military advice to Croatia and maintains that its classes focused on the more mundane issues licensed by the State Department. According to General Soyster in 1995, the instruction MPRI offered "has no correlation to anything happening on the battlefield today."[124] Officials at various levels in the Pentagon support MPRI's rendition of events and argue that MPRI had nothing to do with the HV's actions in Operation Storm.[125] According to the Croatian government, its military success was the result of its consolidation of power in the period before the offensive, and the simultaneous demoralization of the Serbs as international pressure mounted. Others have speculated that Milošević and Tudjman may have

---

[119] Silverstein, *Private Warriors*, p. 172.
[120] For various accounts, see Graham, "US Firm Exports Military Expertise"; Eagar, "Invisible US Army Defeats Serbs"; Economist, "Croatia: Tudjman's New Model Army." Several US defense officials claimed it was highly unlikely that Tudjman would have come up with the idea to contact MPRI himself. Interviews with defense officials June 1999, November 1999, January 2000.
[121] Vankovska, "Privatization of Security," p. 18.
[122] Roy Gutman, "What did the CIA Know?" *Newsweek*, 27 August 2001. Gutman's sources include Tudjman's son, Miro Tudjman then Chief of Secret Services.
[123] These were primarily reports from British, French, and Canadian observers in the field. See William Norman Grigg, "Selective 'Justice' Turns a Blind Eye to Croatian Atrocities," *New American* Vol. 13, No. 21 (October 1997); Scott Taylor, *Inat: Images of Serbia and the Kosovo Conflict* (Ottawa: Esprit de Corps Books, 2000).
[124] Cohen, "US Cooling Ties to Croatia," p. 1.
[125] Interviews with Pentagon officials, April 2002.

agreed to the military outcome of Operation Storm ahead of time: "The very facts that the Operation took only four days, it was almost bloodless and the Croatian forces advanced 145 square kilometers on a heavy mountainous terrain offers ground for a suspicion that it was faked military action [sic]."[126] Indeed, Tudjman told Paddy Ashdown, leader of Britain's Liberal Democrats, that he would retake the Krajina in a campaign that would last less than eight days and cost less than 1,000 battle deaths at a dinner in May 1995. Ashdown, a former Royal Marine officer, expressed doubts about that outcome given the difficult terrain and Serb capacities. Later in testimony at The Hague, Ashdown claimed to be convinced that Operation Storm's success was made possible by a prior agreement with Milošević.[127]

In fact, these two views may not be as far apart as they seem. MPRI must have helped the Croatians in some ways over the course of the conflict.[128] Why else would Tudjman, with no control over about one-third of his territory in 1994, opposition to his rule mounting in Croatia, and engaged as an aggressor in Bosnia, worry about (and spent significant funds for) garnering training for civil–military relations and democratic reforms in his army?[129] Part of what helped the Croatians, though, may have been the contract's political effects that fed into the Croatian Army's battlefield performance. Even before it had been implemented, the contract signaled US support for the Croatian government. Indeed, the MPRI contract itself was part of the "international pressure" that the Croatian government's official story points to. Whatever the impetus to the contract, bringing MPRI to Croatia was a significant achievement for Susak and enhanced both his and President Tudjman's political power *and* the power of Croatia relative to Serbian claims. This was true even before MPRI took any action training forces.[130] Tudjman cited the contract as an example of

---

[126] Vankovska, "Privatization of Security," p. 20. This claim is made in interviews and memoirs of General Martin Spegelj, the first Defense Minister of independent Croatia. Vankovska cites an interview with General Martin Spegelj, "HVO I dejelovi Hrvatske vojske su izvrsili agresiju na BiH," in Martin Spegelj, *Sijecanja vojnika (Memories of a Soldier)* (Zagreb: Znanje, 2001).

[127] See Tribunal Update 68 16–21 March 1998, "Blaskic Trial: Paddy Ashdown's Testimony," http://www.bosnet.org/archive/ bosnet.w3archive/9803/msg00152.html.

[128] See, for instance, Zarate, "Emergence of a New Dog of War"; Bradley Graham, "US Firm Exports Military Expertise: Role in Training Croatian Army Brings Publicity and Suspicions," *Washington Post*, 11 August 1995, p. A1; Eagar, "Invisible US Army Defeats Serbs"; Economist, "Croatia: Tudjman's New Model Army."

[129] Vankovska, "Privatization of Security," p. 17.

[130] See Dubravko Horvatic and Stjepan Seselj, "Croatian Culture and the Croatian Army," *Hrvatsko Slovo* (27 December 1996) cited in Vankovska, "Privatization of Security," p. 17.

the "alliance" between the US and Croatia and sold it to the Croatian public as evidence of US and international support for the Croatian cause. The military leadership in the HV also viewed the contract with MPRI as evidence that the US was on their side. Regardless of any change in the capacity of the HV, then, the contract with MPRI had real domestic political benefits for Susak and Tudjman and international benefits for the Croatian government. Indeed, this impact was probably as important as any skills the Croatian forces gained.

In the wake of Operation Storm, which retook the Krajina region of Croatia from the Serbs, the HV engaged in an ethnic cleansing campaign that was, until the war in Kosovo, "easily the largest single instance of 'ethnic cleansing' of the Yugoslav war."[131] Though MPRI expressed regret at these incidents, they did not suspend their training efforts. Instead one official claimed that the behavior of the Croatian troops demonstrated their need for democratic assistance.[132] Further-more, much of MPRI's work to transform the Croatian Army into a western style army involved the rooting out of communist "dead-wood." This played into the HDZ's platform to create an ethnically pure army because many of the officers with experience were also officers who had served in the YPA. Intentional or not, MPRI's efforts had some questionable effects on social control in the short run.

MPRI's contract with the government also circumvented parliamentary oversight. As of 1996, Croatian law required that the signing and implementation of international agreements be discussed and approved by both the government and the parliament, but this procedure was not followed for the MPRI contracts.[133] Even the budgetary category for MPRI's contract (intellectual services) evaded discussion of the contracts as military or defense related expenditures.[134] Many members of Parliament, including the head of the Parliamentary Committee on International Affairs and National Security, did not know of the MPRI contract in 2001 until asked about it by an academic researcher.[135]

Gradually MPRI's work in Croatia expanded to include an Army Readiness Training Program (CARTS) and then, after Croatia's admission to the PfP program in 2001, assistance and support in implementing that program's requirements.[136] In 2003, MPRI's

---

[131] Mark Danner, "Operation Storm," *New York Review of Books* Vol. 45, No. 16 (22 October 1998).
[132] Background interview with MPRI employee, January 1999.
[133] Vankovska, "Privatization of Security," p. 25.
[134] Other problematic expenditures for weapons and the Bosnian war were handled in the same way.
[135] Vankovska, "Privatization of Security," p. 24.
[136] http://www.mpri.com/subchannels/int_europe.html.

Table 3.1. *US military aid appropriations for Croatia, 1995–2003ᵃ*

Fiscal Year	IMET ($)	FMF ($)	Total ($)
1995	105,000		105,000
1996	218,000		218,000
1997	427,000		427,000
1998	455,000		455,000
1999	435,000		435,000
2000	514,000	4,000,000	4,514,000
2001	1,032,000		1,032,000
2002		5,000,000	5,000,000
2003		6,000,000	6,000,000

Note: ᵃFederation of American Scientists database on US military aid appropriations. http://www.fas.org/asmp/profiles/aid_db.php?regionin=euro&ctryin=hrv&fy1in=1990&-fy2in=2003&appin=1

webpage boasted the continuation of all four of these programs. The Croatian government, though, gradually paid less of the bill. The US Defense Department's contributions to these efforts grew from $105,000 in 1995 to $6,000,000 in 2003 (see table 3.1).[137]

Meanwhile, Croatia consolidated control over its territory – though stability in the country was mixed while President Tudjman was alive. In 1997 the IMF granted the country $486 million credit over the next three years and the Fund's statement praised Croatia for its efforts in reform despite regional military conflict (citing its 5.5 percent real growth estimates with inflation of 3.5 percent and a government deficit limited to 3 percent of GDP).[138] Observers reported the decision as a boost for the Croatian Democratic Party in its efforts to win re-election on 13 April, and indeed, Tudjman and the Croatian Democratic Union were re-elected in 1997.[139] On 27 May 1998, US Ambassador to Croatia, William Montgomery, praised Croatia for its efforts to improve its military with the assistance of MPRI and millions of US dollars.[140]

[137] Croatia also receives support for military training through the State Department.
[138] "Croatian Government Welcomes IMF Credit," *Agence France Presse*, 14 March 1997.
[139] Chris Hedges, "Nationalists in Croatia Turn Away from West," *New York Times*, 27 April 1997, p. A9.
[140] Montgomery speech available at http://www.usembassy. hr/speeches/980527.htm (accessed 4/1/2002).

However, by 1999 Croatia looked less successful with tales of unsettling developments. Economic growth slowed to less than 3 percent with the official unemployment rate at 17.6 percent. Reports claimed that Tudjmen's cronyism had lined the pockets of HDZ elite. He kept inflation at a moderate 5.4 percent but resisted sweeping economic reforms because they threatened the preservation of his political support.[141]

Tudjman's death in December 1999 proved to be a watershed event for enhancing Croatia's stability. A democratic election was held in January 2000 and a peaceful transfer of power to a coalition of opposition parties yielded a new president, Stipe Mesic, who was inaugurated on 19 February 2000. At that time Washington promised to increase foreign aid to Croatia (from $12 million to $20 million) and push for Croatia to become part of NATO's PfP.[142] Under Mesic, the Croatian government made some significant and tough decisions with regard to its military that reflect attention to the principles of democratic civilian control and human rights. In September 2000 Mesic fired seven generals who criticized the government's crackdown on war criminals.[143] In July 2001, the Croatian parliament decided to cooperate with the Hague Tribunal to extradite two Croatian generals – Ante Gotovina and Rahim Ademi – who were indicted for war crimes.[144] Though Mesic's reform capacities were hindered by an awkward constitutional structure that has opponents in charge of key posts in the government, the US government has noted improvements in democratic practices and military reform.[145]

---

[141] Jeffrey Thomas Kuhner, "Croatia at Crossroads: Tudjman has Choice of Embracing Pro-Democracy Movement or Trying to Crush it," *Gazette* (Montreal) Op-ed, 19 August 1999, p. B3.

[142] Bob Drogin, "A Success Story in the Balkans: Croatians Celebrate Mesic's Inauguration," *Gazette* (Montreal), 19 February 2000, p. A20.

[143] The generals protested and claimed Croatia was becoming unstable – as did the Defense Minister who claimed the president's action was "drastic . . . and taken without consultations" with the Ministry. Associated Press, "Generals Criticize War Crimes Crackdown," *St. John's Telegraph*, 30 September 2000, p. 16.

[144] This move was politically difficult for a number of reasons. Many Croatian operations have allegedly included military misbehavior vis-à-vis civilians and some, like Operation Storm, seem to indicate hundreds of civilian murders and a mass exile (150,000–200,000) of Serb civilians. The extent and character of the crimes seem to suggest greater political involvement and thus may come back to haunt alive and serving government officials. Stojan Obradovic, "Indictment not only against Generals," *Network of Independent Journalists Weekly Service* Issue 231, 20 July 2001. See for NIJ (founded by the Institute for Democracy in Eastern Europe in 1993) http://www.idee.org/nij.html.

[145] Drazen Budisa, the party that posed Mesic's key opposition for the presidency, was given the post of Defense Minister. Vankovska, "Privatization of Security," p. 31.

Croatia joined the PfP program in 2001 signaling its commitment to the Charter of the United Nations and the principles of the universal Declaration on Human Rights and its commitment to facilitating transparency in national defense planning, ensuring democratic control of the armed forces, maintaining capability and readiness, developing cooperative military relations with NATO countries, and developing forces better able to operate with NATO forces.[146] Croatia now participates in the highest level of military–military exchanges with the US outside the NATO structure.[147] MPRI is happy to take credit for helping Croatia design and implement the military reforms and members of the US government back their claims.

State contracts for security and the control of force in Croatia

Even without arguing that MPRI had a significant effect on the operational capacity of Croatian troops during Operation Storm most agree that the government's contract with MPRI did have a positive effect on the functional capacity of the Croatian Forces. Though there are some critics of MPRI's approach to training the Croatian Army on purely functional grounds,[148] on balance most agree that the Croatian military is significantly improved from its initial form and that Croatia's security has been enhanced by its contract with MPRI.[149] According to one source, "the Croatians are the premier fighting force in Southern Europe," due to their training from MPRI; according to another, with MPRI's help "the Croatians can do anything."[150] Tonino Picula,

---

[146] "NATO Partnership for Peace: Framework Document."

[147] Interview with John Erath, Pentagon Croatian Desk Officer, 16 April 2002.

[148] Croatian military experts argue that MPRI brought proposals pertinent to the US experience but less applicable to the local context. They particularly point to MPRI's push to upgrade the non-commissioned officers corps (NCO) as something that fitted uncomfortably with Croatian military culture and history. They also point out that strategic documents drafted by MPRI have yet to be accepted and have required much input from local experts to fix the "US-centric bias." Furthermore, this argument questions whether spending on training from MPRI was the best use of scarce Croatian resources. They claim that MPRI had no competition and that the government might have found more cost-effective advice had they looked for a competitor. Also, they suggest that the private alternative allowed the US to influence events in Croatia on Croatia's dime. Without MPRI, the US may have relied on traditional military to military exchanges at no cost or less cost to the Croatian government (and more to the US). Vankovska, "Privatization of Security," pp. 26, 29. The US did begin funding a larger portion of the military training in Croatia coincident with the democratic elections.

[149] Interview with former NATO Special Assistant, June 1999; interview with State Department staff, June 2000, interview with Pentagon staff, April 2002.

[150] Interviews with officials at the State Department, Defense Department, and Joint Staff, June 1999, April 2002.

Croatian Foreign Minister, claims that MPRI's aid was significant in helping Croatia achieve its rightful independence.[151] Even critics of MPRI's training concede that it had effects on the defense establishment.[152] Due to both the contract's impact on morale (evidence that the US was on its side) and its long term reformulations of the defense department and the structure of the forces, the contract is widely hailed as enhancing the abilities of the Croatian armed forces.[153] Almost uniformly, American defense officials claim – the "results speak for themselves."[154]

The impact of MPRI's contract also changed the balance of political power over force in Croatia. It accorded more power to one portion of the government – Tudjman and the HDZ, less power to the parliament, and skirted constitutional procedures. MPRI's training aided the HDZ simply as a result of the contract itself, which brought significant political benefits to the party. It also aided the HDZ's platform by facilitating the removal of communist officers, which played into Tudjman's plans for an ethnically based army in Croatia. MPRI reported to only a small portion of the executive branch of government. Furthermore, the contract enhanced the leverage of the US government. By freezing the contract, the US could damage Tudjman's credibility and MPRI, with a strong commercial interest in keeping the US happy, emphasized its attention to the US government's goals in its contract with Croatia.

The relationship between the government's contract with MPRI and the Croatian army's integration with international values in the country is somewhat more complicated to evaluate. The ethnic cleansing campaign undertaken after Operation Storm did not reflect attention to international values and some have claimed that units of the HV trained by MPRI took part in ethnic cleansing campaigns.[155] That very serious episode aside, however, US reports to Congress point to a gradual increase in the integration of the Croatian military with

---

[151] "A Nation Resolved to Overcome its Tough Heritage," *International Special Reports – Croatia* 10 March 2002 available at http://www.internationalspecialreports.com/europe/01/croatia/ anationresolved.html.

[152] Vankovska, "Privatization of Security," pp. 20–21.

[153] Indeed, the State Department credits MPRI with significant effect on the Croatian military. Interview with State Department Official, April 2002.

[154] Interviews with Pentagon and State Department officials, April 2002.

[155] One site of atrocities in southwestern Bosnia, Mrkonjic Grad, where the bodies of 185 Serb civilians were found, was alleged to have been committed by a Croatian Army Unit that had been trained by MPRI. Grigg, "Selective 'Justice' Turns Blind Eye to Croatian Atrocities," http://thenewamerican.com/tna/1997/vol3no21/vol3no21_croatian.htm, downloaded 12 March 2002.

international values.[156] Also writing for the PfP consortium, Rudocar Vukadinovic and Lidiji Cehulic suggest that there were advocates of democratic standards, respect for human rights, and extended democratic control over the armed forces in the late 1990s.[157] The justification for the US to license MPRI's contract with Croatia in 1994 when the country was under an arms embargo was based on the benefits that professional contacts would have on democratization. The contract specified courses and training that focused specifically on appropriate professional behavior and international law as it applied to military personnel. These training units, common in US professional military education, teach about the system of democratic civil–military relations (at least as it exists in the US) and use case studies and other methods to teach appropriate military responses to difficult situations. Croatia's acceptance to the PfP program demonstrates at least US acceptance of the progress its military has made on this front and even though they offer a report of only modest change, Vukadinovic and Cehulic do suggest some improvement in the social control of Croatian forces.[158]

Critics claim, however, that the participation of MPRI enhanced the capacities of radical ethnic elements in Croatia and thus facilitated a particular kind of state – one that the international community is now trying to reform.[159] These critics claim that if MPRI's task was to democratize the military, it should have been attuned to Tudjman's strategy and tried to improve the culture of national security, spreading the word on the objectives of security sector reform. These same critics point out that having commercially motivated retired officers preaching democratic principles is an awkward juxtaposition – as was the fact that MPRI was teaching classes on the importance of transparency and accountability while their contract with the government evaded both.[160] Only a lucky accident – Tudjman's death and the transfer of power to the opposition – moved Croatia closer to western values.

---

[156] The Foreign Military Training Report FY 1999 and 2000 claims, "Along those lines, IMET Funds have fostered appreciation among Croatian military officers for the proper role of the armed forces in a democracy." See US Department of State, *Foreign Military Training and DOD Engagement Activities of Interest, Vol. I* Joint Report to Congress 1 March 2000, ch. III, European Region, p. 5.

[157] Vukadinovic and Cehulic, "Development of Civil–Military Relations in Croatia," p. 70.

[158] Ibid.

[159] Despite the democratic gain that Croatia has made, a 2002 ICG Report still faults the country on repression of the Serb minority and failure to end discriminatory practices. See ICG Report, "A Half Hearted Welcome: Refugee Returns to Croatia," 13 December 2002, available at http:// www.intl-crisis-group.org/projects/balkans/balkansregion/ reports/ A400848_13122002.pdf.

[160] Vankovska, "Privatization of Security," p. 20.

Though the critics' points are well taken, there are indications that – particularly after Tudjman's death – many of the control mechanisms posited by economists and sociologists appear to be working in concert in Croatia – with some of the positive impacts on control I have hypothesized. Even before his death, MPRI's contracts did help the Tudjman government consolidate power. Before that point, there was little control – on anyone's part – over the use of violence in the country. The contracts also did focus specifically on democratic control of the military and introduced military professional standards.[161] Individuals employed by MPRI referenced these values as did the formal contract itself.[162] Despite reports that MPRI personnel sometimes behaved improperly while in Croatia, and thus may not have been the best examples of military professionals, courses MPRI taught were steeped in international values – attention to human rights, democratic control of the military, and the laws of war. Identical to courses taught in US military academies, they did not simply preach the acceptance of civilian control of the military and appreciation of human rights, but claimed and demonstrated how these principles were related to military effectiveness. Over a period of ten years, a significant number of Croatian military personnel were educated in these principles. Partly because of the cache of American training, partly because of the lure of the PfP program, education by MPRI also enhanced the individual careers of those in the Croatian military who participated.[163] The reorganization of the Croatian Defense Department further enhanced these policies. Finally, the political shift also elevated the role of the US in decisions about the use of force – and the principles enunciated in the PfP program.[164] Promises (and then delivery) of US financing for continued military reform have further reinforced the standards for

---

[161] E-mail correspondence with Srecko Domljanovich, Croatian student at Industrial College of the Armed Forces (ICAF), National Defense University (NDU), June 1999.

[162] Interviews, June 1997, June 1999, September 2001. The degree to which the introduction of these values affected the behavior of military personnel in Croatia is, of course, an open question.

[163] Interview with Ed Soyster, MPRI, April 2002; interview with Pentagon official, March 2002; interview with State Department official, March 2002.

[164] Though the connection of this consolidation to the progress toward democracy we see today is questionable, the consolidation of Tudjman's power did generate greater stability in the country than may have otherwise been the case. And some have argued that stability may be a greater prerequisite for movement toward lasting democratic reforms than any other factor. See, for instance, Jack Snyder and Edward Mansfield, "Democratization and the Danger of War," *International Security* vol. 20, No. 1 (summer 1995), 5–38. See also Samuel Huntington, *Political Order in Changing Societies* and *The Third Wave: Democratization in the Late Twentieth Century* (Norman: University of Oklahoma Press, 1991); Roland Paris, *At War's End: Building Peace after Civil Conflict* (Cambridge: Cambridge University Press, 2004).

military professionalism in Croatia. The long-term aims of the training and the fact that they were sustained over a several year period also gave more time for these effects to be felt. By introducing new values, connecting them with effective military performance and promising military aid for continued changes, the participation of MPRI in training the Croatian military appears to have nudged improvements in the social control of force.

The participation of PSCs under contract with the Croatian government improved the functional control of force, changed the political control of force, and improved the integration of force with international values. It is unclear that Croatia would have started down this path without the private option. The contract between MPRI and Croatia was a way around the international embargo in the Balkans – sending US troops to train the Croatian forces would have been very difficult given the embargo. The contract proved crucial to Tudjman's consolidation of political power and the ability of Croatia to expel Serbian forces from its territory and allowed for the beginning of a process of state building in Croatia. However the ultimate result in Croatia (a greater fit between functional, political, and social control of force) is a testament not just to PSCs, but to their use within NATO's PfP program, which required an extended training program and issued significant external incentives for Croatian political, and military leaders to work toward international standards of military professionalism. This high conditionality – along with some lucky junctures – led private advice and training to enhance long term control over force in Croatia.[165]

US contracts for military services

Unlike Sierra Leone and Croatia, the United States is a fully capable state, the only remaining superpower, clearly the most powerful state in the world. It is also a country with strong democratic traditions and long-standing, well-established institutions. Still, the US has hired PSCs to perform services – particularly in the realm of advice and training – similar to those performed in Sierra Leone and Croatia. How has outsourcing affected US control of force?

[165] For the term "high conditionality" and another positive view of its effects, see Alexander Cooley, "Western Conditions and Domestic Choices: the Influence of External Actors on the Post-Communist Transition," in Adrian Karatnycty, ed., *Nations in Transit 2003: Democratization in East Central Europe and Eurasia* (Lanham, MD: Rowman & Littlefield, 2003), pp. 25–38. See also Jon Pevhouse, "With a Little Help from my Friends? Regional Organizations and the Consolidation of Democracy," *American Journal of Political Science* Vol. 46, No. 3 (July 2002): 611–22.

The US government has a long history of contracting for military services.[166] Up until the beginning of World War II, most of these services were in the area of logistics support and weapons procurement. Contractors were used to supply basic rations, make uniforms, transport supplies, etc.[167] Also, as the arms industry began to grow, the government turned to private suppliers for small arms, bayonets, and ramrods (the most famous of these contractors was Eli Whitney, who supplied interchangeable parts.)[168] During World War II, the US government contracted out additional services such as constructing airfields and training pilots.[169]

With the advent of the Cold War, US interest in stabilizing foreign governments under siege from communist insurgent forces opened more opportunities for private firms. In many cases, the stabilization of foreign governments included military assistance and training and some of this was contracted out. In the Vietnam intervention, for instance, university teams funded by the Pentagon provided military and police training to the South Vietnamese forces, contractors to the US Army provided electronics training to the South Vietnamese and Booz Allen developed a program to train Vietnamese officers.[170] Also in Vietnam, Vinnell Corporation had 5,000 people in the country at the height of its involvement building military bases, repairing equipment, staffing military warehouses and, according to some reports, performing tasks

---

[166] Though the first official statement on contracting did not come out until 1954. See Althouse, "Contractors on the Battlefield." See also, chapter four, footnote 20.

[167] It was periodic dissatisfaction with the quality or reliability of supply that led to the establishment of such things as the commissary system. See Russell Weigley, *History of the US Army* (Bloomington: Indiana University Press, 1984); James Nagle, *A History of Government Contracting* (Washington, DC: George Washington University, 1992); Erna Risch, *The Quartermaster Corp: Organization, Supply, and Services*, (Washington, DC: GPO, 1995).

[168] Nagle, *History of Government Contracting*, pp. 81–82.

[169] In response to a tight time line and neutrality concerns, the US contracted with companies in the airline industry. Pan-Am Airlines and its subsidiaries were hired to construct airfields in the West Indies and throughout Latin America that were used to supply Europe and Africa. Pan-Am was also contracted to fly lend-lease bombers to Africa. When the Army did not have the capacity to train and supply air personnel as quickly as was needed, TWA was contracted to hire and train personnel as well as to provide supplies and facilities for air services to the US Army. The Pan-Am contract allowed the US to build airstrips on some bases in the British West Indies (acquired through the Lend-lease Program) without violating its neutral status, and the contract with TWA allowed the army to quickly train new pilots. After Pearl Harbor, President Roosevelt nationalized the airline industry. Ibid., pp. 454–55.

[170] Sidney Lens, *The Military Industrial Complex* (Philadelphia: Pilgrim Press, 1970), pp. 129–30; James Collins Jr., *The Development and Training of the South Vietnamese Army, 1950–1972* (Washington, DC: Department of the Army, 1975), pp. 111–12; William Proxmire, *Report From the Wasteland* (New York: Praeger, 1970), pp. 9–10.

the US forces could not do for legal reasons or lack of resources.[171] In the wake of Vietnam and the concerns it engendered over US intervention, the 1980s brought an increased focus on military training as a substitute to direct US involvement and private firms played a role here as well. In the wake of the Iran/Contra scandal numerous accounts emerged of US contracts with private (and often quite unsavory) individuals and organizations.[172]

Throughout the 1970s and 1980s service branches of the US military also launched several initiatives to transfer education and (some) training of their recruits and enlisted forces to private, or at least non-military, entities.[173] The policy established by OMB Circular A-76 in 1983 provided a rationale (and eventually a push) for additional contracting by requiring that government rely on commercial entities to provide those services that are not inherently governmental – so as not to have government "compete" with its citizens.[174] Though Circular A-76 was not to apply to the Department of Defense during declared war or military mobilization, it did apply during peacetime and caused the beginning of a more systematic examination of what kinds of services the Department of Defense might effectively privatize.

By the end of the Cold War, then, contracting with private companies for the delivery of military services was hardly new in the US. Since the end of the Cold War, though, the use of private contractors for military services has grown precipitously. As the US government downsized the military after the Cold War, it found itself committing troops in a broader and less predictable array of conflicts. The government turned to contractors for a wider array of services – and contractors mobilized to provide these. By 2002, the use of contractors was so pervasive that, according to (the late) Colonel Kevin Cunningham, then Dean of the Army War College, "the US cannot go to war without contractors."[175]

---

[171] William Hartung, "Mercenaries, Inc.: How a US Company Props up the House of Saud," *Progressive* Vol. 60 (April 1996).

[172] Cynthia Arnson, *Crossroads: Congress, the President, and Central America, 1976–1993* (University Park, PA: Pennsylvania State Press, 1993); Jonathan Feldman, *Universities in the Business of Repression: the Academic–Military–Industrial Complex and Central America* (Boston: South End Press, 1989).

[173] Most of these programs were in concert with established institutions, community colleges, technical institutes, or proprietary schools. Lawrence Hanser, Joyce Davidson, and Cathleen Stasz, *Who Should Train? Substituting Civilian Provided Training for Military Training* (Santa Monica: RAND, 1991), ch. 2.

[174] http://www.whitehouse.gov/omb/circulars/a076.pdf. See also chapter four, footnote 20.

[175] Statement at panel on "New Directions in Civil–Military Relations" at the 2002 annual meeting of the International Studies Association Meeting, New Orleans, 24–27 March.

Private training for US forces – outsourcing Army Reserve Officer
Training Corps (ROTC)

In the 1990s, the Army outsourced a number of education and training programs. The prevailing rationale was to make better use of scarce personnel. MPRI, alone, provided support to the US Army Force Management School, US Army ROTC program, US Army Combined Arms and Services School, and Training and Doctrine Command (TRADOC) Pilot Mentor Program at the Command and General Staff College.[176] Of the more controversial among these is the Army's outsourcing of its ROTC program.

ROTC programs are designed to produce officers for each service branch.[177] Indeed, 75 percent of all Army officers are produced through the ROTC program.[178] The program also allows college students who think they might want a leadership career in the military an introduction to the service. Its primary aim, though, is to professionalize future officers during their educational careers at civilian universities.[179] Students take leadership development and military skills classes and ROTC serves as their army home while they are going to school. In an effort to re-deploy active duty personnel, though, the Army began an experiment (in the 1997–98 academic year) to contract out some of the positions in this program.[180] As of 2002 a portion of ROTC

---

[176] http://www.mpri.com/subchannels/nat_business.html. Outsourcing of education and training is consistent with Department of Defense guidelines. Education and training are listed as commercial activities that could be (but not necessarily should be) outsourced. See http://www.acq.osd.mil/inst/icim/icim/newpriv/newpriv.htm. Cites Appendix 2, Office of Manpower and Budget Circular No. A-76, Revised Supplemental handbook, "Performance of Commercial Activities," March 1996. The Army also used MPRI's support in the development of doctrine – including, ironically, the doctrine for using contractors on the battlefield.

[177] Note that the discussion focuses on the Army. As yet, Navy and Air Force ROTC have not been outsourced.

[178] http://www.armyrotc.com/whatis.html.

[179] In a typical ROTC program as recently as 1997, there were five authorized officers (though typically the positions were staffed at only four), three training non-commissioned officers (NCOs) and one general schedule (GS) civilian. Among the officers, one lieutenant colonel served as the professor of military science and commander of the battalion, while one major (often an Active Guard or Reserve officer) and two captains served as assistant professors of military science. Two of the NCOs were responsible for organizing and conducting training while one handled supply and logistics. See Charles A. Goldman, Bruce R. Orvis, and Rodger Madison, *Staffing Army ROTC at Colleges and Universities: Alternatives for Reducing the Use of Active-Duty Soldiers* (Santa Monica: RAND, 1999), pp. 7–8.

[180] Particularly, it proposed that two of the assistant professors of military science and two NCOs – one trainer and the one responsible for logistics and supply – could be contracted out. Ibid., p. 12.

training was outsourced at over 200 universities and colleges across the country.[181]

MPRI was hired in this initial experiment.[182] The plan was to replicate the existing program – but with private personnel. This contract shifted discretion over the screening and selection of the personnel that would train future officers to a PSC – but with a number of requirements. Strict standards were set for those retired officers who could serve in the ROTC program. They must have been retired no more than two years, wear a uniform during performance of their duties, meet height and weight standards, pass the Army Physical Fitness Test, and participate in ROTC advanced and basic camps during the summer.[183] The personnel MPRI hired met these standards continually, but some have nonetheless worried that there are other features important to ROTC instructors and trainers that are harder to measure – enthusiasm for the job, experience, and professionalism. MPRI claims that it does pay attention to these less tangible values and that it has fielded a good force of instructors and trainers. There have been no complaints from the Army about the quality of staff MPRI has provided.

As is often the case, however, the cost of garnering the exact same service from the private sector was higher.[184] Indeed, from the start, the privatization of ROTC was expected to cost more than the alternative of using active duty personnel. The RAND Corporation estimates suggested that each year it cost about $10,000 more per instructor for

---

[181] http://www.mpri.com/subchannels/nat_ROTC.html. The majority of positions that have been contracted out are assistant professors of military science. Trainers and logistics positions have also been outsourced, but not to such a degree, and administrative positions have been outsourced the least.

[182] Interestingly, in designing the plan for the Army, the Arroyo Center considered and rejected the possibility of having ROTC programs hire retired military personnel directly because of administrative hurdles. Particularly, if a military retiree accepts a position with any organization of the federal government, they must, by law, forfeit all or part of their retirement pay. Also hiring former military members as civilians would subject the Army to limited civilian personnel ceilings, the requirements of which would negate any cost savings from the outsourcing effort. See Goldman et al., *Staffing Army ROTC*, p. 3.

[183] http://www.mpri.com/subchannels/nat_ROTC.html.

[184] Though sophisticated Center for Naval Analyses studies have demonstrated that privatization often results in cost savings, they tie these savings to *competition* rather than privatization, per se. See R. Derek Trunkey, Robert P. Trost, and Christopher Snyder, "Analysis of DOD's Commercial Activities Program," Center for Naval Analyses, CRM December 1996, 96–63. Data on privatization in other arenas suggest that privatization only saves money if the contractor is given flexibility to do the job differently *and* there is competition. Donahue, *Privatization Decision*. Interview with GAO analyst, May 2001. For an excellent discussion of the components of military compensation for enlisted persons see M. Rebecca Kilburn, Rachel Louie, and Dana Goldman, *Patterns of Enlisted Compensation* (Washington, DC: RAND, 2001).

private staffing of ROTC training in the United States.[185] In 2002, the contract for ROTC training was re-competed and MPRI lost the contract on cost concerns. Many worried, though, that the new contractor (Communication Technology or COMTek) would field less-qualified staff.[186] They pointed out that officials from MPRI routinely participate in intellectual forums sponsored by the Army – partly because MPRI has such an impressive array of retired, high level staff – and thus MPRI is considered well positioned to do a better job keeping up with the implicit requirements for ROTC instructors and trainers (enthusiasm, experience, professionalism). Paying attention to cost alone, these people argued, would generate a less impressive program.[187]

Regardless of who hires retired military personnel to work in the ROTC program, all go through a similar socialization process in the Army, and both the Army's strong professional networks and the requirement that personnel be retired for no more than two years create an atmosphere that should lend stability to social control of force.[188] Critics of the experiment in ROTC outsourcing recognize this (though they are quicker to point out the variation among individuals and their internalization of professional norms) and acknowledge that private ROTC trainers may not be so different from their active duty counterparts in the short run.[189]

Portions of the Army's leadership and retired leadership, however, have voiced worry about a different kind of effect on social control. Given the importance of the personnel that staff ROTC programs as role models for future officers, some have questioned the wisdom of having for-profit companies staff the programs with retired officers. It is not a matter of whether MPRI or COMTek fields good retired officers, but whether the use of a commercial company can instill the ideals of a profession whose defining tenet is self-sacrifice. As James Burke put it, reliance on PSCs for ROTC training "may subtly teach new entrants into the profession that, despite the rhetoric of self-sacrificing leadership, market logic trumps other considerations."[190]

This may contribute to a trend analysts have labeled the "de-professionalization" of the military. The outsourcing of ROTC training, by turning over the mission of educating and modeling professional

---

[185] Goldman et al., *Staffing Army ROTC*, p. 12 (figure 3).
[186] Interview with retired Army officers, December 2002.
[187] Interview with retired Army officers, May 2000.
[188] Interview with retired Army officers, April 2001, May 2002.
[189] Ibid.
[190] Burk, "Expertise, Jurisdiction and Legitimacy of the Military Profession," p. 35.

behavior to profit-seeking firms, goes along with the identification of military service with side-payments (like education, travel, acquiring technical skills, etc.) in defining military service as a job rather than a profession.[191] If privatization of ROTC further promotes the de-professionalization of the army, it may have longer-term effects on the overarching values that motivate military service in the first place.[192] The switch from MPRI to COMTek amplified these worries. COMTek does not have the same staff or interest and some worried that it would not be attuned to what the army really needs. Others claimed that the only way COMTek would be able to implement the contract at the cost they bid was to hire less experienced personnel in a way that would undermine the effectiveness of the program.[193] Though there have been no serious complaints about COMTek two years into the switch, these worries remain.[194]

The effects of privatizing this program on the functional control of force are mixed – adding flexibility but at increased cost.[195] The effects on political control of force are subtle. The decision shifted discretion over hiring to a PSC. It also left Congress out of the loop as Congress had no information about the initial outsourcing or about the switch of venders.[196] Furthermore, the re-deployment was one of many taken in the 1990s to keep the military beneath what was considered an "appropriate" size but still do an increased number of missions. Thus it can be seen as a way of increasing the effective size of the force without generating political agreement on this increase. Though such arrangements are often sold

---

[191] See Charles Moskos and Frank Woods, eds., *The Military: More than Just a Job?* (McLean, VA: Pergamon-Brassey's, 1988).
[192] For a discussion of the development of the modern motivation for military service, see Cohen, *Citizens and Soldiers*.
[193] Interview with retired Army General, May 2002.
[194] Elizabeth Stanley-Mitchell, "The Military Profession and Intangible Rewards," in Cindy Williams, ed., *Filling the Ranks: Transforming the US Military Personnel System* (Boston: MIT Press, 2004).
[195] The impact of privatization on cost should vary with the flexibility accorded to the contractor and the level of competition. Calculating cost savings is complicated as military compensation and cost includes more than just pay. Approximately 70 percent of military compensation is cash pay, the remaining 30 percent consists of in-kind pay and benefits. See US Department of Defense, *Report of the Ninth Quadrennial Review of Military Compensation* (Washington, DC: US Department of Defense, March 2002); Carla Tighe Murray, "Transformation of In-Kind Compensation and Benefits," in Cindy Williams, ed., *Filling the Ranks* (Boston: MIT Press, 2004), p. 191. The compensation balance for enlisted personnel is slightly different, with 81 percent in basic pay and 19 percent in other categories. See Kilburn, Louie, and Goldman, *Patterns of Enlisted Compensation*, table 5.7.
[196] Congress did retain access to "fire-alarm" oversight, though. There have been protests at some campuses over the use of private instructors that has alerted congress members to a potential problem.

publicly as cost-saving devises, as we saw above, it was *more* costly. The most significant concerns about the program have to do with the social control of force – particularly the impact of outsourcing core professionalization activities to a commercial entity – and are worries about the future. ROTC candidates may not have the same sense of service if they perceive that MPRI or COMTek and not their country is responsible for their training. Also, as PSCs do more of the curricular development as well as training, the Army is ceding control over the shape of a core element of its professionalism to commercial firms that may be influenced by the variety of consumer demands rather than the US government's alone. Over the long term, if the shape of professionalism changed in a way that reduced the professionalism of the Army, at the extreme perhaps making dying (or killing) for one's country less legitimate, one could imagine such changes eroding the fit between the dimensions of control and decreasing military effectiveness.

Private advice and training for foreign forces – stabilization efforts

Training foreign militaries has a long history in the US and is used to pursue a number of different US foreign policy objectives: to improve the performance of foreign forces, to enhance the professional and democratic nature of foreign forces, to enhance the ability of foreign forces to interface with US forces or work toward US goals, and to reward friendly nations.[197] Foreign military training became a centerpiece of the

[197] Many of the post-Cold War military training efforts have been conducted under the International Military Education and Training (IMET) program. Basically, the IMET program provides scholarships for students to come to Professional Military Education (PME) programs in the US. Congress created IMET in 1976 to strengthen mutual understanding between the US and its friends and allies and to enhance these countries' ability to insure their security. The legislation separated military training from the Military Assistance Program (MAP) and set up funding to help countries unable to purchase US military training. IMET refers to this program of assistance. The general program to sell US training to personnel from other countries operates under the Foreign Military Sales (FMS) Act – this will be discussed in chapter four. IMET was amended in 1978 to increase the participating countries' awareness of human rights. Then in 1991, an amendment entitled Expanded IMET (E-IMET) focused on defense resource management, respect for and grasp of democracy and civilian rule, military justice in a democracy, and human rights. Additional legislation made possible civilian and NGO participation in the program. John A. Cope, "International Military Education and Training: an Assessment," McNair Paper 44 (Washington, DC: Institute for National Strategic Studies, National Defense University, October 1995), pp. 5–6.

General foreign military training takes place either at one of the US professional military education (PME) establishments or outside US territory by a Mobile Training Team (MTT). Both IMET and E-IMET are regulated by the State Department's embargo list. Any legal restrictions on a country by the US or the UN or informal policy holds engendered by human rights abuses or other infractions lead military–military exchanges and training to halt.

US grand strategy after the Cold War, both to enhance stability and democratization in post-communist states and to help stabilize post-conflict states.[198] The budget for the Department of Defense (International Military Education and Training, or IMET) programs alone increased fourfold from 1994 to 2002.[199] In the wake of the 11 September attacks and the wars in Afghanistan and Iraq, these efforts have intensified. In 2002, the US trained at least 100,000 foreign police and soldiers from more than 150 countries.[200] The Department of State's budget for military training in FY 2005 requested nearly $5.2 billion under military assistance (including a variety of programs that provide security assistance: IMET, Foreign Military Financing [FMF], and Peacekeeping Operations).[201]

As the US has increased its focus on foreign military training, it has also increasingly turned to PSCs to carry it out.[202] Private firms such as MPRI, SAIC, Vinnell, DynCorp and others have worked for the US government training army and police forces in the Balkans, the Newly Independent States (NIS), former Warsaw Pact countries, the Middle East, Latin America, Africa, and Asia. In Africa, PSCs played a significant role in both the African Crisis Response Initiative (ACRI now the African Contingency Operations Training Assistance, or ACOTA) and the African Center for Strategic Studies (ACSS) as well as in initiatives to train in individual countries such as Nigeria.[203] In the wake of the US war in Iraq, PSCs played a wide variety of training roles.

---

[198] It is received wisdom in the Pentagon and elsewhere (though wisdom that calls out for validation through empirical research) that "low visibility defense instruction has exceptional value in promoting both democracy and military cooperation." Cope, "International Military Education and Training," p. 41.

[199] Funds for foreign military training come from both the State Department and the Department of Defense. Lora Lumpe, "US Foreign Military Training: Global Reach, Global Power, and Oversight Issues," *Foreign Policy In Focus* Special Report (May 2002).

[200] US Department of State, "Testimony of Colin Powell before the House Appropriations Subcommittee on Foreign Operations, Export Financing and Related Programs," 13 February 2002. Cited in Amnesty International, "US Training of Foreign Military and Police Forces: the Human Rights Dimension," 2002.

[201] See FY 2005 Congressional Budget Justification for Foreign Operations: Military Assistance. Available at http://www.state.gov/documents/organization/28973.pdf.

[202] PSCs also sell training directly to foreign governments via FMS – see chapter .

[203] The ACRI, which trained troops from African countries in peacekeeping, began as a program run with US troops in 1996 and subsequently privatized some, and then all, of its training. The purpose was to work with international partners and African nations to enhance African peacekeeping and humanitarian relief capacity. Particularly, the US would offer training and equipment to African nations dedicated to democracy and civilian rule that would like to improve their peacekeeping abilities. The US intended to use the ACRI to coordinate its African peacekeeping approach with the Organization for African Unity (OAU) and other interested parties (Britain, France, etc.). In December 1997, representatives from these countries, interested donors, and troop

Vinnell won an umbrella contract from the US Army to train the Iraqi
Army, with subcontracts going to MPRI, SAIC, Eagle Group
International, and Omega Training Group.[204] CSC's DynCorp won a
contract to train and support the Iraqi police.[205] There was also
a contract issued by the Coalition Provisional Authority (CPA) to train a
private security force, the Iraqi Facilities Protection Force, to defend oil
facilities and pipelines in the country. Erinys, a South African company,
won that contract.[206]

Evaluating the effects of foreign military training, even when carried
out by US military forces, is complicated.[207] Many factors inhibit a
strong relationship between military training efforts and US goals.
Improved performance among foreign forces depends on what the
forces are called upon to do and how well this tracks with their training.
Also, the democratic (or not) nature of foreign forces may be influenced

contributors met at the UN Department of Peacekeeping Operations in New York for
the first peacekeeping support-group meeting ever.

The ACSS (modeled after the Marshall Center in Garmisch, Germany) was envisioned with contractors in mind. Announced in April 1988, it aims to provide a forum
for senior military and civilian officials to explore together complex defense policy issues
and provide training to strengthen civil–military relations in burgeoning democracies.
See discussion by Susan Rice, Assistant Secretary for African Affairs, in a speech to the
City Club of Cleveland, Cleveland, Ohio, 17 April 1998.

[204] According to a US Department of Defense Contract Announcement issued on 25 June
2003, the cost-plus-fixed-fee contract was for $48,074,442 for work beginning 1 July
2003 and ending 30 June 2004. See also, http://www.export.gov/iraq/market_ops/
contracts03.html.

[205] http://www.policemission.com/iraq.asp. See also, http://www.export.gov/iraq/market_
ops/contracts03.html.

[206] The contract was for $39,500,000 and was signed August 2003. The PSC was to
improve security along the northern pipeline immediately (via expatriate personnel)
and then to recruit, screen, and train some 6,500 Iraqis for the long-term force. Richard
Giragosian, "Targeting Weak Points: Iraq's Oil Pipelines," *Asia Times*, 27 January
2004; Gordon Fellers, "Coalition Works to Make Iraqi Pipeline Protection a Top
Priority," *Pipeline and Gas Journal* Vol. 231, No. 3 (1 March 2004).

[207] Though many agree that military training provides access to, and ties with, foreign
military personnel, there is very little regularized examination of the relationship
between military training and US goals – or the effect of military training on the nature
of foreign forces. There are a variety of studies relying on anecdotal evidence from one
or more cases. There is little systematic study, however, that compares efforts across a
variety of cases or uses sophisticated indicators to judge effects. Many US foreign
education and training missions have not gone without criticism. The former School
of the Americas, located in Panama and then in Fort Benning, Georgia, was criticized
and dubbed the School of Assassins and Dictators. In July 1999 the House voted to
eliminate funds for training foreign officers at the facility. See John Lancaster, "House
Kills Training Funds for School of the Americas, Army Facility Accused of Fostering
Human Rights Abuses," *Washington Post*, 31 July 1999. In its place, the Western
Hemispheric Institute for Security and Cooperation (WHINSEC) was initiated.
http://www.benning.army.mil/whinsec/.

by many factors (including the political goals of the leaders in their country) not related to military training. Furthermore, pursuing one US goal may undermine another. For instance, there are reports that US forces working with warlords in Afghanistan to gain access to al Qaeda hideouts (one US goal) may work against President Karzai's efforts to consolidate control over the country by training a national Afghan Army (another US goal).

The changes introduced by contracting with PSCs for this training provides some functional advantages given the structure of US forces. PSCs can draw on a deeper pool of personnel with area experience. In the ACRI program, for instance, MPRI was able to provide French-speaking instructors for francophone African states that would not be available from the ranks of the Special Forces.[208] In Iraq, the US has relied on PSCs from a number of countries to train forces, and these PSCs have recruited internationally, providing a much larger labor pool. Contractors can also provide greater stability in training programs. While personnel rotate through units quickly in the active duty forces, PSCs can provide teams in which the same personnel stay in a country for several years.[209] Finally, contractors can move personnel to the field more quickly in some circumstances, providing what some have called "surge" capability.[210] As the US went about the monumental task of training the Iraqi Army, police, and other security forces, PSCs offered a vehicle for a rapid increase in trainers that bolstered the capacity of thinly stretched coalition forces.

Frequently, however, using contractors reduces the chances that training will comply with US policy goals in fluid political situations. The nature of the contract instrument reduces US policy flexibility to adjust to changes in events on the ground. The contract specifies tasks to be done and payment to be received for a specific period of time. During that time, however, US priorities may change. The contract, however, enshrines the original agreement and makes it possible for those with different interests – including both the host government and the contractor – to exercise their leverage to prevent change. Those involved in the policy process describe this particular feature as issuing a

---

[208] Interview with Ed Soyster, MPRI, 12 April 1999; Interviews with Jean-Michel A. Beraud and Clifford L. Fields, MPRI (ACRI program), 31 January 2000; Interview with Scott Fisher, State Department, ACRI program, 31 August 1999.

[209] Comments of Theresa Whelan, Deputy Assistant Secretary of Defense for Africa, at the International Peace Operations Association Dinner, Washington, DC, 19 November 2003.

[210] Ibid. Interviews with Ed Soyster, MPRI, 1999, 2000, 2002; Stacey Rabin, PA&E, comments at SAIS/IPOA Conference, "Enhancing Public–Private Peace Operations: Evaluations and Opportunities," Washington, DC, SAIS, 20 November 2003.

constant challenge in Bosnia.[211] The Dayton Accords necessarily enshrined contradictory principles in order to get an agreement. In this context, the expectation was that the course would be adjusted as the peace unfolded. Key tensions surrounded the degree to which the implementation of the train and equip program could proceed simultaneously with the creation of institutions to oversee it and the relationship between the train and equip program and other elements of the Dayton Accords.[212] Pentagon officials working in Bosnia argue that the use of contractors impeded this adjustment. For instance, as US interests in Bosnia shifted their priority to the development of institutions to oversee defense policy from training the Bosnian Defense Force, per se, MPRI was reluctant to adjust.[213] This was partly due to the investment the contractor had made in the training facilities and efforts. Also, though, the host government had political interests in preserving the status quo and worked in concert with MPRI. Those who stood to gain from the contract as it stood were reluctant to change and could use the contract instrument to resist US pressures.[214] Pentagon overseers report struggling with these issues constantly in the Balkans and describe private contracts for foreign military training as "rigid tools for fluid environments."[215]

This rigidity was also apparent in the reaction to Vinnell's contract to train the Iraqi Army. In June 2003 Vinnell won a one year, $48 million contract to train nine battalions (1,000 men each) for the new Iraqi army.[216] Much of the actual training, though, was sub-contracted to MPRI, SAIC, and several other firms.[217] There were early indications that the training was not going well. Vinnell and others sent "classroom

---

[211] In the late 1990s, I witnessed a general divide among those in the Pentagon between the Deputy Assistant Secretary level of government where PSCs were generally viewed quite favorably and those working below that level or at the Joint Staff where PSCs were viewed with much greater suspicion. The details of the policy process provided by those working below the level of the Deputy Assistant Secretary allowed me to extrapolate the following process.

[212] United States Institute for Peace Special Report, "Dayton Implementation: the Train and Equip Program," September 1997, available at wysiwyg://261/http://www.usip.org/oc/sr/dayton_imp/train_equip.html. See also, Jane M. O. Sharp, "Bosnia: Begin Again," *Bulletin of the Atomic Scientists* Vol. 53, No. 2 (March/April 1997).

[213] Interview with Pentagon official, April 2002.

[214] Ibid.

[215] Interview with military officers at the Joint Staff, April 2002.

[216] Pentagon Contract Announcement, US Department of Defense, 25 June 2003.

[217] Eagle Group International, Omega Training Group, and Worldwide Language Resources, Inc. Geoff Fein, "Training Iraqi Army is a Wild Card," *National Defense Magazine* (December 2003). Interview with Colonel Paul Hughes, Senior Military Fellow, NDU and former official with ORHA and then the CPA, May 2004.

guys, not drill instructors"[218] and put too much emphasis on classroom studies of strategy and tactics and not enough on basic combat skills. Reports suggested that the drill instructors were overweight, discipline was loose, the curriculum was confused (perhaps complicated by the number of subcontracts) and when the first battalion graduated on 4 October, its commander concluded that he would have to redo much of the training.[219] In December the problem was even more apparent as almost one half of the recruits abandoned their jobs just before they were to leave training camp.[220] When it became clear that there was a problem with a contract, though, it was hard to adjust because "the contract is a rigid tool. When the situation has changed, you [the US military] are in a worse situation and need to fix things quick but the contractor has the bargaining power and he wants things to stay the same [as they were in the initial contract]."[221] Vinnell kept the contract and completed its obligation to train nine battalions.[222]

Using PSCs to train foreign militaries also poses problems for evaluating the effectiveness of training for meeting US policy goals. The contractor is frequently a main source of information about progress on goals related to the training contract – with the other being the host government. Both the contractor and the host government have an interest in documenting progress so that the money will continue to flow from the US government even if no progress is being made. If both the contractor and the host government cooperate to claim progress, it is hard for US government personnel to dispute this information – short of a battlefield "test." Again, Pentagon officials reported this being an issue in the contract to train the Bosnian military, but they also said that such problems were common to all contracts for foreign military training paid for by the US.[223] Indeed, several mentioned this kind of collusion in a variety of contracts between the US government and PSCs in Bosnia, Croatia, and Macedonia.[224] Ironically, the extent of insecurity in Iraq led the army to be tested – and found wanting – early on.

---

[218] Interview with Colonel T.X. Hammes, USMC, Senior Military Fellow at NDU, July 2004.
[219] Ibid.; Dean Calbreath, "Iraqi Army, Police Fall Short on Training," *San Diego Union Tribune*, 4 July 2004; Ariana Eunjung Cha, "Recruits Abandon Iraqi Army," *Washington Post*, 13 December 2003, p. A1.
[220] Cha, "Recruits Abandon Iraqi Army."
[221] Interview with Col. TX Hammes.
[222] Calbreath, "Iraqi Army, Police Fall Short on Training"; Cha, "Recruits Abandon Iraqi Army."
[223] Interview with military officers at the Joint Staff, April 2002.
[224] Ibid.

Finally, the contractor can use the complexity of US goals to suit their interests in the continuation of a contract. When it looks as if their contract might be frozen because a host country is violating human rights concerns or misbehaving in some other way, a company may claim that its contract should not be frozen because "engaging" human rights abusers may lead to improvements in civil–military relations and democratization that may enhance attention to human rights in the long term. In a number of instances, these kinds of arguments have allowed a contract to continue even when a legal embargo is in effect.[225] When confronted with evidence that the same company's contract may be in violation of local laws or used politically by host country politicians in violation of human rights norms, though, the company can turn around and claim that it is serving US interests by enhancing the capacity of the host government's forces or rewarding cooperative behavior internationally. More than once, contractors told me that, "it is not our job to insure that our boss [the host country] abides by its own laws."[226]

Thus, there are many possibilities for contradictions in US military training even when it is conducted by US troops. In some instances, the use of PSCs only aggravates existing tensions. But some concerns are not so prominent when US military personnel are doing the training. When training is scaled down, active duty personnel salute smartly and move on to their next posting. If the host government is uncooperative making training efforts less effective, active duty personnel have less to lose by reporting the truth.[227] Those military personnel conducting training have fewer vested interests in continuing the training at a cost to US policy. While there may be debates over training programs – particularly at the higher levels of government – those on the ground from whom the various government officials receive information have fewer incentives to exaggerate when they are active duty personnel.

There are a variety of additional functional concerns raised about contracting out foreign military training missions. It deprives active duty US personnel of "engagement" opportunities (or chances to make long-term personal contacts with military personnel in foreign countries) that

---

[225] See footnote 113 this chapter and the discussion of Croatia and Equatorial Guinea in chapter four.

[226] Interviews with MPRI officials.

[227] Interview with military officials at the Joint Staff, April 2002. When challenged with evidence that active duty personnel sometimes did report rosier than justified progress in Vietnam, these officers admitted that information asymmetry is a problem in general, but still claimed that it was a greater problem when contractors were involved.

are one of the rationales for increased attention to training in the first place.[228] Also when the US sends PSCs and not military personnel the host country perceives a lower level of US commitment and generally values this training less highly – there is a certain cachet attached to being trained by US troops.[229] And there are questions about the relative costs of these missions.[230] The policy slippage and frequent cost increases that occur when the US contracts for foreign military training reduces functional control.

Perhaps most importantly, however, the private option enables US government officials to forgo investment in (or reorganization of) military forces for new problems – using PSCs one time makes it more likely that they will be used in the future.[231] While the private option provides flexibility in the short run, then, it is harder to control and frequently more costly than its public alternative and reduces incentives to reorganize the force.[232] This is most dramatically illustrated by the US use of DynCorp for fielding international civilian police. Initially DynCorp allowed the US to field a force of international civilian police in Haiti that it had no other way of fielding. Over the long term, however, the DynCorp option has allowed the US government to avoid the creation of an international civilian police capacity. Civilian police have been routinely sent abroad over the last fifteen years and much evidence suggests that relying on contracts has resulted in poor training, little strategic vision, and, ultimately, less effective policy.[233]

---

[228] Interview with Pentagon officials, April 2002. Comments of Theresa Whelan, Deputy Assistant Secretary of Defense for Africa, at the International Peace Operations Association Dinner, Washington, DC, 19 November 2003.

[229] Comments of Theresa Whelan, Deputy Assistant Secretary of Defense for Africa, at the International Peace Operations Association Dinner, Washington, DC, 19 November 2003.

[230] Decisions to outsource these missions are generally to reduce stress on personnel not to save money – but many point to [assume] cost saving to justify the privatization. A variety of Pentagon staff, however, have expressed confusion about the relative cost and suspicion that the cost is higher. There are no good empirical studies of the relative cost of public v. private foreign training.

[231] Thomas McNaugher, "The Army and Operations Other than War," in Don Snider and Gayle Watkins, eds., *The Future of the Army Profession* (New York: McGraw Hill, 2002).

[232] See Goldman et al., *Staffing Army ROTC*, p. 12; Susan Gates and Al Robbert, "Personnel Savings in Competitively Sourced DOD Activities" (Washington, DC: RAND [MR-1117-OSD]); US General Accounting Office, "Contingency Operations: Army Should Do More to Control Contract Cost in the Balkans," GAO/NSIAD-00-225 (September 2000).

[233] Interview with Robert Perito, June 2004. See Perito, *American Experience with Police*; Robert Perito, *Where is the Lone Ranger When You Need Him? America's Search for a Post-Conflict Stability Force* (Washington, DC: United States Institute for Peace Press, 2004); David Bayley, *Democratizing the Police Abroad: What to do and How to do it* (Washington, DC: National Institute of Justice, 2001).

Contracting for foreign training also changes political control, or who has a role in deciding about how such missions will be carried out. The participation of PSCs in providing information or shaping the lens through which policy makers view a problem is a form of agenda setting. When a PSC is given this role in the policy implementation process, it acquires influence over a piece of the process. For instance, the US hired MPRI to evaluate the progress the Croatian Army was making toward PfP criteria – even as the US was paying the same company to train the Croatian Army.[234] The particulars of this evaluation may have been perfectly reasonable, but the decision to contract with an entity that has a commercial stake in the result of the evaluation opens avenues for commercial interests to affect the shape of US policy.

In addition, private training changes the balance of control between the executive and legislative branches of government. The executive branch hires contractors, not Congress. Though Congress approves the military budget, it does not approve individual decisions to contract out training. It is harder for Congress to oversee PSC behavior. The annual consolidated report on military assistance and sales, for instance, does not include information on who is conducting particular training missions.[235] Examples of executive use of PSCs to evade congressional restrictions abound. For instance, when Congress institutes stipulations on the numbers of US troops, the executive has used contractors to go above this number. Sometimes Congress has innovated and stipulated an upper limit on the number of contractors, but this has simply led PSCs to hire more local personnel.[236] Thus, the executive branch, in its decisions to hire contractors and in its day-to-day implementation of policy is advantaged vis-à-vis Congress. Indeed, this change is often touted by members of the executive branch as one of the benefits of contracting out.[237]

---

[234] Interview with Pentagon official, June 2003. Examples of this kind of problem also abound in non-training missions. In the lead up to the 2003 US war with Iraq, for instance, Kellogg, Brown, and Root (KBR) received an open-ended contract to restore Iraqi oil fields after the conflict without having to compete with any other entity. The rationale for the non-competitive process was a classified contingency plan for rebuilding Iraq's infrastructure, which stated that KBR was the only company with the skills, resources, and security clearances to do the job on short notice. Fair enough, but the contingency plan was written by none other than KBR under another contract to the Army, Logcap (Logistics Civil Augmentation Program), which put KBR in charge of a host of logistics support operations for the next ten years. See Dan Baum, "Nation Builders for Hire," New York Times Magazine, 22 June 2003, p. 34.
[235] Lumpe, "US Foreign Military Training."
[236] Ibid.; Baum, "Nation Builders for Hire," p. 36.
[237] For instance, Theresa Whelan claimed that one of the advantages of contractors is that they "ease" FMF rules for training foreign militaries. Comments of Theresa Whelan,

This is not to suggest that congressional oversight of foreign training is easy or that the executive does not have an advantage in this oversight in the first place. The institutional safeguards that give Congress indirect means of control over military forces, however, are not present with PSCs. For instance, Congress has long-standing ties to military organizations and can write laws to change them, which affect incentives for individual service members and provide mechanisms for congressional control. These mechanisms are not so readily available for PSCs. As Representative Jan Schakowsky (D, IL) notes, contractors "don't have to follow the same chain of command, the military code of conduct may or may not apply, the accountability is absent and the transparency is absent – but the money keeps flowing."[238] I am not arguing that there are no other ways to avoid congressional scrutiny – through the use of covert operations, for instance, or other programs in which congress has less input.[239] PSCs simply add another tool to this list.

Also (as will be discussed in greater detail in chapter four) PSCs not only sell foreign training to the US, but also sell it directly to foreign governments through Foreign Military Sales (FMS). This possibility opens the way for an even greater role for the executive branch relative to Congress and even less transparency over foreign policy.[240] In licensing the contract with Croatia, for instance, a few members of the executive branch managed to retain the neutral status of the US and still change events on the ground such that strategic bombing by NATO could push the Serbs to the negotiating table – the results of which were the Dayton Accords (and another contract for MRPI to train and equip the Bosnian military).[241] We should not confuse an assessment of the

Deputy Assistant Secretary of Defense for Africa, at the International Peace Operations Association Dinner, Washington, DC, 19 November 2003.
[238] Quoted in Baum, "Nation Builders for Hire," p. 36.
[239] For example, in a series of articles, the *Washington Post* reported that US Special Operations Forces frequently conduct Joint Combined Exchange Training (JCET) with foreign troops that would be precluded from receiving military training otherwise. JCETs proceeded in Colombia during 1996 and 1997 even as the Clinton administration "decertified" Colombia for military assistance because of its failure to comply with US anti-narcotics policy. In Indonesia a congressional ban on training Indonesian officers and a checkered human rights record has not prevented forty-one JCET training exercises since 1991. Similar stories in Papua New Guinea, Equatorial Guinea, Rwanda, Suriname, and elsewhere have led some to suggest that these programs undermine, or work at cross-purposes with, US diplomatic efforts. Dana Priest, "Special Alliances: the Pentagon's New Global Engagements," *Washington Post* 12 July 1998, p. A01; Lynne Duke, "Africans Use Training in Unexpected Ways," *Washington Post*, 14 July 1998, p. A01.
[240] Bruce Grant, "US Military Expertise for Sale," Chairman of the Joint Chief of Staff Strategy Essay Competition, National Defense University, 1998; available at http://www.ndu.edu/inss/books/essaysch4.html.
[241] Ibid, pp. 72–73.

benefits (or costs) of this policy with an assessment of whether change has occurred. Many argue that without the increase in Croatian capacities, there would have been no NATO intervention and no end to the conflict. The human rights abuses in the Krajina region in the wake of Operation Storm, however, also may not have occurred.[242] Regardless of how one assesses the costs and benefits, though, it is clear that the policy process is different. When the executive branch has greater power over foreign policy decisions, policy (whether "good" or "bad") can be put in place more quickly without so many checks.

To the degree that PSCs working for the US government generally draw from American retired military personnel who are well socialized in international values and claim to conduct their work accordingly, social control is preserved. The work that MPRI did for the ACRI program drew personnel with good area and language skills and generally operated well within the bounds of integration with social values. Similarly, MPRI's conduct of ROTC training was not criticized for the behavior of the personnel doing the jobs. Though in some instances, government officials in the US have reported opportunistic behavior by retired US forces working for PSCs that drifted from the high standards of integration with social values in the US Armed Forces, for the most part American PSC behavior in the 1990s was consistent with patterns of social control among US forces.[243] PSCs pulled directly from US professional military education in designing their curriculum. Though some cited this as a functional cost, complaining that US PSCs simply offer warmed over West Point or Fort Leavenworth curriculum not relevant to the threats host governments face, this curriculum is carefully designed to represent international values (not simply supporting civilian control of the military and respect for human rights, but claiming that these are integrally related to success on the battlefield). Adopting this curriculum does model a particular type of military professionalism – and one that is consistent with what active-duty US troops would present.

The US hiring pattern in Iraq, however, has weakened social control. The US has hired non-American companies and the American companies it has hired have recruited much more internationally. Partly a feature of the surge in demand precipitated by the role of PSCs in Iraq and partly a natural unfolding of the transnational market, this pattern

---

[242] Cohen, "US Cooling Ties with Croatia"; Mark Danner, "Endgame in Kosovo," *New York Review of Books* Vol. 44, No. 8, (6 May 1999): 8.

[243] The behavior of some MPRI personnel working in Macedonia and Colombia was reportedly unprofessional. Interview with officers at the Pentagon, May 2002, September 2002.

nonetheless has yielded a more heterogeneous set of employees and companies that portends more potential change in the social control of training. Though mostly retired American soldiers worked for Vinnell and MPRI training, the Iraqi army and retired American police and military officers work for DynCorp to train the Iraqi police, the US contract with Erinys to train a private facilities protection force brought in expatriates from South Africa, Nepal, and the UK, among others.[244] The questionable background of Erinys executives and the fact that it was such a new company led many to be surprised that it won the contract.[245]

The Erinys bid was undoubtedly less expensive – according to a DynCorp official, the DynCorp bid was three times the cost.[246] But the DynCorp bid also included helicopter surveillance – something that has since been awarded to another company, AirScan.[247] This led some to conclude that the CPA was making decisions on the basis of cost alone in ways that sacrificed professionalism. Others have suggested that the dicey backgrounds of Erinys executives – who have worked securing oil lines for BP and mines for Ashanti Gold – may have been precisely what the CPA was looking for given the "Wild West" environment in Iraq.[248] Regardless, however, the Erinys contract is part of a trend in Iraq that blurs the US's message about whether professionalism and proper behavior on the part of PSCs is important to its purchasing decisions. Many have claimed that this has lowered the level of professionalism in the country. According to Jerry Hoffman, CEO of ArmorGroup, "What you don't need is Dodge City out there any more than you've already got it."[249] Richard Fenning, CEO of Control Risks Group, claimed that, "The danger is that unless the legal and operational status of such companies is clarified and institutionalized, responsible companies, conscious of their liabilities and reputation, may be driven from the arena." [250]

---

[244] DynCorp advertisements for police officers specify a requirement for US citizenship. See http://www.policemission.com/iraq.asp.

[245] Jim Vallette and Pratap Chatterjee, "Guarding the Oil Underworld in Iraq," *CorpWatch* (5 September 2003); Knut Royce, "Start up Company with Connections," *Newsday*, 15 February 2004.

[246] Knut Royce, "Start up Company with Connections," *Newsday*, 15 February 2004.

[247] Ibid.

[248] Interview with former CPA official.

[249] David Barstow, "Security Companies: Shadow Soldiers in Iraq," *New York Times*, 19 April 2004.

[250] Richard Fenning, "The Iraqi Security Business Urgently Needs Rules," *Financial Times*, 27 May 2004.

State contracts for security and the control of force in the US

Institutional hypotheses suggest that while the US may gain short-run flexibility by outsourcing advice and training, it is also likely to suffer functional losses. US military forces are well trained, disciplined, and capable. When PSCs are hired according to military stipulations (as with ROTC), contracting is likely to increase costs because private personnel are generally more expensive.[251] Contracting for foreign military training that stipulates acceptable criteria equal to that of US forces is also less likely to save money. The examples above largely support these hypotheses. They also suggest that foreign military training creates additional possibilities for control slippage because of the interaction between the nature of US goals and the complicated relationship between the interests of the US government, the contractors, and the host country.

The dynamics of contracting in the US, though, does imply that there may be tasks for which contracting will yield short-run functional gains. When tasks arise that the US military does not have expertise in, does not have the personnel for, or is poorly organized around, contracting can produce functional benefits – at least in the short term. As has been apparent in Operation Iraqi Freedom, PSCs can provide surge capacity: when chaos ensued after the collapse of the government in Iraq, the US and other coalition forces hired PSCs to bolster law and order efforts in the country – both by training Iraqi forces and by providing site security and personal protection to coalition facilities and personnel.[252] The initial use of DynCorp to field international civilian police also illustrates this benefit. Furthermore, as chapter four will point out, the private option for training also opens the way for new kinds of US influence – over direct contracts between US PSCs and foreign governments. The ability to license US firms to provide training to foreign countries directly offers a new tool that sometimes costs the US government nothing and thus enhances functional control.

Using private contractors changes the political process. Sending PSCs abroad causes fewer government decision makers to be involved than

---

[251] This was clear in the Army's contract with MPRI to do ROTC training. Also, a state department internal audit in 2000 noted that it is much more expensive to rely on contractors instead of Colombians in the anti-drug war. A DynCorp pilot receives $119,305 per yr as compared with $45,000 for contractors hired by the Colombian National Police. "Lawmakers Seek End to Anti-Drug Contractors in Peru, Colombia," *Fort Worth Star-Telegram*, 8 May 2001.

[252] Press reports of these activities have been rampant. For just two examples, see Catan and Fidler, "With Post-War Instability still a Pressing Concern"; Daragahi, "In Iraq, Private Contractors Lighten the Load on US Troops."

sending US troops would. The use of PSCs is often regarded as a lower political commitment that reduces the need to mobilize public support for foreign engagement activities. Indeed, congressional leaders and the public appear to be less aware, interested, and concerned about sending PSCs than sending US forces. The use of PSCs to conduct foreign military training makes decisions to use this kind of force abroad less visible and less transparent. It thus enhances the authority of individual decision makers in the executive branch and reduces the processes of inter-agency cooperation and institutional wrangling.

When the US uses PSCs staffed with retired US military personnel to accomplish military advice and training missions, these retired officers are well steeped in American military professionalism and appeal to the same values that their public counterparts would. In fact, one Deputy Assistant Secretary of Defense exclaimed, "MPRI is not a private company, it is an extension of the US government."[253] MPRI's work in the Balkans and Africa, particularly, appeared to reinforce the international values represented by military professionalism and thus the social control of force. When the US uses PSCs staffed with international personnel who have different professional backgrounds, however, social control is more likely to be eroded.

Furthermore, the relationship between these dimensions over time suggests the potential for friction among the mechanisms of control and between these mechanisms and existing US institutions. First, every time a military training mission is privatized, it sends a message to military personnel that training is not a core mission. The increasing reliance on the private sector for training makes it less likely that well-qualified people within the service will choose to do this task. Also, using private contractors to conduct military training invests in private rather than public capacity. As more training is privatized, there will be less of this capacity among military forces and more reliance on PSCs in the future, but less retired personnel to select from. Though this chapter has focused on training, the US uses PSCs for many other tasks – international civilian police, weapons system support, logistics support, and more. In each instance the use of the private sector over time decreases the likelihood that the public sector will retain (or gain) capacity in these arenas. The short run flexibility of private solutions may impede public innovation.

Second, the shift in influence over screening, selection, and oversight associated with privatization introduces a process that changes the institutional basis of future military professional development. While hiring retired military personnel well entrenched in professional networks may be seen to stabilize the immediate effect of privatization on the social control of force, it alters the process through which professional norms are created in the future. This is particularly the case when PSCs are hired to perform tasks closely related to the development of professionalism – like ROTC training, creating doctrine, foreign military training, and the like.[254] Outsourcing the educating and training of US forces loosens the hold of public organizations on the military profession. Because educating and training its own members are critical tasks for maintaining the profession's internal control system, outsourcing this mechanism may lead to less control of the profession on the part of public military professionals.[255]

The privatization of foreign military training poses a set of related issues. The importance of US military organizations is tied to their role in US defense. If training foreign armies plays a more significant role in the defense strategy of the US and more of this has been ceded to PSCs, the role of public forces in national defense has shrunk. Also, if one goal of foreign training is to further US contact, when PSCs do the job, this contact is with private entities rather than military officers. Furthermore, the model of civil–military relations the US is presenting for emulation by other countries is a model with a significant private component. Having companies that sell military training also opens the way for a new process by which military knowledge is shared and spread. Companies like MPRI, Cubic, or DynCorp offer military knowledge outside the structure of the US military. Their position outside the US government may give them a vantage point from which to offer different variants of knowledge that competes with the military's line. Or they simply may sell knowledge derived from the US military in a way that the military has little influence on (unclassified field manuals, for example, are in the public domain). Either way the process by which professional knowledge and norms spread is altered. To the degree that the US hires international PSCs with differing types of professional background, this change is likely to accelerate.

Third, relying on private rather than public forces promises to alter the value Americans (civilian and military) place on public military service in general.[256] As more and more of these jobs are contracted out,

---

[254] Deborah Avant, "Privatizing Military Training: a Challenge to US Army Professionalism," in Don M. Snider and Gayle L. Watkins, eds., *The Future of the Army Profession* (Boston: McGraw-Hill, 2002).
[255] Ibid.
[256] Feigenbaum and Henig, "Political Underpinnings of Privatization."

they are likely to be seen as less important or less a part of what governments do. This may have feedback effects on recruitment, retention, military structures, and military attitudes in general. Already there are tensions between active-duty personnel and PSC personnel surrounding differences in legal rights and responsibilities, representation of US policy, and inequities surrounding day-to-day job performance. Indeed, stresses between active-duty personnel and contractors are almost inevitable when the US government has contractors and active-duty personnel performing the same task.[257]

Finally, when tasks vital to US security goals are outsourced, the different policy process by which these tasks are accomplished is likely to yield different policy. When policy is created with fewer interests represented, fewer interests mobilized, and among those with a stake in the policy, it can open the way for what Gowa calls "political market failures" or the tendency for resource endowments to benefit special rather than general interests.[258] This can happen in a wide variety of ways – PSCs can report information that encourages training programs that are not worth their cost, PSCs can encourage relationships with governments that do not support US interests, can encourage investment in areas that do not serve US interests, etc. This also gives political officials leeway to make decisions that enhance their welfare or that of a segment of the polity rather than the polity as a whole. One of the results may be more adventurous policy than would otherwise be the case. If a leader can use force in a way that reduces or eliminates mobilizing troops, the visibility, sacrifice, and political cost of using force go down. If the costs of using force go down, all things being equal, force is more likely to be used.[259] Reducing the process of political mobilization required for action opens the way for leaders to take action more readily. Moreover, the private option reduces the incentives for politicians to

[257] Interview with Joe Collins, Deputy Assistant Secretary of Defense for Stability Operations, November 2003.

[258] Joanne Gowa, "Democratic States and International Disputes," *International Organization*, Vol. 49, No. 3 (summer 1995): 517. The general logic of market failures as applied to the political realm also underlies Williams' analysis. For other applications, see Robert Keohane, "The Demand for International Regimes," *International Organization* Vol. 36, No. 2 (spring 1982): 325–55.
Kenneth Oye, Robert J. Lieber; and Donald Rothchild, eds., *Eagle in a New World: American Grand Strategy in the Post-Cold War Era* (New York: Harper Collins, 1992).

[259] Exactly this logic is used in a recent Refugees International Report which claims that reducing the cost of intervention with the use of new military technology can increase the potential to intervene. See Clifford H. Bernath and David Gompart, *The Power to Protect: Using New Military Capabilities to Stop Mass Killing* (Washington, DC: Refugees International, July 2003).

build coalitions that support new policies, potentially leading to even less public support.

Some suggest this is the culmination of liberalism and will rationalize ideas and institutions in the American context, allowing the US to do what is in its "objective" interests despite the pressures of public opinion or the intransigence of the bureaucracy.[260] By reducing the political costs of action abroad, private options allow the US to pursue increases in its relative power and advantage the US relative to other countries that do not employ private options.[261] Others claim that the benefits the US has enjoyed domestically and abroad result from its democratic processes, which enhance policy stability and restraint.[262] These processes have been linked to effective international commitments and military effectiveness.[263] This private option may produce democratic deficits and reduce the benefits associated with democratic foreign policy.[264] Regardless of one's normative evaluation, privatization changes the processes for deciding on appropriate functions and generating social norms.

Whether the destabilization of this fit will lead to disruptive change, though, is unclear. The history of US defense procurement lends some insights to how a similar process has unfolded in the past. This history demonstrates that defense procurement costs more, delivers less, and often fails to enforce accountability.[265] The military industrial complex Eisenhower warned of is alive and well and so much a part of US politics that it is hardly noticed. As James Fallows points out, the F-22 Raptor plane, developed under George W. Bush's administration, will cost well over $100 million each and "the expense is mainly for measures that would allow the aircraft to penetrate a Soviet air defense system that

[260] This is the logic, of course, behind Theodore Lowi's classic analysis of the problem with American foreign policy. See Theodore Lowi, "Making Democracy Safe for the World: on Fighting the Next War," in G. John Ikenberry, ed., *American Foreign Policy: Theoretical Essays* (New York: HarperCollins, 1989). From a different perspective, the argument in David Shearer's analysis of the benefits of private military companies bears the same logic. See Shearer, *Private Armies.*
[261] See Cohen, "Defending America's Interests in the Twenty-First Century"; Philip Bobbitt, *The Shield of Achilles: War, Peace and the Course of History* (New York: Knopf, 2002), pp. 316–32.
[262] Alexander George, "Domestic Constraints on Regime Change in US Foreign Policy: the Need for Policy Legitimacy," in G. John Ikenberry, ed., *American Foreign Policy: Theoretical Essays* (New York: HarperCollins, 1989), pp. 583–608.
[263] Charles Lipson, *Reliable Partners: How Democracies Have Made a Separate Peace* (Princeton: Princeton University Press, 2003); Lake, "Powerful Pacifists." See also Immanuel Kant, *Perpetual Peace* (New York: Columbia, 1939); Doyle, "Kant, Liberal Legacies, and Foreign Affairs."
[264] Silverstein, *Private Warriors.*
[265] Donahue, *Privatization Decision*, p. 102.

disappeared more than a decade ago."[266] In what some have described as the most corrosive effect of the military industrial complex, soldiers anticipate their future jobs as consultants to this industry when making decisions while they are still in uniform.[267] This phenomenon, though, has generated little political controversy.[268] Few criticize the fact that the US spends as much as the next twenty-four countries combined – even though the expenditures are hard to match with the nature of the threat to the US.[269] Whether due to the strong performance of these weapons systems in practice (albeit against extremely weak enemies) in the conflicts of the 1990s and early part of the twenty-first century or the fact that the defense industry generates employment opportunities in the US, Americans appear resigned to (if not at ease with) the role of the private sector in procurement.[270] Indeed, some have argued that the private defense industry in the US generated support for greater defense expenditures that enhanced US security during the Cold War.[271]

It is possible to imagine a similar process in the outsourcing of services. Indeed, since the turn of the twenty-first century large weapons companies have purchased a number of the defense service companies, simultaneously suggesting that these companies see financial growth in services and extending their sophisticated lobbying techniques to the

[266] Ibid.

[267] Ibid., p. 48. See also, David Vandergriff, *Path to Victory: a Critical Analysis of the Military Personnel System and how it Undermines Readiness* (Novato: Presido Press, 2002).

[268] Partly this has come about through the co-optation of congress. Intriguingly, the growth of congressional involvement in the procurement of weapons was not a brake but an accelerator to this process. The parceling of defense contracts to the districts of key Congress members led Congress to be a key partner in building weapons systems that benefit their constituencies rather than exercising judgment about the security needs of the country.

[269] James Fallows, "Whatever Became of the Military–Industrial Complex?" *Foreign Policy* (November/December 2002): 47.

[270] See Stephen Biddle, "Victory Misunderstood: What the Gulf War Tells us About the Future of Conflict," *International Security* Vol. 21, No. 2 (autumn 1996): 139–79; Daryl Press, "Lessons from Ground Conflict in the Gulf: the Impact of Training and Technology," *International Security* Vol. 22, No. 2 (autumn 1997): 137–46, for a debate on the importance of weaponry for Gulf War. Biddle's analysis does not dispute the performance of weapons, only their importance relative to military skill.

For arguments about the employment in defense industries and related political support for defense spending, see Kenneth Mayer, *The Political Economy of Defense Contracting* (New Haven: Yale University Press, 1991). See also Markusen and Costigan, *Arming the Future*; Peter Trubowitz, *Defining the National Interest: Conflict and Change in American Foreign Policy* (Chicago: University of Chicago Press, 1998).

[271] See Dwight R. Lee, "Public Goods, Politics, and Two Cheers for the Military Industrial Complex," in R. Higgs, ed., *Arms, Politics, and the Economy: Historical and Contemporary Perspectives* (New York: Homes and Meier, 1990), pp. 22–36. See also Harvey M. Sapolsky and Eugene Gholtz, "Restructuring the US Defense Industry," *International Security* Vol. 24, No. 3 (winter 1999/2000): 5–51.

security services sector.[272] If these companies can convince Congress of their political benefits and spread the economic benefits widely enough in the US, it is possible that the privatization of services may follow in the footpath of the weapons industry – generating new services at increased cost but not stimulating a political backlash.

The tensions mentioned above, however, also hold the potential to induce instability in the relationship between the American polity and the control of force. If changes in the core capacity of the military lead to a highly visible role for PSCs, congress and the electorate might be increasingly uncomfortable with their use and see associated policy as less legitimate. The blurring of lines between the military and PSCs may also call into question the esteem with which Americans view the military, changing the value placed on military service, causing difficulties with military recruitment and/or retention, and diminishing US military effectiveness. Any of these could spur disruption and change that could feed into a disintegrative challenge to the control of force in the US.

Comparisons

These cases suggest that well-functioning states with capable forces do suffer some functional control losses when they privatize advice and training. Though private contractors offer some flexibility, they are often more expensive than their public counterpart, less responsive to government direction, or both. As expected, the professionalism of retired officers lends stability to the values represented in training under contract to the US even when these services are outsourced – thus maintaining the integration of this task with larger international values, though as standards for professionalism are less clear, this effect is less pronounced. Furthermore, private delivery alters political processes. The political changes that accompany contracting make it easier to move ahead with advice and training missions in ways that some (particularly those in the executive branch) regard as a benefit even as it shifts control and reduces transparency in ways that others regard as costs.

States with less capable forces pay more for services, but gain more effective forces, often resulting in short term functional gains. In weak states, PSCs are also more likely to introduce international values and precipitate potential improvement in the social control of force – though

---

[272] See, for instance, the analysis of DynCorp contracts and CSC profitability in Alex Pham, "Federal Contracts Help CSC Post Solid Net Income Gain," *Los Angeles Times*, 18 May 2004.

the lasting effect of improvements in social control is highly variable. The political changes that accompany contracting out in weak states are quite dramatic – they eviscerated Tudjman's opposition in Croatia and empowered a parallel force and led to a coup in Sierra Leone. In both Sierra Leone and Croatia, the ability to use PSCs required financial backing and thus greater political input from external actors, though in Sierra Leone these actors were commercial and in Croatia, they were generally from the US and other governments.

How the dimensions of control add up and fit together in the two weak-state cases varies – with important consequences for the reinforcing process of control, the military effectiveness, and state building in the two countries. In Sierra Leone, the functional gains were short lived, complicated by the changes in political control and while PSC personnel may have behaved in greater accordance with international values than the local forces, there is little evidence that interaction with PSCs had a durable effect on the behavior of local forces. Aside from brief respites in fighting, then, contracts with PSCs did little to help the government consolidate sovereign power, improve long term military effectiveness, or enhance the integration of force with international social values. Croatia provides a more positive outcome. The functional control gains came alongside a long term and sustained effort to transform the values and political structures surrounding the organization of forces. Even though the political redistribution initially solidified Tudjman's power, the country moved relatively easily to nascent democracy after his death and its military progress was dubbed successful enough to be included in the US PfP program.

Differences in the source of financing (and associated interests), the involvement of state institutions (and the relationship of those trained with the state), along with differences in professional networks of the PSCs that worked in the two countries, the focus of the contract on professional norms, and the length of time the PSC spent in the country are all important in explaining the different effects. All of these affected the degree to which control mechanisms worked together or not in these cases. In Croatia, the US government underwrote some of the expenses, the money was funneled through state institutions, and the PSC worked exclusively with the Croatian military – all of which consolidated authority in the state. Also, the contract specified attention to military professionalism and was carried out by a company with strong professional ties in the US. Finally, the overarching conditionality requirements to be a part of the PfP program and eventually NATO issued consequential incentives to political leaders that reinforced military professional norms.

Table 3.2. *Effects of private provision of advice and training on the control of force*

Case	State strength	Functional control	Political control	Social control	Mechanisms	Fit?
United states	Strong	Mixed • Increased cost with little improved performance • Greater flexibility	Changed • Advantaged executive • Lowered transparency • New actors via agenda setting influence for PSC	Mixed • US PSCs have ongoing ties with military professional values and networks • PSCs in Iraq represent a broader mix with fewer ties to military professional values and networks	Chafing • Questions about transparency and foreign policy • Questions about adventurous foreign policy (left and right) • Tension between public and private forces • Uncertain process of developing military norms	Uncertain • Private military advice and training has provided surge capacities in engagement and the war on terrorism but potentially unsettled a reinforcing process of control over force

Table 3.2. (cont.)

Croatia	Weak	Increased • Improved performance • Initial increased cost offset by US aid over time	Changed • Advantaged president • Advantaged US • Lowered transparency	Improved • Increased integration with international military professional values • PSC personnel closely linked to professional networks in US	Reinforcing • Consolidation of central government control • Professional development goals in contract • Complimented by international incentives (NATO)	Enhancing • Private military advice and training laid the groundwork for the reinforcing process of control over force
Sierra Leone	Weak	Increased • Improved performance • Increased cost offset by private financiers	Changed • Advantaged financiers • New (or enhanced) actors: PSCs, mining interests, CDF	Not improved • Short-run increase in integration with international military professional values • PSC personnel weakly linked to professional networks in RSA and UK	Chafing • CDF vs. RSLMF • Commercial financing vs. state control of violence	Eroding • Private military advice and training delivered to the state did not lead to the development of a reinforcing process of control over force

In Sierra Leone, while the government paid for PSC services, the payment was financed through commercial mining companies. The government did not receive and redirect the money; instead it went directly from the commercial sector to the PSCs. Also, both EO and Sandline's work with the civil militias worked against a consolidation of power in the government. All of this led to a diffusion of control over violence in the country. The short-term nature of the contracts, their lack of attention to military professionalism, and the weaker links between (particularly) PSCs and associated professional military networks decreased the chance that contracts would lead to a reinforcing process of control. Finally, there was no overarching international structure for inducing proper political behavior in Sierra Leone.

In the US, outsourcing advice and training yields some short run benefits, but opens many possibilities for tension and change. The use of PSCs opens the possibility that American forces will not contain the capacity for key functional tasks. Outsourcing training also opens the way for changes in the hold of public institutions on the development of military norms, changes in the value attached to military service, and changes in policy resulting from a different policy process. Different people will undoubtedly come to different conclusions about the costs and benefits of this change, however, and the jury is still out on whether this will disrupt the existing "fit" or be folded into a long-standing process of control.

4   Dilemmas in state regulation of private security exports

In the modern era, state control over force has not only meant control of the force they field, but also control over the force that emanates from their territories.[1] States have acted to control the violent activities of their citizens outside their borders, restricting their actions on behalf of other states and regulating trade in the instruments of violence. This chapter investigates the impact of the market for security services on states' control of the force that emanates from their territories. Optimists suggest that using well-established norms will allow states to control the export of security services and argue that these exports provide a flexible new tool by which to generate state security. Pessimists, however, worry that the export of these services will frustrate states' consequential controls and that export industries may influence the articulation of state interests in ways that undermine "national" security.

The literature on the arms trade provides some useful context. Analysts of arms exports have recognized that industries that produce tools of war present states with dilemmas. Some of the same dilemmas are articulated in the debate between optimists and pessimists about the export of security services.[2] On the one hand, PSCs draw on the skills learned in their state's military and share skills along with information about effective military organization with their employer state in ways that their home state might want to control. Also, a company's behavior might affect the reputation of its parent state or implicate it in conflicts to which it is not a party. To the degree that a PSC's activities enhance the capacities of future enemies, are at odds with government policy, or implicate the government in conflicts, they risk a decrease in functional control – as would similar exports of arms.[3]

---

[1] Thomson, *Mercenaries, Pirates, and Sovereigns*; Avant, "From Mercenary to Citizen Armies"; Herbst, "Regulation of Private Security Forces."

[2] Krause, *Arms and the State*; William Keller, *Arm in Arm: the Political Economy of the Global Arms Trade* (New York: Basic Books, 1995); O'Prey, *Arms Export Challenge*.

[3] In the seventeenth and eighteenth centuries states were implicated in conflicts and even fired upon by non-state purveyors of force. Thomson, *Mercenaries, Pirates, and Sovereigns*, pp. 43–68.

This industry, though, is also a mechanism by which states can garner additional wealth and power, and therefore something they may want to encourage. Trade in services can enhance a state's influence abroad. A strong security services industry – built in part by exports – can also be used by the home state. Furthermore, commercial sales of security services can influence relationships abroad without necessarily implicating the state – opening the way for a new tool for executing foreign policy. To the degree that PSCs further their government's policy abroad, bring income home, or advantage other industries abroad, they can offer increases in functional control – again, as would arms exports.

States avoided these dilemmas in the security services sector in much of the modern era by harnessing the services of their citizens to deliver security through state organizations – military organizations, alliances, and international organizations. Indeed the somewhat surprising paucity of regulation surrounding the export of services (as opposed to arms) may be a result of the assumption that military services would be monopolized by states – an assumption that Janice Thomson and others have argued became a fundamental feature of the sovereign state system.[4]

As states looked increasingly to the market for security services in the 1990s, however, these dilemmas returned. Furthermore, as the literature on globalization and the service sector tells us, these dilemmas have been exacerbated by particular characteristics within the current market and industry that decrease the usefulness (or increase the costs) of state regulation.[5] Particularly, the market's increasingly transnational character – that is neither supply nor demand fit within state borders – and the glut of supply – if demand cannot be satisfied by one supplier, there are many others in line – increase the costs of regulation. Meanwhile, the industry's low capitalization, fluid structure, and the lack of commitment to territory – a PSC frustrated with one state's regulation can simply move abroad, or melt and reconstitute itself differently to avoid it – decrease the usefulness of the kinds of authoritative controls often associated with states.[6]

States, however, need not only rely upon authoritative controls. The market offers states a different kind of tool for control: consumer demand. To the degree that states purchase security services from the market, they can both affect the behavior of PSCs with their

[4] Ibid.
[5] Porter, *Competitive Advantage of Nations*, pp. 657–82.
[6] Herbst, "Regulation of Private Security Forces"; Porter, *Competitive Advantage of Nations*, pp. 239–76; Drucker, "Trade Lessons From the World Economy"; Feketekuty, *International Trade in Services*; Kostecki, *Marketing Strategies for Services*.

procurement and give firms incentives to abide by authoritative controls. When the government is a consumer, PSCs may choose to abide by regulation to preserve their government contracts. Firms may also abide by regulation if they believe that doing so is important to enhance their competitive advantage over other PSCs or to attract other customers. Furthermore, through consumer demand states can affect the values to which PSCs attend and the degree to which they move toward or away from the military professional model. State consumption thus provides a social control mechanism as well.

The institutional synthesis proposed in chapter two, however, alerts us to the trade-offs facing states as they decide how best to control the export of security services. First, strategies to maximize functional control through market mechanisms also change political control. The conditions most favorable to government influence over the behavior of their PSCs abroad also redistribute power over foreign policy making and enhance the influence of PSCs in the foreign policy process. Thus the first trade-off states face is between influencing the behavior of PSCs abroad and maintaining the integrity of political processes of foreign policy making.

Second, strategies that maximize an individual state's influence on the values PSCs attend to by purchasing their services also undermine the notion that states, collectively, monopolize the legitimate use of violence. The conditions most favorable for an individual state's effect on the values PSCs attend to also suggest a model of defense that holds a role for private entities and alters the process by which professional knowledge and norms develop. This is the second trade-off, between maintaining the value surrounding the role of the state in security and influencing professional military values PSCs attend to. Though states may manage these trade-offs in different ways, no state should be able to avoid them altogether.

In this chapter, I examine how the three largest exporters of military services: the US, the UK, and South Africa have managed these dilemmas. Each has chosen a different strategy – but each has also experienced associated consequences for government influence of PSCs abroad, the preservation of political processes surrounding foreign policy, and the values represented in the process.[7]

---

[7] Some states have not sought to control the violent actions of their citizens abroad. Similar to Palan and Abbott's category of states that are "not in the game," the incomplete and fragile nature of these states makes them incapable and political incentives make them uninterested in regulation – except as such regulation might generate personal payoffs. For the most part, the lack of capacity also makes these states less sought-after suppliers of security services – though some do supply the "down-market"

The United States

The US government's strategy is most likely to maximize functional control of PSCs abroad. The US sees PSCs as an opportunity, not a threat and has sought to use PSCs to the government's advantage. The success of this strategy has been enhanced by the US government's procurement of private security services. In the US PSCs appear to work in concert with US policy and members of the US government report satisfaction with their behavior. The mechanisms that government officials use to affect the behavior of US firms, however, accrue mainly to the executive branch and present oversight hurdles even there. Furthermore, the participation of PSCs as both contractors to the US and contractors to other governments has opened the way for PSCs to use information to reshape agendas within government, affecting foreign policy decisions on a country-by-country basis. The process through which PSCs are influenced, then, has re-allocated power within government and opened additional avenues for private influence over foreign policy. Furthermore, while the US government's segment of market demand has given it a large influence on the values PSCs profess, the fact that the US government purchases security services from the market undermines the overarching norm that defense is best served through public institutions.

The market for US PSCs and the range of providers and services

With threats diminished in the 1990s US forces were downsized, but not reorganized to meet the demands of new engagements.[8] As documented in chapters one and three, to cope with the resulting stress on US forces, policy makers increasingly turned to private contractors. The Commission on Roles and Missions set up by Congress in 1993 to recommend ways to eliminate duplication among the branches of the military focused on privatization.[9] A Defense Science Board (DSB) Report in 1995 suggested that the Pentagon could save up to $12 billion annually by 2002 if it contracted out all support functions except actual

---

demand for protection among illegal commodities such as drugs, armaments, and persons. See Palan and Abbott, *State Strategies*, pp. 185–98. See also Christopher Clapham, *Private Patronage and Public Power: Political Clientelism in the Modern State* (London: Pinter, 1986).

[8] US White House, "A National Security Strategy of Engagement and Enlargement," Washington, DC: The White House, February 1995; McNaugher, "Army and Operations Other Than War."

[9] Bradley Graham, "Consensus is Building to Privatize Defense Functions," *Washington Post*, 20 March 1995.

warfighting.[10] Though the cost savings associated with outsourcing many missions are not well documented and many are less sanguine about reducing costs,[11] outsourcing has been common.[12] In 2001, the Pentagon's contracted workforce exceeded civilian defense department employees for the first time.[13]

The US government purchases a wide range of services from PSCs. Chapter three looked at advice and training missions in some detail, but that is the tip of the iceburg.[14] Site security is provided at West Point by Alutiiq-Wackenhut,[15] ICI provides transport to US forces in Africa, and KBR has the contract for logistics support generally – the Logistics Civil Augmentation Program or LOGCAP, under which it does everything from fixing trucks to warehousing ammunition to peeling potatoes, doing the laundry, and building bases abroad.[16] PSCs provide operational support for weapons and other military systems in the US, abroad and during conflicts.[17] The American use of PSCs in Iraq provides the most recent and extensive example of the broad range of services the US is willing to contract for – from training the police

[10] Vago Muradian, "DOD Can Save Billions By Outsourcing Work, DSB Says," *Defense Daily* Vol. 193, No. 1 (1 October 1996).

[11] See Gary Pagliano, "Privatizing DOD Functions through Outsourcing: a Framework for Discussions," CRS Report 96–700F (6 August 1996). He states, "Since many outsourcing efforts to reduce DOD's infrastructure costs are relatively new, little information or data exists to evaluate their efficacy with any degree of accuracy. Even with such information, it will be difficult to measure most outsourcing initiatives because of DOD's numerous and incompatible management systems."

[12] See, for instance, "Improving the Combat Edge through Outsourcing," DOD Report, March 1996. See also, Dr. Paul Kaminski (the Under Secretary for Defense Acquisition and Technology), "Meeting the Defense Modernization Challenge," speech to the AFCEA Spring Gala, City Tavern, Georgetown, 22 April 1996 and DOD, "Improving the Combat Edge through Outsourcing," Address to the Atlanta XXII conference, Atlanta, Georgia, 24 April 1996. See also reports such as the Report of the Tail to Tooth Commission chaired by Warren Rudman and Joash Weston and press reports: Sean D. Naylor, "Civilians Could Save Troop 'Spaces' at Training Center," *Army Times*, 3 August 1998; Steven Saint "NORAD Outsources," *Colorado Springs Gazette* 1 September 2000; James Murphy, "DOD Outsources $500m in Spare Parts Work," *PlanetGov.com*, 29 September 2000.

[13] Ellen Nakashima, "Pentagon Hires Out More Than In," *Washington Post*, 3 April 2001, p. A19.

[14] See chapter three; Larry Grossman, "The Privatization of Military Training," *Government Executive* (March 1989); David Isenberg, *Soldiers of Fortune, Ltd.: a Profile of Today's Private Sector Corporate Mercenary Firms*, Center for Defense Information Monograph (Washington, DC: CDI, 1997); www.mpri.com; "Private US Companies Train Around the World," *US News and World Report* (8 February 1997).

[15] "Private Guards to Take Over at West Point," *Associated Press*, 21 January 2004.

[16] Wynn, "Managing the Logistics-Support Contract in the Balkans Theater"; GAO Report, "Contingency Operations," p. 4; Nelson, *Business of Peace*, p. 91. See also Baum, "Nation Builders for Hire."

[17] Colonel Steven J. Zamparelli, "What Have We Signed Up For?" in *Issues and Strategy 2000: Contractors on the Battlefield, Air Force Journal of Logistics*, (December 1999).

force[18] to training the army[19] to protecting US officials, guarding buildings, and conducting interrogations. US contracts with PSCs, though hardly new, grew markedly in the post-Cold War era and have continued to grow in the context of the war on terrorism.[20]

Growth in the US government's demand for these services, however, has been complemented by a newer demand for military and other security services from foreign governments. In the mid-1970s Vinnell became the first US firm to sell military training directly to a foreign government, when in 1975 they signed a $77 million contract to train Saudi Arabian Forces to defend Saudi oil fields.[21] At the end of the Cold War, this foreign market boomed. European and other western states provide one part of this client base. For example, American firms such as KBR and the Carlisle Group have contracts with the British and Australian governments to provide a variety of military support services.[22] Non-western states eager for US expertise in defense organization, civil–military relations, and military professionalization offer another layer of demand. For instance, Hungary hired Cubic to help upgrade its military to NATO requirements, MPRI has contracts with Croatia and Equatorial Guinea to provide military advice and training, and MPRI worked for the Bosnian defense department to train its military under the Dayton Accords.[23] The range of services purchased from US PSCs by foreign governments and private entities matches the broad range purchased by the US government.

Finally, at the Cold War's end, a non-governmental market also grew as private companies, IOs, and INGOs sought to accomplish their goals in unstable parts of the world. Corporate, IO, and INGO consumers

[18] See Erin E. Arvedlund, "Privatized Warriors," *Barron's* (8 August 2003). See also CPA website, http://www.cpa-iraq.org/security.html.
[19] BBC, "US Firm to Rebuild Iraqi Army"; Robert Burns, "New Iraqi Army to Cost $2 Billion to Build," *The Associated Press*, 18 September 2003.
[20] The first official statement on contracting, the 1954 Budget Bureau Bulletin 55–4 (revised in 1955, 1957, and 1960), was renamed OMB Circular A-76 in 1966. It is still in effect but was revised again in 1967, 1979, 1983, and 1999. It states that government agencies should seek to obtain products and services through the private sector except in cases of national interest. See Althouse, "Contractors on the Battlefield"; http://www.whitehouse.gov/omb/circulars/a076.pdf.
[21] Kim Willenson with Nicholas Proffitt, "Persian Gulf: this Gun for Hire," *Newsweek*, 24 February 1975, p. 30.
[22] Anthony Bianco and Stephanie Anderson Forest, "Outsourcing War: an Inside Look at Brown and Root," *Business Week* (15 September 2003); "US Firm to take over state defense group," *Financial Times*, 5 September 2002; "Is Big Business Bad for Our Boys?" *Guardian*, 2 March 2003; http://www.mod.uk/business/index.html; http://www.halliburton.com/gov_ops/sl0252.jsp.
[23] http://www.cubic.com/ (accessed 15 December 2000); http://www.mpri.com/subchannels/int_europe.html.

purchased a more limited array of services including logistics, site security, crime prevention, and intelligence. ICI Oregon has worked for the World Food Program and commercial firms, as well as for the US government and foreign governments.[24] KBR supported UN operations in Haiti and Rwanda.[25] US Defense Systems offers support to the UN as well as to US embassies.[26] Other companies like Total Security Services International specialize in providing services to the private sector.[27]

In the US, the same companies that sell military services to foreign governments also sell services to the US government and US contracts are lucrative. The fact that PSCs sell similar services to the US government that they sell abroad (combined with the fact that the US government is a very good customer) gives American PSCs a market incentive to pay attention to US policy and to stay in tune with government regulatory initiatives.

Regulatory environment

The International Transfer of Arms Regulations, ITAR (part of the Arms Export Control Act), governs services sold to another government by PSCs.[28] The legislation was designed specifically to deal with the functional control dilemma outlined above. By regulating what is sold to other governments, the US hoped to insure that arms sales would further the government's interest. The clause on services was originally intended to license the kind of training that frequently went along with the sale of complex weapons systems. It provided a convenient regulatory structure, however, as security service exports boomed in their own right.

The process of licensing military service exports uses standard tools to enforce general principles – that the US should export these services to reliable countries that abide by the norms the US supports. The Department of State's Office of Defense Trade Controls oversees the

[24] http://icioregon.com/.
[25] Nelson, *Business for Peace*, p. 91.
[26] Thomas Boyatt, "Privatization of OOTW" paper presented at the "Feed 'Em or Fight 'Em" symposium sponsored by the Patterson School of Diplomacy and International Commerce and the US Army War College, University of Kentucky, 22–24 September 1995, pp. 54–55.
[27] http://www.totalsecurityservices.com/.
[28] A "defense service" is defined as assistance, technical data, or training related to military units. This regulation does not apply to law enforcement or sales of security advice to private entities. "International Traffic in Arms Regulations," (22 CFR 120–130) as of 1 April 2001 (United States Department of State, Bureau of Political–Military Affairs, Office of Defense Trade Controls).

150   The Market for Force

process.[29] Before a license is granted, the appropriate regional office, political–military bureau, desk office for the country, and others (such as the Bureau of Democracy, Human Rights, and Labor) are invited to comment. There are different standards for different kinds of services. Lethal training is more closely scrutinized than non-lethal training.

In the event that a country with no restrictions wants to buy non-lethal training, the license should be readily approved. On the other extreme, a contract with a country listed on the State Department Embargo Chart should not receive a license. When in-between cases arise, a variety of offices make their case and the Assistant Secretary makes a final decision.[30] Even once a license is issued, the export of security services falls under general guidance for arms exports. For instance, MPRI was issued a license to sell training in Angola, but its work was stopped before it began due to an informal policy hold.[31]

This process appears to fold the export of security services into a well-designed system for insuring that these services are consistent with US goals. The idiosyncratic nature of the licensing process, however, combined with inadequate and sometimes problematic oversight means that the US government may not have good information about what an individual PSC is doing in a particular country – potentially leading to a decrease in functional control. In its actual working the process is somewhat ad hoc. The Defense and State Department offices that have input into the process vary from contract to contract. For instance, when MPRI first applied for a license to export services to Equatorial Guinea, the inter-agency process only included the Africa desk at the Department of State. When it applied for the same license some time later, the Office of Democracy, Human Rights, and Labor was also consulted.[32]

Furthermore, there is no formal reporting or oversight process required by the ITAR.[33] Once a license is issued, there is no formal

---

[29] US Congress, "Arms Export Control Act," (P.L. 90–629) *Legislation in Foreign Relations Through 1999*, Vol. I-A (Washington, DC: Government Printing Office, 2000); US State Department, "International Traffic in Arms Regulations." Companies must be registered with the US government before they can apply for a license. In 2004, the Department of State announced a new, electronic licensing system for defense exports – D-Trade. See http://www.pmdtc.org/.
[30] Interviews with State Department Officials, July 1999.
[31] Ibid.; interview with Ed Soyster, MPRI, April 1999.
[32] Ibid.
[33] Interview with State Department Official, August 1999. Under Section 40A of the Arms Export Control Act, there is a requirement that the Office of Defense Trade Controls monitor the end use of licensed transactions. This, so called, "Blue Lantern Program" did result in 410 checks in FY 2001 and 71 unfavorable determinations. See "End Use Monitoring Report for FY 2001," available at http://pmdtc.org/docs/End_Use_FY2001.pdf (as of October 2002).

process by which to insure that what was licensed was really what was delivered.[34] In its day-to-day work, of course, the State Department monitors the behavior of other countries. If a country commits egregious acts, the State Department can freeze contracts (just as it can freeze weapons transfers). In some cases, for instance the "Train and Equip" program in Bosnia, significant oversight structures are put in place. In others, there are no reporting or oversight mechanisms aside from routine monitoring by embassy staff. And sometimes licenses are granted to companies doing work in countries where the US has no embassy.[35]

Also, those nominally responsible for overseeing the behavior of PSCs in the State Department often do not see themselves as overseers. "When asked whether his office would pursue the employees of AirScan who had coordinated air strikes in Colombia that killed civilians, including nine children, one State Department official responded, 'our job is to protect Americans, not investigate Americans.'"[36] Similar difficulties come up in the relationship between the defense attachés that conduct monitoring in many cases and the retired military personnel that staff PSCs. In several cases, defense attachés have found themselves "overseeing" past bosses – and feeling quite uncomfortable with the idea.[37] This, too, impedes the oversight process.

The way service exports are regulated also redistributes political control over policy. The licensing procedures feed information to (and ask for advice from) the executive branch. In the process State Department offices and sometimes offices within DOD are invited to comment. Only if the license is for a contract of more than $50 million in services, however, is Congress notified before the license is approved. The first Vinnell contract with Saudi Arabia was for over $50 million, required congressional notification, and generated a lot of controversy. Since that time contracts have often been written for less than $50 million. There is nothing to prevent a company from selling several separate contracts for services to avoid the $50 million bar. Though there has been periodic criticism of PSCs from Congress in the wake of particular scandals, most of this activity stays below congressional radar.[38]

---

[34] Interview with Ed Soyster, MPRI; interview with State Department official, August 1999.
[35] Though a nearby embassy would take charge, the oversight in these situations is likely to be minimal.
[36] Singer, *Corporate Warriors*, p. 239.
[37] Interview with former defense attaché, June 1998.
[38] Representative Jan Schakowsky (D, IL) introduced legislation to restrict the use of PSCs and legislation was introduced to prohibit funding of private contractors for

The control trade-off

PSC employees express attention to the goals of US foreign policy when describing their sales to other countries. ICI Oregon touts its work for a multi-national peacekeeping force in Liberia as working toward stability in the region that enhances US goals.[39] MPRI claims that its contracts with countries like Croatia and Equatorial Guinea carry out US policy at no cost to US taxpayers.[40] Those working for PSCs say they operate within received standards of civil–military relations and further US interests abroad.[41] Indeed, PSC employees express beliefs that their work furthers US interests in the world – and free of charge because other countries pay the bill.[42]

Government officials – particularly at the upper levels of the executive branch – profess happiness with PSC behavior in their contracts with other governments abroad.[43] US military personnel also often have a favorable view of companies like MPRI, though it varies from contract to contract. US Army personnel reported enthusiastic support for MPRI's work in the lead up to Operation Iraqi Freedom, but there were more stresses between active duty Army personnel and MPRI in the Balkans and Colombia.[44] Many claim that PSCs give US policy makers more flexible foreign policy tools. The fact that PSCs like MPRI exist opens the way for the US to affect military capacities abroad without sending US forces – or even US money. The ability of the US to license a private firm to train foreign military forces or offer other kinds of security services abroad opens the potential for "foreign policy by proxy."[45] Many in the executive branch regard this as a net functional gain – a new tool in the US foreign policy quiver.

As discussed in chapter three, MPRI's contract with Croatia is an example of this new tool for US governmental influence. When Croatia and MPRI signed a contract in September of 1994 and the State Department licensed the project, the US wanted to change the Balkan game. Senior State Department officials admitted that Croatia became a

military or police work in the Andean region following the mistaken shooting down of a missionary plane in Peru. Neither made it out of committee. Lora Lumpe, "Special Report: US Foreign Military Training," *Foreign Policy in Focus* (February 2002): 20.
[39] http://icioregon.com/nomination.htm.
[40] Interview with Ed Soyster and Carl Vuono, 27 October 2000.
[41] Interview with General Carl Vuono, 27 October 2000.
[42] Interviews with personnel working for MPRI.
[43] Based on over thirty interviews at the Pentagon and Department of State between 1998 and 2002. Upper levels refers to Deputy Assistant Secretary and above.
[44] Mark H. Milstein, "GIs in Gym Suits," *Soldier of Fortune* Vol. 23, No. 5 (May 1998): 67; interview with retired Army officer who had served in Bosnia, 10 April 2002.
[45] Ken Silverstein quotes Dan Nelson. See Silverstein, "Privatizing War."

de facto ally – that arms flowed in despite the embargo and top retired American generals were allowed to advise the Croatian Army.[46] Richard Holbrook recounts the contents of a note passed to him by Bob Frasure before his death that said, "We 'hired' these guys to be our junkyard dogs because we were desperate. Now we need to control them . . ."[47] MPRI's mere presence was evidence of this "alliance." It changed the strategic environment in Croatia, provided benefits to Tudjman in his effort to consolidate political power,[48] and boosted Croatian Army morale.[49] Finally, MPRI presence provided to Milošević a signal of American commitment to Tudjman – some have argued that Serbs in the Krajina put up less resistance once they realized that Milošević was not going to back them up with JNA forces.[50] Croatian military successes that followed changed events on the ground such that strategic bombing by NATO could push the Serbs to the negotiating table – the results of which were the Dayton Accords.[51] By licensing MPRI, the US retained its official neutral status while changing events on the ground in the direction favored by the US government.[52]

Even in the Croatian case, though, there are some potential long-term functional costs to this choice. PSC contracts with foreign governments frequently lead to contracts funded by the US government. MPRI remained working in Croatia, but the US gradually took over the bill. As described in chapter three, there are also numerous potential functional losses associated with private delivery of foreign military training – policy is less responsive to changes in US goals and both PSCs and host country governments gain greater influence on US decisions – potentially leading to continued funding for failing programs.

The use of PSC exports as a foreign policy tool also changes political control over force. First, the influence of the government on these exports is linked to its market demand – and as we saw in the previous chapter, government consumption alone redistributes political control.

---

[46] Cohen, "US Cooling Ties with Croatia."
[47] See Richard Holbrooke, To End A War (New York: Modern Library, 1999), p. 73.
[48] Vankovska, "Privatization of Security."
[49] Zarate, "The Emergence of a New Dog of War"; interview with Pentagon Official, January 2000, April 2002.
[50] Some have suggested that Tudjman and Milošević made a deal: little Serb resistance in Krajina in return for Tudjman's support for Milošević in Bosnia. See Vankovska, "Privatization of Security," p. 20.
[51] Ibid., pp. 72–73.
[52] Even those who refuse to admit any MPRI influence on the Croatian Army during Operation Storm nonetheless state that MPRI allowed the US to influence events on the ground when it would have been politically untenable to use US troops for such a task. Interview with Pentagon official, June 1999; interview with Pentagon official, January 2000; interview with Pentagon official, April 2002.

But the flexible new tool offered by PSC contracts with foreign governments furthers this redistribution. First, it evades processes that give Congress checks on executive power. Congress has little information about most export contracts and few consequential tools with which to exert its influence. The process also reduces the amount of information the electorate is likely to have about foreign policy and the overall transparency of foreign policy. If a company like MPRI violates the terms of its license in a country like Croatia under informal executive branch guidance, there is a good chance that no one who could make a fuss would find out. It may be that the government enhanced the capacity of its "junkyard dog" in Croatia and altered the environment in the Balkans in ways that evaded public and congressional scrutiny because MPRI was there to help. MPRI's presence and likely effect was not widely noticed. The new policy tool is flexible precisely because it avoids established processes.

Second, PSC exports open the way for PSC influence (and foreign influence) over the process by which foreign policy interests are defined.[53] Take MPRI's contract with Equatorial Guinea as an example. When MPRI first requested a license to evaluate Equatorial Guinea's defense department and need for a coastguard in 1998, the regional affairs office for Africa at the State Department rejected the request because of Equatorial Guinea's poor human rights record.[54] Officials from MPRI then visited the Assistant Secretary for African Affairs and congressional members to suggest looking at the license from a different perspective.[55] There are benefits, MPRI argued, to "engaging" with a country rather than punishing it; in the case of Equatorial Guinea engagement would foster better behavior (fewer human rights abuses) in the future and enhance US (as opposed to French) oil interests, especially given that Equatorial Guinea was going to hire someone (if not MPRI, it could be a less savory company or one less interested in the needs of American companies abroad).[56] These arguments, coming from esteemed, high level (albeit retired) military officers and reflecting a deep understanding of the ins and outs of American defense policy, had an impact.[57] When the application was submitted again, it was approved by the regional office but held up in the office of Democracy,

---

[53] Silverstein, *Private Warriors*.
[54] Interview with Ed Soyster, MPRI, 1 December 1998.
[55] Ibid.
[56] Several US oil companies, including Exxon and Chevron, have discovered significant petroleum reserves off the coast of Equatorial Guinea. See Ken Silverstein, "US Oil Politics in the 'Kuwait of Africa,'" *Nation* (22 April 2002).
[57] Interview with State Department Official, January 1999.

Human Rights, and Labor. Again, MPRI went to visit and explain their case, to the Assistant Secretary, to more members of Congress, and officials at Democracy, Human Rights, and Labor.[58] In the spring of 2000, the contract was approved – on the basis of a different set of guidelines than it was originally rejected.[59] One may find MPRI's logic persuasive or not, but the standard for licensing a contract shifted with no new information about the impact of such a contract on Equatorial Guinea's human rights processes and no change in MPRI's contract with them. Some may argue that MPRI simply gave more power to those in government who were arguing for this approach to begin with. This is true, but beside the point. These people were losing the argument before MPRI joined forces.[60]

Because US PSCs sell the same services abroad that they sell to the US government, there are market incentives to stay in step with US policy. This leads PSCs to behave in ways that are mostly satisfactory to US government officials. It also, however, leads to changes in the policy process that redistributes power within the government. The process by which exports are authorized accords more control to the executive branch. The ad hoc nature of the licensing procedure and the fact that there is little required monitoring open avenues for government policy by proxy that violates the official US line. Furthermore, the licensing process opens the way for PSCs to influence the standards by which their contracts are judged, thus opening the way for commercial interests to affect public policy.

Some decry this as a circumvention of the democratic process and argue that bad policy will come of it.[61] Peter Singer suggests that it has placed influence over and control of important decisions one step further away from the public and their elected representatives, in a way that is likely to decrease accountability.[62] Bruce Grant claims that it has upset the Clausewitzean trinity between the government, the military,

---

[58] Ibid.

[59] Interview with Ed Soyster, MPRI, April 2000, Interview with Bennett Freeman, Department of State, Office of Democracy, Human Rights, and Labor, 24 April 2000.

[60] The story did not end here. Once MPRI did its assessment for Equatorial Guinea, the State Department approved only a portion of what the Equational Guinea government wanted to purchase from MPRI. MPRI was lobbying not only the State Department and the Congress, but also the Pentagon for help in moving the approval forward. An April 2001 memo suggests the result of the lobbying, "[MPRI] may need our help or moral support . . ." "The Curious Bonds of Oil Diplomacy," ICIJ Report, *The Business of War*, available at http://icij.org/dtaweb/icij_bow.asp.

[61] See Marcus Raskin's analysis of the Kosovo crisis. *Washington Post*, 7 May 1999, editorial page.

[62] Singer, *Corporate Warriors*, p. 215.

and the people.[63] Ken Silverstein claims that it has poured money into policies that do not serve the general US interest.[64] Others could argue that this is a good thing—avoiding public debate over every foreign excursion will allow more "rational" foreign policy.[65] No matter your view on the relative benefits or costs, however, the process is different. Had US troops been the only option for engaging with the Croatian military, US officials would have had a tougher choice.[66] Had US troops been working with the Croatian military at the time of Operation Storm, the subsequent ethnic cleansing would have been associated with the US, and embarrassing to US policy makers. Even though foreign governments associate MPRI with the US government, the US electorate is less likely to see the connection.

In many cases, American PSCs do abide by similar values as their public counterparts. MPRI's training of militaries in the Balkans and Africa includes many features of curriculum and attention to values similar to training by US forces.[67] American PSCs' reliance on US professional military education encourages attention to the budding set of international military professional values. The US control strategy has undoubtedly encouraged this behavior. When a company like MPRI sells training both to the US government and directly to other governments, it is more likely that both sets of training will rely on similar values. This is true for other services as well. ICI, for instance, has provided support for the US government (even earned an award as US contractor of the year) but also provides similar support for IOs and INGOs in Africa. ICI also touts its reliance on retired American military professionals and attention to professional military values – though within the parameters of doing what it takes to get things done.[68] KBR similarly provides significant logistics capacities for the US but also for IOs, foreign governments, and the private sector abroad. It also touts its attention to professional values and its ability to spread these values abroad through its interaction with the local personnel it hires. In all of

---

[63] Bruce Grant, "US Military Expertise for Sale: Private Military Consultants as a Tool of Foreign Policy," National Defense University Institute for National Security Studies, Strategy Essay Competition, 1998 (http://www.ndu.edu/inss/books/essaysch4.html).

[64] Silverstein, *Private Warriors*, p. 143.

[65] Lowi, "Making Democracy Safe for the World."

[66] Interviews with State Department and Pentagon officials, 1999.

[67] Interviews with Jean-Michel A. Beraud and Clifford L. Fields (ACRI), 31 January 2000; interviews with Pentagon officials, 2002.

[68] As PSCs work in less-governed arenas, there is a greater likelihood that what it takes to get things done will butt up against values such as the protection of human rights, the laws of war, and democratic control of force. Indeed, in less-governed arenas, these values may conflict with one another. This was a frequent complaint in the Balkans. Interviews with State Department personnel, 1999, 2000, 2002.

these situations, American PSCs refer to professional military values in their plans, advertisements, and decisions. Thus the US strategy – particularly the fact that the US government purchases services from the private sector – appears to buy influence over the values to which PSCs ascribe.

This strategy, however, also communicates a model for security that holds a prominent role for the private sector. This is perhaps most apparent in Iraq. The US efforts at stabilization include private sector training for the Iraqi Army, the Iraqi police force, and Iraqi gendarmes, and a private Iraqi force to guard the oil fields.[69] Furthermore, the CPA has required contractors to demonstrate that they can provide their own security to avoid wasting reconstruction money. How these different forces will work together, and whether the new Iraqi government can control these forces – and the booming private security industry in Iraq – is still an open question.

Furthermore, as discussed in chapter three, the strategy enhances new processes of military professional development in which PSCs have a significant role in planning, training, writing doctrine, and serving as the conduits for military professionalism. Military professionalism has been dominated by military organizations and academies in the public sector and aimed at public service. The increasing use of PSCs, however, is changing that practice and opening the way for private military professionals. This development not only changes the process by which military professional norms are formed, it also portends a different relationship between citizenship, military service, and the state – undermining what has been argued to be one of the central features of sovereignty in the modern era.[70]

South Africa

The almost simultaneous end of apartheid and the Cold War led to a revolution in the way South Africa approached security. South Africa's "Total Strategy" spelled out in its 1977 White Paper on Defense had seen the enemies of apartheid and communist forces combining in a total onslaught to overthrow the South African State. South African society was militarized, security forces operated with impunity, and vast

---

[69] "Extra Guards for Iraq Oil Sites," *The Australian*, 5 September 2003; "Guarding the Oil Underworld in Iraq," CorpWatch, 5 September 2003 (www.corpwatch.org/issues/ PID.jsp?articleid=8328).

[70] Thomson, *Mercenaries, Pirates and Sovereigns*. See also, Moskos, Williams, and Segal, *Postmodern Military*; Snider and Watkins, *Future of the Army Profession*.

resources were dumped into the creation of a war machine. The new ANC government in a new international environment saw a greater likelihood of peace and a declining relevance of sovereignty and national interest. This led them to reject national security and endorse human security.[71]

Given the fact that South African PSCs were generally staffed with apartheid-era personnel, it is not surprising that the relationship between post-apartheid South African governments and PSCs has been tenuous at best, hostile at worst. As the government undertook the restructuring of its defense forces, there was a great deal of political uncertainty over how the military would be organized and what its goals would be. In this context, Executive Outcomes (EO), a company originally set up to train the apartheid South African Defense Forces (SADF), began to recruit from the restructuring army, particularly from special operations regiments.[72] EO was attractive to those worried about what they perceived to be a politicized working environment in the restructuring army.[73] Though some claim that Nelson Mandela's government facilitated EO's activities as a way of getting otherwise troublesome personnel busy outside of South Africa's borders,[74] others argue that PSC recruitment pulled competent soldiers from the army and put them in private companies rather than transforming their allegiance to the new government.[75] Regardless, the ANC government had little trust in the rising number of South African PSCs. The fact that employees of PSCs worked against the ANC during apartheid left some concerned about individuals' motivation and the feeling that the government of South Africa was still in a transition or consolidation phase left many believing that private security undermined the state at the very moment that it was being reconstructed.[76] By 1997 the government expressed this distrust more clearly as it moved to de-legitimize PSC activities.

---

[71] Peter Batchelor and Susan Willet, *Disarmament and Defense Industrial Adjustment in South Africa* (New York: Oxford University Press, 1998), ch. 3.
[72] EO also allegedly had a contract to train Umkhonto weSizwe (the armed wing of the ANC) personnel as part of a bridging exercise. See Kevin O'Brien, "Private Military Companies and African Security, 1990–1998," in Musah and Fayemi, *Mercenaries*.
[73] Interview with former South African government official, February 2000.
[74] Shearer, *Private Armies and Military Intervention*, pp. 54–55; Rubin, "An Army of One's Own"; p. 54; Steve McNallen, "South African Headhunters," *Soldier of Fortune* (May 1995).
[75] Interview with Rocky Williams, ISS, 28 February 2000.
[76] Interviews with South African academics, government officials, and former government officials in February/March 2000.

The market for South African PSCs and the range of providers and services offered

The South African government has not manifested the enthusiasm for private solutions found in the US.[77] This is partly a result of its apartheid predecessor. As apartheid ended, the National Party (NP) began a privatization process to "shrink the size of the state the ANC would inherit . . ."[78] Also the fact that PSCs were made up of retired apartheid-era military personnel who had been in direct confrontation with the ANC hardly generated trust. For both reasons, despite periodic reports that PSCs might help secure banks from robbery or patrol farms to prevent stock loss along the Lesotho border, PSCs in South Africa have not looked to the government for contracts.[79] To the degree that South African PSCs have pursued work in South Africa, it is with private citizens and businesses.[80]

The end of the Cold War, however, enhanced international demand for PSCs in Africa. The strategic importance of many African countries to the west evaporated – and with it military assistance to Africa. South African PSCs saw this vacuum as opening a potentially lucrative market. Governments that needed professional military assistance might purchase it on the market. Not all governments in need can afford such a service, but PSCs have targeted governments with access to extractive resources, or wealthy commercial patrons who can afford to pay. EO, Lifeguard, Saracen, TransAfrica Logistics, Falconer Systems Pty Ltd, and Ibis Air, for instance (as well as a variety of other PSCs including Sandline and Alpha 5) all had reported links to the "Branch Group," which includes diamond and oil conglomerates DiamondWorks, Ltd., Heritage Oil and Gas, and Branch Energy.[81] A wide variety of corporations operating in unstable parts of Africa, Asia, and the Middle East as well as INGOs, and IOs, round out the market further.[82] Finally,

---

[77] International guidance did generally attempt to push the new government in this orthodox economic direction. James Hentz, "Privatization in Transnational South Africa," *Journal of Modern Africa Studies* Vol. 38, No. 2 (2000): 203–23, p. 205.

[78] Ibid.

[79] "Mercenary Groups Hired to Halt Rustlers," *Africa News Service*, 14 September 1998; Christopher Munnion, "Banks May Use Mercenaries to Fight Robbers," *Daily Telegraph*, 26 January 1998.

[80] For an examination of private police, see Jenny Irish, "Policing for Profit: the Future of South Africa's Private Security Industry," Pretoria, Institute of Security Studies Monograph, No. 39 (August 1999).

[81] O'Brien, "Freelance Forces," p. 43.

[82] See Greg Mills and John Stremlau, "The Privatization of Security in Africa: an Introduction," in Greg Mills and John Stremlau, eds., *The Privatization of Security in Africa* (Johannesburg: SAIIA Press, 1999); Lock, "Africa: Military Downsizing and the Growth in the Security Industry," in Jakkie Cilliers and Peggy Mason, eds., *Peace,*

US actions in Afghanistan and Iraq after the 11 September 2001 terrorist attacks has opened another portion of the market for South African PSCs.[83]

Many South African PSCs offer a wide range of services – from the provision of troops through advice and training, operational support, logistics support, site security, and crime prevention services.[84] EO was close to a private army and offered support, training, and procurement through conduct of harassment, political propaganda, and sabotage and even the waging of "total guerilla warfare behind enemy lines,"[85] and worked for governments (Angola, Central African Republic, Rwanda, and Sierra Leone) as well as mining companies in these countries. There are a variety of other South African PSCs, though, which offer logistics, operational support, advice and training, site security and crime prevention services. Saracen has worked for governments, commercial industry, and INGOs conducting operational support, training, logistics, site security, crime prevention, and intelligence.[86] Southern Cross Security (SCS) provides site security as well as transportation and other logistics support for the INGO community around Sierra Leone to this day. FND has contracts with a variety of private entities including some oil companies in the Sudan and expressed desire to sell its services to governments – even the South African government.[87] Gray Security aims at commercial security markets in South Africa as well as protection for mining in Angola and other parts of Southern Africa.[88] Other companies including Lifeguard, Omega Support Limited, Shibata, and Strategic Resources Corporation offer similar services.[89] Particularly

Profit, or Plunder? (Pretoria: Institute for International Studies, 1999); Mark Malan, "The Crisis in External Response," in Jakkie Cilliers and Peggy Mason, eds., *Peace Profit or Plunder?* (Pretoria: Institute for International Studies, 1999).

[83] Beauregard Tromp, "Hired Guns from SA Flood Iraq," *Cape Times*, 4 February 2004.

[84] See EO website, archived, available at http://web.archive.org/web/19980703122204/ http://www.eo.com/; Ruben, "An Army of One's Own"; Shearer, *Private Armies and Military Intervention.*

[85] Khareen Pech, "Executive Outcomes – a Corporate Conquest," in Jakkie Cilliers and Peggy Mason, eds., *Peace, Profit, or Plunder?* (Pretoria: Institute for International Studies, 1999), p. 85.

[86] Interviews with INGO personnel in Washington, January 2000, interviews with journalists and PSC personnel in Pretoria and Johannesburg, South Africa, March 2000.

[87] Interview with PSC personnel in Pretoria, March 2000. "Oil Companies to Hire Mercenaries to Protect Oil Fields," *Africa News Service*, 25 November 1996. In February 2002, NCACC (chaired by Kadar Asmal) announced investigation into FND's work in Sudan.

[88] Interview with PSC personnel in Pretoria, March 2000. "South African Security Consultant in Angola Murdered for Food," *Reuters.*

[89] *Electronic Mail & Guardian*, "SA Mercenaries Working for the UN" (17 July 1998); available from http://www.mg.co.za/mg/news/98jul2/17jul-mercenrary.html; Thomas Adams, "The New Mercenaries and the Privatization of Conflict," *Parameters* Vol.

after EO's demise PSCs in South Africa became smaller and more specialized, largely offering non-combat services.[90] Initially, some South African PSCs reported a hope their government might eventually be a customer.[91] As tensions between PSCs and the government increased, however, PSCs conducted their activities more clandestinely or in a way that did not elicit governmental attention or response.

Regulatory environment

In the early 1990s there was little regularized interaction between the government and PSCs. Some reported that executives from EO did meet with government officials to inform them of its activities. The government acknowledged meetings but denied coordinated action.

In the wake of EO's high profile contracts in the mid-1990s, the government embarked on a campaign to "leash" the dogs of war and passed the Regulation of Foreign Military Assistance Act in May 1998. According to officials, the Act had both a moral and a pragmatic motivation. Morally, South Africa was pledged to have an ethical foreign policy and a human security doctrine, both of which required regulation of PSCs. Practically, it saw EO and PSCs like it as a threat to the stability of the government and its control of its own foreign policy – it needed to keep track of shady activities on the part of enemies of the regime.[92]

The legislation claims that it aims to "regulate the rendering of foreign military assistance by South African juristic persons, citizens, persons permanently resident in the Republic, and foreign citizens who render such assistance from within the borders of the Republic."[93] Justifications for the refusal of authorizations include any action that may be in violation of international law, South African obligations or interests, or may cause human rights abuses, support terrorism, endanger the peace, escalate regional conflicts, or "be unacceptable for any other reason."[94]

29, No. 2 (summer 1999): 109; Misser and Versi, "Soldier of Fortune", pp. 1–4; Reno, "Privatizing War in Weak States," p. 1; Vines, "Mercenaries and the Privatization of Security in Africa."

[90] Howe, *Ambiguous Order*, p. 218.

[91] Interview with Chris Grove of Frederick, Nicholas, and Duncan, Pretoria, 29 February 2000.

[92] Interview with former South African government official, February 2000; interview with South African academic, March 2000.

[93] Republic of South Africa, "Regulation of Foreign Military Assistance Act," No. 18912, 20 May 1998, available at http://www.gov.za/acts/98index.html.

[94] Ibid., Section 7.

EO argued publicly that it welcomed the legislation, and was licensed to provide services in 1998.[95] By 2000, though, both PSCs and many government officials agreed that the Act's intent was to de-legitimize private security and put companies like EO out of business.[96]

The legislation has been criticized on many counts. Analysts argue that it is both too vague and casts too broad a net, trying to regulate much activity that is far from military.[97] Indeed, what constitutes foreign military assistance is both unclear and potentially problematic. For instance, "advice and training" was taken by some to mean security advice in the form of activities conducted by NGOs and think tanks and "procurement of equipment" was taken to mean supplies of mundane items (like backpacks) to other militaries.[98] In 2000, many in the government reported spending their time trying to inform suppliers that they might be subject to regulation and claimed that there was a good deal of uncertainty about this issue – even among those doing the regulating.[99] Furthermore, an important exception in the legislation excludes from regulation "humanitarian or civilian activities aimed at relieving the plight of civilians in an area of armed conflict."[100] Though it sounds sensible, it allows PSCs to deliver services to protect commercial property in conflict zones, potentially allowing a loophole for the continued participation of PSCs under contract to extractive industries in conflict zones. These are just the kinds of activities that may enhance instability and discourage the consolidation of government control in unstable areas – and prove problematic to South Africa's human security agenda.[101]

PSC officials have criticized the Act for being unclear, but more importantly, they did not trust that it would be fairly executed.[102] This has caused some to aim at less regulated markets – like domestic security or security for extractive industries abroad. It caused some to break up

[95] Howe, *Ambiguous Order*, p. 212. See also O'Brien, "PMCs, Myths and Mercenaries," p. 1.
[96] Herbst, "The Regulation of Private Security Forces," p. 119. The Act prohibits citizens or permanent residents of South Africa from rendering foreign military assistance to other states or groups unless he or she has been granted approval from the government.
[97] Interview with Mark Malan, February 2000; interview with South African defense official, 7 March 2000.
[98] See RSA, "Foreign Military Assistance Act," Definitions, 1., iii., a and v.
[99] Interview with defense official, South Africa, 7 March 2000.
[100] See "Foreign Military Assistance Act," Definitions, 1., iii., d.
[101] See the discussion in chapter five. See also, Mats Berdal and David Malone, *Greed and Grievance: Economic Agendas in Civil Wars* (Boulder: Lynne Rienner, 2000); Karen Ballentine and Jake Sherman, *The Political Economy of Armed Conflict: Beyond Greed and Grievance* (Boulder: Lynne Rienner, 2003).
[102] Interviews with PSC personnel in Pretoria and Johannesburg, February and March 2000.

and either move off-shore or reconstitute themselves clandestinely. Within a year of the bill's passage EO had closed its doors for business.[103] EO personnel did not stop selling their wares, however. Several other firms cropped up in its wake, some with the former EO employees at their helm, and EO employees were reportedly working in Sierra Leone with Lifeguard.[104] Despite significant PSC activity abroad, however, less than a handful had even applied for an export license as of March 2000.[105]

Indeed, the most serious criticism of the Act is that the South African government's heavy-handed approach led PSCs to move further out of governmental reach. According to Kevin O'Brien, "By engaging in dialogue with these private military companies, the government could have successfully co-opted them into legitimate operations. Now, the closure of EO may well signal the end of this effective dialogue and the emergence of much more covert – and therefore much more potentially damaging – firms engaging in entirely unregulated activities outside of South Africa's borders."[106]

Though the Act extends its regulation to all South African citizens and passport holders, enforcement has proved difficult. South Africa did prosecute its first successful case under the Act in 2003 and another in 2004, but these prosecutions seem like a small number when compared to the activities of South African PSCs.[107] The government is now faced with deciding how to handle reports that Iraq is flooded with South African PSCs and South African citizens working for PSCs – all potential contraventions of the Foreign Military Assistance Act and all involved in a war South Africa did not support.[108]

In short, the regulation of security services is difficult and confusing and the legislation may work to curb activities that the government is not worried about while allowing activities the government is worried about. Furthermore, the prevention of core military services exports is hard to enforce without cooperation from PSCs (or other countries). In the

---

[103] Howe, *Ambiguous Order*, O'Brien, "PMCs, Myths and Mercenaries."
[104] "Can Anyone Curb Africa's Dogs of War?" *Economist*, 16 January 1999, p. 41.
[105] Interview with South African government official, 4 March 2000.
[106] O'Brien, "PMCs, Myths and Mercenaries."
[107] "SA ex-Air Force Officer in Hot Water in Swellendam," *SABC News*, 4 February 2004, available at www.sabcnews.com/southafrica/crimejustice/0,2172,73352,00.html; Melanie Gosline, "Pilot Held as Suspected Mercenary," *The Star*, 4 February 2004; "South Africa: Authorities Target Alleged Mercenaries," UN IRIN-SA 4 February 2004.
[108] According to Kader Asmal, NCACC chairman, "the government has become aware that South African citizens and South African companies may be rendering security and related services in Iraq." "South Africa: Authorities Target Alleged Mercenaries," UN IRIN-SA.

absence of that cooperation, the legislation appears to have simply pushed what was an above board business underground.[109]

The control trade-off

The relationship between PSCs and South African foreign policy goals are disputed. As I mentioned earlier, some have argued that having former employees of the SADF employed outside South Africa in the initial years of the post-apartheid government was a security benefit for the ANC government[110] and even claimed that EO carried out unofficial South African policy.[111] Though it is not clear that EO's actions were coordinated with the government, many reports suggest that EO informed Mandela's government of its actions and its actions were largely consistent with government policy. Some claim that EO met regularly with South African government officials and even shared intelligence information during its actions in both Sierra Leone and Angola.[112] Before regulation, many South African PSCs appeared to further – or at least not undercut – the ANC government's foreign policy goals. For instance, EO worked in Angola with a government that many EO personnel had seen as their enemy just a few years before.[113] Also, in Sierra Leone, EO's work enhanced the stability of the Strasser regime (an ally of South Africa) at least in the short term. Though some press reports cited EO abuses of civilians, most reported restraint.[114] EO worked toward humanitarian goals in Sierra Leone – including the return of school children and teachers to their homes and the de-mobilization of child-soldiers.[115] Former EO personnel claim to have allocated medicines and passed out Bibles in Freetown as evidence of their attention to international values.[116] According to one South African government official, the worst problem occurred when an EO

---

[109] O'Brien, "PMCs, Myths and Mercenaries."

[110] Ibid., pp. 54–55; Rubin, "An Army of One's Own," p. 54; McNallen, "South African Headhunters."

[111] A British intelligence report links the ANC government with EO and concludes that the government sanctioned EO's foreign contracts. Lynne Duke, "South Africa's Ex-Soldiers Becoming 'Dogs of War': Apartheid Commandos Peddling Skills," *Houston Chonicle*, 24 March 1996, p. 129; Zarate, "Emergence of a New Dog of War," p. 102. Both EO and the ANC government deny this link.

[112] Jeremy Harding, "The Mellow Mercenaries," *Guardian*, 8 March 1997; Zarate, "The Emergence of a New Dog of War."

[113] Duke, "South Africa's Ex-Soldiers"; Zarate, "Emergence of a New Dog of War," p. 102.

[114] Rubin, "An Army of One's Own"; Donald G. McNeil Jr., "Pocketing the Wages of War," *New York Times*, 16 February 1997, p. 4 for reports of humanitarian abuses.

[115] Harding, "Mellow Mercenaries"; Zarate, "Emergence of a New Dog of War," p. 97.

[116] Interview with Chris Grove, March 2000.

employee from Angola shot another EO employee from South Africa in a long-standing feud.[117] The company's general good behavior and humanitarian efforts also accorded with South Africa foreign policy. Government officials, however, professed dissatisfaction with EO and other PSCs' actions. Rusty Evans, the Director-General of the South African Foreign Affairs Department in 1996, called EO a "dangerous criminal and destructive force in Africa."[118] Some claim that EO posed dilemmas for Mandela's government; even if the company did not undermine South African foreign policy directly, it was seen to undermine governmental authority and South Africa's new security agenda.[119] Also, EO's recruiting embarrassed the government and caused it to lose competent soldiers.[120] The uneasy juxtaposition of PSCs with South Africa's new security agenda led to government worries despite EO's purported consistency with South Africa's foreign policy. Indeed, many argue that regardless of their behavior, the existence of PSCs alone caused the South African government discomfort. "The decision to intervene and to take sides in an armed conflict is a political one, whether it is made by an international organization, a regional organization, a coalition of states, or a single state. When private individuals and companies are allowed to make such decisions, the concept of international law loses all meaning."[121] The apartheid experience of EO and other PSC employees exacerbated this discomfort, leading officials to worry that PSCs could not be trusted to follow government guidelines.[122] The government's search for a way to end EO's participation in Angola, even though it supported the government's policy, demonstrates this concern. The South African government also attempted to persuade its partners in the OAU to take a position against EO. Next, they passed the Regulation of Foreign Military Assistance Act.[123] Finally, they began to prosecute those selling security services abroad.

---

[117] Interview 3 March 2000, Pretoria.
[118] Michael Ashworth, "Privatising War, by 'The Executives'," *Independent*, 16 September 1996, p. 1.
[119] Rubin, "An Army of One's Own," p. 51; Jacklyn Cock and Laurie Nathan, *Society at War: the Militarization of South Africa* (New York: St. Martins Press, 1989); Jacklyn Cock and Peggie Mckenzie, *From Defense to Development: Redirecting Military Resources in South Africa* (Ottowa: International Development Research Centre, 1998).
[120] Interview with Rocky Williams, ISS, Pretoria, 28 February 2000.
[121] Mark Malan and Jakkie Cilliers, "Mercenaries and Mischief: the Regulation of Foreign Military Assistance Bill," Institute for Security Studies, Occasional Paper No. 25 (September 1997), p. 1.
[122] Interview, Pretoria, 29 February 2000.
[123] Duke, "South Africa's Ex-Soldiers"; Pech, "Executive Outcomes," pp. 94–95.

South Africa's strategy, however, had consequences for its ability to control the behavior of PSCs. Before the South African government's passage of the Act, PSCs in South Africa worked hard to enhance their legitimacy. As EO's documentation suggests, many PSCs saw their capacity to make money tied to their ability to sell themselves as legitimate entities in the international marketplace. The efforts of PSCs demonstrate their belief that financial gain is tied to their ability to become legitimate international actors. EO also made efforts to inform the government of its actions. As O'Brien suggests, the South African government could have used this good will to co-opt PSCs into working for the interests of the South African government. The government's strategy to de-legitimate the private provision of security, however, removed this option. Whatever informal coordination occurred between the government and PSCs in the early 1990s evaporated. Though some PSCs claim to have restricted their activities, selling only site security and crime prevention services and only to private actors,[124] others have simply moved their offices out of South Africa or broken into smaller companies and moved underground.[125] Companies like Lifeguard, SCS, and Saracen now operate from outside South African territory and companies like FND operate more or less underground. PSCs based on retired South African military personnel continue to sell their services, but the government's influence over and knowledge of their activity is reduced. In effect, South Africa's regulatory strategy led the government to reduce its influence over the behavior of PSCs abroad. The participation of South African PSCs providing key services to the US-led occupation in Iraq – an occupation the South African government does not support – is the most recent and dramatic example of this control loss.

Moreover, while the government's strategy to de-legitimize private security exports in South Africa pushed PSCs further away from South African governmental influence and control, the transnational market for South African PSCs impeded the government's attempts to put the companies out of business. It is also unclear that the South African government's strategy alone will erode PSC legitimacy, particularly when South African PSCs work for a range of international bodies, INGOs, and even the US government. Indeed, some South African PSCs have pursued a strategy of seeking legitimacy through appeals to international bodies like the UN and international values rather than to the South African state.[126] The South African strategy, then, has also

---

[124] Interview with representative from Gray Security, March 2000.
[125] Howe, *Ambiguous Order*, pp. 226–29.
[126] Interview with Chris Grove, FND, 29 February 2000.

reduced the potential for the government to influence the values to which South African PSCs attend.

Reduced government influence over the behavior of PSCs, though, has maintained *political* control over violence. It has reduced the opportunities for PSCs to affect government policy or preferences in South Africa. While executives from EO met privately with South African officials before the Act, they do not have the same access in its wake. PSC officials report feeling that they have little political influence or power.[127] If South Africa considers the use of force abroad, it considers the use of public forces, governed by standard political processes. Foreign policy by proxy is not an option, but this also means that foreign policy decisions are less likely to change political procedures.

Furthermore, though the government has given up resources to influence the values to which PSCs adhere, it has preserved the value of *public* security. Indeed, government officials and academic analysts emphasized just this point.[128] By focusing on the "fact" that PSCs should be seen as they are – as mercenary companies – the South African government preserved its proper role in the defense of the country and its ability to determine foreign policy independently. Efforts to control PSCs, these officials suggest, would also have legitimized their role. Allowing PSCs to operate legitimately, in turn, would work to undermine the government's capacity to set its own agenda for security – and even the authority of the state. Faced with the choice between a strategy that enhanced their influence over PSCs abroad by legitimating their activity and a strategy that gave up influence for de-legitimation, South African officials believe they made the right choice.[129] The South African government officials reported that the political cost of effective functional control was simply too great.

The United Kingdom

British PSC activity also flourished in the 1990s, but the government remained aloof. Though it sometimes acted as a booster for British PSCs, the government purchased few of the services its PSCs exported and maintained a long-standing policy of "plausible deniability" with respect to its PSCs' activities abroad. The coordination of British government policy and British PSCs has thus been ad hoc and episodic.

---

[127] Ibid.
[128] Interview with Rocky Williams, February 2000; interview with Jackie Cock, February 2000; interview with South African defense officials, March 2000.
[129] Ibid.

The British have suffered some guilt by association with their firms, though, and experienced scandals involving PSCs and poor policy coordination. These led the parliament to commission a Green Paper on the regulation of mercenary activity, which points toward the US model in its recommendations. The lack of a government market for the kinds of services they seek to regulate, however, may lead regulation to have a different impact in the UK than it does in the US unless the British government also increases its consumer demand for security services.

The market for British PSCs and the range of providers and services offered

In the 1990s, the British government provided only a limited market for a small segment of security services. Though the British government faced challenges similar to those faced by the US, and issued initiatives to encourage private solutions in defense, outsourcing in the UK was more limited.[130] In 2000, the Private Finance Initiative (PFI) had led to twenty-six contracts with an estimated capital value of £1 billion and the government claimed "there are no 'no go' areas for PFI in the MOD."[131] A sample of government contracts included the provision of vehicles to British Forces in Germany and the UK; the outsourcing of the Army Logistics Agency IS/IT requirements; the Naval Recruitment and Training Agency strategic partnership; a management information system for the Army Training and Recruitment Agency; the provision of Material Handling Equipment; the Defence Helicopter Flying School; provision of an information system on the handling of hazardous substances.[132] Private companies also work for the Department for International Development (DFID) doing such things as landmine removal, and for the Foreign and Commonwealth Office (FCO) providing security at embassies and commissions abroad.

The MOD has hired PSCs (even foreign PSCs) to run bases and construct particular projects. Though it has not hired PSCs to conduct the range of operational support and training missions as in the US[133] (indeed, reports that battlefield support services were to be open to

---

[130] As of 1998, British defense expenditure had dropped 23 percent in real terms since 1990. "Strategic Defense Review," MOD White Paper, July 1998.

[131] Ibid.; "UK Outlines Revised Plans to Privatise Defense Research," *Jane's Defense Weekly*, 26 March 2000.

[132] See "Public/Private Partnerships in the MOD: the Private Finance Initiative in Government," www.mod.uk/commercial/pfi/intro.htm.

[133] Interview with Rt. Hon. Bruce George MP, Chairman House of Commons Defense Select Committee, 31 May 2000; interview with FCO officials, September 1999, interview with MOD officials, September 1999.

private competition spawned great angst in 1999[134]), the Blair administration has moved further down this path. The pursuit of Better Quality Services (BQS) has led to an increase in privatization of defense functions. As of 2003, the UK PFI had increased to forty-two projects with an estimated value of £2 billion and the British MOD has increased the scale and scope of commercial involvement in the theater of military operations with its "Contractors On Deployed Operations" (CONDO) policy and related initiatives.[135] Thus, while PSCs offering operational support, training, and even logistics and site security have not looked to the British government as their prime (or even a major) customer, this could be changing.[136]

British exports of military services to foreign governments, however, are significant. The current trend began in the late 1960s when retired British Special Air Service (SAS) Colonel Sir David Stirling founded WatchGuard International in 1967 to serve the needs of sultanates of the Persian Gulf.[137] Other companies, such as KMS and Saladin, and then Defense Systems Limited (DSL), were founded well before the Cold War's end. Since then, the numbers and activities of PSCs have risen precipitously. Aims Limited, Rubicon International, Sandline, Northbridge, and others have cropped up in the post-Cold War era and aim their services to foreign and private markets. British firms have worked for governments and the private sector in Europe, the Persian Gulf, Africa, Latin America, and Asia.[138]

The range of services British companies export is almost as broad as South African PSCs. Some PSCs provide operational support on the battlefield, very close to combat support. Different companies offer different ranges of services, however, and have different reputations. Sandline listed the widest array of services ranging from advice, training, operational support, and intelligence support to humanitarian support and law and order services. It had no restrictions on its personnel carrying weapons or participating in operations. Sandline sold military

---

[134] "Army to Privatise Some Key Units," *Guardian*, 14 February 1999.
[135] Matthew R. H. Uttley, "Private Contractors on United Kingdom Deployed Military Operations: Issues and Prospects," paper presented at the International Security Studies Section (ISSS) Meeting of the International Studies Association, US Army War College, Carlisle, PA, 1 November 2003.
[136] Interview with Noel Philp, Managing Director of ArmorGroup's DSL, London, 2 June 2000; interview with Michael Grunberg, advisor to Sandline, London, 31 May 2000.
[137] O'Brien, "PSCs, Myths, and Mercenaries," p. 60.
[138] Ibid; Goulet, "DSL: Serving States and Multinationals"; Andromidas, "Defense Systems Ltd."; Reno, "Privatizing War in Weak States," p. 1; Peter Lagerquist and Jonathan Steele, "Company Acts after Guardian Investigation," *Guardian*, 9 October 2002; O'Brien, "Freelance Forces: Exploiters of Old or New-Age Peacebrokers?" *Jane's Intelligence Review* (August 1998).

services to states such as Papua New Guinea and Sierra Leone and many others according to company officials.[139] Sandline also boasted of its status as a UN service provider and listed a variety of services that might assist not only the UN but also INGOs.[140]

DSL (now ArmorGroup International) has a more circumscribed list of capacities but still boasts services such as site security, manned guarding to crisis management, and security advice and training, to humanitarian support, electronic security, and more. DSL aims at the high end of the market, selling to international organizations such as the UN and the World Bank, INGOs such as CARE, and many private companies that operate in the riskiest environments. DSL has procedures and guidelines to regulate its own actions and appears to have closer connections to the British government than did Sandline – though, as with many PSCs, these guidelines change on a contract-by-contract basis. DSL undertook tasks closer to the "tip of the spear" in Mozambique and Colombia.

Other PSCs focus more specifically on a particular market or client base. For instance, Control Risks (established in 1975) focused on the private sector market in the 1990s and Crown Agents (a formerly public entity that was privatized in the late 1980s) has sold services mostly to the public sector. These specializations are subject to abrupt changes, however: Control Risks has sold security services to a wide range of governmental and non-governmental entities in the wake of the 11 September terrorist attacks and the wars in Afghanistan and Iraq.[141]

In addition, British PSCs list less senior retired personnel (fewer generals and more colonels than in US-based firms) and draw largely from the SAS. Again, however, this is something that is in flux. As British PSCs provide more in the way of logistics and other services, they have begun to draw from a broader array of military organizations.

Regulatory environment

The British regulatory environment is informal. Laws that regulate the export of arms in the UK do not extend to services. The Defense Export Services Organization in MOD provides advisory services to companies wishing to export defense products and services. It acts as a booster to the UK defense industry, facilitating interaction between UK companies and foreign governments, providing advice on a variety of legal, financial,

---

[139] Interview with Michael Grunberg, advisor to Sandline, 31 May 2000.
[140] Tim Spicer's comments, 17 March 2000.
[141] They are among the fifteen "Essential Security Providers" for Iraq. See http://issues.topikmail.com/gingg/?I=2008.

military, and political issues, and generally greasing the wheels for UK industry in other countries.[142] Because there is no law regulating the export of services, its work does not extend to legal advice.[143]

In the absence of a formal process, the interaction between the government and PSCs is ad hoc. There are several avenues for communications. The MOD Office of Defense Export Services, the FCO, the embassy or commission abroad all serve as points of contact for PSCs. In many cases, if PSCs coordinate with the government, it is with government officials serving in the field. The communication is not mandated, though, and therefore depends on the initiation of the PSC. Furthermore, communication on the part of a PSC with one part of the government may not be communicated with other parts. For instance, when Sandline was working for exiled President Kabbah, officials from the company did communicate with the High Commissioner and others on the ground in Sierra Leone. Sandline claimed to have gone ahead with its work advising President Kabbah on arms acquisitions and training the Kamajors assuming it had the approval of the British government.[144] What communication did take place, though, never reached members of the FCO in London. In the event, Sandline purchased weapons from the Bulgarian Arsenal and arranged to have them flown into Sierra Leone with help from Sky Air Cargo Service.[145] As the plane landed in Lungi airport, however, Nigerian troops operating in Sierra Leone on behalf of ECOMOG intercepted it and impounded the weapons on the grounds that they contravened a UN arms embargo. The disclosure that Sandline delivered arms to Sierra Leone in contravention of a UN and UK Arms Embargo led to a scandal.[146]

Even though the British government does not regulate security services exports, it has pushed forward contracts between British PSCs and other countries in specific instances. For example, the British government loaned money to Mozambique so the government could hire DSL to train its soldiers that were assigned to protect Lonhro's tea

---

[142] See Joanna Spear, "Britain and Conventional Arms Restraint," in Mark Hoffman, ed., *UK Arms Control in the 1990s* (Manchester: Manchester University Press, 1990), pp. 174–6. See also, Frederic S. Pearson, "The Question of Control in British Defense Sales Policy," *International Affairs* Vol. 59, No. 2 (spring 1983).

[143] http://www.dgcom.mod.uk/dgcom/dss/exports.htm.

[144] "Out of Control: the Loopholes in UK Controls of the Arms Trade," Oxfam GB Policy Paper (December 1998) available at http://www.oxfam.org.uk/policy/papers/control/broker.htm.

[145] Arsenel is Bulgaria's largest state owned arms manufacturer known for the quality of its AK-47 assault rifles. See "FO Muddle Leaves Boss in Firing Line," *Sunday Times*, 17 May 1998 (FOCUS). See also Malan and Cilliers, "Mercenaries and Mischief."

[146] "Sierra Leone: Second Report," Foreign Affairs Committee, House of Commons, Session 1998–99, Vol. 1, p. vi.

and sugar estates as well as the rail lines on which they were transported from Resistancia Nacional Mocambicana (RENAMO).[147] The activities of Sandline and the scandal that erupted over its behavior in Sierra Leone, and the "arms to Africa affair" led the UK to begin a process evaluating whether mercenaries (or military service exports) should be regulated more formally. A Green Paper on this subject was commissioned in the wake of the Sandline Affair in Sierra Leone and released in February 2002.[148]

The Green Paper does not suggest policy, but puts forth the case for regulation and several regulatory options. Regulation, the Green Paper suggests, could bring PSCs under government control so as to insure that PSCs do not cut across government interests, assist forces the British government might confront in the future, affect the British government's reputation, or put British lives at risk.[149] Regulation could provide additional benefits by setting guidelines for the industry and establishing a respectable and thus employable industry. It argues that regulation could insure that PSCs operate within the interests of British foreign policy, set guidelines for the industry, and establish a way of distinguishing between reputable and disreputable PSCs. All of these would help British PSCs meet the international demand for security services more effectively.[150] Though it notes that costs and effectiveness could be difficulties, it suggests that the difficulties are not insurmountable.[151] Options for regulation, the paper suggests, range from (1) a ban on all military activity abroad (amending the 1870 Foreign Enlistment Act) to (2) a ban on military recruiting abroad (following up on the Diplock Report of 1967) to (3) a licensing regime for military services to (4) registration and notification to (5) general licenses for PSCs to (5) self-regulation. The paper lays out arguments for and difficulties with each of these options, but appears to lean toward some kind of licensing regime.[152]

---

[147] Interview with former MOD official, London, 30 May 2000. Interview with Noel Philp of DSL, 2 June 2000.

[148] Green Papers lay out broad policy options and the logic behind them. The Green Paper was scheduled to be released in the fall of 2000, but was delayed for a variety of reasons and only released 12 February 2002. "FT Investigation of the Private Military Business: Foreign Office Faces Opposition to Regulation Green Paper, Downing Street Blocks Publication until after Election," *Financial Times*, 18 April 2001. See *Private Military Companies: Options for Regulation* (London: Stationary Office, 12 February 2002, HC 577).

[149] *Private Military Companies: Options for Regulation*, p. 21.

[150] Ibid., pp. 20–26.

[151] Ibid.

[152] This is my reading of the report. Several others share this reading. See, for instance, Richard Norton-Taylor, "Let Mercenaries be Licensed, says Foreign Office,"

A heated debate about the report and its options ensued, with Labour backbenchers calling the proposals "repugnant"[153] while members of the industry hoped for more government support.[154] As of 2005, though, the British government had taken no action to regulate, ban, or otherwise clarify the British government's control of security service exports.

The control trade-off

British PSCs have generally supported British foreign policy goals. Sandline's work for exiled President Kabbah in Sierra Leone is a case in point. The British government clearly supported Kabbah and wanted his government reinstated. After the coup, the military junta in Sierra Leone was suspended from the Commonwealth and Tony Blair issued a personal invitation to Kabbah to attend the Commonwealth meeting in Edinburgh (October 1997).[155] The British High Commissioner to Sierra Leone, Peter Penfold, also maintained close contact with Kabbah throughout the affair. Sandline's work on behalf of restoring Kabbah to power, then, appears in line with British goals.[156] In other instances, DSL, Control Risk, Northbridge, and others have also appeared to support British foreign policy goals.

Government opinion of British based PSCs varies and government officials report mixed levels of satisfaction with their behavior.[157] Some argue that PSCs like Sandline have been beneficial and promise to be advantageous in the future – having a few cowboys ready to do dirty work can be quite useful in complicated situations.[158] Others are concerned that PSCs implicate British policy and sometimes are a poor reflection on the UK because they are not coordinated or regulated.[159]

Guardian, 13 February 2002; Cathy Newman, "UN to hire mercenaries for policing peace," *Financial Times*, 13 February 2002; "Peace Role for Mercenaries," *Sky News*, 13 February 2002; "Straw Seeks to Rein in Mercenaries," *Reuters*, 12 February 2002; David Isenberg, "Regulated Private Military Firms have a Role," *Defense News*, 11–17 March 2002.

[153] "Peacekeeping 'Role' for Mercenaries," *BBC News*, 13 February 2003; Peter Waugh and Nigel Morris, "Mercenaries as Peacekeepers Plan under Fire," *Independent*, 14 February 2002.

[154] Jimmy Burns and Andrew Parker, "Ex-SAS Soldiers Hope for New Lease on Life," *Financial Times*, 14 February 2002.

[155] Nicholas Rufford, "Diamond Dogs of War," *The Times*, 10 May 1998.

[156] As indicated in chapter three, though, many of Sandline's efforts on behalf of Kabbah came to naught when the arms were embargoed at Lungi airport.

[157] Even Sandline's action in Sierra Leone was consistent with stated British objectives.

[158] This sentiment was expressed in interviews with members of the FCO, MOD and House of Commons September 1999 and June 2001.

[159] Chaloka Beyani and Damian Lilly, *Regulating Private Military Companies: Options for the UK Government* (London: International Alert, 2001).

There is a general suspicion of the activities of PSCs (often termed mercenaries) in the UK. This is partly due to the fact that the activities of companies like Sandline are seen to be infringing on the tasks of the military. For instance, the British Army sees foreign military training tasks as one of its key missions and active duty officers believe that outsourcing foreign military training would infringe on their profession in ways that US Army officers do not.[160] Also, the practice of retired military personnel selling their expertise on the market has been traditionally frowned upon in the UK.[161] Related to this, many (military and civilian) in the UK do not view PSCs as military professionals.

Finally, British PSCs do not see themselves as carrying out British policy and neither do British civilians.[162] The fact that British PSCs do not consider the British government a prime customer gives them less incentive to attend as closely to British policy as American PSCs.[163]

Many British PSCs do have a global presence, however, and worry about how their behavior in one place will affect their reputation in others. Many also clearly look to international organizations and INGOs as potential clients and aim their public relations appeal in that direction with their claims to abide by international laws and norms. British PSCs do claim attention to principles of self-regulation and transparency, and argue that they abide by international law, the rule of law, and human rights.[164] Sandline was a loud voice for the importance of international norms and the possibility for self-regulation among PSCs. It also had a policy that required it to work only for internationally recognized states, international institutions, or internationally recognized and supported liberation movements.[165] It claimed that it would not become involved with embargoed regimes, terrorist organizations, or other international criminal activity. Sandline was in a number of scrapes, however, that belie these claims. In its involvement with Papua New Guinea and with Sierra Leone, Sandline was accused of either undermining British policy and/or skirting international law.[166] DSL also is a strong proponent of

---

[160] Interviews with British Army and Navy officers, September 1999, June 2000. Though they rarely suggested competition with PSCs would infringe on their turf, several suggested that it would be inappropriate to outsource such a task.
[161] Interviews with employees at Sandline, DSL, officials at MOD, FCO, and House of Commons, September 1999 and June 2001.
[162] Ibid.
[163] Interview with Tim Spicer (Sandline), March 2000; Michael Grunberg (consultant to Sandline), June 2000; Noel Philp (DSL), June 2000.
[164] Interviews with officials at Sandline, DSL, June 2001.
[165] Much relevant information was available on their website, http://www.sandline.com/site/index.html (accessed November 2003).
[166] Dinnen, Regan, and May, *Challenging the State*; "Sierra Leone: Second Report," Foreign Affaris Committee, House of Commons.

corporate social responsibility.[167] To the degree that British firms nod to the normative context in which they operate, however, they tend to mention international norms, not the pursuit of British values or interests.[168]

The strategy that leads PSCs to be less clear "tools" for British policy than in the US, though, also restricts the presence of British PSCs in policy circles relative to their American counterparts. To the extent that PSCs affect British foreign policy it is by association. Assumptions that these PSCs are British firms and therefore reflect British policy may cause embarrassment to the British government. In Sierra Leone, for instance, the fact that Sandline arranged for arms on behalf of Kabbah's exiled government in the face of a UN arms embargo caused embarrassment to British officials and affected foreign perceptions of British policy. As of yet, however, PSCs do not have the kind of access to government officials or impact on foreign policy processes that PSCs in the US do.[169]

The British strategy, however, may be changing. The 2002 Green Paper suggests that if Britain were to regulate its PSCs, it could both increase their attention to British foreign policy and boost the market appeal of those that maintain their reputations.[170] Taking up the arguments that Sandline and others floated, it even suggests that PSCs could be hired to perform international peacekeeping missions more cost effectively than the UN. Some portions of the government appeared to believe that regulation would facilitate the participation of British firms in the international market and open the way for new private efforts to facilitate international peace. Because government purchases span a smaller range of services than do exports, though, it is unclear that British regulation would have the same effect as regulation in the US – unless, of course, there is also an upswing in government purchasing.

Transnational markets and political trade-offs

The market for force complicates the ability of states to control the use of force by its citizens abroad. The transnational nature of the market and the particular structure of the security service industry leads states to face trade-offs in their management of the market for force.

---

[167] Nelson, *Business of Peace.*
[168] Interviews with employees at Sandline, DSL, officials at MOD, FCO, and House of Commons, September 1999 and June 2001.
[169] Ibid.
[170] *Private Military Companies: Options for Regulation,* House of Commons.

Table 4.1. *Export control trade-offs*

	Functional control	Political control	Social control – firms	Social control – state
US	Improved	Changed	Improved	Impaired
UK	Moderately improved	Some change	Some improvement	Some erosion
RSA	Impaired	Unchanged	Impaired	Improved

Particularly, market mechanisms allow some states more influence on their PSCs' behavior abroad in ways that enhance the tools of force available to that state. The strategies that lead to the greatest influence, however, also alter political processes within the state, redistributing power over the definition of national security goals and policies. See Table 4.1.

The US strategy offers new tools for achieving their international goals and appears to generate policies in keeping with the government's preferences. This strategy reflects the US government's procurement and the associated market incentives for firms to stay in tune with US policy. The private provision of security services, however, causes the foreign policy process to work differently, enhances the power of the executive over the legislative branch and opens new avenues for PSCs to affect foreign policy regulatory standards. The close relationship between PSCs and the government and an acceptance of private participation in defense lead to a situation where regulation appears to work relatively well, but the export of military services allows the government to pursue policies that it would not if it had to send American troops, and creates opportunities for PSCs to influence foreign policy.

On the other extreme, South Africa's strategy has maintained the process of foreign policy making and kept private security actors from affecting governmental preferences. However, it has cost the government influence over and information about the activities of its PSCs abroad. More private security activity simply takes place outside the purview of the government. The US risks folding private interests into the policy process, the South Africans risk pushing private military capacity underground and out of its influence. The UK is dancing between these two – and is subject to more moderate variations on both kinds of risks. The Green Paper on the regulation of the private security industry and the increasing British consideration of commercial contractors in military operations suggest that Britain may be moving closer to the US model.

The transnational nature of the private security industry and its service nature have limited the effect of some strategies. Were the security industry capitalized or tied to territory, the South African government's strategy might be more successful in shutting the industry down or making its firms uncompetitive. As it is, however, South African PSCs can simply carry on their business outside the bounds of the state. And though the de-legitimation strategy preserves political processes in South Africa, it has not undermined PSCs' *international* legitimacy. So long as PSCs provide services demanded by other governments, IOs, INGOs, and corporations, South Africa, alone, cannot undermine their international legitimacy.

The transnational nature of the industry is also likely to play a role in the effectiveness of British regulation. Much is made of the relationship between US regulation and the US government's satisfaction with the activities of its PSCs abroad. US regulation, however, is undergirded by market incentives. Indeed, the overwhelming dominance of the US in defense spending suggests that other governments will have only limited consumer impact on the behavior of PSCs. Regulation by other governments is likely to yield less satisfaction unless they step up their consumption of security services.

5 Private financing for security and the control of force

Thus far, I have focused on the changes in the control of force associated with private delivery of security services. In this chapter I look at the private financing of security – examining how non-state actors, directly or not, affect the resources through which violence is controlled. As chapter one suggests, non-state actors – particularly transnational non-state actors – dedicated to maintaining a presence in parts of the world where the state is weak are an important source of demand for private security.[1] Non-state actors finance security in a variety of ways, though, subsidizing state, rebel, or paramilitary forces as well as hiring PSCs. It is increasingly the case that non-state actors have both direct and indirect impact on the financial resources available for security in weak states. This chapter explores the consequences of that impact for control of force in weak states.

The optimists and pessimists once again suggest different conse-quences. Pessimists argue that transnational financing is a fundamental challenge to the state's control of consequential incentives that may also undermine the coherence and legitimacy of states. More optimistic visions see non-state financing of security as simply an indication of state weakness – and a tool that can bolster security in a way that enhances short-term functional control. The rosiest scenario might imagine that non-state financing could, particularly when reinforced with education about the proper behavior of security forces, even subsidize order so as to help generate the political coherence necessary for improving the strength of a weak state, potentially contributing to greater coherence, and improving the likelihood that force will be integrated with prevailing international norms.

---

[1] Private individuals and other non-state actors may also finance security. See David Bayley and Clifford Shearing, *The New Structure of Policing: Description, Conceptualiza-tion, and Research Agenda* (Washington, DC: National Institute of Justice, 2001); Jeremy Gans, "Privately Paid Public Policing: Law and Practice," *Policing and Society* Vol. 10, No. 2 (August 2000): 183–206.

The budding literature on transnational actors' increased influence in world politics provides one way to think about this – suggesting hypotheses that link the motivation of the transnational financier to one or another dimension of control over violence. Studies of INGOs often argue that they are motivated by values and examine their positive effect on the kinds of norms or values reflected in an issue area – or social control.[2] Studies of transnational corporations, on the other hand, often assume these actors are motivated by interest and examine their mostly negative effect on the distribution of power (and material resources) – or political control.[3] Thus we might expect that INGOs that finance violence will improve the social control of force and TNCs that finance violence will change the political control of force.

The synthesis of institutional approaches I have suggested, however, re-focuses attention from motivations to the way transnational actors deploy social and material resources to meet their goals. Whether INGOs and TNCs have varying effects should depend not only on their motivations but also on their strategies for action (often influenced by the social and material constraints on transnational actors themselves) and how they affect the consequential and normative mechanisms of control. Furthermore, we should examine how transnational financing affects all three dimensions of control over force and whether the dimensions of control fit together.

Transnational financing for security should have its clearest effect on the political control of force. By definition this redistributes political influence to the transnational financiers and often also changes the balance of political power over violence within a territory. Its effect on

---

[2] Ann Marie Clark, "Non-Governmental Organizations and their Influence on International Society," *Journal of International Affairs* Vol. 48, No. 2 (1995): 507–25; Florini, *Third Force*; Keck and Sikkink, *Activists Beyond Borders*; Ronnie Lipschultz, "Reconstructing World Politics: the Emergence of Global Civil Society," *Millennium: Journal of International Studies* Vol. 21, No. 3 (1992): 389–420; M. J. Peterson, "Transnational Activity, International Society, and World Politics," *Millennium: Journal of International Studies* Vol. 21, No. 3 (1992): 371–88; Wapner, "Politics Beyond the State"; Peter Willetts, *"The Conscience of the World": the Influence of Non-Governmental Organizations on the UN System* (Washington, DC: Brookings, 1996).

[3] Frynas, "Political Instability and Business"; Global Witness, "Crude Awakening"; Pegg, "Cost of Doing Business." Fewer analyses have examined the implications of transnational actors in terms of function. For exceptions, see Cooley and Ron, "NGO Scramble"; and Pamela Aall, "What Do NGOs Bring to Peacemaking?" in Chester Crocker, Fen Osler Hampson, and Pamela Aall, eds., *Turbulent Peace: the Challenges of Managing International Conflict* (Washington, DC: United States Institute of Peace, 2001). Also, Ann Florini discusses the degree to which NGOs are moving from advocacy alone to implementing policy, which may bring with it concerns about functionality. Florini, *Third Force*, p. 213.

functional control should vary, however, with whether it centralizes or diffuses control and whether it generates agreement or disagreement over security functions. Centralization and agreement tend to increase functional capacity, while diffusion and disagreement tend to erode functional capacity. Transnational financing's effect on the social control of violence should vary with the degree to which financing is interwoven with other social appeals to professional norms, education, and reinforcements of proper behavior in day-to-day processes. The particular change in political control of violence (who power is redistributed to) should also have important feedback effects on both functional and social controls and the way the dimensions of control fit together.

Tracing the processes through which three different types of transnational financiers – oil companies in Nigeria, relief INGOs in the Goma Camps, and conservation INGOs in Garamba National Park, Democratic Republic of Congo – I find more support for the relevance of institutional mechanisms as a predictor of a transnational financier's effect on the control of force than actor motivation. INGOs, with the best of intentions, change the political control of force and erode the functional control of force in a way that is similar to the effects of "money-grabbing" TNCs. Similarly, TNCs that link their investments to international norms about appropriate uses of force also appear to affect the social control of force – though, like their "value motivated" counterparts, in ways not always supported by political change. In these cases, however, the changes do not appear to introduce the reinforcing process that optimists hope for. Though transnational payment for violence changes the political control of force in each case, increasing the potential influence of transnational actors, the social and material incentives for transnational actors (sometimes combined with their lack of expertise in security issues) frequently lead transnational actors to strategies that (intentionally or not) increase neither functional nor social control of violence – thus leaving politics changed, but states still weak. Though the more optimistic scenario is possible, its conditions appear to be hard to meet.

Transnational corporate financing and the control of force

Transnational corporations have a long history of investment in far-flung places where governance may be weak. The search for extractable resources, inexpensive labor, and new markets has led TNCs to invest despite state weakness and then take steps to guarantee their property and workforce.[4] These steps range from pleas for government help (accompanied by reminders of the benefits of foreign direct investment [FDI] and threats of withdrawal) to TNC financial support for either the state's general security capacity or a portion of the state security apparatus specifically charged with protecting TNC property, to TNC payment for a private entity such as a PSC to provide protection services. After the Cold War, increased instability in many parts of the third world opened another chapter in this history.

Studies connecting FDI and what I have called the political control of force are legion.[5] Case study research has suggested a particular relationship between foreign investment in oil, diamonds, and other minerals and a repressive state's security apparatuses that is perceived to work first and foremost on behalf of the property rights of foreign investors in Latin America, Africa, the Middle East and Asia.[6] The logic of the argument is that foreign direct investors supply the state with needed revenue, eclipsing the state's need to build support among its populace in return for taxes. The resulting "rentier" state is beholden to external investors rather than internal support – this is said to erode the potential for democracy and harness coercive forces for the protection of foreign property.[7] This investment thus changes the political control of force – enhancing the influence of foreign investors and their domestic allies. At the same time it decreases (or does not improve) the social control of force – as security forces ignore international norms, particularly those regarding human rights to protect TNC investments. Evaluating its impact on the functional control of force is complicated, though. Many times it builds a strong and well-equipped force, which could be argued to improve the functional control of force – at least in the short run. Using violent repression as a solution to societal demands,

---

[4] Of course, TNCs also can take other steps to enhance stability. Nick Butler talks about corporate engagement to insure community development. See Butler, "Companies in International Relations," pp. 158–62. Others have talked about a role for business in conflict resolution and the like. See Nelson, *Business of Peace.*

[5] Literature regarding the so-called "resource curse" and its affect on politics in the state is relevant here. See for instance, Karl, *The Paradox of Plenty*; Michael Ross, "Does Oil Hinder Democracy?" *World Politics* Vol. 53, No. 3 (April 2001): 325–61; Douglas Yates, *The Rentier State in Africa: Oil Rent Dependency and Neocolonialsim in the Republic of Gabon* (Trenton, NJ: Africa World Press, 1996); Hazem Beblawi and Giacomo Luciani, eds., *The Rentier State* (New York: Croom Helm, 1987).

[6] See Tornquist, "Rent Capitalism"; Karl, *Paradox of Plenty*; Clark, "Petro-Politics in Congo"; Skocpol, "Rentier State." Quantitative analysis of these relationships has been more guarded. Michael Ross finds that oil exporters demonstrate greater military spending, but that other mineral exports are negatively associated with military spending. See Ross, "Does Oil Hinder Democracy?"

[7] Ross, "Does Oil Hinder Democracy"; Skocpol, "Rentier State"; Tornquist, "Rent Capitalism."

however, often spawns a cycle of violence that erodes security and the capacity of even strong forces in the long run.

In a twist on this logic, others have pointed out that foreign investment can lead in more perverse directions – instead of building repressive state instruments of coercion, rulers may opt to guarantee foreign property with a variety of non-state coercive instruments. Though the enhanced influence of external investors on security decisions is similar, worries about internal threats may lead rulers to funnel foreign funds into privately controlled security rather than into state bureaucracies. In these instances, the effect of foreign financing on functional control is reversed, leading to "quasi-states," "shadow states," and "warlords."[8] Rulers use the trappings of external sovereignty for commercial opportunities and political alliances but operate without even a semblance of regard for the collective good – often erasing social controls on the use of force. Such strategies not only affect the domestic population, but also cultivate illicit economies and undermine order in the country and in surrounding territories.[9]

The wealth of research on transnational commercial financing of security, then, comes to the uniform conclusion that foreign investors, involved in the financing of security, change the political control of force. TNCs gain sway over security goals, and this leads away from an improvement in the social control of force but can lead to different effects on the functional control of force – sometimes enhancing functional control in the short run (with serious long-run risks), other times decreasing functional control even in the short term – depending largely on whether funds are directed into a state military or non-state security apparatuses.

Oil in Nigeria

The history of oil companies in Nigeria illustrates how transnational financing and specific payments to security forces has led to the more functional of the two outcomes, but also reveals the inherent instability associated with changes in political control and short-run functional gains that are not accompanied by improvement in social control. The particular unfolding of events in Nigeria, however, also illustrates how the political changes can lead transnational corporations to pursue new strategies – with associated differences in the social control of violence.

[8] See Robert Jackson, *Quasi-States: Sovereignty, International Relations and the Third World* (New York: Cambridge University Press, 1990); Reno, *Warlord Politics*; Reno, "Shadow States and the Political Economy of Civil War."
[9] Reno, *Warlord Politics*.

The relationship between oil companies and the use of force in Nigeria has obtained almost paradigmatic status.[10] Nigeria became an oil exporter in 1958 – two years before independence. Both oil and the military have been involved in Nigerian politics since independence.[11] The state is highly reliant on oil – though oil contributes only 13 percent of Nigeria's gross domestic product, it supplies more than 80 percent of the federal government's revenues.[12] Unsurprisingly, then, petroleum policy has been generally stable despite the frequent changes in Nigerian governments – over the course of almost forty years, from 1960 to 1998, relations with oil companies were an element of continuity across the ten governments.[13]

The Nigerian economy's heavy dependence on oil has led it to track closely with oil revenue and the Nigerian government's income to fluctuate wildly depending on the international price of oil.[14] In and of itself, this has contributed to instability as boom and bust oil cycles play on the economy. Over-concentration on oil has also eroded the country's capacity for food production, and led to a decline in manufacturing exports. The fact that most Nigerians see little of the benefits from even the boom cycles – an estimated 90 percent of national wealth is held by only 10 percent of the population, an oil enriched elite of former military officers and their networks – has led this potentially wealthy state to rank near the bottom (148 out of 173) of the UN's 2002 Human Development Report.[15] The relationship between poverty and the incidence of civil war is well established.[16] This is one

---

[10] Commercial oil companies have been involved in Nigeria since the 1930s, though oil exports only took off in the 1960s. The Nigerian government gradually imposed greater terms on these companies through the 1960s and 1970s and the 1979 constitution claims government ownership over all minerals, oil, and gas. Bronwen Manby, *The Price of Oil: Corporate Responsibility and Human Rights Violations in Nigeria's Oil Producing Communities* (New York: Human Rights Watch, 1999), p. 26.

[11] By the early 1990s oil production accounted for 90 percent of the country's foreign exchange receipts and oil exports for 97 percent of total oil receipts. Frynas, "Political Instability and Business," p. 457. The petroleum sector comprises more than 40 percent of GDP. Manby, *The Price of Oil*, p. 25.

[12] Okechukwu Ibeanu, "Oiling the Friction: Environmental Conflict Management in the Niger Delta, Nigeria," *Environmental Change and Security Project Report*, No. 6 (summer 2000), p. 21. See also Salih Booker and William Minter, "The US and Nigeria: Thinking Beyond Oil," *Great Decisions* 2003 (available at www.greatdecisions.org), p. 44.

[13] Frynas, "Political Instability and Business," p. 460; Sarah Ahmad Khan, *Nigeria: the Political Economy of Oil* (Oxford: Oxford University Press, 1994).

[14] "Royal Dutch/Shell in Nigeria," Harvard Business School Case 9–399–126, 20 April 2000, p. 5 and Exhibit 6.

[15] Booker and Minter, "US and Nigeria," pp. 45–6.

[16] Fearon and Laitin, "Ethnicity, Insurgency, and Civil War"; Gurr, Marshall, and Khosla, *Peace and Conflict*; Collier, "Doing Well out of War."

variation of the pattern the oft-cited resource curse literature has found in numerous instances – foreign resources cause a state to be beholden to FDI rather than its citizens, which leads to poor investment decisions, corruption, and instability.

In Nigeria, though, oil companies have also contributed more directly to the financing and direction of force.[17] The unequal distribution of oil benefits combined with the often devastating environmental consequences of oil extraction in the Niger Delta led to a "petro-movement" that incited rebellion and violence against the state and oil facilities.[18] In the early 1990s, the Ogonis, led by Ken Saro-Wiwa, formed a movement for the Survival of the Ogoni people to protest massive oil operations accompanied by meager investment in public services (like electricity and water). In the wake of this movement, a variety of additional protests – including among the more numerous Ijaw in Delta state also sprang up.[19] In response to these protests, oil companies worked to generate security for themselves.

Details of the arrangements between oil companies and public or private Nigerian security forces are opaque.[20] Some have claimed that "on countless occasions, oil companies have called out directly the police, the army and the navy to quell disturbances on their installations, without applying to the government for help."[21] The so-called "Shell police" were assigned to protect Shell facilities.[22] Shell also admitted to paying field allowances to Nigerian military units associated with the disruption of popular protests in particular instances.[23] There are reports that Shell Petroleum Development Company of Nigeria (the Nigerian subsidiary of Royal Dutch/Shell Group of Companies) both purchased weapons and used its helicopters and boats to transport the Nigerian military.[24] Shell is not the only company that participated in this more direct financing of force, Chevron helicopters transported troops to the site of a protest at the Parabe oil platform where protesters were shot.[25]

---

[17] Pegg, "Cost of Doing Business."
[18] Booker and Minter, "US and Nigeria," p. 45; Ibeanu, "Oiling the Friction"; Manby, *Price of Oil.*
[19] Frynas, "Political Instability and Business," p. 466. Ken Saro-Wiwa and the "Ogani 8" were executed in 1995.
[20] Manby, *Price of Oil,* p. 167.
[21] Ibeanu, "Oiling the Friction," p. 22.
[22] "Companies were responsible for paying, training, and equipping the police assigned to their facilities, including providing them with arms as necessary," Harvard Business School, "Royal Dutch/Shell in Nigeria," p. 5.
[23] Ibid., p. 170.
[24] Pegg, "Cost of Doing Business."
[25] Ibid.

The transnational financing of oil has had significant political effects in Nigeria. By virtue of their importance to the government, oil companies have a variety of mechanisms for influencing policy – access to government officials and financial support for weaponry and troops being only the most obvious and direct.

The behavior of the Nigerian police and military in a large part of the 1980s and 1990s did not accord with international norms about the proper use of violence.[26] Opponents of Shell implicate the company and its interests directly – arguing that Shell hired security forces that behaved in opposition to international norms. For instance, the 1990 president of the Movement for the Survival of the Ogoni People (MOSOP), Dr. G. B. Leton, claimed, "[T]he Ogoni case is of genocide being committed in the dying years of the twentieth century by multi-national oil companies under the supervision of the Government . . . of Nigeria."[27]

The participation of the Nigerian police and military in the protection of oil enriched the resources available to the security forces in ways that one might think would make it more capable and increase functional control.[28] The huge sums of money paid by oil companies for security, however, have also been a magnet for corruption. Former military ruler Sani Abacha, for instance, is estimated to have siphoned off $4 billion to foreign bank accounts. The corruption also extends down into the forces.[29] Both the police and military in Nigeria have been distracted by money-making potential in a way that decreases their capacity. The use of patronage and payoffs by Abacha's regime played into this strategy, which bordered on warlordism in the mid-1990s.[30] Though there are many examples of the way corruption has impinged on the capacity of the Nigerian police,[31] some of the most obvious problems come up in the military's behavior abroad. Both officers and common soldiers

---

[26] See Amnesty International, "Security Forces: Serving to Protect and Respect Human Rights?" *Amnesty International* (19 December 2002).

[27] "Royal Dutch/Shell in Nigeria," p. 9.

[28] Claude E. Welch, Jr., discusses some of the improvements the Nigerian military made, see "Civil–Military Agonies in Nigeria," *Armed Forces and Society* Vol. 21, No. 4 (summer, 1995), pp. 604–07.

[29] Sayre P. Schatz, "Pirate Capitalism and the Inert Economy of Nigeria," *Journal of Modern African Studies* Vol. 22, No. 1 (March 1984). See also Welch, "Civil–Military Agonies in Nigeria," p. 608.

[30] Reno, *Warlord Politics*, ch. 6.

[31] See Amnesty International "Security Forces: Serving to Protect and Respect Human Rights?"; Human Rights Watch Report, "THE BAKASSI BOYS: the Legitimation of Murder and Torture," May 2002; Department of Justice, "International Criminal Investigative Training Assistance Program (ICITAP): Nigeria," http://www.usdoj.gov/criminal/icitap/nigeria.html.

subsidize their salaries with private money-making activities. In the officer corps, this takes the form of administrative assignments, payoffs, and involvement in illicit trade; in the force at large, it takes the form of looting.[32] Nigerian troops' peacekeeping capacities are diminished by these activities. Leading the ECOMOG regional peacekeeping force in Liberia in 1997, the Nigerians reportedly engaged in systematic looting – including shipping entire buildings to be sold for scrap abroad, trafficking in heroin, and child prostitution.[33]

Furthermore, though Nigeria's national interest is tied to oil and oil money, the particular use of forces in Nigeria did not yield stability for the production of oil. Indeed, some have argued that had Nigerian forces been deployed to respond to citizen needs and complaints surrounding the oil fields, they might have better insured a more sustainable and peaceful continuation of oil pumping and processing. The access of oil company personnel to high level politicians and the ability of the oil companies to direct resources into particular areas (protecting oil fields) demonstrated a political impact from transnational financing that arguably undermined functional control in the long run.[34]

Business for peace?

The behavior of Nigerian troops, and police, and its reflection on oil companies led to a transnational campaign targeting oil investment in Nigeria. Particularly when the Nigerian government executed Ken Saro-Wiwa and "the Ogoni 8," many communities in the Niger Delta, where people saw little difference between the oil companies (particularly Shell) and the Nigerian state, joined with transnational INGOs in a campaign for retaliation that mounted specific boycotts on Shell.[35]

The company responded (as several did at the time) by undertaking a worldwide campaign to better understand its reputation and "engage"

---

[32] Reno, *Warlord Politics*, ch. 6 (particularly, pp. 196–97, 199–200, 204–08), Kenneth Cain, "Send in the Marines," *New York Times* 8 August 2003, p. A21.

[33] Cain, "Send in the Marines."

[34] The propensity of the Nigerian military to coup – and its existence as a political machine – adds yet another dimension to this political equation. See Welch, "Civil–Military Agonies in Nigeria"; Julius O. Ihonvbere, "A Critical Evaluation of the Failed 1990 Coup in Nigeria," *Journal of Modern African Studies* Vol. 29, No. 1 (1991). See also Robin Luckham, *The Nigerian Military* (Cambridge: Cambridge University Press, 1973).

[35] See Ibeanu, "Oiling the Friction," p. 21, http://www.essentialaction.org/shell/, http://www.moles.org/ProjectUnderground/motherlode/shell/nig.html. Concerted efforts by INGOs in the 1980s and 1990s often targeted transnational investment as well as states for human rights and environmental abuses. See Keck and Sikkink, *Activitsts Beyond Borders*; Florini, *Third Force*.

with stakeholders – both internationally with INGOs and locally with communities where it worked. In 1998 the company began a process to hold regular meetings with key institutional investors to discuss non-financial issues such as human rights and the environment.[36] Shell thus joined a handful of international businesses that have "expressed interest in working in partnership with civil society organizations and governments to make a positive contribution to peace and stability."[37] In 1999, the company reported that it had processes in place to engage with communities on local concerns in ninety-one countries and efforts to measure the effectiveness of their efforts in forty-eight of those.[38] Shell has also supported the United Nation's "Global Compact" and in 2002 joined efforts to support the "Voluntary Principles on Security and Human Rights."[39]

In an effort mounted by International Alert, the Council on Economic Priorities, and the Prince of Wales Business Leaders' Forum, a document was produced called "The Business of Peace," that outlines the ways in which the private sector might be a partner in conflict prevention and resolution. This document highlights Shell's efforts along with the efforts of British Petroleum (implicated in human rights abuses in Colombia). Responsible TNCs, the document argues, should at the very least comply with national regulations and benchmark their local practices against internationally agreed upon laws, conventions, and standards. Beyond this, companies should be aware of their impacts – particularly as they relate to violent conflict – and should develop policies to minimize damage that may result from their practices. Finally, it suggests that companies can create positive value through social investment, consulting with stakeholders, building civic institutions, and engaging in collective action with other companies.[40]

"The Voluntary Principles" negotiated between TNCs, INGOs, and the US and UK governments further guide TNCs' security decisions when working in unstable territories.[41] The principles suggest attention to risk assessment and awareness of the security situation before

[36] Wales, *Business for Peace*, p. 134.
[37] Hauffler, "Is there a Role for Business in Conflict Prevention?" p. 659.
[38] Ibid. See also http://www.shell.com/home/Framework?siteId=home.
[39] Bennett Freeman, "Managing Risk and Building Trust: the Challenge of Implementing the Voluntary Principles on Security and Human Rights," remarks at Rules of Engagement: How Business Can Be a Force for Peace conference, The Hague, 13 November 2002. See also "Voluntary Principles on Security and Human Rights," US Department of State, Democracy, Human Rights, and Labor.
[40] Nelson, *Business of Peace*, p. 7.
[41] "Voluntary Principles on Security and Human Rights," US Department of State, Democracy, Human Rights, and Labor.

investing in a territory, a series of consultations with the host country to both assess the company's impact and communicate the requisite international standards the company wishes the government to follow. They suggest that companies should use their influence to promote adherence to applicable international law. In the event that a government cannot provide security and a company engages a PSC, the guidelines suggest that the company insure the PSC observes the policies of the company, maintains adequate professional proficiency, acts in a lawful manner, observes rules of engagement, and conducts only preventative or defensive security measures. Furthermore, the company should insure that the PSC's employees are screened for human rights abuses and should investigate all uses of force, particularly any reported human rights abuses.[42]

Since 1998 Shell has unmistakably linked its efforts to claims about principles rather than merely profits. Its actions are also an indicator that the company believes its future revenues demand that it take some responsibility for the way governance works in weak states. And the company has shifted from a strategy of negotiating only with the central government (and writing off any damages to failures by the government) to a strategy that involves more actors – Memoranda of Understanding (MOUs) with stakeholders. The increasing inclusion of other stake-holders changes the political process by which Shell engages with the Nigerian government.

Shell's actions initially corresponded with a tentative improvement in the social and functional control of force in Nigeria.[43] The government committed itself to reform and President Obasanjo "quickly retired the so called 'political soldiers' who had held public office while on active duty and reinforced those officers committed to military professionalism."[44] Also, the government has embarked on an effort to re-professionalize the military and police.

Any improvement in the behavior of the Nigerian forces, though, was likely the product of a variety of factors. Particularly, Nigeria experienced two democratic elections and with President Obasanjo's commitment to reform has come a massive infusion of US military aid (much of it is for training and reorganization and is being conducted by MPRI).[45] The cost of this program is great, and any evaluation of

---

[42] Ibid.

[43] Interviews with Defense Department personnel, fall 2003.

[44] Booker and Minter, "US and Nigeria," p. 50.

[45] Interview with Bernd McConnell, January 2000, Ed Soyster, MPRI, Bill Klontz, MPRI, November 2003. See also, "Nigeria: Defense Ministry Promotes Democratic Value in Army," *Africa News*, 11 December 2003.

functional improvements would have to balance the cost with the improvements – some in Nigeria have complained that the cost is too great and not a worthwhile use of Nigerian funds.[46] Though the jury is still out on the benefits (or costs) of the reform effort, it is intended to work in the same direction as any improvement in Shell's behavior would. The professional training for the Nigerian military and police, particularly, is important. As we shall see in the cases that follow, transnational actors frequently lack the expertise necessary to push for or oversee such professional training. The fact that the US is paying for part of this training and overseeing it should increase the chance that Shell's efforts to support a more professional force will have its intended effect.

Furthermore, assertions of improvement, particularly in the social and political control of force, are hotly disputed. Shell's efforts with the MOUs are said to be elitist and may involve more social groups and INGOs but do little to meet the "simple needs" of the vast majority.[47] In 1999 an (admittedly violent) attack by Ijaw youths on policemen in Odi led to chilling reprisals by the army.[48] Furthermore, disputes continue to rage over the responsibility for environmental damage caused by abandoned Shell facilities – with Shell claiming that the damages were caused by sabotage and thus it is not liable (by law, oil companies are not liable for damages caused by sabotage to their facilities), while the community claims that the facilities are old and have not been maintained. Regardless, the disputes delay clean up and the environmental problems provide impetus to more protest and violence. In response to these continued frustrations in the communities, Obasanjo's creation of a paramilitary force to combat those vandalizing petroleum pipelines was seen as a step toward repressive action.[49] Furthermore, Human Rights Watch argued that violence in the Niger Delta during the 2003 springtime elections was "par for the course" – similar to what it had been before Shell changed its strategy.[50] Continued violence throughout the year and into 2004 (including a potential coup plot) led

---

[46] Total US expenditure on military training in Nigeria was $256,213 in 2000, $579,989 in 2001, $193,559 in 2002, and $467,738 in 2003. See US Department of State, "Foreign Military Training and DOD Engagement Activities of Interest," Joint Report to Congress, Department of State, Bureau of Political Military Affairs, available at http://www.state.gov/t/pm/rls/rpt/fmtrpt/.

[47] Ibeanu, "Oiling the Friction," p. 29.

[48] Youths took several policemen hostage and tortured them to death. In return over 100 civilians were killed and the town was razed. Ibid., pp. 30–31; Booker and Minter, "The US and Nigeria," p. 45.

[49] Ibeanu, "Oiling the Friction," p. 31.

[50] Human Rights Watch Report, "The Warri Crisis: Fueling Violence," 17 December 2003.

to further skepticism about Nigeria's direction and the extent to which Shell's role had changed.[51] Some suggested that, even given its new strategy, Shell's capacity to influence the control of force in the country was limited. Indeed, a Shell funded report in June 2004 concluded, "The basis for escalated, protracted, and entrenched violence is rapidly being established . . . It would be surprising if [Shell] is able to continue onshore resource extraction in the Niger Delta beyond 2008, whilst complying with Shell Business Principles."[52] If there has been improvement in the control of force in Nigeria, then, it has been modest and Shell's efforts should be seen as only part of this result.

Tough choices for TNCs

The corporate social responsibility movement – with Shell in Nigeria as an epitome – has led to a debate about what role TNCs should play in governance. This movement was designed to improve the behavior of TNCs, asserting that TNCs must be part of the solution to avoid being part of the problem.[53] The logic behind corporate social responsibility is that corporations have many resources at their disposal that can be harnessed for the social good. It is true that Shell in Nigeria has much freedom of action – more than will be the case in either of the following INGO cases, where the reliance on donors or other fundraising limits their range of choices.

Shell, however, has frequently argued that its role is less consequential than many assume and has expressed worries about moving outside of a "proper" commercial role. For instance, in the early 1990s the Ogoni argued that Shell could persuade the government to behave better by threatening to pull out of the country.[54] Shell officials, however, stated that such a threat would have limited impact. Furthermore, they held that action to threaten the government would violate the proper role for a commercial company. Shell business principles committed the company to an apolitical role. "Shell companies should endeavor always to act commercially, operating within existing national laws in a socially responsible manner and avoid involvement in politics."[55] Even as it has moved to embrace corporate social responsibility, Shell has been uneasy about too large a role in "governance" that would violate this principle. Indeed, concerns about the legitimacy of its role as the guardian of

---

[51] "Nigerian Sources Deny Probability of New Coup, but Highlights Failure of US Approach to Reshaping Army," *Defense and Foreign Affairs Daily*, 12 April 2003.
[52] Karl Maier, "Shell May Have to Quit Nigeria," *Bloomberg News*, 11 June 2004.
[53] Nelson, *Business of Peace*.
[54] Ibid., p. 11.   [55] Ibid.

democracy and human rights led Shell officials to balk at some of the demands made by critics of the government.[56] While Shell was engaging in an effort to broaden its role in the community and clean up its image, it was unwilling to exert direct effort to affect government behavior, believing that such action was "political" and well beyond its proper mandate as a commercial entity.

Some have supported this reticence, claiming that asking companies to play the role of modern day missionaries spreading western values is illegitimate and unlikely to work.[57] It is illegitimate because TNCs have no right to be the guardians of democracy and human rights. It is unlikely to work because companies that attend to such issues are unlikely to profit – and even if they do profit are unlikely to be trusted purveyors of democratic values. This perspective has a long history. The idea that a corporation has responsibilities other than maximizing profits for its shareholders, according to Milton Friedman, undermines the fundamental tenets of a free economy.[58] David Henderson made a similar argument in his liberal critique of corporate social responsibility, arguing that it is premised on intellectual misconceptions and is detrimental to the functioning of a market economy. "Welfare may be reduced, not only because businesses are compelled to operate less efficiently, but also because new forms of intervention arising out of the adoption of corporate social responsibility, including closer regulation, narrow the domain of competition and economic freedom."[59] More recently Marina Ottoway argues that oil companies are designed to find, extract, and distribute oil – not to guarantee democracy and respect for human rights – "taking on the role of imposing change on entire countries does not fit the nature of these organizations."[60] Despite some general support for the notion of corporate social responsibility, this debate has yet to be resolved. Critics from the right worry that social responsibility taken too far will undermine profits and critics from the left worry that asking corporations to guarantee democratic practices is like asking the fox to guard the hen house.

These worries, however, may have as much to do with discomfort about the movement of non-governmental forms into governance

---

[56] Harvard Business School, "Royal Dutch/Shell in Nigeria"; see also, Jedrzei Frynas and Scott Pegg, *Transnational Corporations and Human Rights* (New York: Palgrave, 2003).

[57] Marina Ottoway, "Reluctant Missionaries," *Foreign Policy* (July/August 2001): 44–55.

[58] Milton Friedman, *Capitalism and Freedom* (Chicago: University of Chicago Press, 1962), p. 133.

[59] David Henderson, *Misguided Virtue: False Notions of Corporate Social Responsibility* (London: Institute of Economic Affairs, 2001), pp. 147–48.

[60] Ottoway, "Reluctant Missionaries," p. 53.

processes as the substantive worries voiced by the critics. As we shall see in the rest of this chapter, similar kinds of debates have emerged in both the conservation and relief INGO communities as they have moved into financing security. When private organizations step into financing violence, they become a de facto part of the governance process, and simultaneously open themselves to claims about the results of their actions that make it hard to maintain an apolitical or "neutral" status. But just as avoiding responsibility is seen to be illegitimate, so often is seizing a greater governance role. The changes in the political control of force associated with private financing of security also disrupt political and social norms in the private sector.

Humanitarian relief in war zones

One can hardly imagine a more pointed contrast in motivations than between transnational corporations and humanitarian relief organizations. While TNCs are driven by profit, relief organizations dedicated to humanitarian principles work at great risk to themselves for little material benefit. Individuals working in the relief community have aided civilians in war zones for some time – aiming to create a humanitarian space within which individuals have access to food, medicine, and shelter even in the midst of conflict.[61] In the 1990s, though, a proliferation of what came to be termed "complex humanitarian emergencies" began, which both increased the danger to relief workers and opened a debate about whether humanitarian relief aggravated the suffering it was designed to forestall.[62] The now infamous results of the relief community's efforts to provide humanitarian aid to Rwandan refugees in the Goma Camps following the 1994 genocide is both evidence of and fodder for these debates.

The efforts and resources of transnational relief actors changed the political control of violence – both indirectly as relief resources affected the power of local coalitions and more directly as humanitarian organizations, through UN financing, tried to limit violence in the camps. The redistribution of political control among local actors, though, enhanced the power of those least likely to abide by humanitarian principles. Despite

---

[61] For a discussion of the difference between humanitarian and human rights organizations and orientations, see Larry Minear, *The Humanitarian Enterprise* (Bloomfield, CT: Kumarian Press, 2002), pp. 37–54.

[62] Ibid., p. 2. CARE, Canada reported that a total of six people working for CARE, Canada or its nine sister operations were killed between 1979 and 1985. The toll from 1985 to 1998 was eighty-seven. See Norma Greenaway, "Aid Agencies Told to Hire Mercenaries for Protection," *Ottawa Citizen*, 28 January 1999.

the deployment of resources in support of humanitarian controls on violence, then, the relief efforts did little to enhance the social control of force. Furthermore, the relief community's resources allowed forces in the camps to become political powers themselves, reducing functional control of violence. Despite very different motivations, the finances of the relief community in the Goma camps had similar effects on the control of violence as have TNCs. Though members of the relief community recognized (and worried about) the effect of their efforts, they had even less latitude than TNCs and found themselves having to choose between "a rock and a hard place."

Indirect transnational financing of security – relief and violence among Rwandan refugees

In 1994 the Rwandan government directed the slaughter of those who supported the implementation of a power sharing agreement with the Tutsi-dominated Rwandan Patriotic Front (RPF). When the RPF fought back and defeated the Rwandan Armed Forces (Forces Armées Rwandaises – FAR), the majority Hutu government fled causing the Hutu population to flee as well into the border areas in Zaire, Tanzania, and Burundi. It is estimated that two million Hutu sought refuge between April (when nearly 170,000 Rwandans crossed into the Ngara district of Tanzania in one twenty-four hour period) and July (when 500,000 crossed into North Kivu, Zaire between the 14th and 17th).[63]

The sudden and dramatic exodus created a public health disaster. The relief community responded by setting up camps, building sanitation facilities, and bringing food and medical supplies to a desperate population.[64] Between the months of April and December 1994, alone, the international community spent $1.2 billion to provide relief to the Hutu population in these camps. The total cost over the

---

[63] Fiona Terry, *Condemned to Repeat: the Paradox of Humanitarian Action* (Ithaca: Cornell University Press, 2002), pp. 155, 171.

[64] Ibid., pp. 170–75. See also Michael Barnett, *Eyewitness to a Genocide* (Ithaca: Cornell University Press, 2002); Scott Feil, *Preventing Genocide: How the Early Use of Force Might Have Succeeded in Rwanda* (New York: Carnegie Commission on Deadly Conflict, 1998). Bruce Jones points out that the relief effort ended up costing the aid community a total of $2.5 billion. Compared to the roughly $3 million for the Arusha process and the $25 million for UNAMIR before the genocide, "money spent on responding to the humanitarian consequences of the genocide exceeded by ninety times money spent on efforts to resolve the Rwandan civil war. See Jones, *Peacemaking in Rwanda: the Dynamics of Failure* (Boulder: Lynne Rienner, 2001), p. 139. For an argument that an international response may have had little effect, see Alan J. Kuperman, *The Limits of Humanitarian Intervention: Genocide in Rwanda* (Washington, DC: Brookings, 2001).

following two years has been estimated at $2.5 billion.[65] These humanitarian actions were based on a well-established international norm that even in the midst of conflict, there are basic human needs that should be tended to.[66] Evoking this norm had an immediate effect – it accorded legal and physical protection to the populations in the camps from the Tutsi-led government in Rwanda.

The problem was that the camps contained a government and an army as well as refugees. In essence, the humanitarian response "permitted war criminals and an entire army to mingle with the refugees and set up camp in Zaire."[67] Even before humanitarian organizations considered financing security directly, their presence, doctrine, and resources changed the political control of force (allowing resources for the government in exile), without enhancing the social control of force (the forces operated without regard for international norms surrounding the proper use of force), and decreased the functional control of force (allowing a foreign/rebel/parallel force to mobilize in the camps).

The resources deployed in the name of humanitarian principles changed the power of political actors over violence – elevating the capacities of extremist elements of the old government. The exiled government already had freedom of movement thanks to (the late) President Mobutu's support, but the relief effort allowed the government in exile a new strategy for regaining power with refugees as the central element. The refugees both guaranteed resources (via the relief effort) and legitimacy (via a constituency) to their effort. Though the FAR had its own camp in Lac Vert (just south of Goma), many soldiers, militiamen, and former political leaders settled in the camps at Goma.[68]

In the ensuing months, the FAR and its allies set up an administrative structure in the camps to serve their remobilization effort.[69] By inflating population numbers, stealing aid supplies, and taxing the local employees of INGOs, the FAR directly lined its coffers. Original estimates of 1.2 million refugees in Goma were revised downward to

---

[65] As Jones points out, the $1.2 billion figure alone exceeds by 20 percent the prewar gross national product of Rwanda. John Borton, Emery Brusset, and Alistair Hallam, *Humanitarian Aid and Effects: Report of the Study III of the Joint Evaluation of Emergency Assistance in Rwanda* (Copenhagen: DANIDA, 1996), pp. 111–18, cited in Jones, *Peacemaking in Rwanda*, p. 139.

[66] For an overview of humanitarian principles, see Jean Pictet, *The Fundamental Principles of the Red Cross* (Geneva: Henry Dunant Institute, 1979); David P. Forsythe, *Humanitarian Politics: the International Committee of the Red Cross* (Baltimore: Johns Hopkins University Press, 1977).

[67] Terry, *Condemned to Repeat*, p. 173.

[68] Jones, *Peacemaking in Rwanda*, p. 140.

[69] Terry, *Condemned to Repeat*, pp. 175–80.

850,000 and then further downward once a census showed 740,000.[70] Robert Hauser from the World Food Program claimed that even that number was too high, "we deliver daily in the camps sufficient food to meet the needs of 740,000 refugees when we know that there are approximately 600,000."[71] Malnutrition rates remained high, though, suggesting that the food was being stolen. Also, refugees used the aid to purchase services (including extortion) that fed more resources to the FAR and its allies.[72]

During the first few months, particularly, violence was the primary tool by which the FAR and its allies controlled the refugee population. "The former politicians and military retained strong control over the refugees through the use of violence, coercion, authority, propaganda, and social networks."[73] It was estimated that 4000 refugees died as the result of violence.[74] The use of violence against the refugees was a direct affront to the social control of force, operating against international norms about the use of force – and the particular humanitarian values that underlay the relief effort. It also created violence and disorder in the camps, undermining the functional control of force. More importantly, the remobilization of the FAR and its supporters was aimed toward a series of armed incursions into Rwanda, which eventually led the new regime in Rwanda under President Kagame to attack the camps in 1996.

Direct transnational financing of security

By August 1994, the level of violence in the camps led the United Nations High Commissioner for Refugees (UNHCR) to claim to the Secretary General and the Department of Peace Keeping Operations (DPKO) that "the situation was beyond their scope as well as their mandate" and to consider actions to correct the security situation.[75] While the DPKO began a discussion of possibilities, the UNHCR began a set of negotiations with the government of Zaire for a force provided by Zaire but directed internationally to provide security for the camps.[76]

---

[70] Situation Report no. 10 (Goma: UNHCR mimeo, 25 September 1995), cited in ibid., p. 187.
[71] Situation Report no. 19, 15 January–15 February 1995 (Goma: UNHCR mimeo, February 1995) cited in Terry, *Condemned to Repeat*, p. 187.
[72] Terry, *Condemned to Repeat*, p. 186.
[73] Ibid., p. 181.
[74] Ibid., p. 175.
[75] Jones, *Peacemaking in Rwanda*, p. 141.
[76] Though successfully negotiated in September, this proposal was put aside until January while the DPKO explored more robust options. Ibid.

According to Jones, the DPKO considered three options. First was a large scale (7,000–4,000 for Goma and 3000 for Bukavu), Chapter VII operation to separate the soldiers from the refugees. Second was a smaller (3,000–5,000 troops) under Chapter VI rules to slowly clean the camps, area by area.[77] The third option was a proposal to use a private security company to provide training and logistical support for Zairean troops that would provide security for the camps. The Chapter VII operation was most clearly designed to meet the real goal but the Security Council would not even consider it. In the wake of the recent experience in Somalia, the Security Council regarded such action as "fantasy." The Secretary General preferred the Chapter VI operation, both because it was more likely to be approved by the Security Council and because it required the formal agreement of the Zairean governments but not the participation of Zairean troops. Given the implicit agreement between Mobutu and the Rwandan government in the camps, he worried that Zairean troops would be reluctant to separate the FAR from the refugees. The private security plan had some support but was ultimately rejected on the basis of cost and principle.[78]

In the end, none of these options was employed and UNHCR's deal with Zaire was resurrected and put in place in January 1995. Under an agreement with the UN, a contingent of 1,500 Zairean military personnel was deployed in the camps at UN expense.[79] The Zairean Camp Security Operation (ZCSO) was civilian in structure and reported to a Civilian Liaison Unit (mainly Dutch police).[80] The force was charged with improving public order in the camps, preventing violence aimed at the voluntary repatriation of refugees, protecting humanitarian facilities and personnel, and escorting convoys to the Rwandan border.[81] The civilian liaison unit had few mechanisms through which to affect the daily practices of the Zairean troops, though, as the UN paid Mobutu and Mobutu paid the troops – who supplemented their incomes by extorting from the refugees.

The presence of the Zairean troops – particularly the first contingent – did appear to quell some of the worst violence, enhancing functional control in the camps. Fiona Terry points out, however, that the deployment of these troops overlapped with the consolidation of

---

[77] Under the UN Charter's Chapter VI, the Security Council can work to solve disputes peacefully. Under Chapter VII, the Security Council can maintain or restore international peace and security militarily. See http://www.un.org/aboutun/charter/.

[78] Ibid., pp. 141–42.

[79] Terry, *Condemned to Repeat*, p. 176.

[80] Jones, *Peacemaking in Rwanda*, p. 144.

[81] Terry, *Condemned to Repeat*, p. 176.

political control by the FAR and increasing worries among its leadership that continued violence would erode international sympathy and
reduce the support they found so lucrative.[82] Terry gives more credit to
the consolidation of political control for the decline in violence than to
the presence of the Zairean troops.

In allowing relief workers to go about their business without death
threats, one could argue that the Zairean troops (particularly the first
contingent recruited from the presidential guard) reinforced the
humanitarian principles that underlay the operation in the first place.
The first contingent of troops was also moderately more attuned to
international norms surrounding the use of force than the FAR and its
allies and could be said to have improved the social control of force. The
second contingent of ZCSC, however, "became the principle source of
insecurity" for the refugees.[83] The Zairean soldiers extorted money,
levied taxes on refugees, and allegedly used the refugees for prostitution.[84] As the UNHCR had no alternative and few tools for action,
though, there was little it could do to punish the force.

Most importantly, the Zairean forces did little to reverse the changes
in the political control of force. Their mission was camp control, not
the eradication of the former government, FAR, and associated militias.
In effect, even if we assume that the ZCSC was responsible for a
moderately less dangerous camp environment, the result forestalled a
pull out by relief organizations and thus allowed the FAR to continue its
use of relief resources to remobilize.[85] And, of course, the continuation
of support for the FAR and its allies allowed them to mount strikes on
Rwanda, which eventually led the new Rwandan government to attack
the camps.

Paths forsaken

The impact of the alternatives not chosen presents interesting counter-
factuals. Had the UN created a peacekeeping force, it would have
changed political control of force – enhancing the power of external
actors, particularly the international community represented by the UN.

---

[82] Ibid., pp. 176–77. See also Jones, *Peacemaking in Rwanda*, pp. 143–44; Mark Frohardt,
Diane Paul, and Larry Minear, "Protecting Human Rights: the Challenge to Humanitarian Organizations," occasional paper #35, Thomas Watson Institute, Brown University, 1999, pp. 70–1.

[83] Terry, *Condemned to Repeat*, p. 177.

[84] Ibid.

[85] On 3 November 1994, many of the agencies working in the Goma camps signed a
declaration demanding that the UN address the dangerous security situation. See
Frohardt, Paul, and Minear, "Protecting Human Rights," p. 71.

A UN force would also have been constituted within the principles and values articulated by the international community. Even within such a framework the behavior of UN troops varies considerably – particularly in unstable environments – but generally they behave in a way much more consistent with international values than the Zairean troops did. There is a general sentiment that the UN often fails to enhance the functional control of force.[86] Indeed, in considering the Chapter VI option, the DPKO thought it would only work with a strong, well-equipped backbone and given the absence of potential contributors, it was "dead before it started."[87] The functional difficulties with UN forces can be traced to political problems (many times forces are not deployed effectively because the parties on the Security Council can only agree on a lowest common denominator and do not deploy enough force or deploy forces without a robust doctrine), to operational problems (particularly in cases such as this one, the forces deployed are from UN member states with the least competent forces, and there are coordination problems with the deployment of a UN force regardless of competence), to expense.[88] It is likely that a UN force would have had at least the functional capacities (man for man) of the Zaireans, probably more. Thus the impact of a UN force under a Chapter VI mandate may have curbed some of the worst offenses of the Zairean troops but would have been unlikely to halt the flow of resources to the FAR supporters.

Advocates of private security generally suggest that private security companies will increase the functional control of violence – i.e., PSCs will allow more effective fighting or will reduce costs.[89] Jones appears to believe that the private option was more likely to succeed – calling it a "truly innovative alternative." In this case, an improvement in functional control could mean that the forces would dampen violence in the camps more effectively, that the force could remove the militia and military personnel from the camps and/or that the cost of the force would be less. In the end, though, Jones tells us that the option was

---

[86] William Durch, *The Evolution of UN Peacekeeping* (New York: St. Martins, 1993); William Durch, ed., *UN Peacekeeping, American Politics and the Uncivil Wars of the 1990s* (New York: St. Martins, 1996); Michael Doyle, Ian Johnstone, and Robert Orr, eds., *Keeping the Peace: Multidimensional UN Operations in Cambodia and El Salvador* (Cambridge: Cambridge University Press, 1997). See also Cindy Collins and Thomas Weiss, *An Overview and Assessment of the 1989–1996 Peace Operations Publications*, Occasional Paper, No. 28 (Providence: Thomas J. Watson Institute, 1997).

[87] Jones, *Peacemaking in Rwanda*, p. 143.

[88] Brahimi, "Report of the Panel on United Nations Peace Operations."

[89] Brooks, "Write a Cheque, End a War," and "Supporting the MONUC Mandate with Private Services in the DROC," IPOA Operational Concept Paper, November 2002.

rejected on the basis of principle and its *high cost* (emphasis added).[90] Decision making parties on the Security Council, then, did not believe that the PSC-directed force would have cost less.[91] Jones does not discuss whether UN funded, PSC-directed Zairean troops would have agreed to remove militia and military personnel from the camps in the first place, but this bears consideration. Zaire was a close ally of the old Rwandan government and speculation abounds about agreements between the FAR and the Zairean government that allowed the FAR to keep its weapons, acquire new weapons, and conduct raids from Zairean soil.[92] Also, there was speculation that Zaire would balk at any formal involvement in UN peacekeeping operations to separate the FAR and associated militias from the population.[93] To assume that Zaire would nonetheless allow its troops to carry out such an operation under the direction of a PSC seems an unlikely stretch. It is possible, however, that the training and supervision of a PSC could have improved the behavior of the Zairean forces. The private option had command and control features and allowed for more monitoring – both of which may have precluded some of the Zairean troops' more exploitative activities.

Though the effects on political control of violence would depend on specifications of the contract that were never made, we can speculate. The infusion of money through the DPKO may have given individuals at the UN a greater ability to call the shots – assuming that the DPKO was able to field the requisite expertise to oversee the PSC's activities in the field and had authority to sanction behavior that it did not condone. A PSC presence may have given more information about the activities of the FAR and militia members in ways that could have enhanced the UN's ability to discourage these. On the other hand, the implication that the UN was funding security in the camp and simultaneously allowing the FAR and militia to operate out of that camp may have incited reprisals against the UN and the PSC by the new Rwandan government and the RPF. Furthermore, sometimes PSC activities exacerbate rifts and shift power within the forces they train in unexpected ways. We must also consider, then, the possibility that whatever Zairean forces

---

[90] An intervention plan by EO was estimated to last six months and cost $600,000/day ($1.5 million total). Singer, *Corporate Warriors*, p. 185.

[91] Though in retrospect, the UN operation cost $3 million/day – more than three times as much as the EO estimate. Ibid., p. 186.

[92] Terry, *Condemned to Repeat*, pp. 156–64. See also, *Rwanda/Zaire. Rearming with Impunity: International Support for the Perpetrators of the Rwandan Genocide*, Human Rights Watch Arms Project, Vol. 7, No. 4 (New York: Human Rights Watch, May 1995); *Rwanda: Arming the Perpetrators of Genocide* AFR 02/14/95 (Amnesty International, June 1995).

[93] Jones, *Peacemaking in Rwanda*, p. 142.

were trained in the camps may have upset the balance of forces among the troops in Zaire. In hindsight, of course, this problem appears particularly worrisome given the now apparent instability in Zaire at the time. Any anticipation of the effects on political control of using a PSC must also bear in mind the PSC's reputation and other clients, both of which would be likely to affect the company's decision making and advice.[94]

Some argue that PSCs also enhance the social control of violence. The companies themselves have argued that they inculcate the troops they train with professional norms and standards in ways that make these troops both more effective and more likely to abide by international norms surrounding human rights, international law, and the proper use of force.[95] Again, given the fact that a contract was never specified, it is difficult to anticipate its effects – as the kinds of training and supervision the troops encountered would matter for our expectations. The potential that a PSC would improve the social control was a possibility, but short-term training alone rarely creates enduring improvements in social control.

Either UN force or the private option for security in the Rwandan camps, then, may have produced a less exploitative camp environment, but neither was likely to change the capacity of the FAR and militia to operate in the camps and profit from them and therefore they were not a way around the larger political and diplomatic problem of separating refugees from the perpetrators of violence.

Tough choices for humanitarians

The exodus from Rwanda was so huge that initially humanitarians were overwhelmed with simply creating the infrastructure to cope with and prevent the recurrence of cholera and other disease. As the situation stabilized, however, and the underlying political dynamic became clear, INGOs were faced with a dilemma. As Terry puts it, "the humanitarian imperative to give aid wherever it was needed clashed with the responsibility to ensure that their aid was not used against those for whom it was intended."[96] Organizations within the relief community

---

[94] Koenrad Van Brabant has suggested that aid organizations considering hiring PSCs address a checklist of questions including this one. See Koenrad Van Brabant, *Operational Security Management in Violent Environments* (Washington, DC: Overseas Development Institute, 2000).

[95] Shearer, *Private Armies and Military Intervention*; Correspondence with James Fennell, Managing Director, Defense Systems Africa and Regional Manager (Central Africa), ArmorGroup, April 2000.

[96] Terry, *Condemned to Repeat*, p. 195.

grappled with this dilemma in a variety of ways but in the end only two organizations withdrew from the camps.[97]

The dominance of the humanitarian imperative was undoubtedly at work in the decisions of those who stayed. Humanitarian organizations, though, were also operating in a highly constrained environment. They were constrained not only by their ethical imperatives and concerns about their proper role, but also by their competitive financial environment and powerful states.

Cooley and Ron argue that the "hyper-competition" among relief organizations in the Goma camps, alone, can explain their behavior. Because the crisis was so huge and all attention was on the exodus, the long-term prospects for individual relief organizations depended on their visibility in the relief effort for the Rwandan refugees. "The combination of vast sums of donor money, short-term contracts, and an overabundance of NGOs created an unstable and competitive environment . . ."[98] Individual INGOs were unwilling to take action that would undercut their ability to raise future funds. Opportunities for self-reflection or protest within the INGO community were often passed up due to worries about how it would affect their long-term organizational interests. In interviews with personnel from one relief organization with the pseudonym "Refugee Help," Cooley and Ron found that people worried that their protest would lead the UNHCR to award contracts to less vocal aid groups because there were so many new aid organizations trying to break in to the relief network.[99] In such a competitive environment it was difficult to generate collective action to protest the presence of military forces, threaten to halt food distribution, or otherwise pressure the UN (or the Zairean military) to drive the militia out. In one case another relief group actually threatened to step in immediately if "Refugee Help" halted its services.[100]

Even the power of the UNHCR, though, was constrained. Fiona Terry reports "fears inside UNHCR that a withdrawal could make the organization irrelevant in refugee contexts of the future, particularly in light of the growing aversion to refugee asylum and erosion of central tenets of refugee protection."[101] She also notes that the dominance of NATO in providing for the Kosovar refugees in 1999 shows that this fear was not unfounded. Indeed, much of the funding for the

[97] The French section of MSF and the International Rescue Committee. Terry, *Condemned to Repeat*, p. 195.

[98] Cooley and Ron, "NGO Scramble," p. 26.

[99] Ibid., p. 29.

[100] Ibid., pp. 29–30.

[101] Terry, *Condemned to Repeat*, p. 198.

humanitarian response came from western governments. Both the UNHCR and the humanitarian organizations it funded were in effect "contractors," for the same western states that had not only eschewed political action to halt the genocide and opted to use the humanitarian response to *avoid* foreign policy engagement, but also refused to authorize a military initiative to separate the refugees from army and government operatives.[102]

A few organizations attempted to overcome this dilemma by asserting control over the aid process so as to undercut the FAR and former government manipulation. This, however, prompted violent reaction against aid workers. Thirty-five local CARE employees (Rwandan "Scouts" hired to help control access to the camp and direct traffic) were murdered after CARE international staff evacuated in response to death threats.[103] Two other organizations opted to withdraw from the camps after the initial crisis, arguing that the diversion of funds and the refusal of the UN or western states to de-militarize the camps were leading aid to be used against those it was designed to protect.[104] Some also worked together to lobby for improved security, improved tracking of refugee numbers, and changes in the payments to local employees to make aid diversion more difficult.[105] In this case, however, their capacity to change the situation was limited.

Though transnational relief in the Goma camps was motivated by humanitarian values, its dominant effect was to change the political control of force, enhancing the ability of violent local actors through their diversion of transnational resources. Changes in the political control of force led to less security for the refugees in the short and long term.

In the wake of the Goma disaster, CARE, Canada published a report advising that relief INGOs consider the hiring of PSCs directly to maintain "humanitarian space."

The notion of an independent, volunteer security force not affiliated with any single nation, and available explicitly to further humanitarian ends was not the subject of our research and remains largely unexamined elsewhere. Since the core dilemma humanitarians face is the ability of predators to prey on civilians and NGO staff at will, and since nations and the UN are increasingly hesitant to

---

[102] Ibid.; Jones, *Peacemaking in Rwanda*.

[103] Terry, *Condemned to Repeat*, p. 176; Jones *Peacemaking in Rwanda*, pp. 145–46. Some mild efforts to reduce the diversion were effective. See Terry, *Condemned to Repeat*, pp. 201–02; Johan Pottier, "Why Aid Agencies Need Better Understanding of the Communities they Assist: the Experience of Food Aid in the Rwandan Refugee Camps," *Disasters* Vol. 20, No. 4 (1996): 324–37.

[104] Terry, *Condemned to Repeat*, pp. 196–97.

[105] Ibid., pp. 201–02.

furnish the necessary means to provide that security, it is worth exploring whether in the face of the privatization of assistance, the privatization of security is also appropriate.[106]

This has added to a heated debate that touches on related arguments about the workability of neutrality and "acceptance" as a security strategy for relief workers, whether INGOs can "do no harm," and whether doing no harm is enough.[107] Some have argued that INGOs and the international community in general must seize a more active role that aims to shoulder the "responsibility to protect" when states shirk that responsibility.[108] That responsibility goes beyond relief to prevention and rebuilding and under the best circumstances should be undertaken with UN tutelage but may be justified by gravity and urgency if the UN does not act.[109] Others have claimed that humanitarianism is not the appropriate instrument for these objectives and that humanitarianism in its purest neutral form may solve significant problems that are too important to give up in the pursuit of the grander vision of human rights.[110] Must relief workers be neutral above all else – even if their actions create outcomes they find abhorrent? If relief does produce evils despite the best intentions, are relief workers responsible? Are there acceptable strategies to manage this responsibility?

This debate is undoubtedly more agonizing and complex than the debate about corporate social responsibility, but its inspiration is similar. Can non-state actors legitimately take on governance tasks? If they cannot, and they also cannot legitimately ignore their effects while avoiding these tasks, where does legitimate non-state action lie? The inadvertent financing of security by relief agencies changed the political control of violence in the Goma camps but (similar to the experience of Shell in Nigeria) it also called into question the political and social norms within the relief community.

---

[106] Michael Bryans, Bruce D. Jones, and Janice Gross Stein, "Mean Times: Humanitarian Action in Complex Political Emergencies – Stark Choices, Cruel Dilemmas," Report of the NGOs in Complex Emergencies Project, *Coming to Terms*, Vol. 1, No. 3 (Center for International Studies, University of Toronto, 1999) available at CARE, Canada's web site: www.care.ca.

[107] See Mary Anderson, *Do No Harm: How Aid Can Support Peace – and War* (Boulder: Lynne Rienner, 1999); see also Tony Vaux, Chris Seiple, Greg Nakano, and Koenrad Van Brabant, "Humanitarian Action and Private Security Companies" (London: International Alert, March 2002).

[108] Gareth Evans and Mohamed Sahnoun, "The Responsibility to Protect," *Foreign Affairs* Vol. 81, No. 6 (November/December 2002): 99–110.

[109] Ibid. See also Lee Feinstein and Anne-Marie Slaughter, "A Duty to Prevent," *Foreign Affairs* Vol. 83, No. 1 (January/February 2004).

[110] David Reiff, "Humanitarianism in Crisis," *Foreign Affairs* (November/December 2002): 111–21.

Conserving nature in the state of nature

Turmoil in the developing world during the 1990s affected conservation strategies as well. The host of new international environmental agreements reached in 1970s and 1980s generally enhanced the role of INGOs in their execution.[111] One way in which INGOs encouraged the cooperation of third world states was to augment their capabilities.[112] Sometimes this allowed weak states to commandeer conservation concerns as a means of controlling valuable economic resources or upgrading their coercive capacities and, inadvertently or not, INGOs played into these strategies.[113] Conservationists became more involved in coercion in the Cold War's wake as they continued to pursue global conservation values and goals in territories where weak states began to fail – Garamba National Park in Zaire and Democratic Republic of Congo is one of these instances.[114]

In the Garamba case, INGO financing for security changed political control of force, enhancing the role of transnational actors over security decisions in the Park. Though transnational financing reinforced conservation and good governance goals, however, the INGO's lack of expertise about professional standards for law enforcement personnel led to little enhancement of the social control of force. Furthermore, despite a multi-decade commitment to security in the Park, there was little functional improvement in the security apparatus. Mired in multiple principal problems and lacking the requisite expertise, the transnational conservation community spent much money for little gain. Lack of expertise, a concern with their non-governmental role, and common practices within these organizations, also hindered conservationists' ability to distinguish between functional and dysfunctional plans to improve guard forces.

Transnational funding for government anti-poaching forces

Garamba National Park occupies about 4,920 km in the northeast of Democratic Republic of Congo on the border with the Sudan. Among

---

[111] Peluso, "Coercing Conservation," p. 46; Keck and Sikkink, *Activists Beyond Borders*, p. 123. Ann Thomson Feraru, "Transnational Political Interests and the Global Environment," *International Organization* Vol. 28, No. 1 (winter 1974): 31–60.

[112] Peluso, "Coercing Conservation," p. 46.

[113] Ibid.; Ken Conca, "In the Name of Sustainability: Peace Studies and Environmental Discourse," in Jyrki Kakonen, ed., *Green Security or Militarized Environment* (Brookfield: Dartmouth Publishing Company, 1994).

[114] Jack Hitt, "The Eco-Mercenaries," *New York Times Magazine*, 4 August 2002, pp. 24–9; NPR Interview: "Tom Clynes Discusses a Controversial Anti-Poaching Program in Central Africa," 30 October 2002.

its many environmental treasures, the Park holds the last population of the northern race of white rhinoceros in the wild.[115] A survey of the animals at Garamba in the mid-1980s revealed an emergency – only fifteen northern white rhinos remained.[116] In response, Garamba National Park was placed on the World Heritage Site Danger List and the World Wildlife Fund (WWF) joined with other international groups (Frankfurt Zoological Society or FZS and UNESCO under IUCN) to support a project undertaken by the local authorities, the Institut Zaïrois pour le Conservation de la Nature (IZCN), to rehabilitate the Park.

The project was designed as a holistic attempt to integrate wildlife and human uses of the natural resources Garamba offers, providing services (health care, water, and food supplies) and education for the local community – but also aiming to improve anti-poaching measures (including reconnaissance flights, airstrips, roads, river crossings, and observation posts).[117] To accomplish these goals, the transnational community provided both equipment (new vehicles, HF – high frequency – walkie-talkie radios, computers, guard uniforms, patrol rations, and solar energy equipment) and offered direct salary support (bonuses) to the guard staff.[118] These measures seemed to have success and the Park was removed from the danger list in 1992.

The security situation, however, continued to worsen. In 1991, the capture of a nearby town by the Sudanese People's Liberation Army (SPLA) caused refugees to spill into Democratic Republic of Congo (then Zaire). By 1993, 50,000 Sudanese refugees had settled on one of the three reserves that surround the Park and poaching in the Park increased. It was not only refugees that were poaching, but also members (or former members) of the SPLA ·armed with automatic weapons, hand grenades, and other military equipment. The Park guards in Garamba were no match for the numbers of refugees and military capacity of the guerilla fighters. More elephants and buffalo fell to poachers and the number of armed contacts between Park guards and

---

[115] People have recorded 138 species of mammals and 286 species of birds in the Garamba ecosystem. Garamba National Park was established in 1938. Its unique beauty and wildlife concentrations led it to be designated a World Heritage Site by UNESCO in 1980. "Garamba National Park," http://www.panda.org/resources/factsheet/general/temp/garamba.htm. "The Fight for Survival," http://www.panda.org/resources/publications/species/african_rhino/box_2.htm.

[116] The survey was conducted under the auspices of the IUCN (created after WWII as an umbrella organization with states, government agencies, and NGOs as members, IUCN frequently serves as a clearinghouse for international projects such as the project in Garamba). See also Keck and Sikkink, *Activists Beyond Borders*, p. 122.

[117] "Garamba National Park," http://www.panda.org/resources/factsheet/general/temp/garamba.htm.

[118] Ibid.

poachers grew.[119] Between 1993 and 1995 there were 121 shoot-outs between Park staff and poachers. Three guards were injured, one was killed, and the project aircraft was shot at. Also between 1991 and 1996 Park guards recovered more than 900 weapons as well as refugee registration, Sudanese identity cards, and Sudanese currency.[120]

The pressing situation soon brought more conservation organizations on board. In 1994 the International Rhino Foundation or IRF joined with WWF.[121] IRF coordinated an effort to purchase vehicles for patrol and in 1995 they began to supply salaries for the Park's guards.[122] Then, in early 1996 two rhinos were killed. A male, Bawesi, and a pregnant female, Juliet, were shot in February 1996 and found with their horns hacked off.[123] The Park was again placed on the World Heritage Site Danger List and transnational activists went on a campaign on behalf of WWF and the conservation community in general to make the international community realize what was at stake in Garamba.[124] The regional representative of WWF Eastern Africa warned in a statement to the Inter Press Service: "It is time for the international community to look at the impact of the civil war in Sudan on this unique ecosystem. If not, by the time the refugees return to their homeland, Zaire will have lost one of the jewels of its natural heritage."[125]

The initial project changed political control over violence – generally by according more influence over the governing of the territory to transnational actors. The Park's remote location and distance from the capital contributed to low interest on the part of Zaire's government. The expatriate staff, working on behalf of WWF and IUCN, used its resources to affect Park security decisions. Expatriates arranged and participated in a "management committee" through which the daily routine and goals were debated and detailed records of the poaching incidents were kept.[126] In fact, the high level of expatriate influence was noted (and criticized) by a 1996 review of the project.[127]

---

[119] Moyiga Nduru, "Environment: Poachers Return to Zaire's Garamba Park," *Inter Press Service*, 8 April 1996. Interview with Kes Hillman-Smith, 26 Feb 2000.

[120] Nduru, "Environment."

[121] The IRF is an American based INGO with a mission to conserve all five species of rhino. See http://www.rhinos-irf.org.

[122] http://www.rhinos-irf.org/programs/garamba.html. Interview with Dr. Tom Foose, International Rhino Foundation, 24 January 2001.

[123] Nduru, "Environment."

[124] Sam Kiley, "Sudanese Poachers Threaten the Last of the White Rhinos," *The Times*, 15 February 1996.

[125] Nduru, "Environment."

[126] Mike Buser, "Law Enforcement Field Report, Garamba National Park, Democratic Republic of Congo," Submitted to World Wildlife Fund (June 1998); interviews with Kes Hillman-Smith, Deborah Snelson, Holly Dublin, February 2000.

[127] This review suggested that to be consistent with WWF's philosophy of working with and through the local government, more authority and responsibility should be given to

Though this effort influenced the social goals for which violence was used – the values important to the transnational conservation community (backed by dollars) directed force to be used for the purposes of anti-poaching and conservation more generally – it did not reflect attention to the standards of professional law enforcement and the associated norms for the proper behavior of security personnel.[128] To begin, appeals to international values regarding conservation and the relationship between conservation and development were not accompanied by appeals to the values surrounding the appropriate use of force.[129] More importantly, the guards were paid and equipped, but were not educated or trained. Furthermore, pay was not tied to appropriate behavior. Indeed, the authority of the transnational community over personnel was unclear.[130]

While one might imagine that the infusion of additional resources would enhance the capacity of forces, there was little improvement. This was primarily due to the unclear legal status of the conservation organizations in Garamba and the effect this had on the chain of command.[131] Officially, the government in Kinshasa hired and fired the Park personnel, but they were supervised and paid by the expatriate staff from WWF. What the expatriate staff was authorized to do in this supervisory role was unclear, though. This lack of clarity extended to the qualifications for being a guard, including even basic operating objectives and performance standards.[132] Without standards, a good portion of the guard force was unqualified to carry out many tasks – for instance, guards were unable to field strip or clean their weapons. There were also no procedures for basic operations – for instance, weapons were not clean, guards had no first aid kits, and there were no guidelines for safely carrying or storing weapons.[133] Furthermore, communication systems between the guards and between patrolling guards and headquarters were not established and communication equipment was

---

the Chief Park Warden and less to the expatriate staff. Interview with Holly Dublin, 25 February 2000, interview with Deborah Snelson, 24 February 2000. To help accomplish this goal, a project manager was appointed to work with the local staff and oversee the Garamba project from WWF's office in Nairobi.

[128] Buser, "Law Enforcment Field Inspection Report," interview with WWF staff member, February 2001.

[129] Interviews with staff from WWF and IRC.

[130] Ibid.

[131] There was no legal official document even authorizing INGO action in the Park until 1990 (long after the project began). And this document only allowed WWF to conduct its business in the country. There was no mention of the authority of its staff over the guard force. Interview with WWF staff member in Washington, DC, February 2001. Correspondence with Mike Buser, consultant to WWF, February 2001.

[132] Buser, "Law Enforcement Field Inspection Report."

[133] Ibid.

not well coordinated – for instance, while radios had multiple channels, the repeater stations had only one.[134]

Much of this reflects a lack of expertise as well as an unclear chain of command. The lack of expertise was further demonstrated by the command and control arrangements in the Park. The management committee, through which the Park was run, allowed debate over the daily routine but did not chart lines of responsibility and/or account-ability, so the chain of command, central to the control of force, was not clear.[135] Without basic professional infrastructure, the money that had been dedicated to anti-poaching in the Park did not build a solid and professional force – or even the foundation for one – but allowed the project to operate in a constant state of "crisis-management." Despite the infusion of resources, the guard force was no larger or better able to perform its duties in 1996 than it had been in the mid-1980s.[136]

Transnational financing for PSCs?

When, later in 1996, full-scale civil war broke out in the country, security in the Park broke down altogether.[137] Over the course of several months (the late) President Mobuto's troops and foreign troops he had hired and then (the late) Kabila's troops (the ADFL) arrived in the Park.[138] Members of the transnational community had to flee for their

---

[134] Ibid.

[135] Correspondence with Mike Buser, February 2001.

[136] Confidential correspondence, 18 February 2001.

[137] In Democratic Republic of Congo, as in many portions of Africa, the end of the Cold War exacerbated long-standing problems states had in establishing security. As Chris-topher Clapham has argued, broad agreement on "the idea of the state" and who should run it has been hard to maintain in many post-independence African states; Clapham, "African Security Systems." Civil unrest became a much more common occurrence on the African continent in the first years of the post-Cold War as the strategic interest (from both the west and the east) in Africa evaporated. The supply of foreign and military aid dried up, leaving governments even more cash starved than they had been during the Cold War. Other events in the 1990s such as drought and famine intensified governance problems, resulting in a stream of revolutions, civil insurrections, ethnic strife, and failed states. The World Bank estimates that per capita Gross Domestic Product (GDP) declined by more than 40 percent between 1965 and 1997 in Democratic Republic of Congo. The civil war began in the fall of 1996. For details on its outbreak see William Thom, "Congo-Zaire's 1996–1997 Civil War in the Context of Evolving Patterns of Military Conflict in Africa in the Era of Independ-ence," *Journal of Conflict Studies* Vol. 19, No. 2 (fall 1999).

[138] See Thom, "Congo-Zaire's 1996–1997 Civil War"; Khareen Pech, "The Hand of War," in Abdel-Fatau Musah and J. Fayemi, eds., *Mercenaries: an African Security Dilemma* (London: Pluto, 2000). Mobutu hired Christian Tavernier to lead a Western European band, "Colonel Dominic Yugo" to pull together a Serbian, eastern European band, and Stabilco to head a South African group of mercenaries. Though Stabilco never did much in Zaire until the very end, members of the Park staff had several interactions with Tavernier and the Serbian forces. See Pech, "Hand of War."

safety and the project's equipment, supplies, and weapons were looted (sometimes by the guards themselves). Without arms or equipment even most guards that were so inclined gave up patrolling, and the poaching pressure from the north (and from the refugees) increased. The local Park leadership did its best to ameliorate the situation and was occasionally able to persuade troops to accompany Park patrols,[139] but when transnational representatives returned to the park in June 1997, they found a disaster. "We are absolutely dismayed by the current situation," claimed Elizabeth Kemf, Species Information Officer at WWF International in July.[140] "There are practically no resources in place with which to fight back at the present; about 90% of the park's equipment was either looted or destroyed during the civil war." Sudanese guerilla fighters took advantage of the situation.[141] An aerial monitoring project survey in July 1997 found forty-nine recently occupied poacher camps along the Garamba River. One rhino, twenty-nine elephants, twenty-four buffaloes and over sixteen hippos were found dead.[142] As the central government failed to consolidate, the troops surrounding the Park were frequently unpaid and had insufficient rations. Armed and unpaid soldiers created a variety of tensions in the Park and surrounding areas – and posed an additional poaching risk! Meanwhile, the guard staff still contained members who had partici- pated in the looting. The guards were still nominally government employees, but with no effective government, there was no one in charge at the top and the INGO staff had no authority to fire personnel.

In the midst of this "state of nature" transnational actors proposed hiring private security to guarantee the survival of the rhinos in Garamba. With the state (or *states* – both Sudan and Democratic Republic of Congo) in turmoil, no international action on the horizon and the extinction of a species on the line, the expatriates argued that private security could provide a solution.[143] While careful to pledge cooperation with the new government and express hopes that the

---

[139] Interview with Mr. Mafuko, Chief Park Warden, Garamba National Park, 24 February 2000. See also letter from Kes Hillman-Smith, "Zaire's Rhinos," *The Times*, 13 May 1997.

[140] "New Congo in Great Need of help to Save Endangered Species," 25 July 1997, wysiwyg://18/http://www.panda.org/news/press/news_140.htm.

[141] Refugees were also a problem for wildlife in general but did not target the rhinos and elephants for their tusks and horns. Interview with Kes Hillman-Smith 26 February 2000.

[142] WWF Press Release, "New Congo in Great Need of Help to Save Endangered Species," 25 July 1997, wysiwyg://18/http://www.panda.org/news/press/news_140.htm.

[143] Interview with Kes Hillman-Smith; Kes Hillman-Smith and Fraser Smith, "Conser- vation Crises and Potential Solutions: Example of Garamba National Park, Demo- cratic Republic of Congo," paper presented at the Second World Congress of the International Ranger Federation, San José, Costa Rica, 25–29 September 1997.

government would take control of the security situation, they observed that national priorities lay elsewhere. Instead they suggested that a training team, synthesizing a wide range of conservation law enforcement, in support of local forces might have both an intervention and training role – simultaneously enhancing the skill and motivation of the guards and deterring the increasing threat from poachers. Such a force might "hold the fort and protect nationally and internationally valued resources in times of crisis."[144]

WWF solicited proposals from a variety of private security entities: the Game Ranger Association (of South Africa), Saracen (of South Africa and Angola), and an independent private security consultant.[145] The two proposals given serious consideration, from Saracen and the independent consultant, suggest very different approaches to security in the park. Though both nod to the need to gain approval from the government of Zaire (or Democratic Republic of Congo), they differ in their attention to the role of INGOs, their duration, and their focus on professional development for the forces.

The Saracen proposal lays out a command and control hierarchy flowing from Zaire's Minister of the Environment through Saracen, Pretoria, Saracen, Uganda, and then the Park headquarters. The role of INGOs is not clear – although there is reference to a donor that would approve and fund the project. The primary goal of the proposed

---

[144] In this paper Smith and Hillman-Smith indicate that they had sought clearance from the Ministry of the Environment for the plan, acknowledge that they would need to re-establish ICCN (IZCN became ICCN as Zaire was renamed Democratic Republic of Congo) authority over arms and equipment before such a contract would be feasible, and state that they had project funds available to carry it out. Hillman-Smith and Smith, "Conservation Crises and Potential Solutions." They recommended that the Game Ranger's Association of Africa (or some other body) explore a mobile training force, in conjunction with the United Nations African Crisis Initiative or the International Green Cross. The International Green Cross was formed under the leadership of Mikhail Gorbachev in 1993. As of now, it operates as an international network to transform values, encourage dialogue, and reconcile trade-offs between the environment and economic development. See http://www.gci.ch/.

[145] "Project Proposal: An anti-poaching training programme by the Game Rangers Association of Africa for guards in Garamba National Park, D. R. Congo." This proposal was based on the training needs assessment. Jack Greef (1997), "Training Needs Assessment (GNP, Zaire, Report)." Both the proposal and the assessment are cited in Hillman-Smith and Smith, "Conservation Crises and Potential Solutions." The Game Ranger Association is a group in South Africa dedicated to representing game rangers to governments in Africa. It promotes standards for training, motivation, and support and works to advocate for game rangers to a variety of governments and other organizations. See http://wildnetafrica.co.za/wildlife/inc/specialist/gamerangers.html. "Concept Proposal for Garamba National Park: Zaire," prepared by Saracen International, Ltd., 17 January 1998. Saracen is a PSC based in South Africa and Angola. Correspondence with Mike Buser, security consultant to WWF, February 2001.

three-month project was to stop poaching in the rhino sector and force unwanted elements out of the central section "by means of offensive activities."[146] By relieving poaching pressure, it was suggested, the existing staff could implement effective management policies. A training program for the guards was listed as a secondary goal. More concretely, it proposed a twelve-man team of expatriates selected by Saracen to be deployed to the Park to patrol with (and potentially train) the local guards. The government and "other partners involved" were to be responsible for visa arrangements for the Saracen employees, air reconnaissance, selection of 128 suitable field rangers, air support, logisitical support for field operations, back-up for Park staff, instruction to military forces to respect the National Park regulation and ownership, and rhino monitoring.[147] At the end of the three-month project, a re-evaluation would determine whether to continue to employ Saracen to enable the Park staff to lead and supervise their own field operations and further train Park wardens and officers to direct law enforcement operations.[148] The proposal lists two personnel by name and back-ground, a project manager and a second in command, both South African with experience in the South African military before (SADF) and after (SANDF) apartheid. The total cost of the three-month operation was US $414,252.

The private security consultant's plan was proposed directly to WWF. It focused on remediation of deficiencies in professional performance standards, human resource management, and operating procedures, and proposed reorganization of the Park's management to facilitate command and control. Key elements for a successful operation were listed as: clearly defined law enforcement mission approved by the government, a command, control, and communications structure, secure base camps, effective logistical and administrative structure, equipment, weaponry, and transportation, air support, field engineering capability, heath care and family support, skilled, motivated, and fit personnel, and a community support program.[149] He noted that a variety of "imposed constraints" including the remoteness of the Park, the difficulty of moving by road during the wet season, and ineffective Government structure and budgets were unlikely to change and that WWF consider whether these prohibited the development of sound objectives – if so, he claimed, the project should be revisited. If not, he

---

[146] Saracen, "Concept Proposal for Garamba National Park: Zaire," p. 11.
[147] Ibid., pp. 11–12.
[148] Ibid., pp. 12–13.
[149] Buser, "Law Enforcement Field Inspection Report, Garamba Naitonal Park, Demo-cratic Rebublic of Congo," June 1998, p. 4.

suggested that WWF aim for clear authorization from the government to carry out durable improvements to the system of law enforcement in the Park.[150] He argued that particular difficulties in command, control, and communication, and a host of other key elements for a successful mission would need to be addressed. The cost of the remediation was estimated at US $1,099,367 – an initial $601,000 in capital investment and a recurring annual cost of $498,367.

Though neither proposal was implemented, they promised quite different effects. The Saracen proposal promised the least change. It did not challenge the formal role of the state, although given the condition of the government in Democratic Republic of Congo (then Zaire) at the time, the proposal's implementation would have given Saracen significant de facto control of its operation. It continued to direct resources to support conservation values, in a way that was consistent with the rough and ready processes the Park had seen for decades, with little in the way of professional training. It was a "crisis-management" plan for the Park – and some argued that this had been the focus of conservation INGOs in that area all along.[151] The plan was costly, aimed at short-term goals, and was unlikely to yield long-term functional gain.

The private security consultant's plan was more radical. The proposal was directed to a conservation INGO, a formal notification of a potential shift in control over violence. It also proposed a plan that would have led to a clear and formal role for the conservation community in the authorization of violence within the Park's territory. The plan promised significant functional reordering and enshrined not only conservation values, but also the values and processes surrounding professional law enforcement, into daily operating procedures. So, the plan promised functional increases (at a cost), an improvement in the social control of force, and a further redistribution of political control over force in a portion of the Democratic Republic of Congo that more clearly contested the exclusive role of the state in general in authorizing and controlling violence.

Tough choices for conservationists

These proposals immediately incited debate within the conservation community. On one side were those who advocated protecting the

---

[150] Mike Buser, "Final Report," from Training Consultant Project ZR 0009 (Mike Buser) to Programme Officer (Sylvie W. Candotti), 17 August 1998.
[151] Interview with WWF staff member, February 2001.

rhinos at all costs, were willing to do whatever it took to conserve species, and were happy for expatriate populations to play a significant role in the process. On the other were those who believed their role as an INGO limited the scope of proper action, were more likely to consider the costs and benefits of different strategies, and were more focused on empowering local actors. Though individuals on both sides can be found in each of the organizations involved, IRF generally has followed the former line and WWF the latter.

Some at WWF, particularly those from WWF US, were appalled at the idea of receiving proposals akin to Saracen's.[152] Their discomfort was deepened by the history of white soldiers of fortune in the region and whom the security personnel would be – former forces from apartheid South Africa or forces that had fought in an immoral Angolan rebellion. Also they pointed out that it was not only SPLA-affiliated troops, but also refugees who were poaching. Even the remote possibility that WWF would fund PSCs from South Africa and Angola who could potentially shoot at refugees trying to stay alive was repulsive to these staff members.[153] The cost of security only solidified this view. From the perspective of these individuals, WWF had already become too involved in governance in Garamba. They believed the project should be run by the local authorities and had already proposed a plan to remove the expatriate presence from the Park. The worsening security environment led WWF to look long and hard at its commitment to the Park. Continuing to work with ICCN representatives, WWF offered to pay for an assessment of the potential to move the rhinos to a safer spot. When the ICCN officials refused this option, WWF decided to withdraw their financial support for the Garamba project and direct rhino conservation money where it would have more success.

The IRF charged that WWF's action to dismiss the expatriate staff and move more authority to the ICCN just when there was effectively no government was a recipe for disaster.[154] IRF claimed that expatriate support was the key to maintaining Garamba's viability, and, even more generally, that INGOs are vital to conserving biodiversity when governments are incapacitated. IRF took up the mantel in Garamba, hired back the expatriate staff, and continued to support efforts to

---

[152] The World Wildlife Fund is organized around an international secretariat (which coordinates policy), national organizations (which raise and disperse funds), and pro- gramme offices (which execute projects). WWF Eastern Africa is a programme office. Its main funding came from WWF US and WWF UK.

[153] Interview with Kate Newman, Director for East and Southern Africa, WWF US, January 2000.

[154] Interview with Tom Foose, International Rhino Foundation, 24 January 2001.

protect the Park. A UN Foundation Initiative to maintain protection in times of anarchy has delivered some support to IRF and the Park (aiming to provide emergency support for the guards as well as to plan and fund further training for them).[155] The legal ambiguities surrounding the project and the Democratic Republic of Congo government in Garamba, however, continued to frustrate many of these efforts. Plans to train Park guards at a facility in South Africa were scuttled twice in 2000 due to problems in getting travel visas and the expatriate staff has continued to look at bringing in South African trainers.[156] In the interim, the Park staff has worked with whatever was available, including the various armed forces that have moved through the area.[157]

Neither side of the debate within the conservation community, however, demonstrated an understanding of what was required for an effective operation in the Park. The question was not whether WWF should hire private security or not, but whether they were willing to insist on an operation that upheld the values and standards underlying professional law enforcement.[158] IRF's response was no better as it only continued the crisis management approach.[159] Some involved in the process claim that misunderstanding of law enforcement issues is a common problem among conservation INGOs. Though increasing evidence suggests the importance of law enforcement efforts for conservation,[160] donor driven INGOs eager to cut costs, gain access, and maintain their neutrality have incentives to ignore the requirements for effective law enforcement.[161] Effective law enforcement is expensive and requires both clear agreements with the government and oversight which INGOs sometimes see as overstepping neutrality. Donor requirements for cost efficiency, though, often lead INGOs to short change security or assume it simply costs too much. Also, in order to gain publicity and receive donor funds, INGOs have to gain access to environmentally threatened areas – and this often leads them to accept whatever terms a government offers rather than insisting on professional

---

[155] Ibid.,p.20;http://www.unfoundation.org/programs/environment/priorities_en.asp; http://www.unfoundation.org/grants/index_environment.asp; http://www.unesco.org/whc/news/newsUNF091299.htm.

[156] Ibid.

[157] As of October 2003, the rhinos were still in danger. Susan Bisset, "Only Twenty-Two Rare White Rhinos Survive the War in Congo," *Sunday Telegraph*, 5 October 2003.

[158] Background interview, January 2001.

[159] Ibid.

[160] See, for instance, Aaron G. Bruner et al., "Effectiveness of Parks in Protecting Tropical Biodiversity," *Science* Vol. 291, No. 5501 (5 January 2001).

[161] Ibid. Background interview with WWF staff member, February 2001.

law enforcement when they have bargaining power (before they enter the country).[162]

These "donor" generated incentives are reinforced by the culture of conservation INGOs. Conservationists pride themselves on working on a shoestring and making do with whatever they have to pursue their goals. This emphasis on heroic action to overcome obstacles, though, contrasts with the practices required for effective security organizations, which centers on standards and routines. INGOs also tend to attract people interested in cooperation and non-hierarchical authority, and suspicious of the use of violence at all. This only reinforces the lack of expertise these organizations field on security issues.[163] Finally, similar to TNCs and relief organizations, conservation INGOs commit themselves to non-partisanship and seek to work with whomever they can in pursuit of conservation goals – dabbling in law enforcement conversations or supporting those better able to issue effective law enforcement is often seen as out of bounds activity.

When conservation INGOs financed security in Garamba, they gained influence over decisions about the use of violence and reinforced not only conservation values, but also the value of using violence – or the threat of violence – to achieve conservation goals. Their lack of understanding about security issues, however, led them to have little effect on the social control of the violence they funded. The lack of expertise combined with an unclear legal status led INGOs to have little ability to tie guard salaries to functional improvements. Despite significant deployment of resources, transnational involvement did not enhance the functional or social control of violence in the Park. Experience in the Park did fuel a larger debate within the conservation community about how they should best pursue their goals. Similar to the experiences of TNCs and relief INGOs, this debate challenged political and social norms within the conservation community.

Comparison

Although INGOs and transnational corporations may be motivated differently, they share dilemmas in financing security. They inevitably

---

[162] Ibid.
[163] Several members of the WWF staff were clearly uncomfortable with the military backgrounds of the PSCs advising them. Daniel Byman notes the mutual lack of familiarity between NGOs and the military. Daniel Byman, "Uncertain Partners: NGOs and the Military," *Survival* Vol. 43, No. 2 (summer 2001): 106–07. See also Laura Miller, "From Adversaries to Allies: Relief Workers' Attitudes Toward the US Military," *Qualitative Sociology* Vol. 22, No. 3 (1999): 181–97.

Table 5.1. *Effects of private financing on the control of force*

Case	State strength	Functional control	Political control	Social control	Mechanisms	Fit?
Shell – in Nigeria	Weak	Decreased/ *moderately* increased	Changed • Enhanced oil companies and their allies (though allies changed with new strategy)	Decreased/ increased? • As Shell strategy changed the discourse on human rights has increased	Chafing/ reinforcing? • Shell efforts to tie investment to better behavior of Nigerian forces (questions about the efficacy and legitimacy of this strategy)	Eroding • Initially no increase Reinforcing • Arguable modest increase since 1997
Relief INGOs – in Goma Camps	Weak/failed	Decreased	Changed • Enhanced relief orgs. and those who served to benefit from the humanitarian crisis (gov't in exile)	Neutral • Enhanced importance of humanitarian norms but not integration of violence with these norms	Chafing • Relief norms pointed in different direction than political gains from relief resources • Competing norms pulling relief orgs. in different directions	Eroding

	Weak/failed	Decreased/no change	Changed	Neutral		Neutral
Relief INGOs – in Goma Camps					• Competition for relief contracts undermined admission of the problem	Neutral
Conservation INGOs – in Democratic Republic of Congo			Changed • Enhanced conservation organizations	Neutral • Enhanced importance of conservation norms but not integration of violence with these norms	Chafing • Competing norms pulled conservation orgs. in different directions • Proper role inconsistent with effective use of guard financing • Guard financing executed by those with low level of security expertise	

redistribute power over the control of force, but often do so in ways that do not improve the functioning of forces or the likelihood that forces will abide by professional norms. In some cases private financing of security does strengthen the use of forces for narrow aims – although often this leads to a backlash that ultimately reduces functional control. In other cases, however, introducing another "principal" in the control of violence leads to less effective forces. In this situation, the private financing of violence may introduce values that the international community supports, but change political control in unanticipated ways that work against these values and enhance external actors' political power, generating competing authorities that erode functional control of violence.

Furthermore, by financing security – directly or not – each of these actors has opened themselves up to claims about the consequences of their actions that go beyond the single-minded pursuit of particular values or commercial interests. To work effectively toward the values they endorse in this situation, transnational actors must attend to the political and functional consequences of their actions. Similarly, to work toward their commercial interests, transnational corporations are compelled to attend to the social and functional consequences of their decisions. Though attending to these consequences should make TNCs and INGOs alike eager to pursue strategies that enhance the capacities of weak states, they rarely do. In the cases I have examined, transnational actors' concerns about the legitimacy of becoming too political have combined with material incentives (and sometimes a lack of expertise) to cause them to choose ineffective strategies. See table 5.1.

These cases demonstrate the greater importance of strategies and their effect on mechanisms of control than motivations, per se, in explaining the impact of private financing of security. They also suggest how difficult it is for transnational financiers to generate reinforcing processes of control and demonstrate that financing security generates political controversy among non-state actors. Resolving some of these difficulties requires action by donors. Others, though, can be eased by awareness in the transnational community about their impact on all three dimensions of control, open debates about the impact of different strategies, and greater knowledge of the requirements for professional security.

6   Market mechanisms and diffusion of control over force

Private security offers opportunities to states and non-state actors. As both have taken advantage of these opportunities, the market for force has affected the control of violence in many, sometimes contradictory, ways. In different instances it has both enhanced and undermined functional control and enhanced and undermined the integration of violence with the values we associate with the international community – democratic principles, human rights, and the rule of law. In each case, however, it has changed the mechanisms by which force is controlled and thereby redistributed power over the control, of violence – spreading that power differently within states and often enhancing the influence of persons and groups outside the state. Two general features of this political change, however – the growing significance of market mechanisms for eliciting control and the diffusion of control over violence – merit more discussion, as they point to the context in which the relationship between the three dimensions of control will work as this market unfolds further.

Market mechanisms

The growing importance of market mechanisms suggests that the control of violence will not only accrue to superiors in a hierarchical sense (for instance, leaders nested in electorates), but to consumers. While states can and have taken advantage of their role as consumers to increase their functional control of PSCs, market mechanisms work differently than hierarchical ones. The characteristics of market mechanisms combined with the global forces that led to the private security market in the first place may change the very professional military norms that optimists hope will stabilize the effect of privatizing security.

The mechanism through which individual values and interests are aggregated to make "consumer demand" is based on purchases. The ecology of the market, shaped by prevailing norms and ideas, can also

219

affect its character by establishing the default "proper" behavior for PSCs and private financiers.[1] Conceptions of proper behavior, such as the codes of conduct and standards in vogue among advocates of corporate social responsibility, can be important in setting expectations and norms within which the market works. The model advanced in this book also suggests that we attend to the interaction between these two: the monitoring and sanctioning capacity of consumers and corporate standards and codes of conduct. In general, market mechanisms are blunt tools and markets offer fewer pathways for consumers to explain their choices than hierarchies offer to superiors. Thus market mechanisms may complicate how standards and codes of conduct work.

Consumers, of course, are those who can pay – suggesting that political power over private violence will be distributed according to access to wealth.[2] There is nothing to prevent a state from being a consumer if it so desires and when consumers are capable states, they may direct security effectively, though, if it is a sovereign task, generally with some additional cost or political slippage.[3] The United States has chosen to play a large consumer role in this market and its choices have therefore had a large impact on the market's ecology. Governments that have chosen to reduce their reliance on the private sector for sovereign tasks (such as South Africa) have abandoned their capacity to affect the development of the market's ecology. Though weak state consumers may gain the potential for effective force when hiring PSCs, they are less likely to direct PSCs effectively or to have much demand on the market's

[1] This focus is common among sociologists. See R. Burt, *Corporate Profits and Cooptation* (New York: Academic, 1983); M. Gerlach, *Alliance Capitalism* (Los Angeles: University of California Press, 1992); J. Pfeffer and G. Salancik, *The External Control of Organizations* (New York: Harper and Row, 1978); DiMaggio and Powell, *New Institutionalism*; J. Meyer and B. Rowan, "Institutionalized Organizations: Formal Structure as Myth and Ceremony," *American Journal of Sociology* Vol. 83: 340–63; Scott and Meyer, *Institutional Environment and Organizations*; John Meyer, David John Frank, Ann Hironaka, Evan Schofer, and Nancy Brandon Tuma, "A World Environmental Regime, 1870–1990," *International Organization* Vol. 51, No. 4 (autumn 1997).

The importance of ecology is not lost on economists. As Bowles and Gintis describe it, the efficiency of neoclassical economics is based on a world where "a handshake is a handshake." In other words, markets work better when individuals (irrationally) do not take advantage of one another. Samuel Bowles and Herbert Gintis, "The Revenge of Homo Economicus: Contested Exchange and the Revival of Political Economy," *Journal of Economic Perspectives*, Vol. 7, No. 1 (1993): 83–102. See also, Joseph Stiglitz, "Post Walrasian Economics and Post Marxian Economics," *Journal of Economic Perspectives*, Vol. 7, No. 1 (1993): 109–14.

[2] The simultaneous growth of vigilantes and militias suggests a different alternative for those who cannot afford other private options. See Ero, "Vigilantes, Civil Defense Forces and Militia Groups."

[3] Benjamin Klein and Keith B. Leffler, "The Role of Market Forces in Assuring Contractual Performance," *Journal of Political Economy* Vol. 89, No. 4 (1981): 615–41.

ecology because PSCs are more likely to respond to larger consumers or the interests that are bankrolling the weak state's efforts. Finally, the fact that consumers need not be states has also opened a role for other actors of means to garner control over force in individual settings and, depending on their level of demand, portions of the market.

Consumer choice is also affected by the level of competition and the flow of information. Competitive markets offer more choices than non-competitive markets and the information consumers have about the industry will affect their ability to make their wishes known through decisions to switch brands. Meanwhile, the competence of consumer judgments will matter for whether consumers lead the industry or vice versa.[4] If there are a variety of PSCs, companies are worried about their reputation and prospective employers can easily know what they are likely to be buying, consumers can exercise the most effective control with purchasing decisions. As Jeff Herbst has argued, "[I]n industries where the barriers to entry are low and where, as a result, companies probably cannot compete on price alone, firms will necessarily attempt to differentiate themselves in other ways." He predicted that a distinction would emerge between upscale firms (that appeal to the UN, INGOs, and other upstanding members of the international community by virtue of their willingness to abide by international law) and downscale firms (that appeal to non-lawful elements).[5]

If wealthy consumers only hire upscale firms, are a significant portion of the demand, and have the requisite information about PSCs' behavior, this may be true. Anticipating this, persons associated with PSCs argue that proper behavior is crucial to their reputation, which has impacts on corporate contracts – and thus their bottom line. As one gentleman at DSL put it, "when we sneeze in Africa, we catch a cold in Asia." DSL, as a global company, has many profit driven incentives, he argues, to pay close attention to its reputation and protect its brand name by avoiding compromising situations. As part of ArmorGroup, DSL's operating principles include legal and professional behavior and attention to human rights.[6] Many PSCs make similar claims. Some have participated in emerging regimes of corporate responsibility, offering to come up with standards for professional behavior, and monitoring by objective groups.[7] There is even an organization for the "self-regulation"

---

[4] Steven Tadelis, "What's in a Name? Reputation as a Tradable Asset," *American Economic Review* Vol. 89, No. 3 (1999): 548–63.

[5] Herbst, "Regulation of Private Security Forces," pp. 122–25.

[6] http://www.armorgroup.com/ mainframe.htm.

[7] For instance, in the "Voluntary Principles on Security and Human Rights."

of international PSCs that provide support for peace operations – the International Peace Operations Association.[8]

The organization of most PSCs, however, introduces some difficulties in monitoring and linking the behavior of individual employees to a PSC's reputation. Although PSCs do operate as long-term corporate entities, and thereby appear to rid worries about fly-by-night operations typical of individual soldiers of fortune, most PSCs operate as databases from which to service contracts and these databases are non-exclusive (individuals often show up on the rosters of several different companies). Thus, someone working for one firm one week may be working for a different firm or simply as an independent consultant the next. Reports that MPRI was training the Kosovo Liberation Army (KLA) in the midst of the war in Kosovo – vociferously denied by MPRI – were due to just this dynamic. Though MPRI's claims were true, persons who had worked for MPRI at one time also did freelance consulting with the Albanian government and may have provided services to portions of the Kosovo resistance.[9] While there is a virtual cottage industry of reporting on the connections between individuals and various firms, and companies do appear worried about their reputations, the fluctuation in personnel makes it hard to track which behavior is attributable to which firm.[10] This complicates the development of corporate reputation as a link to accountability or control by clouding the information available.

The deeper ecology of the market suggests an additional control tool. While many point to security as a sector that is more dominated by *intergovernmental* relations than many other sectors, even security has seen a rise of formal and informal relations in the form of security organizations and military–military contacts.[11] Evidence of this is found in academic studies, but also in policy makers' statements. For instance, in a speech at The Hague on 9 May 2001, the Secretary General of NATO, Lord Robertson, addressed the issue of "Democratic Civil–Military Relations and Reform." He argued that although there are unique cultural, political, and military traditions in each country, there are common denominators essential for proper civil–military relations

---

[8] http://www.IPOAonline.org/.
[9] Personal interviews, December 1999, June 2001.
[10] See, for instance, Pech, "Executive Outcomes: a Corporate Conquest"; Silverstein, *Private Warriors*; Musah and Fayemi, *Mercenaries*.
[11] Meyer et al., "World Environmental Regime," argue that security is dominated by governments. Jepperson, Wendt, and Katzenstein, "Norms, Identity, and National Security," however, suggest that even security is being affected by norms.

in a democracy and proceeded to outline these.[12] The emerging acceptance of expert judgment about security and the role of security professionals is a step toward the definition of universal principles among security professionals.[13] DiMaggio and Powell have argued that such universal principles will influence individual behavior most clearly when they are reinforced in an individual's day-to-day activities.[14] The career and network patterns among professionals in some parts of the world suggest that this may be a more robust control mechanism than the reputation of firms. Many individuals working for PSCs began their careers in military service but have since moved back and forth between service to the UN, service to PSCs, and service to INGOs.[15] Indeed, by the turn of the twenty-first century there was a relatively small cosmopolitan community surrounding relief, development, and peace-keeping efforts in the Balkans and Africa where individuals knew each other through work together in different arenas over time. While it may be difficult for the press or INGOs to track the reputation of PSCs when individuals working to promote security and other goals in conflict zones know each other and predict that their future employment depends on their reputation for professionalism, they should be more likely to behave according to professional norms. If professional security expertise and networks of individuals become linked and the market splits between less savory firms pulling from a different pool of individuals than more savory firms, the effect of reputation on social control could rise.[16]

This scenario, however, rests on the idea that those who abide by professional military values are most effective. Indeed, the acceptance of universal principles among security professionals has been bolstered by the claim that militaries and police are most effective when they practice within received political structures and international social norms. In US military training, for instance the values associated with professional military education are presented in the context of effective action. It is

[12] Lord Robertson, "Perspectives on Democratic Civil–Military Relations and Reform," Speech at the Centre for European Security Studies Conference, Taking Stock on Civil–Military Relations, The Hague, 9 May 2001.
[13] Margaret Keck and Katherine Sikkink talk about the importance of expertise for the building of networks. Though their focus is on advocacy networks, one could extend the analysis to other varieties such as security professionals. See Keck and Sikkink, *Activists Beyond Borders*, ch. 6.
[14] DiMaggio and Powell, "Iron Cage Revisited."
[15] For instance, James Fennell at DSL used to work for the United Nations.
[16] The war in Iraq introduced a different dynamic when the US hired many with little background in post-conflict reconstruction to do relief and development work for the CPA that frustrated the potential for this kind of control. See Ariana Eunjung Cha, "In Iraq, the Job Opportunity of a lifetime," p. A1.

argued that abusing human rights is problematic not only because it is wrong, but also because it reduces military effectiveness; democracy and civilian control of the military are means to a more effective military organization.[17] Though these claims are routine in any western professional military education facility, officers teaching the courses will admit that there are difficulties applying the law of war to conflicts, like the ongoing civil conflict in Colombia, where the military is fighting a criminal force.[18] Similarly, in the training MPRI did for the ACRI, it taught human rights within the context of the law of war, but instructors acknowledged that many of the personnel had experienced combat situations where the ends they sought – perhaps quite noble – would have been undermined had they abided by a strict interpretation of the law of war. MPRI employees admitted that it was sometimes tough to walk the line between advocating strict and clear adherence to the laws of war and developing a mutual understanding with the personnel they were training so as to better influence their judgments and behavior in the future.[19]

The very global changes that have led to the private security market in the first place, though, have also enhanced the difficulty of walking this fine line by calling into question the connection between universal security principles and effective action. The proliferation of less savory private, sub-state, transnational, or otherwise non-state actors who participate in violent activity – militias, paramilitaries, local or transnational crime syndicates, and others – makes it more likely that conflict will operate outside conventional rules and lead forces to believe that "appropriate" behavior will reduce rather than enhance functional effectiveness.[20] While this was an issue for weak states in many areas of the world throughout the 1990s, it increasingly became an issue for strong states as witnessed by the US prosecution of the war on terrorism. In deciding how to treat captured Taliban and al Qaeda forces during the conflict in Afghanistan, for instance, the US judged the detainees not to be prisoners of war partly because members of the Bush

---

[17] See descriptions of "Mil-To-Mil Contact Programs for FSU," May 1994 USAF Briefing, JCTP Briefing Papers, HQ EUCOM, November 1997, JCTP mission statement in HQ USAFE Military to Military briefing May 1995, all in Marybeth Ulrich, *Democratizing Communist Militaries: the Cases of the Czech and Russian Militaries* (Ann Arbor: University of Michigan Press, 1999), pp. 50–66.

[18] Conversations with officers at WHINSEC, September 2003, December 2003. Analyses of the success of mil-to-mil efforts suggest these contradictions are an enduring problem in a variety of contexts. See Ulrich, *Democratizing Communist Militaries*.

[19] Interview with Jean-Michel A. Beraud and Clifford L. Fields (ACRI), Alexandria, VA, 31 January 2000.

[20] See Friman and Andreas, *Illicit Global Economy and State Power*; Andreas, "Clandestine Political Economy of War and Peace."

administration believed that treating terrorists according to the laws of war would disadvantage the US. These judgments extended to the conflict in Iraq as the insurgency heated up and detainees were seen as targets for better intelligence. Though the exact chain of events that led to the abuses at Abu Ghraib prison remains unclear, it is increasingly apparent that some in the US believe that prosecuting the war on terrorism will be undermined rather than enhanced if it abides by military professional values that embrace human rights and the laws of war.

When what is appropriate and what is functional appear to diverge, the hold on social control among military professionals should weaken. The market pressures on PSCs should lead this weakening to happen even more quickly in the private sector. After all, it is through the delivery of a function that these organizations establish professional authority at all.[21] While serving, military personnel still respond to hierarchical organizational incentives and face military justice systems. As is described below, PSCs face murkier legal accountability and have to make judgments about the trade-offs between different approaches, knowing that other companies are available for hire if their "customer" is dissatisfied with the outcome. The bluntness of market mechanisms offers less obvious means for consumers to explain their preferences.

These conditions cause functional concerns to loom large. If acting in accordance with the going professional norms leads a PSC to be less effective, it may diminish its professional reputation and market share. Take, for instance, the difference between GSG and EO in Sierra Leone. GSG refused to go beyond its contract and participate in operations with the RSLMF or provide the RSLMF with security during its training out of fear that it might anger another customer – the British government – and out of a desire to preserve its "non-mercenary" reputation. A few months later, EO came on the scene promising to do whatever it took to generate security in Sierra Leone and proceeded to help the RSLMF and then the civil-defense forces to effectively dislodge the RUF from many areas of the country. EO's pure functional capacity led many – even in the UN and INGO community – to sing its praises and many even urged that it be brought back into Sierra Leone when tensions re-emerged in May 2000.[22] EO placed functional concerns first

---

[21] Gerth and Mills, *From Max Weber*, p. 299. See also discussion in Barnett, "Authority, Intervention, and the Outer Limits of International Relations Theory," pp. 59–65.

[22] See Simon Barber, "Bring Executive Outcomes Back to Fight in Sierra Leone," *Business Day*, 12 May 2000, available at wysiwyg://187/www.bday.co.za/bday/content/direct/0,3523,613273-6078-0,00.html; comments by William Shawcross, 29 August 2000 available at http://www.abc.net.au/foreign/interv/shawcross.htm; Johan Schulhofer-Wohl,

and abided by political and social concerns to the degree that they did not get in the way of the (short-run) goal, while GSG was quite worried about the political and social control issues and these conditioned the range of functions the firm saw as appropriate.[23] Even though its impact is debated, advocates still boast of EO's ability to get things done and GSG in Sierra Leone is generally touted as an example of PSC failure.[24] Which was the proper or "professional" role? Though which company followed the "right" path can be debated, the general point is that when social norms and functional needs point in different directions, we should expect continued – and disruptive – change, or a situation that we perceive as loosened control of force.

More importantly, in this situation we also may see change in the definition of professional. Indeed, the meaning of professional in the world of "new wars" or "the post 9/11 world" is increasingly disputed. Among PSCs, two different models of professionalism have emerged – the "cowboy" model that privileges the effective use of force and the "starched shirt" model that privileges international values. While one could argue that there are also different approaches to military professionalism within military forces (between regular and special forces, for instance), professional change inside the forces is debated and must be squared with formal rules – as witnessed by the struggles over proper interrogation techniques between the US Departments of Justice, State, and Defense. PSCs, though, react more swiftly to market pressures. As they compete for customers, who is hired is the mechanism through which the preferred model of professionalism is communicated. If customers choose "cowboys" more often, they will (intentionally or not) reshape professional norms.

In this context, examining US choices – by far the largest consumer of security services – is suggestive. Particularly in Iraq, the US has chosen some cowboys. As discussed in chapter three, the CPA hired Erinys, to guard oil facilities in Iraq and train a private Iraqi force to carry on in their wake.[25] As the handover of Iraqi sovereignty approached, the office monitoring reconstruction projects in Iraq, the Program Management Office, solicited bids for a PSC to provide armed bodyguards and

---

"Peacekeeping in Sierra Leone Could be Privatized," *International Herald Tribune* (15 May 2000); Alexander Rose, "Hurray for Soldiers of Fortune," *National Post* (Canada) (30 August 2000). See also Sebastian Mallaby, "Paid to Make Peace," *Washington Post*, 4 June 2001.

[23] The difference between the alternate private security plans for Garamba Park reflect a similar split.

[24] On the other hand, EO has since folded and GSG continues to work.

[25] Vallette and Chatterjee, "Guarding the Oil Underworld in Iraq"; Catan and Fiddler, "With Post-War Instability." See Erinys' website at http://www.erinysinternational.com.

coordinate security among the thousands of private contractors employed by the more than fifty PSCs operating in the country. The solicitation requested as many as seventy-five two-man personal security details a day to protect Program Management Office personnel and stipulated that these personnel should have skills such as "mobile vehicle warfare" and "counter-snipping," and should be able to protect sites against indirect fire and attacks by small units.[26] Rather than hiring an established company that recruits from those with strong links to professional networks, however, the US awarded the $293 million contract to Aegis Defense Services.[27] Aegis is headed by (now defunct) Sandline's Tim Spicer. The company was only founded in 2002, has been primarily engaged in anti-piracy efforts, and has an unclear base of recruitment. Spicer's colorful history – he was implicated in breaking the arms embargo in Sierra Leone and arrested for his activities in Papua New Guinea, his advocacy for an increased international role for PSCs, and his willingness to engage in a wide variety of security activities, though – places him squarely in the cowboy camp. It also appears that Aegis was not the lowest bid. US Army spokesman, Gary Tallman, reported that Aegis was chosen from among six bidders "based on the criterion that was sought and Aegis's technical capability, not so much cost."[28] But exactly what expertise was the US looking for? Many have speculated that it was precisely Spicer and his reputation that the US hired – that his history and record of taking on dicey tasks may have led him to be more attractive than the companies that play more strictly by the rules.[29] While the security director for the Program Management Office claimed that the selection of Aegis did not indicate a more offensive posture in Iraq, PSCs are unlikely to buy this argument. According to one in the industry:

The USG [US government] needs an organ that is from outside the US, far less accountable, and already tainted, albeit slightly, with a whiff of dirty tricks. And that is the crux of the matter. The powers that be want mercenaries, for mercenary activity. Dirty stuff doable, non-accountable and at no extra cost to boot!! I am sure that Tim will recruit as many non-US citizens as he can, which will lessen the body-bag impact on the US voter population. And I can also tell you now there will be layers to the onion, somewhere hidden in Tim's set-up will be groups, teams, actions that will have nothing to do with defensive operations

[26] Mary Pat Flaherty, "Iraq Work Awarded to Veteran of Civil Wars," *Washington Post*, 16 June 2004.
[27] The contract is being protested by DynCorp. See Paul Lashman, "Spicer's Security Firm in Battle with DynCorp over $290m Deal," *Independent*, 4 July 2004.
[28] Ibid.
[29] Pratap Chatterjee, "Controversial Commando Wins Iraq Contract," CorpWatch (9 June 2004); interview with former CPA official.

or man-guarding. Tim, with Aegis, will be controlled by whomever holds the purse strings. Therefore they will do what is required, otherwise they get canned.[30]

The Aegis contract comes on the heels of Erinys' no-nonsense approach to oil facilities security, it also follows Blackwater's toothy efforts at personal protection that bordered on counter-insurgency.[31] Indeed, some US officials admit that they need PSCs that act like soldiers, not businessmen, in Iraq and that some of the problematic experience training the Iraqi Army was due to a "starched-shirt" approach.[32]

The US selection of PSCs that are willing to take risks may make sense for short-term function needs in Iraq. The potential long-term social effect, however, should not be missed. When market mechanisms are the primary tools through which social control standards are communicated to PSCs and the US plays a large consumer role, the more the US chooses cowboy firms the more it is likely to influence a change in the norms that govern PSCs. Whether professional norms provide a stabilizing impact and lead to private security activity that is in keeping with the professional rules that traditional militaries adhere to, or whether they are a tool for altering these professional norms without the bureaucratic stickiness associated with traditional militaries, depends on who are the wealthy consumers in the market and the choices they   make.

Diffusion of control

Though private security sometimes strengthens elements of individual states' control over force, the growth of the market for force simultaneously diffuses control over violence among a variety of non-state entities, undermining states' *collective* monopoly over the control of force. It enhances the role for non-state actors in shaping decisions about the use of force and presents states and non-state actors with additional tools for accomplishing their goals. This development has implications for a debate about the likely global institutional trajectory. On one side of this debate, Held et al. contend that in the Cold War's wake, the global reach of the great power rivalry and conflict, the global arms dynamic, and the expansion of agreements regulating organized violence have moved the world into an era where the military sphere is

---

[30] E-mail from Cobus Claassens, Southern Cross Security, July 2004.
[31] Knut Royce, "Start-up Company with Connections," *Newsday* (15 February 2004); interview with former CPA official.
[32] Interview with Pentagon employee, May 2004.

increasingly globalized and institutionalized. Defense policy and decisions about the use of force, they argue, are "embedded in a matrix of institutionalized bilateral and multilateral consultative and cooperative mechanisms, both official and unofficial."[33] The increasing use of violence for international (rather than national) goals and through the mechanisms of international institutions, they claim, potentially opens the way for a transformation from the "national security state" to the "post-military state," reflecting a shift of the structural balance from warfare to welfare with the military institution existing to a greater and greater degree on the periphery of society. Others have questioned the depth or the direction of this institutionalization. Frederic Cooper writes, "It is debatable, in today's context, whether such discourses encourage a thick notion of social citizenship and political accountability within or among nation-states, or whether they imply a thin notion of the individual as an economic actor or rights-bearing entity, with weak reinforcement by sovereign governments and piecemeal intervention by international organizations against the most publicized violations."[34] Mark Duffield argues that the liberal governance networks of the 1990s merged security and development in a way that set up impossible goals (the transformation of social systems in the developing world) and often reinforced the use of violence and shadow economies (the very processes they were trying to transform).[35]

The logic of the institutional argument I have presented leads us to expect that as international institutions were built on a platform of a particular kind of state, the redistribution of power within states and between states and other entities might just as easily undermine as enhance international institutions. As power is redistributed to a variety of actors with different constituents, roles, and claims to authority, it is not at all clear that international institutions will be useful forums for these actors. The diffusion of control over violence, then, might weaken not only the collective monopoly of states over the control of violence, but also the international institutions that were built on that state monopoly.

---

[33] They cite the increasing institutionalization of security regimes, the rising density of financial, economic, and trade connections, the diffuse and non-military nature of security threats, the transnationalization of the arms trade and the global infrastructure of arms regulations, and the degree to which great power (i.e., the US) behavior sets the standard for other state behavior. Held et al., *Global Transformations*, p. 144.

[34] Frederick Cooper, "Networks, Moral Discourse, and History," in Thomas Callaghy, Ronald Kasimir, and Robert Latham, eds., *Intervention and Transnationalism in Africa* (Cambridge: Cambridge University Press, 2001), p. 44.

[35] Duffield, *Global Governance and the New Wars*.

There is evidence that the diffusion of control over violence has already disrupted some mechanisms for international governance of violence – it has complicated interpretations of international law, complicated relations within and among states, and disrupted the functioning of international institutions. It has also opened new paths for global political action outside of established international institutional channels. Looking back at the previous eras where control was widely diffused reveals a similar dynamic – contracted force led to change rather than the solidification of existing institutions. A contrast between this dynamic in the Holy Roman Empire and some Italian City States, however, reveals that contracted force can sometimes yield new reinforcing processes of control. Whether contracted force leads to the potential for increased conflict or to new institutions of control depends on whether the mechanisms of control push against or reinforce one another.

Complications in international law

Much of international law relevant to security has been created by states and for states. Decisions by private actors to break these rules in order to gain advantage have created one set of complications. The US has faced these kinds of complications in prosecuting its war on terrorism. Should it treat non-state enemy combatants as prisoners of war? Or are they a new category of combatant? Established categories in international law do not provide guidance for this decision. Treating these actors as states' combatants might elevate their status,[36] treating them as "criminals" might reduce the options that states have in dealing with them. Treating them as neither, though, opens the US up to other states' accusations that it is behaving improperly. Combating other types of private actors that have engaged in violence – militias, paramilitaries, local or transnational crime syndicates – has introduced similar difficulties for a wide variety of states.

PSCs who claim to be on the legitimate side of international action have also rendered legal questions. The first question was what to call them. Mercenaries are illegal. In 1987, the United Nations Commission on Human Rights appointed a Special Rapporteur on the use of mercenaries to address increasing concerns about their use. A specific aim of this mandate was to encourage states to ratify the "International Convention against the Recruitment, Use, Financing, and Training of

---

[36] Sir Michael Howard, "What's in a Name? How to Fight Terrorism," *Foreign Affairs* (January/ February 2002): 8–20.

Mercenaries."[37] Although the 1990s demonstrated more mercenary involvement in armed conflict since the 1960s, according to International Alert, the complexities introduced by the PSC phenomenon fit uncomfortably with the Special Rapporteur's mandate. Instead of redefining the mercenary issue to deal with the phenomenon at hand, though, the UN office continued its focus on ratification of the "International Convention" (successfully, it came into force in 2002) and largely side-stepped the issue of PSCs.[38]

The passage of the International Convention did clarify the illegality of mercenaries, but it has many loopholes. First is the ambiguous definition of mercenary. Article 1, paragraph 2 defines a mercenary as someone who is specifically recruited for the purpose of participating in a concerted act of violence aimed at overthrowing a government or undermining the territorial integrity of a state, is motivated by the desire for private gain and material compensation, is neither a national nor a resident of the state against which such act is directed, has not been sent by a state on official duty, and is not a member of the armed forces of the state on whose territory the act is undertaken.[39] Many have noted that the definition alone opens the largest loophole as it relies primarily on the motivation of an individual – something that is near impossible to determine.[40] Other complaints have to do with the statute's reliance on states for enforcement, and lack of international monitoring or enforcement capability.[41] Furthermore, the UN's focus on the (very) narrow aim of outlawing mercenaries missed an opportunity to begin discussions on regulating PSCs.[42]

Even if we remove debates over the mercenary issue, the uses of PSCs have an unclear status in international law. The laws of war specify the qualities of combatants in ways that exclude most PSC employees.[43] Specifically, the International Law Concerning the Conduct of

---

[37] International Alert, "An Assessment of the Mercenary Issue at the Fifty-Fifth Session of the UN Comission on Human Rights," May 1999.

[38] See Fifty-Sixth General Assembly, A/SCH/ 3600, Third Committee, 31 October 2001, 26th meeting. Discussion of document A/56/224 summarizing the activities of the Special Rapporteur.

[39] "International Convention against the Recruitment, Use, Financing and Training of Mercenaries," UN General Assemby Resolution 44/34, 4 December 1989.

[40] Zarate, "Emergence of a New Dog of War," p. 121.

[41] International Alert, "The Mercenary Issue at the UN Commission on Human Rights: the Need for a New Approach," January 2001, pp. 29–30.

[42] Ibid. This document suggests continued focus on definitions, a new framework for regulation – possibly along the lines of the UN conventional arms register – and dialogues with users and providers of private security services, among others.

[43] Zamparelli, "What Have We Signed Up for?" See also discussion in Zarate, "Emergence of a New Dog of War," pp. 120–33.

Hostilities states, "To be commanded by a person responsible for his subordinates; to have a fixed, distinctive sign recognized at a distance; to carry arms openly; and to conduct their operations in accordance with the laws and customs of war."[44] Also Article 43 of Protocol I of the Geneva Convention states, "The armed forces of a party to a conflict consist of all organized armed forces, groups and units that are under a commander responsible to that party for the conduct of its subordinates . . . Such armed forces will be subject to an internal disciplinary system that, inter alia, shall enforce compliance with the rules of international law applicable in armed conflict."[45] PSCs frequently operate out of uniform and beyond the reach of military law.

In some cases, PSC personnel have been commissioned by a government and fought as combatants. This was true for EO in Sierra Leone and Sandline claimed that it sometimes operated in this way.[46] In the absence of such commissioning, persons employed by PSCs would generally fit into the category of non-combatants. Though the law of war has recognized the right of non-combatants to be present on the battlefield, and even to be accorded prisoner of war status, this is not guaranteed. Strategies that blur the distinction like guerilla tactics or PSCs engaged in activities more directly related to a war effort are likely to increase the chance that PSC employees will be treated as illegal non-combatants.

This risk led US military planners to worry that contractors performing operational support duties (providing battlefield mainten-ance for various weapons Systems) effectively forfeit their non-combatant status and risk execution if captured.[47] Concerns over contractor safety escalated in the early part of the new century as US PSCs were targeted in Afghanistan and Iraq and kidnapped in Colombia in 2003. The juxtaposition of three incidents, in particular, demonstrate uncertainties about the status of private security personnel, their relationship to military forces, and their relationship to their parent state that indicate the variety of risks contractor personnel face. In April when hundreds of Iraqi insurgents attacked US headquarters in Najaf, it was not US forces, but eight Blackwater security personnel that repelled

---

[44] See Collection of the Hague Conventions and Some Other International Instruments, International Committee of the Red Cross, p. 7 cited in Zamparelli, "What Have We Signed Up for?"

[45] Article 43 of Protocol I of the Geneva Convention, dated August 1949, cited in Zamparelli, "What Have We Signed Up For?" p. 15. Note that the difficulties with combatant status do not only extend to PSCs. Special forces in civilian clothing or clandestine state forces would also be subject to these difficulties.

[46] Interview with Tim Spicer, Washington, DC, 17 March 2000.

[47] Zamparelli, "What Have We Signed Up For?"

the attack, even relying on their own helicopter to re-supply the forces and ferry out a wounded Marine.[48] The next day in Kut, however, when five Hart Group employees were involved in intense fighting and their position was overrun, coalition forces did not come to their rescue and one Hart employee bled to death on the top of a building.[49] Thus while contractors are taken to be an integral part of coalition forces in Iraq, the rights of these personnel and their ability to count on regular military forces to back them up is not clear. Similarly, in January 2003 a plane carrying four contractors and a Colombian soldier was shot down doing surveillance over FARC territory. After executing one of the contractors and the soldier, the FARC took the other three into custody, calling them prisoners of war. The US government, however, denied them that status – referring to them as "kidnappees." There are several other irregularities about this incident – the contractors were originally working for a company called California Microwave Systems, but their contract was transferred ten days after their capture to a newly formed company, CIAO, Inc.[50] All of this is simply to illustrate that uncertainties over status can lead not only the enemy, but also the contracting state, to make decisions that compromise the safety of PSC personnel. PSC personnel do not have the clear rights that soldiers have.

The uncertainties also have implications for how and whether PSC personnel can be held responsible for their conduct. While the operation of troops abroad is governed by national systems of military justice, PSCs, as private entities, are not normally subject to military justice.[51] In the US, "typically, the only recourse commanders have for punishing contractor crimes . . . is to send them home . . ."[52] Depending on Status of Forces Agreements, US contractors may be subject to the local and criminal law for misdeeds. However, in situations where the local government is not functioning effectively, this may lead to less than

---

[48] Dana Priest, "Private Guards Repel Attack on US Headquarters," *Washington Post*, 6 April 2004.
[49] Jamie Wilson, "Private Security Firms Call for More Firepower in Combat Zone," *Guardian*, 17 April 2004.
[50] Vanessa Arrington, "Videotape Shows Colombia Captives Alive," *Associate Press* 28 August 2003; "60 Minutes II," CBS television transcript, 8pm 8 October 2003; John McQuaid, "Citizens, Not Soldiers," *New Orleans Times Picayune*, 11 November 2003; John McQuaid, "US Hostages in Colombia Mark One Year," *New Orleans Times Picayune*, 13 February 2004.
[51] In the US, the Supreme Court held that prosecuting civilians under military law was unjust in the 1950s. See Glenn Schmitt, "Closing the Gap in Criminal Jurisdiction Over Civilians Accompanying the Armed Forces Abroad – A First Person Account of the Creation of the Military Extraterritorial Jurisdiction Act of 2000," *Catholic University Law Review* Vol. 51, No. 1 (fall 2001): 55–134.
[52] Zamparelli, "What Have We Signed Up For?" p. 16.

satisfactory outcomes. This was the case when DynCorp employees
working for the US (doing aircraft maintenance for the Army) or for the
UN (part of the UN's International Police Task Force) were implicated
in prostitution (or worse) rings in Bosnia.[53] About the time the
DynCorp scandals were unfolding the US passed legislation, the
Military Extraterritorial Jurisdiction Act or MEJA, which promises to
hold personnel who have committed criminal acts under contract with
the Department of Defense to account in US Federal Courts.[54] Though
there are many uncertainties about how this law will work in practice
and it covers a fairly narrow range of PSC activity (PSCs under contract
to the US DOD), it does close the loophole under which the DynCorp
employees doing aircraft maintenance for the Army evaded responsibility for their actions.[55] Contractor involvement in the abuses at Abu
Ghraib prison in Iraq has led the US Justice Department to begin a
criminal investigation under the MEJA.[56] The passage of the Patriot Act
in 2001 extends US Federal law to crimes committed by or against US
citizens on lands or facilities designated for use by the US government.[57]
In 2004 an independent contractor working for the CIA was charged
under the Patriot Act for abuses of a prisoner in Afghanistan that led to
the prisoner's death.[58] Finally, the US has taken additional steps to

[53] Patricia O'Meara Kelly, "Broken Wings," *Insight Magazine* (29 April 2002); Robert
Capps, "Outside the Law," Salon.com News, 26 June 2002.
[54] http://caselaw.lp.findlaw.com/casecode/uscodes/18/parts/ii/chapters/212/toc.html. The
passage of MEJA was not expressly tied to the DynCorp case. How to prosecute
civilians accompanying troops overseas had been an issue for quite some time. The
immediate impetus for the bill that became MEJA was a constituent complaint to
Senator Jeff Sessions (R, Alabama) about an unpunished crime by the son of a service
person on a US base in Germany. See Schmitt, "Closing the Gap."
[55] Andrew D. Fallon and Theresa A. Keene, "Closing the Loophole? Practical Implications of the Military Extraterritorial Jurisdiction Act of 2000," *Air Force Law Review*
(22 March 2001). For more discussion of the difficulties with this act and the legal
responsibilities of PSCs more generally, see Peter Singer, "War, Profits, and the
Vacuum of Law: Privatized Military Firms and International Law," *Columbia Journal
of International Law* Vol. 42 (2003): 521; Seth Stern, "Contractors Hover in Gray Area
Regarding Legal Liability," *Congressional Quarterly Weekly Report* (8 May 2004);
Michael Sirak, "ICRC Calls for Contractor Accountability in War," *Jane's Defence
Weekly* (19 May 2004), p. 4. See Schmitt, "Closing the Gap," pp. 133–34 for a
discussion of why the act did not originally apply to contractors working for other US
agencies. The 2004 National Defense Authorization Act amends MEJA to extend its
reach to all US government contractors that support the mission of the Department of
Defense overseas.
[56] Renae Merle, "Contractor Investigated by Justice," *Washington Post*, 22 May 2004.
[57] "CIA Contractor Indicted for Assaulting Detainee Held at US Base in Afghanistan,"
Press Release, US Department of Justice, 17 June 2004.
[58] See CPA Official Documents, Order #17, "Status of the Coalition, Foreign Liaison
Missions, their Personnel and Contractors," available at http://www.cpa-iraq.org/
regulations/ CPAORD17Status_of_Forces.pdf.

clarify the legal responsibilities of contractors in particular situations. For instance, in Iraq the CPA's top authority, L. Paul Bremer, issued an order specifying that contractors are subject to the law of their parent country and not Iraqi law for any action they take as part of their contract.[59]

How legal liability works for PSC personnel who are non-US nationals, however, is not so clear. Many countries do not have laws covering extraterritorial behavior. Though the CPA attempted to stipulate that jurisdiction should lie in a contractor's country of origin, countries like South Africa, who argue that its citizens are serving in PSCs in Iraq illegally, may be less than willing to prosecute them at home. Furthermore, there are situations where the extension of US legal jurisdiction outside its territory may overlap with or contradict orders like CPA Order No. 17 in Iraq. Both the Patriot Act and MEJA specify conditions under which US jurisdiction applies to third party nationals – for MEJA it is if they commit criminal acts under contract to the US DOD, for the Patriot Act it is if they commit criminal acts against a US citizen in a territory designated for use by the US government.[60] Thus there are situations that could result in jurisdictional confusion between the US and the accused individual's parent country. If a PSC is not working for the US DOD and commits a criminal act against a non-US citizen, US law would not apply, and prosecution would depend on the law and interest of either the host territory or their parent countries. And, it is not hard to imagine situations under which PSC employees of different nationalities face quite different legal ramifications from criminal deeds that they commit together. All of this simply reiterates that the proper legal authority under which to hold PSCs liable for potential misdeeds is unsettled.

There is the potential to hold the company responsible, instead of (or in addition to) the individual. The US rules for defense acquisitions (DFARS), for instance, do open the possibility that firms can be punished, even prevented from future competition for US contracts, if they field employees that commit criminal behavior. This possibility was raised in the wake of revelations that personnel working for US defense contractors, CACI and Titan, may have been involved in the abuses at Abu Ghraib.[61] Iraqis who were injured by contract employees

---

[59] The Patriot Act amended the definition of "special maritime and territorial jurisdiction" (SMTJ 18 USC 7). See http://caselaw.Lp.findlaw.com/ scripts/ ts_Search.pl? title=18&sec=7.

[60] Schmitt, "Closing the Gap."

[61] Anitha Reddy and Ellen McCarthy, "CACI in the Dark on Reports of Abuse," *Washington Post*, 6 May 2004.

could also sue the companies under the Alien Tort Statute – though corporate defendants could shield themselves through a "military contractor defense" if they had followed government specifications in their hiring.[62]

Finally, there is the question of the legal responsibility of those who finance violence. Here again, plaintiffs (and their allies in the human rights community) have increasingly sought to use US law and legal venues, and particularly the Alien Tort Statute to hold companies liable for repressive practices by the security forces they finance.[63] Royal Dutch/Shell, ExxonMobil and Unocal were all sued in US Courts for the behavior of the forces they financed. In 2001, the International Labor Rights Fund filed suit in Washington Federal Court against ExxonMobile, claiming that it and its Indonesian subsidiary could be held liable for the murder, torture, and sexual crimes committed by the Indonesian troops it financed.[64] In March 2002, a US Federal Court ruled that a civil lawsuit charging Shell with complicity in the execution of Ken Saro-Wiwa and the other Ogoni activists could go forward.[65] In June 2002, a California Court agreed to hear a case against Unocal – one of America's largest oil and gas exploration companies – to determine its responsibility for human rights abuses during the construction of a natural gas pipeline in Burma (Myanmar).[66] Paradoxically the use of US courts may eviscerate the capacity and legitimacy of local courts in ways that may be detrimental to the long-term interests of plaintiffs (in a good legal system) and the companies they sue (in having cases tried where local conditions are better understood).[67]

Disruption of existing institutional arrangements

Rather than reinforcing existing institutions, private security often appears to change or disrupt the way these institutions work. The nine cases in this book illustrate these disruptions as they affect state institutions and state building enterprises in a variety of ways. As the US

---

[62] Stern, "Contractors Hover in Gray Area Regarding Legal Liability."

[63] Elliot Schrage, "Judging Corporate Accountability in the Global Economy," *Columbia Journal of Transnational Law* Vol. 42 (2003).

[64] "ExxonMobil-Sponsored Terrorism?" *Nation* (14 June 2002). In an interesting twist in this case, ExxonMobil argued that if the judge prosecuted the case, he could hinder the US war on terrorism by issuing judgment on a US ally.

[65] EarthRights International, 5 March 2002.

[66] Elliot Schrage, "A Long Way to Find Justice: What are Burmese Villagers Doing in a California Court?" *Washington Post*, 14 July 2002, Sunday Outlook Section, p. B2.

[67] Ibid.

case in chapter 3 demonstrates, private security frequently changes the balance of power within strong states and allows new actors access to the policy process (PSCs employed by strong states can collude with the host government to frustrate the plans of their employer). Furthermore, as the cases in chapter 4 demonstrate, PSCs from one state under contract to another undermine the international institution that the state controls the violent actions of its citizens abroad. PSCs can implicate their home state causing embarrassment – as Sandline involvement in Sierra Leone and the political fallout in Britain demonstrates. The current participation of South African personnel and PSCs under contract with the US government and the CPA in Iraq is also calling into question South African law.[68] Finally, as seen in chapter five, transnational financing of security has often contributed to the disruption of (admittedly already weak) state institutions. In Nigeria, for instance, the influence of oil financing encouraged forces to seek funds outside the state, which has sometimes distracted them from security tasks and contributed to the de-professionalization of both police and military forces. Also in Garamba, the fact that financing for guards came from INGOs and control over personnel came from the government contributed to a situation where no one had effective control over the forces in the Park.

It is not only states that are impacted by this change, however. When private transnational actors finance security, their involvement often leads to disruptions in the institutions that govern their actions as well. As discussed in chapter 5, INGOs and TNCs that finance security also violate norms regarding their status or mandate as non-governmental actors. This frequently opens disputes within issue communities about proper behavior and leads to splits within these communities that make it harder for them to reach their goals. The cases in chapter five demonstrate that the institutional structures of both INGOs and commercial companies have been disrupted by their participation in governance roles. The very meaning of being a "non-governmental" actor depends on having a government. Similarly, without an effective government, "commercial" companies may be drawn to a variety of activities that cannot be judged by looking at the "bottom line" alone.[69]

The cases in this book do not address the question of how this market for force will impact the United Nations, though they do hold

---

[68] UN-IRIN, "South Africa: Authorities"; Tromp, "Hired Guns from SA Flood Iraq."
[69] Thus new references to the "double" or "triple" bottom line. See www.sustainability. com.

implications for that question. For the past several years there have been periodic queries about whether PSCs could help make the UN – UN peacekeeping, in particular – function more effectively. For instance, David Shearer's Adelphi Paper advocated the use of PSCs within an international structure including the UN so as to foster more effective intervention. More recently, Peter Gantz of Refugees International argues, "If nations with first class militaries refuse to put their troops in harm's way in remote locations, and if the UN is saddled with troops from developing nations that are not up the task, then perhaps the UN should hire the private sector to save the day."[70] PSCs have worked with the UN to supply peace operations and the UN has directly contracted with PSCs to provide such services as armed guard for convoys.[71]

There are hints, however, that private security could just as easily undermine as enhance the relevance of the UN. Private security may provide a platform that competes with the United Nations as a tool for "international" force. Again, Iraq is a case in point. Operation Iraqi Freedom was conducted without a UN mandate and UN peacekeeping forces were not forthcoming for the post-war stabilization. As insecurity ensued, PSCs were deployed to provide a wide variety of security related functions. Given the general antipathy with which the "international community" viewed the operation and the difficulty the US has had gaining support from other states, one could view private security as an alternative mechanism for gaining additional personnel. It is not only analysts that think this way. One American Army Staff Sergeant claimed, "We're trying to get more international participation here and the contractors can hire internationally."[72] As easily as being a tool for enhancing UN operations, then, in some circumstances PSCs may also offer tools that compete with the UN. The private option may be seen as an alternative that avoids sticky political debates and can take quick action when that is required. By offering a tool that works in an array of different forums, private security may reduce the need to work through the political processes that states have set up through multi-lateral institutions.

---

[70] Peter Gantz, "The Private Sector's Role in Peacekeeping and Peace Enforcement," *Refugees International Bulletin* (18 November 2003); www.refugeesinternational.org/cgi-bin/ri/bulletin?bc=00681.

[71] "Use of Military or Armed Escorts for Humanitarian Convoys," UN OCHA Discussion Paper, the United Nations, New York, 2001.

[72] Borzou Daragahi, "For Profit, Private Firms Train Iraqi Soldiers, Provide Security, and Much More," *Post-Gazette* 28 September 2003 (http://www.post-gazette.com/pg/03271/226368.stm).

Feedback effects: private stabilization, conditionality, and state building

Not only was the role for PSCs in Iraq huge, Iraq also presents a different model of stabilization than the Balkans. Some of the PSC presence in Iraq was a continuation of the trends begun in the 1990s. Support for US and British troops continued, for instance, though the PSC role in providing some tasks, such as interrogations, was dramatically enhanced.[73] Also PSC work in training – though more significant in efforts to train the Iraqi army and Iraqi police force than it had been in similar efforts in the Balkans – was still largely consistent with past activities.[74] The lack of UN peacekeepers, though, combined with the fact that coalition forces were stretched thin, led to a much greater use of PSCs to provide site security, convoy protection, personal security details, and the like.[75]

These efforts were not coordinated by a single overarching entity. PSCs not only worked for the CPA, the US Central Command, and the British Army, they also worked for ABC News, the Triangle Research Institute, Catholic Relief Services, Bechtel, Parsons, and others. Virtually anyone working in Iraq required private security.[76] The rules by which PSCs operated, however, were initially unclear – and often set by individual employers, or even the PSCs themselves.[77] As the insurgency heated up, PSCs ostensibly providing low-level security found themselves in situations indistinguishable from combat. PSC employees were shot and killed, and shot and killed others. Though the CPA did attempt to issue some regulation, specifying limits on the weaponry PSCs should carry, the circumstances under which PSCs could use deadly force, and the legal bodies to which contractor personnel would be liable, a good amount of authority was devolved to those who issued the contracts.[78]

All of these issues became more apparent when four Blackwater employees escorting a convoy through Faludjah were attacked, killed,

---

[73] Highlighted by contractor involvement in the abuses at Abu Ghraib. See Seymour M. Hersh, "Torture at Abu Ghraib," *New Yorker*, 6 May 2004.

[74] Fein, "Training Iraqi Army is a Wild Card."

[75] Catan and Fidler, "With Post-War Instability Still a Pressing Concern."

[76] Michael Stetz, "Private Bodyguards are Essential in Iraq," *Union Tribune*, 3 June 2004.

[77] Carolyn Aldred, "Standards Sought for Iraq Security Firms," *Business Insurance* (26 April 2004); Stephen Gray, "Iraq Targets Private Guards," *Sunday Times*, 6 June 2004.

[78] Coalition Provisional Authority, Official Documents, Order Number 17, 31 December 2003. Deadly force is permitted for self defense, the defense of people or property specified in their contract, and the defense of civilians. See also CPA Order Number 17 (revised) "Status of the Coalition Provisional Authority MNf-Iraq, Certain Missions and Personnel in Iraq," available at http://www.iraqcoalition.org/regulations/20040627_CPAORD_17_Status_of_Coalition_Rev_with_Annex_A.pdf.

and then mutilated by the crowd.[79] Days later, Blackwater employees fought off an insurgent attack on US Marines. These events highlighted the presence of PSCs in Iraq and engendered requests for more information from the press, NGOs, the US Congress, and the British Parliament. In response to these pressures, the CPA intensified its regulatory efforts, requiring that PSCs be insured and setting up systems for standards and vetting with the Iraqi interior ministry.[80]

Even as it was doing more to coordinate the private sector, however, the CPA was also insuring its continued existence. When the insurgency (and associated looting) began to take a toll on rebuilding efforts, the CPA required that those receiving coalition money build security into their bids, in effect encouraging private responsibility for security.

How the private security sector will affect the fledgling Iraqi government's ability to control force remains to be seen. The fact that many features of private security in Iraq bear more resemblance to Sierra Leone than Croatia, however, should lead to tentative pessimism. The PSCs coordinating private security in Iraq and training the facilities protection force have close ties to oil and mining interests.[81] Also, authority over force is spread outside the state, to the oil sector and to local companies, some with ties to local militia forces. Add to this the tribal and ethnic claims to the control of force already in the country and the lack of a multi-lateral organization through which to impose conditionality and one is left with many of the factors that led to chafing control mechanisms in Sierra Leone. Ironically, to the extent that PSCs compete with and undermine the importance of multi-lateral institutions, the effect is to remove one of the more important ways in which political and social control over violence can be coordinated through conditionality.

Institutional innovations

Even as many traditional institutions have been eroded by private options, however, new institutional innovations are already apparent.[82]

---

[79] James Dao, "Private US Guards Take Big Risks for the Right Price," *New York Times*, 2 April 2004.

[80] Aldred, "Standards Sought"; Gray, "Iraq Targets Private Guards"; Mary Pat Flaherty and Dana Priest, "More Limits Sought for Private Security Firms," *Washington Post*, 13 April 2004.

[81] Thomas Catan and Ruth Sullivan, "Morrison Heads High Risk Security Group," *Financial Times*, 26 March 2004; Knut Royce, "Start Up Company with Connections," *Newsday*, 15 February 2004; Flaherty, "Iraq Work Awarded to Veteran of Civil Wars."

[82] For general analyses of networks, see Walter Powell, "Neither Market nor Hierarchy: Network Forms of Organizations," in L. L. Cumings and B. Staw, eds., *Research in*

One of these, the Chad–Cameroon pipeline deal, could be characterized as "networked governance," with private firms cooperating with IOs, INGOs, and local civil societies to direct the proceeds from oil extraction toward agreed upon governance goals to avoid the need for the repressive forces often associated with extractive resources (oil in particular). The other prominent innovation is the US use of PSCs in Iraq, which one could argue provides the basis for a US imperial force.

Networked governance

In anticipation of just the kind of criticism Shell had received in Nigeria, a group of oil companies led a process to legitimize their extraction of oil from Chad. They initiated consultations with a number of stakeholders to strike an innovative deal that allows TNCs access to oil and (they hope) shields them from responsibility for any improper behavior that the governments of Chad and Cameroon might undertake. The deal struck between Exxon, the World Bank, interested INGOs, and the governments of Chad and Cameroon includes arrangements to avoid the channeling of oil money through these governments.[83] Under the terms of the agreement, several oil companies (ExxonMobil, Petronas, and ChevronTexaco) drilled for oil and the World Bank loaned Chad and Cameroon the money to construct a pipeline to the sea. Instead of oil money going into government coffers, however, some repays the World Bank loan directly. In Chad the rest of the money is spent under the supervision of a nine member "revenue management college" composed of representatives from civil society, the government, and the courts. In Cameroon no similar local measure was set up but the general project is overseen by an International Advisory Group (IAG) and monitored by the External Compliance Monitoring Group (ECMP).[84] Each country made commitments to spend its oil proceeds on health,

---

Organizational Behavior (Greenwich, CT: JAI, 1990), pp. 295–336; W. Powell and L. Smith-Doerr, "Networks and Economic Life," in Neil Smelser and Richard Swedberg, eds., *The Handbook of Economic Sociology* (New York: Russell Sage, 1994); Oliver Williamson, "Comparative Economic Organization: the Analysis of Discrete Structural Alternatives," *Administrative Studies Quarterly* Vol. 36 (1991): 269–96.

[83] Ironically, Exxon was not one of the participants in the "Voluntary Principles." Ibid.; Bennett Freeman, "Drilling for Common Ground," *Foreign Policy* (July/August 2001), p. 50.

[84] See http://www.worldbank.org/afr/ccproj/; Ian Gary and Terry Karl, "Bottom of the Barrel: Africa's Oil Boom and the Poor," Catholic Relief Services Report, June 2003, available at http://www.catholicrelief.org/get_involved/advocacy/policy_and_strategic_issues/oil_report_full.pdf; Emily Wax, "Bottom of the Barrel," *Washington Post*, 21 March 2004.

education, infrastructure, and rural development projects, plus 5 percent must return to the areas from which oil is pumped and 10 percent must be set aside in a future generation's trust.[85]

This agreement was intended to ensure that payments from the oil companies do not go disproportionately into a repressive state security apparatus or the pockets of corrupt politicians.[86] It was also designed to spread the wealth from oil in a broader way, potentially avoiding the uneven distribution of oil wealth that some argue is bound to lead to violence and security concerns in the longer term. The plan anticipated and prepared for some security concerns – particularly regarding sensitive environmental areas that will be more easily accessed given the pipeline construction.[87] INGOs, including WWF Cameroon, were involved in the execution of conservation activities with the government providing the requisite personnel for park guards, etc.[88]

The result is an unprecedented intervention in the politics of Chad and Cameroon not by other states, but by commercial and non-commercial transnational actors allied with functionally based international organizations and local NGOs. Oil began flowing through the pipeline in 2003 and the pipeline was formally inaugurated in June 2004.[89] Even if successful, this project portends significant changes in the political control of violence that may have unanticipated functional effects. For instance, how will the anti-poaching forces be governed (will the use of government forces be an avenue through which the government can continue to divert resources to its security apparatus)? One worry is that multiple principals will leave no one with control of forces (or of accountability for their actions).[90] A Congressional

---

[85] Ottoway, "Reluctant Missionaries," pp. 52–53. The World Bank Group, "The Chad–Cameroon Petroleum Development and Pipeline Project," http://www.worldbank.org/afr/ccproj/project/pro_overview.htm; The World Bank Group, "IFC Participants Meeting: Oil and Gas," Washington, 4–5 June 2002 available at http://www.ifc.org/syndications/pdfs/Kaldany.pdf.

[86] Although in the midst of political unrest in Chad the government reportedly used some $4.5 million of a $25 million signing bonus for its defense budget. Charles Cobb, Jr., "Chad–Cameroon Pipeline Considered by Congressional Subcommittee," allAfrica.com NEWS 18 April 2002 available at http://allafrica.com/stories/printable/200204180864.html.

[87] Two new national parks are to be established in Cameroon via the "Off-site Environmental Enhancement Program," and three sensitive areas along the pipeline are to be protected through an "Induced Access Management Plan," that combines physical barriers with rules on hunting and inspections. See http://www2.exxonmobil.com/Chad/People/Programs/ Chad_PG_IndAccess.asp.

[88] The World Bank Group, "Chad–Cameroon Petroleum Development and Pipeline Project."

[89] "3.7B Oil Pipeline Official," Toronto Sun, 13 June 2004.

[90] Ottoway, "Reluctant Missionaries," p. 53.

Research Service (CRS) report in 2003 suggests that there are many loopholes for government discretion, but more importantly for the purposes here, the political changes brought by this project are not what was expected. The IAG's mandate is murky and is under-resourced and the "revenue management college" in Chad has already ceded to unanticipated (and undue) intervention from political authorities, perhaps made possible by the government's control over the committee's resources.[91] While governance networks of the type set up over this project have the potential to yield more effective control of force (and public goods more generally), their success will depend on their distribution of power to people and organizations competent to do their jobs (or trained to be competent) and with an interest in the success of the experiment toughened by belief in the values that underlie it.

An imperial force

Prominent in policy debates are arguments about whether the US should accept the imperial role many associate with its relative power and develop more effective tools for imperial rule.[92] If the US steps fully into an imperial role instead of seeing itself as leader in a multi-lateral world, there are likely to be more and more situations in which the US and its traditional allies do not agree. The more the US acts unilaterally, the more difficult it will be to get cooperation from other states. This will leave the US hard pressed to meet the demands of its actions.[93] The way the US has used PSCs in Iraq suggests that the private sector might contribute to an imperial force.

As indicated above, the US has turned to the private sector to fill in for the lack of stabilization forces. Though the nature of these contracts and their uncoordinated nature may not have contributed to public security, they have protected important people and assets in Iraq. Because the US used PSCs based in many different countries and these companies have recruited from all over the world, it vastly increased the pool from which to draw security personnel. This strategy also reduced the costs – retired personnel from South Africa and seconded personnel

---

[91] Gary and Karl, "Bottom of the Barrel," p. 74.

[92] Niall Ferguson, "A World Without Power," *Foreign Policy* (July/August 2004): 32–39; Eliot Cohen, "History and the Hyperpower," *Foreign Affairs* (July/August 2004): 49–63; Thomas Barnett, *The Pentagon's New Map: War and Peace in the Twenty-First Century* (New York: Putnam, 2004); Bobbitt, *Shield of Achilles*; Chalmers Johnson, *The Sorrows of Empire: Militarism, Secrecy, and the End of the Republic* (New York: Metropolitan Books, 2004).

[93] For this reason, Barry Posen suggests that the US eschew such a strategy. See Posen, "Command of the Commons."

from Fiji are less expensive than retired US personnel.[94] Furthermore, contracting directly with PSCs that can recruit internationally may give the US more control over forces than would be the case if it had to negotiate with another government for troop contributions. Though the US continues its efforts to train foreign militaries (an effort accomplished with the help of PSCs), using foreign troops (or retired foreign troops) under contract may provide a more controllable set of forces.

How this strategy will play – at home and abroad – however is still unclear and there are many potential pitfalls. As mentioned in chapter three, recruiting internationally reduces social control. If PSC employees behave poorly, it may also affect the legitimacy of US actions abroad and their acceptance at home. Other countries may not approve of PSC recruitment of their citizens and take steps to prevent it, making the practice more risky and raising costs. The US has been reluctant to assume the mantle of empire partly because the concept sits uncomfortably with the essential ideals on which democracy rests – and these are the very ideals that Americans see themselves upholding.[95] Finally, as mentioned in the section on stabilization efforts above, it is unclear that PSCs provide a strong basis for long term stability. If using PSCs creates more territories with weak state control, there will be more and more areas for the US to police, potentially driving up the costs of an imperial strategy – and the demand for more private security.

While both of these innovations are seen to have promise by some, neither is assured to generate an effective process of control – the networked governance experiment risks generating multiple principals with overlapping claims to authority over force and a decline in functional control. The US use of a privately recruited imperial force promises political changes that may be seen as illegitimate and risks decline in the social control of force. Neither will be effective unless these risks are managed. Looking back to early modern Europe demonstrates that market forces were sometimes quite disruptive, leading to less control and other times useful tools on which to build new governance platforms. A quick look at the different contractual relationships of the time demonstrates that those relationships deemed successful were those where control mechanisms reinforced one another – leading to a fit between function, political power, and values.

---

[94] E-mail correspondence with PSC employees in Iraq who claim that as more Iraqis and other internationals have flooded the market, salaries are decreasing markedly.
[95] Cohen, "History and the Hyperpower," p. 54.

Competing mechanisms, conflict, and change in history

Bernard Guenee sums up the fourteenth and fifteenth centuries as "the era of the contract forces."[96] There are many similarities between that era and today's. Then as now, disjunctures between rulers' security goals and the prevailing structure of force precipitated contracting. Then, as now, contractors varied in the degree to which they provided security effectively. Then, as now, contracts prompted political change. Then, as now, contracted forces often introduced new values into the decision making process. The market in that era, however, led to quite distinct effects on the control of force in different situations.[97] Market forces and the diffusion of control caused instability and change where control mechanisms competed in the territories of the Holy Roman Empire, but led to advances in controlling force where they reinforced one another in some Italian City States.

Historical analyses of the rise of private forces in the late middle ages tie these forces to changes in the societal context which led to the demand for different functions. The growth of trade, and with it merchants and towns, brought security requirements that were not well met by the personalistic and largely rural organization of feudal forces.[98] In response to new demands, a variety of military enterprisers sprung up to work, via contract, for a plethora of different employers.[99] Princes contracted with companies within their territory – akin to MPRI's work for the US government. They also frequently looked to companies outside their territory – akin to MPRI's work for Croatia or Equatorial Guinea. Not only princes, but also overarching authorities such as the Emperor and the Pope hired forces – akin to DSL's work for INGOs and TNCs around the work. During the Thirty Years War, one of the most infamous of these enterprisers, Wallenstein, used his resources and enterprisers to fight against other political units.

---

[96] B. Guenee, *States and Rulers*, p. 142.

[97] Others have looked back at this period for analogies. See, for instance, Phillip Cerny, "Neomedievalism, Civil War, and the New Security Dilemma: Globalization as Durable Disorder," *Civil Wars* Vol. 1, No. 1 (spring 1998).

[98] William H. McNeill, *The Pursuit of Power: Technology, Armed Force and Society since AD 1000*, (Chicago: University of Chicago Press, 1982), pp. 63–65; Spruyt, *Sovereign State and its Competitors*.

[99] See Trease, *Condottieri*, Redlich, *German Military Enterpriser*. Fritz Redlich distinguishes these military enterprisers from the foreign adventurers, criminals, and partners of warlords that immediately preceded them. While foreign adventurers might flock to the warlord's banner expecting plunder or a share in his conquests, military enterprisers hired a workforce and paid them a wage. They contracted with employers in need of military services for payment of a set amount in exchange for the services of so many men. Vol. 1 (pp. 4–5).

The private forces of this time were frequently raised, trained, and "regulated" by feudal lords.[100] As Redlich describes it, contractors of the late middle ages had obligations to their feudal lords even as they sold their services elsewhere. "By necessity each of them had two masters: his feudal lord and the one with whom he made a contract."[101] They even sometimes refused contracts that would break these obligations. For instance, in May 1364 the Archpriest employed by the King of France refused to fight at Cocherel because he held lands from the Captal de Buch who commanded for the King of Navarre and thus fighting would violate his oath of fealty.[102] The Holy Roman Empire enacted principles to support lords in their regulation of these contractors with the 1495 Diet at Worms, which declared it an established principle that permission by any estate was required to raise troops, even by the Emperor.[103] The Swiss chose a different strategy, making military training universal and then allowing it to be sold (exported) through individual cantons.

The values that underlie the legitimate use of force were based on just war. Aquinas proposed three requirements for just war: authority, just cause, and just intention.[104] The primary concern was authority, "since princes were instituted by God to further the common good, they had the duty to defend it."[105] Because the feudal order still provided the legitimate mechanism for waging war, though, increasing conflict between the Pope and the Emperor created many gray areas where the application of just war norms was contested. Indeed, the whole doctrine of just war depended on legitimate authority and it was legitimate authority that was under dispute. Similarly, chivalry rooted in the personal and private world of ancient Germanic tradition, and based on notions of loyalty, honor, and self-sacrifice, became less relevant as men fought by contract further from their homes.[106] As the moral code

---

[100] Though analogous with the situation today, the style and strength of that regulation varied. Mocker argues that the Condottieri took the form they did in Italy because of the weakness of feudalism there. See Mocker, *Mercenaries*, ch. 3.

[101] Redlich, *German Military Enterpriser*, Vol. 1, p. 95.

[102] Mockler, *Mercenaries*, pp. 33–34. For evidence of contracts that excused enterprisers from fighting their friends, see Redlich, *German Military Enterpriser*, Vol. 1, p. 95.

[103] Ibid., p. 38.

[104] Russell, *Just War in the Middle Ages*, p. 268.

[105] Ibid., p. 268.

[106] The writings of churchmen in the middle ages about the proper ordering of Christian society divided estates between the clergy – to cater to spiritual needs, the warriors – to uphold justice, protect the weak and defend the Church, and labourers – to till the soil and provide for physical needs. This division had a profound influence on establishing the ideal behavior of warriors, which came to be known as chivalry. See Keen, *Chivalry*, pp. 3–5.

of feudalism unwound, military service was increasingly taken up in pursuit of financial gain rather than personal duty.[107]

In this environment, the church, feudal relationships, towns, and emerging states competed for legitimate authority, all of them exercising authority over the use of force in one place or another. The general interpretation of this era suggests that violence was rife and hard to control (not altogether unlike the recent environment in Africa and the Balkans). Military contracting has been cited as an enabling feature for the level of conflict that beset Europe during this time. While the basis of feudal obligations frequently made offensive action difficult (knights were obligated for a limited number of days each year and not required to serve abroad) contractors could fight more flexibly. Thus, according to Thomson, "it appears that the European market for mercenaries was largely a creation of war-makers seeking to escape the constraints of feudal military obligations."[108] The overlapping entities with control over violence also led to misunderstandings, misperceptions, and misjudgments – all of which escalated the potential for conflict. For instance, McNeill describes the failure of rulers to think about the financial requirements of conflict and the likely benefits. "War was an affair of honor, prestige, heroic self-assertion . . . Hence no one routinely calculated the balance between the costs of military enterprises and the likely returns . . ."[109] Also, competing claims to authority led to conflict. The Diet of Worms, for instance, yielded a Proclamation of Perpetual Public Peace and established an Imperial Chamber of Justice to eliminate feuding privileges. To fund this instrument, it also enacted a tax – the common penny, which led Switzerland to reject the decision and obtain independence via the Swabian War of 1499.[110] The devastating Thirty Years War, begun in Bohemia as the Protestant aristocracy rose up against Spanish authority, was both a product of overlapping authority and enabled by the vast array of contracted forces.[111]

---

[107] Felix Gilbert, "Machiavelli," in Peter Paret and Gordon Craig, eds., *The Makers of Modern Strategy* (Princeton: Princeton University Press, 1986), p. 15. See also M. E. Mallett and J. R. Hale, *The Military Organization of a Renaissance State* (Cambridge: Cambridge University Press, 1984).

[108] Thomson, *Mercenaries, Pirates and Sovereigns*, p. 27; Mockler, *Mercenaries*, Richard A. Preston and Sydney F. Wise, *Men in Arms: a History of Warfare and its Interrelationships with Western Society* (New York: Praeger Publishers, 1970).

[109] McNeill, *Pursuit of Power*, p. 105.

[110] Hermann Kinder and Werner Hilgeman, *The Anchor Atlas of World History* (New York: Anchor, 1974), Vol. 1, p. 219.

[111] Geoffrey Parker and Simon Adams, eds., *The Thirty Years War* (New York: Routledge, 1997); Kalevi J. Holsti, *Peace and War: Armed Conflict and International Order, 1648–1989* (Cambridge: Cambridge University Press, 1991), pp. 25–70; McNeill, *Pursuit of Power*.

These examples lend fodder to pessimists who might expect the combination of market forces and diffusion of authority to erode the existing reinforcing process of control.[112] In the Holy Roman Empire, the diffusion of control most clearly supports the pessimistic case. Religious splits and the overlapping authorities prevented rulers from establishing strong controls over military contractors. Though military enterprisers had greater incentives to fight effectively,[113] the financial wherewithal of some proved to be de-stabilizing,[114] and the license they were given to loot fit poorly with traditional notions of chivalry and just war.[115] Competing authorities, competing norms, and political opportunities led to more (and more poorly governed) conflict.

In Italy, though, the practice unfolded differently. The beginnings were similar – as they emerged, companies would, in effect, blackmail towns by pillaging and then offering to halt in return for payment.

---

[112] Silverstein, *Private Warriors*; Williamson, "Public and Private Bureaucracies"; Donahue, *Privatization Decision*. Samuel Bowles even describes the way market forces can transform preferences in such a way as to undermine potential for future trust. See Samuel Bowles, "Endogenous Preferences: the Cultural Consequences of Markets and other Economic Institutions," *Journal of Economic Literature* Vol. 36 (March 1998).

[113] Contracting was a path toward social achievement particularly for the lower nobility, but also for commoners. Fritz Redlich writes of a rudimentary shoemaker from Augsburg who played a role in the siege of Neuss (1475), then fought under Englebert of Nassau for Maximillian I and before long became a Swiss colonel. He went on to service with the Yorks and died leading 2,000 Swiss and German mercenaries to invade Lancashire. Redlich, *German Military Enterpriser*, pp. 107–08. Also, contractors had more military experience than peasants and more incentives to fight effectively. See Parker, *Thirty Years War*, pp. 190–95.

[114] During the Thirty Years War, Wallenstein had wealth and ambition enough to try and leverage his military capacity for political power.

Mansfield is another, lesser known example. In 1621 while Mansfield was under contract with the fugitive Protestant king of Bohemia, he simultaneously negotiated with Duke Maximillian of Bavaria to switch sides and evaded a Baviarian–Austrian pincer movement under way. He then negotiated with Infanta Isabella of the Spanish Low Countries and then negotiations were broken off, he was discharged and became a military enterpriser on his own account and risk. He received a variety of bids from the States General, Infanta Isabella, again, and both the Huguenots and the French king. In 1622 he went into service for the Dutch, then on his own again. In 1624 he extracted 3000,00fl from the Frisian estates to pay off his work force, dissolve his organization, and disappear. His retirement was quite short and he was negotiating in Paris by April 1624, then with England. In 1625 he appeared in Germany supporting King Christian IV of Denmark and then fighting in Lower Saxony. Only his death in 1625 put him out of service. Redlich, *German Military Enterpriser*, pp. 291–95, See also pp. 231–36 and McNeill, *Pursuit of Power*, pp. 120–21.

[115] As Maurice Keen puts it, "Pay in these conditions was rather more like a return (quite a handsome return) on an investment than a wage in the modern sense." Though excessive force or looting was frowned on, some force and looting was expected, and the lines between some and excessive were not clear. The feudal notions of chivalry (not so clearly strong in the best of circumstances) appear to have weakened further with the rise of the military enterpriser. Keen, *Chivalry*, p. 225.

Trease claims, however, that the condottiere's financial incentives suggested a basis for new controls. "True, they had a vested interest in war, but it would be more accurate to say that their interest lay in defense expenditure than in carnage."[116] This possibility led some Italian City States to propose that both employer and employee had an interest in long-term contracts where both employment and absence of plunder were guaranteed.[117] Along with this long-term employment came greater oversight, and, through muster and review, the standardization of personnel. Italian cities such as Venice used a number of mechanisms to generate control. They divided contracts among different condottieri to keep any one from growing too strong and usurping power. They also undertook efforts to engage contractors in local customs and values – bestowing civic honors and gifts upon successful condottieri to and even arranging marriages with suitable Venetian aristocracy.[118] By bestowing honor on these men as military "professionals" or creating ties with the aristocracy through marriage, Venetian nobility managed to dampen the pursuit of power via force. Local authorities played a greater and greater role in this process causing something like a corps of officers and a regular standing army to emerge in the better-governed City States of Italy during the first half of the fifteenth century.[119] "By inventing administrative methods for controlling soldiers and tying their self interest more and more closely to continued service with the same employer, these cities altered the incidence of instability inherent in market relationships."[120]

Thus, while contracted military services allowed a number of different entities to exercise military power and enhanced the options for using violence, the use of violence varied between the ruthless commercial ventures of Wallenstein and Mansfield in the Holy Roman Empire and the use of contractors by Italian City States for defense. Machiavelli's disdain for the unreliability of the condottieri should prevent too rosy a reading of the Italian mercenaries and some have suggested that City States such as Venice slipped back into neo-feudal relationships that inhibited their competition with sovereign states.[121] Nonetheless, some Italian City States did use the market to begin a process of organizing

---

[116] Trease, *Condottieri*, pp. 341–42.   [117] McNeill, *Pursuit of Power*, p. 75.
[118] Ibid., p. 76.   [119] Ibid., pp. 75, 77.
[120] Ibid., p. 78. Of course, the efficiency of the Italian cities' system led to naught when they were invaded by the Spaniards. McNeill reports that this was one of the few invasions that paid. By substituting the Spanish soldier for the Italian condottieri who had previously drawn pay for defending the same territory, the tax system in place allowed empire to be built without too much strain on the Castilian taxpayer. McNeill, *Pursuit of Power*, p. 109.
[121] Spruyt, *Sovereign State and its Competitors*.

violence around post-feudal principles and practices where political and social control mechanisms reinforced one another. After the Thirty Years War, McNeill argues, France took action very similar to that which Venice had taken centuries earlier.[122] In both cases, the development of a notion of service was based on payment, but payment tied to the development of a different process of public finance – taxation by the state and regular pay for the military rather than plunder. It also noted and reinforced the idea of professional military service and tied the fate of soldiers to the fate of the political entities through contracts.

An in-depth review of the roots of the different strategies for dealing with contracts is beyond this analysis. It is important to note, though, that the overlapping claims to violence in the Holy Roman Empire appear to have been one key issue in preventing the emergence of a reinforcing process of control.[123] The uncomfortable fit between the values of chivalry and market forces also played a greater role in the German territories. In the communes of northern Italy, feudalism never took hold as deeply and the landed nobility in Italy became urbanized and engaged in mercantile pursuits.[124] Finally, the Italian City States had experimented with contracting as a mechanism for overcoming disputes before – the podesta was an outsider brought in to perform executive functions – particularly policing power.[125] Experience with this political form may have generated more effective contracting capabilities at a later date.

Whatever their roots, these different strategies had significant effects on the control of force, suggesting that actors can either exacerbate the instability associated with market mechanisms and the diffusion of control or use markets as tools for building new structures of governance. The key to the latter outcome is building agreement between functions, political arrangements, and values.

---

[122] McNeill, *Pursuit of Power*, p. 125.

[123] Others have examined these differences. See, for instance, Hendrik Spruyt's discussion of the different material bases of towns in Germany, Italy, and France. Spruyt, *Sovereign State and its Competitors*.

[124] Ibid., p. 138; see also Daniel Waley, *The Italian City-Republics* (London: Weidenfeld and Nicolson, 1969).

[125] Spruyt, *Sovereign State and its Competitors*, p. 142. See also Avner Grief, "Self Enforcing Political Systems and Economic Growth: Late Medieval Genoa," in Robert Bates, ed., *Analytic Narratives*, (Princeton: Princeton University Press, 1998). For the general point that a variety of institutional forms can produce collective goods, see Paul Milgrom, Douglass North, and Barry Weingast, "The Role of Institutions in the Revival of Trade: the Law Merchant, Private Judges, and the Champagne Fairs," *Economics and Politics* Vol. 2 (1990): 1–23.

Discussion

The fact that market mechanisms for controlling violence suggest different routes of action and the diffusion of control pulls actors in different directions has complicated the operation of existing institutions. It has exacerbated disagreement among committed multi-lateralists – over whether to call PSCs mercenaries or regulate them; among governments – over the propriety of using PSCs; among "like-minded" activists – over the proper behavior of INGOs in conflict zones; and among allies – over the role of PSCs in peacebuilding. It has also generated strange bedfellows – between human rights activists and PSCs to facilitate humanitarian intervention, between TNCs and INGOs to promote development plans that avoid violent repercussions. These all suggest that private security arrangements are more likely to lead to change than to the solidification of existing institutional arrangements.

The logic of competing mechanisms of control exercised by different institutions also suggests increased potential for conflict. Previews, of course, can be seen in those parts of the world where this variety of actors have been most prolific. Will Reno describes the result as warlord politics,[126] Mark Duffield calls it non-territorial network war,[127] and Mary Kaldor labels it "new war."[128] In the Sudan, Sierra Leone, Liberia, Democratic Republic of Congo, Bosnia, and elsewhere there is much evidence that the market's forces – even the more legitimate portions – have often reinforced the potential for conflict, even when their purpose was to avoid it.[129] Without legal consequences for misbehavior, forces in conflict zones often take advantage of opportunities for profit and plunder – even when it goes against the political aims for which they fight or norms of proper professional behavior. Without other forces that play by the rules, "professional" forces are forced to choose between proper behavior and effective behavior in the short run, but functional forces that undermine established political control or run counter to prevailing measures of social control may erode reinforcing processes of control.

The market, however, may also generate new reinforcing processes of control. New institutional innovations that solve functional needs within a structure of social and material control mechanisms that support one another can offer paths that lead to different, but still effective, control.

---

[126] See Reno, *Warlord Politics*; Reno "Privatizing War in Sierra Leone."
[127] Duffield, *Global Governance and the New Wars*.
[128] Kaldor, *New and Old Wars*.
[129] As have a variety of other forces, see Collier, "Doing Well out of War."

If history is our guide, successful innovations will take advantage of market mechanisms to generate political agreement on new functions. Though the diffusion of control may be problematic, it is less important than the qualities associated with the diffusion – overlapping claims to control are particularly difficult to translate into agreement on functions or social and political controls that reinforce one another. Finally, attention to functional concerns alone may yield short-term "effective" uses of force, but may also prompt social and political backlash.

7   Conclusion

Though the legitimate use of force is presumed to be the realm of the state, during the 1990s and into the first decade of the twenty-first century, the private sector's role in security burgeoned. Global forces, new ideas, and political choices combined to enhance the opportunities for private delivery of and private financing for security services. A growing market for force now exists alongside, and intertwined with, state military and police forces.

I have argued that this development holds significant implications for the control of force that poses states, firms, and people with a number of trade-offs. Individual states can sometimes enhance the capacity of their forces, and thereby increase functional control. At the same time, though, the market undermines the *collective* monopoly of the state over violence in world politics, and thus a central feature of the sovereign system. Without that collective monopoly, states face increasing dilemmas about whether to hire from the private sector for security and how best to regulate the export of security services. Furthermore, even as privatization may increase the capacity of some states, it also changes who has influence over the use of force. The changes in political control are most dramatic when transnational private actors finance violence in weak states, but apparent even when PSCs deliver security services to strong states. Moreover, though non-state actors gain influence over force when they finance it, along with that influence comes responsibility for the behavior of the forces they finance – a development that frequently leads to political debates within communities of non-state actors. Though some point to the strength of international norms of military professionalism as something that will check the effect of these shifts, there are also signs that with market mechanisms of control and the decline of the state's monopoly in the use of force will come changes in the relationship between citizenship and military service, with associated changes in the process by which norms of military professionalism are created – and military professional norms, themselves.

The debate between optimists and pessimists about the consequences of privatizing security missed these important changes. Each side of the debate emphasized only a part of the control problem, which caused the pessimists to ignore potential functional and social control gains and the optimists to ignore potential functional control losses, political control changes, and long-term changes in social control. Neither side pointed out the inevitable trade-offs states, firms, and people will have to make in deciding how to manage this market. The rush to normative judgment about whether the privatization of security was "good" or "bad" impeded analysis of the range of privatization's effects and clouded understanding of the dilemmas associated with private security. Better understanding will not only lead to more satisfactory political science, but also to more effective analysis and political action.

Institutional mechanisms and political processes

Struggling with how to analyze privatization's effects on all three dimensions of control led me back to an article by James March and Johan Olsen about the "new institutionalism." This was a very influential article that described a movement afoot among social scientists to look at institutions not just as "arenas" where behavior driven by more fundamental factors occurs, but as "structures that define and defend interests" and enable processes that "affect the flow of history."[1] Though that article points out the many, sometimes contradictory, forms "institutionalism" takes – a point that has spilled much ink in the past twenty years as the variety of institutionalists have fought about the relative effectiveness of their tools – their essay also reveals links between different institutional approaches.

The theoretical approach I developed drew on this latter insight. I first juxtaposed rationalist, economic arguments that focus on functional and political control with constructivist, sociological arguments that focus on functional and social control. The hypotheses I drew from these accounts led me to expect that the functional control gains or losses from privatizing security would depend on how privatization interacted with a variety of intervening variables – particularly, state strength and the nature of the security task. Social control gains or losses, I deduced, should also vary – with the strength and consistency of norms and their relative hold on public and private purveyors of force. In practice, this suggests potential gains in functional and social control when security,

---

[1] March and Olsen, "New Institutionalism," pp. 734, 738, 739.

even a sovereign service, is privatized in weak states. It also suggests that although there may be functional control losses when strong states privatize sovereign tasks strong professional networks often maintain social control. Almost inevitably, though, private financing or delivery of services redistributes power over force – changing who has influence and thus the political control of force.

The redistribution of power turns out to be crucial for expectations about whether privatization will lead toward or away from a reinforcing process of control – the situation when forces deliver a function a collective wants according to political processes and undergirded by values the collective views as legitimate. I claim that this is more likely when control mechanisms (social and material) reinforce one another in their micro-governance of individual behavior. Who gains in the redistribution of power over the control of force, what they believe is legitimate, and the strategies of action they choose hold the key to how these mechanisms will interact.

In most of the cases I have examined, the shifts in political control generated by privatizing military advice and training have led to control mechanisms that chafe against one another and spur more change rather than a reinforcing process of control. In the one instance where private security contributed to the arguable beginnings of a reinforcing process of control (MPRI's delivery of advice and training to Croatia), a variety of variables encouraged the mechanisms of control to work together: links between training and human rights education, close collaboration with the US and multilateral conditionality requirements.[2] Of the four other cases where security was privatized in weak states, in one – Sierra Leone – the government was so weak that it relied on PSCs for control of operations. Maximizing short run functional gains led EO to rely on civil militia, enhancing their power in a way that undermined national control of force. Also, continued and enhanced influence from commercial miners (prominent security consumers) decreased the incentives for politicians to build democratic or capable institutions. In another – Nigeria – Shell's financing led to repressive forces that engendered a backlash. Shell's efforts to link its financing to international values corresponded with some moderate functional gains in Nigerian forces. These changes have as much to do, however, with the simultaneous US efforts to reconstruct the forces via private training. Also, they have been implemented without the benefits of the multilateral conditionality that tipped the balance in Croatia and thus

[2] Cooley, "Western Conditions and Domestic Choices."

far have not consolidated a reinforcing process of control. In the two other cases in the Democratic Republic of Congo, INGOs financing security did not even lead to short-run functional gain nor did either engender political changes that would support international values surrounding the control of violence. Despite INGO good will, the lack of expertise on security issues combined with reticence to tread too closely to governance roles led INGOs to simply feed more resources into poor systems of control rather than to transform them.

In strong states, privatization has often bought new security tools in ways that opened the way for a broader variety of functions, sometimes at increased cost and with still uncertain effects on professionalism within the military (and thus the long-term military effectiveness). The strong state cases all experienced less impact from privatization than weak states. South Africa's decision not to engage the industry led it to forgo either functional gains or political changes. Given other states' decisions, though, South Africa gave up its influence over those who chose to participate in the security industry and thus lost relative power. The US's enthusiastic endorsement of the industry led to overarching gains in effectiveness, contracting for delivery of services, and using training exports as a new tool for achieving foreign policy goals – at increased cost. It has also, however, engendered non-democratic political changes and a process that may speed modifications in the social control of force, leading away from international values. The UK's more moderate endorsement of the industry has also led to functional gains (though less dramatic than in the US) and more moderate political changes.

Whether privatization of security in strong states will lead to disruptive change in military effectiveness or will be folded into a new reinforcing process of control is the $64,000 question. In the recent Iraqi conflict, well-publicized cost overruns from outsourcing, dramatic scenes of private personnel abused and abusing, unclear coordination between public and private forces, and a higher than average separation of special forces personnel from both the US and UK to take higher paying private security jobs, all seem to point toward an eroding process of control. At the same time, however, if using PSCs allows the US to withdraw from Iraq more quickly, the potential for high salaries in the private sector prompts an upsurge in military recruitment, Americans' stock portfolios rich with defense services companies continue to rise, and private security is associated with effective action, perhaps private forces will be folded into the future of American foreign policy as a necessary dimension in a new military era.

Globalization, the state, and the sovereign system

Beyond its effects on the control of force in individual countries, the shifts I have identified are clearly pertinent to debates about globalization, sovereignty, and the state. Many of these debates have focused on whether states are losing power and the sovereign system is being eroded – perhaps replaced by global institutions, markets, or networks – or whether states and the sovereign system remain robust. Those arguing for the "power shift" have emphasized globalization's erosion of state capacities – in revenue generation, agenda-setting power, and authoritative control of markets or networks.[3] Looking at arms industries, for instance, some have claimed that the transnationalization of the industry has enshrined international regulation, making it "not something which is carried on simply in UN forums but is constitutive of the military and arms procurement practices of many states."[4] Less rosy scenarios suggest that in this system where the state is losing power, war is no longer "politics by other means," but its own end.[5] Skeptics have dismissed both claims by pointing out the continued salience of states. International organizations are made powerful by, and may be changed by states.[6] Furthermore, TNCs retain close and dependent relationships with their home states.[7] The very existence of international interdependence, realists point out, is predicated on the preferences of major powers.[8] And without states, the outcomes for which transnational networks advocate, cannot be realized.[9] Finally, some have argued that the sovereign system has never been as clear and uncontested as the literature suggests and so violations of sovereignty are neither new nor important.[10]

[3] Mathews, "Power Shift"; M. Shaw, *Post Military Society* (Cambridge: Polity Press, 1991); Florini, *Third Force*; Keck and Sikkink, *Activists Beyond Borders*; Van Creveld, *Transformation of War*.
[4] Held et al., *Global Transformations*, p. 133.
[5] Van Creveld, *Transformation of War*.
[6] Pauly, *Who Elected the Bankers*.
[7] P. Hirst and G. Thompson, *Globalization in Question* (Cambridge: Polity Press, 1996).
[8] Kenneth Waltz, *Theory of International Politics* (New York: Random House, 1979), Robert Gilpin, *The Political Economy of International Relations* (Princeton: Princeton University Press, 1987).
[9] Miles Kahler, "The State of the State in World Politics," in Ira Katznelson and Helen Milner, *Political Science: the State of the Discipline* (New York: W. W. Norton, 2002), p. 62. See also the discussion of globalists and skeptics in David Held and Anthony McGrew, *Global Transformations Reader: an Introduction to the Globalization Debate* (Cambridge: Polity Press, 2003), pp. 3–8.
[10] Stephen Krasner, *Sovereignty: Organized Hypocrisy* (Princeton: Princeton University Press, 1999).

The analysis in this book joins other recent arguments to claim that the connection between state power and sovereignty is not so clear. Individual states may gain power even as their actions erode the sovereign system. Furthermore, a focus on the relative power of states and markets (or other actors) leads both sides of the debate to miss what may be globalization's most important effects – changes in the practice of statehood.[11] Technological changes, marketization, and factor mobility issue challenges to states.[12] Though individual states often choose to meet these challenges differently, their decisions will have consequences for the policies they pursue, their power relative to other actors, and the relevance of individual state preferences for global outcomes.[13] While hyper-globalists and skeptics argue about the state's power relative to other actors, what states do and how they do it has shifted in the past and appears to be shifting again today. Furthermore, as states work differently, other institutional forms – from international organizations to markets to voluntary organizations – encounter challenges as well. Even though states continue to be powerful players, these changes alter expectations about the way international politics works. The following three sections offer hypotheses about the way the changes described in this book should matter in three sets of literature.

The market, adventurous foreign policy, relative power, and stability

Having a market alternative for military services changes the options available to states for the conduct of foreign policy. The use of market alternatives, however, through government contracts or regulation, operates differently from using modern military organizations, and advantages some portions of the government more than others. Particularly, using market allocation generally advantages executives relative to legislatures, reduces transparency, and reduces the mobilization required to send public forces abroad. Furthermore, the use of market alternatives often involves the private sector in decision making – giving those with commercial interests in policy influence on its formation and implementation. Because of these changes, the market

---

[11] See Held and McGrew, *Global Transformations*, introduction; Jonathan Kirshner, "Globalization and National Security," in Jonathan Kirshner, ed., *Globalization and National Security*.

[12] This definition of globalization draws from Jonathan Kirshner, "Introduction," in Kirshner, *Globalization and National Security*.

[13] Kirshner, *Globalization and National Security*.

option makes it easier to undertake adventurous foreign policies – or actions that do not have widespread support in a polity. According to retired Air Force Colonel Sam Gardiner, "When you can hire people to go to war, there's none of the grumbling and the political friction."[14] This alternative should be particularly important for expectations about the behavior of strong, democratic states.

Strong states that take advantage of the market buy increased power in the form of raw capacity to project their interests abroad.[15] The US has taken particular advantage of this market. In the 1990s, US use of PSCs opened the way for initial involvement in the Balkans when the use of US military forces seemed unfeasible. From Somalia through Kosovo, Afghanistan, and Iraq, the use of PSCs to support US forces reduced the numbers of US forces needed. PSCs have been particularly important in Iraq, where they not only supported US troops via logistics and operational support missions, but also deployed quickly to the country to train Iraqi forces and provide security as stability unraveled in the wake of Saddam Hussein's fall from power. Sometimes these choices have been more costly than using US military forces, other times less, but as one US official put it in 1999, "it is easier to get money out of the Pentagon than people."[16] Indeed, the US can afford additional relative costs. It far outstrips any other country in both its raw economic power (producing 23 percent of Gross World Product [GWP]) and defense spending (the US spends 3.5 percent of its GDP, which is close to 1 percent of GWP on defense, more than the next twenty-four countries combined).[17]

Though US raw military power was already dominant without it, its use of private security has further enhanced its relative capacity to project military force. Those who believe that the US must have increased military capacity to secure its interests around the globe have expressed concern that the US lacks the will to undertake the tough ground actions necessary to solidify its hegemonic position.[18] PSCs provide a way around this problem. The US can use PSCs as force multipliers for its own troops, to train and supervise other troops, and even as a tool for recruiting something like an imperial force. As chapter six described, in Iraq the US has hired PSCs and personnel from a variety

[14] As quoted in Jane Mayer, "Contract Sports," *New Yorker*, February 2004, p. 87.
[15] See, for instance, Bobbitt, *Shield of Achilles*.
[16] Interview with US official at the Pentagon, September 1999.
[17] See Posen, "Command of the Commons," p. 6.
[18] Barnett, "Pentagon's New Map of the World." Posen argues that given the expense of ground force, the US should pursue a more modest policy of selective engagement rather than dominance and rely on allies in its efforts to contain contested areas. Posen, "Command of the Commons."

of different countries including Fiji and South Africa who work for a variety of PSCs providing security in Iraq and training for Iraqi private security forces.[19]

The US strategy vis-à-vis the market for force is strikingly different from South Africa's. South Africa's efforts to sideline the market have not only led it to forego new policy tools, but also decreased its ability to control the violent actions of its citizens abroad. This is particularly poignant as South African personnel and PSCs have poured into Iraq under contract with the US to support stability operations in the wake of a war that the South African government did not support.[20] Even as the South African government decries these individuals as "mercenaries," US members of the CPA were boasting about the South Africans that work for them, the companies that employ them, and the work they were doing to stabilize Iraq.[21]

This US strategy, though, increases one element of power in a way that may undermine others and has international consequences that stretch beyond relative power, alone. Arguments that democratic states fight less among one another, are better able to make and keep commitments, and win the wars they fight all rely on elements within democratic polities that promote transparency and restrain the use of raw coercive power.[22] Analysts have built on these insights to claim that the US has been uniquely successful because its more benign exercise of power has been less costly to the economy, generated fewer military threats, and built a system of institutions through which international political order is maintained without US empire.[23]

---

[19] Daragahi, "In Iraq, Private Contractors Lighten Load on U.S. Troops"; Catan and Fidler, "With Post-War Instability Still a Pressing Concern."

[20] "Are We Fighting Foreign Wars?" *The Star*, 10 February 2004.

[21] Conversation with former CPA official.

[22] Michael Doyle, "Liberalism and World Politics," *American Political Science Review* Vol. 80, No. 4 (December 1986): 1151–69; Carol R. Ember, Melvin Ember, and Bruce Russett, "Peace between Participatory Polities: a Cross-Cultural Test of the 'Democracies Rarely Fight Each Other' Hypothesis," *World Politics* Vol. 44, No. 4 (July 1992): 573–99; Lake, "Powerful Pacifists"; James D. Fearon, "Domestic Political Audiences and the Escalation of International Disputes," *American Political Science Review* Vol. 88, No. 3. (September, 1994), pp. 577–92; Lipson, *Reliable Partners*; Reiter and Stam, *Democracies at War*; see also Dan Reiter and Allan Stam, "Understanding Victory: Why Political Institutions Matter," *International Security* Vol. 28, No. 1 (summer 2003): 168–79.

[23] See, for instance, Aaron Friedberg, "Why Didn't the US become a Garrison State," *International Security*, Vol. 16, No. 4 (spring 1992); G. John Ikenberry, *After Victory: Institutions, Strategic Restructuring and the Rebuilding of Order after Major War* (Princeton: Princeton University Press, 2001); G. John Ikenberry, *America Unrivaled: the Future Balance of Power* (Ithaca: Cornell University Press, 2002).

The availability of private options may erode some of these benefits. The loss of transparency, shift of power away from the congress, and increased influence of PSCs, for instance, may reduce restraint. The ability to hire an international force may curb the willingness of American leaders to bargain with other governments to build effective international coalitions. Finally, the tensions between PSCs and active-duty soldiers may undermine the loyalty, initiative, and fighting power of soldiers. Though there are many who argue that the democratic peace and democratic military effectiveness of democracies are overstated, even these critics should agree that if leaders engage in foreign policies that do not have widespread support, the potential for conflict will be enhanced and that a decline in the initiative and loyalty of military personnel would decrease military effectiveness.[24]

Thus, the US may be making an implicit trade-off between increased relative power and capacity for action and the maintenance of institutions that have encouraged stability in the system and effective action. Furthermore, both the democratic peace and democratic military effectiveness may rely on the particular kind of relationship between citizens and the exercise of military power that has been prominent in the modern nation-state system. By choosing to increase its relative power using market forces, the US may be also enhancing the prospect for conflict and risking its military effectiveness in the future.

The diffusion of control and durable disorder

At the same time that state choices regarding private security change the balance of power and potential for stability among states, privatization also shifts power over violence outside the bounds of state machinery. This is most obvious when non-state actors finance security, which accords influence over security decisions to actors both outside the territory of the state and outside of government. In individual instances, transnational financing often diffuses power over the control of force. From a broader perspective, this diffusion of power should also lead us to expect a greater variety of actors to have influence over the use of force, and more competing institutions with overlapping jurisdictions over force. Both accord with analyses arguing that the world is entering a neomedieval period.[25]

---

[24] See Gowa, "Democratic States and International Disputes"; Michael Desch, "Democracy and Victory: Why Regime Type Hardly Matters," *International Security* Vol. 27, No. 2 (fall 2002): 5–47.

[25] This is one of the six conditions that Philip Cerny claims mirrors medieval conditions. Others of the six conditions, such as contested property rights and legal boundaries, also

Cerny argues that neomedievalism issues a new "security dilemma" to states that will likely lead to what he calls "durable disorder" rather than global empire or global democracy. "In this situation, attempts to provide international and domestic security through the state and states system actually become increasingly dysfunctional. They create severe backlashes at both local and transnational levels, backlashes that further weaken the state and undermine wider security."[26] The trade-offs facing the states examined in chapter four seem to exemplify some features of this dilemma. The South African government sacrificed international power considerations to maximize the integrity of its political processes. The US has seized PSCs as a potential new resource for exercising its power abroad. This has enhanced the power of the strongest state in the world in a way that some argue is likely to increase the imperial role of the US.[27] The potential for backlash, however, is certainly present. It could take the form of a backlash from the electorate as huge bills from Halliburton raise questions about the efficiency, and private inter-rogaters' participation in prisoner abuses raise questions about the legitimacy of US policy. A backlash could also come from international entities who perceive US behavior as threatening and mobilize to counter it. There is also the potential for private entities to pursue their own goals in ways that undermine effective US policy.

My focus on institutional mechanisms generates less in the way of predictions about whether global empire, global democracy, or durable disorder will ensue but instead outlines the conditions under which disorder and change versus order and stability might take hold. As we saw in the historical examples in chapter six, market allocations of violence can lead to different outcomes for control, stability, and accountability. The market's consequences depend on its structure (will there be one global market or several different segments and how competitive will the market be?) and the organizational ecology of PSCs and private financiers (what kinds of features will select winners and losers, what will be considered legitimate activity, what are the mechanisms through which standards are communicated and enforced,

---

are supported by my findings. See Cerny, "Neomedievalism, Civil War and the New Security Dilemma." The term neomedievalism comes from Bull, *Anarchical Society*, pp. 254–55.

[26] Cerny, "Neomedievalism, Civil War and the New Security Dilemma," p. 40.

[27] Others have noted this trend for a variety of reasons. See, for instance, George Steinmetz, "The State of Emergency and the Revival of American Imperialism: Toward an Authoritarian Post-Fordism," *Public Culture* Vol. 15, No. 2 (2003); Tarak Barkawi and Mark Laffey, "The Imperial Peace: Democracy, Force and Globalization," *European Journal of International Relations*, Vol. 5, No. 4 (1999): 403–34.

do the mechanisms reinforce one another, etc.?). Those actors that play roles as consumers, standard setters, and legitimators are likely to have influence over both the structure of the market and its organizational ecology. Attention to both who these actors are and the strategies they employ will be important for generating expectations about the market's impact as it unfolds.

Changes in states also change markets and networks

Both Cerny's analysis and the rosy or risky scenarios he criticizes assume a certain amount of continuity of functions within states and markets. This is a common feature of the literature that seeks to understand when ideal type institutional forms – hierarchies, markets, or networks – are advantaged. The analysis in this book suggests, though, that at any particular historical moment, the structure of institutions may stray far from their ideal form. Furthermore, institutional forms are not independent of one another. The "ideal" form of markets can only function effectively when the state is also playing its "ideal" role. Similarly, NGOs, to play their ideal role, rely on a government.

Thinking of institutions this way suggests that changes in the nature of states will not "advantage" other institutional forms so much as pose challenges and prompt changes in them as well. As states change their collective function, pressures on non-state actors arise that promise a shift in their function as well. Chapter five documented the debates within both commercial and non-commercial entities about their proper role in situations where the government does not assume its proper role. The cases are just the tip of the iceberg. As western governments increasingly outsource a wide variety of foreign policy tasks to private firms and INGOs, these dilemmas will only increase.

My analysis suggests that expectations about how markets and voluntary associations will work based on ideal types are not so useful for analyzing change. The privatization of security does not so much transfer power from one institution (the state) to another (the market) as pose challenges to the way both states and markets have functioned in the modern system. Instead of focusing on ideal types of states and markets (based in large part on historically specific renditions of each), I suggest we examine the variety of institutional forms that are emerging, the way they are functioning, and think about their viability in terms of whether they generate mechanisms that work together, potentially generating reinforcing processes, or chafe against one another, generating continued change. Such a strategy can help generate expectations about the general level of stability in the system, and also the conditions under which we should expect islands of stability versus "gray zones" where extra-legal activity is the norm.[28]

The market for force has undermined states' collective ability to monopolize violence in the international system. This has not made states, per se, less important, but opened the way for changes in the roles states and other actors play in controlling force on the world stage. Changes in the nature of states and the practice of sovereignty may be ubiquitous,[29] but they are also vitally important for understanding the likelihood of conflict, the purpose violence serves, and to whom it answers at a particular point in time.[30] Increases in the market allocation of violence have had serious consequences for politics and political order in the past and promise to have similarly serious consequences in the future.[31] Rather than arguing about its overall costs or benefits, both policy makers and their constituents would be well served by thinking about the trade-offs involved in the different strategies for participating in and managing this market.

---

[28] Ibid. The idea of gray zones – or "zones grises" – comes from Alain Minc, *Le Nouveau Moyen Age* (Paris: Gallimard, 1993).

[29] Krasner, *Sovereignty.*

[30] Barkin and Cronin, "State and the Nation."

[31] Thomson, *Mercenaries, Pirates, and Sovereigns*; Cohen, *Citizens and Soldiers*; Avant, "From Mercenary to Citizen Armies."

Bibliography

Aall, Pamela, "What do NGOs Bring to PeaceKeeping?" in Chester Crocker, Fen Osler Hampson, and Pamela Aall, eds., *Turbulent Peace: the Challenges of Managing International Conflict* (Washington, DC: United States Institute of Peace, 2001).

Abbott, Andrew, *The System of Professions: An Essay on the Division of Expert Labor* (Chicago: University of Chicago Press, 1988).

Abdullah, Ibrahim, "Bush Path to Destruction: the Origin and Character of the Revolutionary United Front/Sierra Leone," *Journal of Modern African Studies* Vol. 36, No. 2 (1998), 203–35.

Adams, Thomas, "The New Mercenaries and the Privatization of Conflict," *Parameters* Vol. 29, No. 2 (summer 1999), 103–27.

Africa Confidential, "Protection," *Africa Confidential*, 12 June 1998.

African Business, "The Mercenary As Corporate Executive," *African Business* (December 1997).

African News Service, "Oil Companies to Hire Mercenaries to Protect Oil Fields," *Africa News Service* (25 November 1996).

"Mercenary Groups Hired to Halt Rustlers," *Africa News Service* (14 September 1998).

"Nigeria: Defense Ministry Promotes Democratic Value in Army," *Africa News Service* (11 December 2003).

Agence France Presse, "Croatian Government Welcomes IMF Credit," *Agence France Presse* (14 March 1997).

Alborghetti, Igor, "MPRI, Croatia – an Example for B&H?" *Globas* No. 254 (October 1995) translated by Srecko Bartl and posted on BosNet 18 November 1995, downloaded 12 March 2002 from http://www.bosnet.org/archive/bosnet.w3archive/9511/msg00448.html.

Alchian A. A. and H. Demsetz, "Production, Information Costs, and Economic Organization," *American Economic Review* Vol. 62 (December 1972).

Aldred, Carolyn, "Standards Sought for Iraq Security Firms," *Business Insurance* (26 April 2004).

Allen, Christopher, "Sierra Leone," in John Dunn, ed., *West African States: Failure and Promise* (Cambridge: Cambridge University Press, 1978).

Althouse, James E., "Contractors on the Battlefield," *Army Logistician* (November/December 1998), 14.

Amnesty International, *Rwanda: Arming the Perpetrators of Genocide* AFR 02/14/95 (Amnesty International, June 1995).

"Security Forces: Serving to Protect and Respect Human Rights?" *Amnesty International* (19 December 2002).

"US Training of Foreign Military and Police Forces: the Human Rights Dimension" (2002).

Anderson, Gary and Robert Tollison, "Apologiae for Chartered Monopolies in Foreign Trade, 1600–1800," *History of Political Economy* Vol. 14, No. 4 (1983), 549–66.

Anderson, Mary, *Do No Harm: How Aid can support Peace – and War* (Boulder, Lynne Reiner, 1999).

Andreas, Peter, "Redrawing Borders and Security in the Twenty-First Century," *International Security* Vol. 28, No. 2 (fall 2003), 78–111.

"The Clandestine Political Economy of War and Peace in Bosnia," *International Studies Quarterly* Vol. 48, No. 1 (March 2004), 29–52.

Andromidas, Dean, "Defense Systems Limited: Crown Jewel," *The Executive Intelligence Review* Vol. 22 (August 1997).

Apter, Andrew, "Death and the King's Henchmen: Ken Saro-Wiwa and the Crisis in Nigeria," in Abdul Rasheed Na'Allah, ed., *Ogoni's Agonies: Ken Saro-Wiwa and the Crisis in Nigeria* (Trenton: Africa World Press, 1998), 121–60.

Arend, Anthony Clarke and Robert J. Beck, *International Law and the Use of Force: Beyond the UN Charter Paradigm* (New York: Routledge, 1993).

Arnson, Cynthia, *Crossroads: Congress, the President, and Central America, 1976–1993* (University Park, PA: Pennsylvania State Press, 1993).

Arrington, Vanessa, "Videotape Shows Colombia Captives Alive," *Associate Press* (28 August 2003).

Arvedlund, Erin E., "Privatized Warriors," *Barron's* (8 August 2003).

Ascher, William, "New Development Approaches and the Adaptability of International Agencies: The Case of the World Bank," *International Organization* Vol. 37, No. 3 (summer 1983), 415–39.

Ashworth, Michael, "Privatising War, by 'The Executives,'" *Independent* (16 September 1996), 1.

Associated Press, "Peacekeeping Helped Cheney Company," *Associated Press* (28 August 2000).

"Generals Criticize War Crimes Crackdown," *St. John's Telegraph* (30 September 2000), 16.

"Private Guards to Take Over at West Point," *Associated Press* (21 January 2004).

"Private Commandos Shoot Back on the Iraq Firing Line," Associated Press (19 April 2004).

Australian, "Extra Guards for Iraq Oil Sites," *Australian* (5 September 2003).

Avant, Deborah, *Political Institutions and Military Change: Lessons from Peripheral Wars* (Ithaca: Cornell University Press, 1994).

"Conflicting Indicators of 'Crisis' in American Civil–Military Relations," *Armed Forces and Society* Vol. 24, No. 3 (spring 1998), 375–88.

"From Mercenary to Citizen Armies: Explaining Change in the Practice of War," *International Organization* Vol. 54, No. 1 (winter 2000), 41–72.

"Privatizing Military Training: a Challenge to US Army Professionalism," in Don M. Snider and Gayle L. Watkins, eds., *The Future of the Army Profession* (Boston: McGraw-Hill, 2002), 179–196.

Bailey, Robert W., "Uses and Misuses," in *Privatization: the Provision of Public Services by the Private Sector* (Jefferson, NC: McFarland & Company, Inc., 1991).

Baldwin, David, "Security Studies and the End of the Cold War," *World Politics* Vol. 48, No. 1 (October 1995), 117–41.

Ballentine, Karen and Jake Sherman, *The Political Economy of Armed Conflict: Beyond Grief and Grievance* (Boulder: Lynne Reiner, 2003).

Ballesteros, Enrique Bernales, "Report on the Question of the Use of Mercenaries as a Means of Violating Human Rights and Impeding the Exercise of Right of People to Self Determination," submitted to the UNHCR, 53rd session, item 7, 20 February 1997.

Barber, Ben, "Feeding Refugees or War? The Dilemma of Humanitarian Aid," *Foreign Affairs* Vol. 76, No. 4 (July/August 1997), 8–15.

Barber, Richard, *The Knight and Chivalry*, revised edition (Woodbridge: Boydell Press, 1995).

Barber, Simon, "Bring Executive Outcomes Back to Fight in Sierra Leone," *Business Day* (12 May 2000), 2.

Barkawi, Tarak and Mark Laffey, "The Imperial Peace: Democracy, Force, and Globalization," *European Journal of International Relations* Vol. 5, No. 4 (1999), 403–34.

Barkin, Samuel and Bruce Cronin, "The State and the Nation: Changing Norms and the Rules of Sovereignty in International Relations," *International Organization* Vol. 48, No. 1 (winter 1994), 107–30.

Barnett, Michael, "Identity and Alliances in the Middle East," in Peter Katzenstein, ed., *The Culture of National Security* (New York: Columbia University Press, 1996).
"Authority, Intervention, and the Outer Limits of International Relations Theory," in Thomas Callaghy, Ronald Kassimir, and Robert Latham, eds., *Intervention and Transnationalism in Africa* (Cambridge: Cambridge University Press, 2001).
Eyewitness to Genocide (Ithaca: Cornell University Press, 2002).

Barnett, Michael and Martha Finnemore, "The Politics, Power, and Pathologies of International Organizations," *International Organization*, Vol. 53, No. 4 (autumn 1999), 699–732.

Barnett, Thomas P. M., "The Pentagon's New Map of the World," *Esquire* (March 2003), 174–182.
The Pentagon's New Map: War and Peace in the Twenty-First Century (New York: Putnam, 2004).

Barry, Brian *Sociologists, Economist and Democracy* (Chicago: Unviersity of Chicago Press, 1970).

Barstow, David, "Security Companies: Shadow Soldiers in Iraq," *New York Times* (19 April 2004).

Batchelor, Peter and Susan Willet, *Disarmament and Defense Industrial Adjustment in South Africa* (New York: Oxford University Press, 1998).

Bates, Robert, Arner Grief, and Smita Singh, "Organizing Violence: Wealth, Power, and Limited Government," *Journal of Conflict Resolution* Vol. 46, No. 5 (October 2002), 599–629.

268   Bibliography

Baum, Dan, "Nation Builders for Hire," *New York Times Magazine* (22 June 2003), 32–38.

Bayley, Charles C., *Mercenaries for the Crimea: the German, Swiss, and Italian Legions in British Service, 1854–1856* (Montreal: McGill-Queen's University Press, 1977).

Bayley, David, *Democratizing the Police Abroad: What to do and How to do it* (Washington, DC: National Institute of Justice, 2001).

Bayley, David and Clifford Shearing, *The New Structure of Policing: Description, Conceptualization, and Research Agenda* (Washington, DC: National Institute of Justice, 2001).

Bazargan, Darius, "High Risk Business," *Guardian* (8 September 1997), T2.

BBC, "PeaceKeeping 'Role' for Mercenaries," *BBC News* (13 February 2003).

"US Firm to Rebuild Iraqi Army," *BBC News* (26 June 2003).

Beblawi, Hazem and Giacomo Luciani, eds., *The Rentier State* (New York: Croom Helm, 1987).

Becker, Elizabeth, "The Danger of Doing Good Deeds," *New York Times Magazine* (6 January 2002), 4.

Bendor, Jonathan, J. Glazer, and T. Hammond, "Theories of Delegation," *Annual Review of Political Science* Vol. 4, No. 1 (2001), 235–69.

Bendor, Jonathan, Serge Taylor, and Roland van Gaalen, "Stacking the Deck: Bureaucratic Missions and Policy Design," *American Political Science Review* Vol. 81, No. 3 (September 1987), 873–96.

Bennett, James T. and Manuel H. Johnson, *Better Government at Half the Price* (Ottowa, IL: Caroline House Publishing, 1981).

Berdal, Mats and David Malone, eds., *Greed and Grievance: Economic Agendas in Civil Wars* (Boulder: Lynne Rienner, 2000).

Berger, Thomas, "Norms, Identity and National Security in Germany and Japan," in Peter Katzenstein, ed., *The Culture of National Security* (New York: Columbia University Press, 1996).

Bergner, Daniel, *In the Land of Magic Soldiers* (New York: Farrar, Straus, and Giroux, 2003).

Bernath, Clifford H. and David Gompart, *The Power to Protect: Using New Military Capabilities to Stop Mass Killing* (Washington, DC: Refugees International, July 2003).

Best, Geoffrey, *Humanity in Warfare: the Modern History of the Law of Armed Conflict* (London: Weidenfeld and Nicolson, 1980).

Beyani, Chaloka and Damian Lilly, *Regulating Private Military Companies: Options for the UK Government* (London: International Alert, 2001).

Bianco, Anthony, and Stephanie Anderson Forest, "Outsourcing War: an Inside Look at Brown and Root," *Business Week* (15 September 2003).

Biddle, Stephen, "Victory Misunderstood: What the Gulf War Tells Us About The Future of Conflict," *International Security* Vol. 21, No. 2 (autumn 1996), 139–79.

Binder, Leonard, "The Natural History of Development Theory," *Comparative Study of Society and History* Vol. 28, No. 1 (1986), 3–33.

Bisset, Susan, "Only Twenty-Two Rare White Rhinos Survive War in Congo," *Sunday Telegraph* (5 October 2003), 19.

Bitzinger, Richard, *The Globalization of Arms Production* (Washington, DC: Defense Budget Project, 1993).

Bland, Douglas, "Patterns in Liberal Democratic Civil–Military Relations," *Armed Forces and Society* Vol. 27, No. 4 (summer 2001), 525–40.

Block, Robert, "African Mercenary Supplier To Close; Marks End of Era," *Wall Street Journal* (10 December 1998).

Bobbitt, Philip, *The Shield of Achilles: War, Peace, and the Course of History* (New York: Knopf, 2002).

Boli, John and George Thomas, *Constructing World Culture: International Non-Governmental Organizations Since 1975* (Stanford: Stanford University Press, 1999).

Bonner, Raymond, "France Linked to Defense of Mobutu," *New York Times* (2 May 1997).

Booker, Salih and William Minter, "The US and Nigeria: Thinking Beyond Oil," *Great Decisions* (2003) (available at www.greatdecisions.org).

Borton, John, Emery Brusset, and Alistair Hallam, *Humanitarian Aid and Effects: Report of the Study III of the Joint Evaluation of Emergency Assistance in Rwanda* (Copenhagen: DANIDA, 1996).

Bourdieu, Pierre, *Outline of a Theory of Practice* (Cambridge: Cambridge University Press, 1977).

Boutwell, Jeffrey, Michael Klare, and Laura Reed, eds., *Lethal Commerce: the Global Trade in Small Arms and Light Weapons* (Cambridge, MA: American Academy of Arts and Sciences, 1995).

Bowles, Samuel, "Endogenous Preferences: the Cultural Consequences of Markets and other Economic Institutions," *Journal of Economic Literature* Vol. 36 (March 1998), 75–111.

Bowles, Samuel and Herbert Gintis, "The Revenge of Homo Economicus: Contested Exchange and the Revival of Political Economy," *Journal of Economic Perspectives*, Vol. 7, No. 1 (1993), 83–102.

Boxer, C. R., *Jan Compagnie in War and Peace, 1602–1799* (Hong Kong: Heinemann Asia, 1979).

Boyatt, Thomas, "Privatization of OOTW," paper presented at the "Feed 'Em or Fight 'Em" symposium sponsored by the Patterson School of Diplomacy and International Commerce and the US Army War College, University of Kentucky, 22–24 September 1995, pp. 54–55.

Brahimi, Lakhdar, "Report of the Panel on United Nations Peace Operations," A/55/305-S/2000/80 (21 August 2000).

Brauer, Jurgen, "An Economic Perspective on Mercenaries, Military Companies, and the Privatization of Force," *Cambridge Review of International Studies*, Vol. 13, No. 1 (autumn/winter 1999), 130–45.

Brecher, Michael and Frank Harvey, "Evaluating Methodology in International Studies," in Michael Brecher and Frank Harvey, eds., *Millennial Reflections on International Studies* (Ann Arbor: University of Michigan Press, 2002).

Brinkley, Joel and James Glanz, "Contract Workers Implicated in February Army Report on Prison Abuse," *New York Times* (4 May 2004).

Brooks, Doug, "Write a Cheque, End a War," *Conflict Trends* No. 6 (July 2000).

"Supporting the MONUC Mandate with Private Services in the DROC," IPOA Operational Concept Paper (November 2002).

"Help for Beleaguered Peacekeepers," *Washington Post* (2 June 2003), A17.

Brown, Justin, "The Rise of the Private Sector Military," *The Christian Science Monitor* (5 July 2000).

Brown, Michael, "The Cause of Internal Conflict," in Michael Klare and Yogesh Chandrani, eds., *World Security: Challenges for a New Century* (New York: St. Martin's Press, 1998).

Bryans, Michael, Bruce D. Jones, and Janice Gross Stein, "Mean Times: Humanitarian Action in Complex Political Emergencies – Stark Choices, Cruel Dilemmas," Report of the NGOs in Complex Emergencies Project, *Coming to Terms*, Vol. 1, No. 3 (Center for International Studies, University of Toronto, 1999).

Bull, Hedley, *The Anarchical Society* (London: Columbia University Press, 1977).

Burk, James, "Expertise, Jurisdiction, and Legitimacy of the Military Profession," in Don Snider and Gayle Watkins, eds., *The Future of the Army Profession* (Boston: McGraw Hill, 2002), 19–38.

"Theories of Democratic Civil–Military Relations," *Armed Forces and Society* Vol. 29, No. 1 (fall 2002), 7–30.

Burns, Jimmy and Andrew Parker, "Ex SAS Soldiers Hope for New Lease on Life," *Financial Times* (14 February 2002).

Burns, Robert, "New Iraqi Army to Cost $2 billion to Build," *Associated Press* (18 September 2003).

Burt, R. *Corporate Profits and Cooptation* (New York: Academic, 1983).

Buser, Mike, "Law Enforcement Field Inspection Report, Garamba National Park, Democratic Rebulic of Congo," submitted to World Wildlife Fund (June 1998).

"Final Report," from Training Consultant Project 2R0009 (Mike Buser) to Programmer Officer (Sylvie W. Candotti) (17 August 1998).

Business Week, "Outsourcing War: an Inside Look at Brown and Root," *Business Week* (15 September 2003).

Butler, Nick, "Companies in International Relations," *Survival* Vol. 42, No. 1 (spring 2000), 149–65.

Butler, Stuart M., *Privatizing Federal Spending: a Strategy to Eliminate the Deficit* (New York: Universe Books, 1985).

Buzan, Barry, "New Patterns of Global Security in the Twenty-First Century," *International Affairs* Vol. 67, No. 3 (1991), 431–51.

"From International System to International Society: Structural Realism and Regime Theory Meet in the English School," *International Organization* Vol. 47, No. 3 (summer 1993), 327–52.

Byman, Daniel, "Uncertain Partners: NGOs and the Military," *Survival* Vol. 43, No. 2 (summer 2001), pp. 106–07.

Byman, Daniel, Ian Lesser, Bruce Pirnie, Cheryl Benard, and Matthew Waxman, *Strengthening the Partnership: Improving Military Coordination with Relief Agencies and Allies in Humanitarian Operations* (Washington, DC: RAND, 2000).

Cain, Kenneth, "Send in the Marines," *New York Times* (8 August 2003), A21.

Calbreath, Dean, "Iraqi Army, Police Fall Short on Training," *San Diego Union Tribune* (4 July 2004).

Campbell, David, "Why Fight? Humanitarianism, Principles, and Post-Structuralism," *Millennium* Vol. 27, No. 3 (1998), 497–521.

Canadian News, "Canadian, Anglo-Italian Firms to Train UK Navy," *Canadian News* (25 July 2000).

Catan, Thomas and Stephen Fidler, "With Post-War Instability Still a Pressing Concern, Western Companies and Government Agencies are Awarding Big Contracts to Ex-Military Personnel with Expertise in Providing Security," *Financial Times* (30 September 2003), 21.

Catan, Thomas and Ruth Sullivan, "Morrison Heads High Risk Security Group," *Financial Times* (26 March 2004).

Cawston, George and A. H. Keane, *The Early Chartered Companies: A.D. 1296–1858* (New York: Burt Franklin, 1896, reprinted 1968).

CBS Television, "60 Minutes II," transcript (8pm 8 Ocotober 2003).

Cerny, Philip, "Globalization and the Changing Nature of Collective Action," *International Organization* Vol. 49, No. 4 (autumn 1995), 595–625.

"Neomedievalism, Civil War, and the New Security Dilemma: Globalization as Durable Disorder," *Civil Wars* Vol. 1, No. 1 (spring 1998).

Cha, Ariana Eunjung, "Recruits Abandon Iraqi Army," *Washington Post* (13 December 2003), A1.

"In Iraq, the Job Opportunity of a Lifetime," *Washington Post* (23 May 2004), A1.

Charlton, Roger and Ron May, "NGOs, Politics, Projects, and Probity: a Policy Implementation Perspective," *Third World Quarterly* Vol. 16, No. 2 (1995), 237–55.

Chatterjee, Pratap, "Controversial Commando Wins Iraq Contract," *Corp-Watch* (9 June 2004).

Checkel, Jeff, "The Constructivist Turn in International Relations Theorizing," *World Politics* Vol. 50 (January 1998), 324–48.

Cillers, Jakkie and Ian Douglas, "The Military as Business: Military Professional Resources, Incorporated," in Jakkie Cillers and Peggy Mason, eds., *Peace, Profit or Plunder? The Privatisation of Security in War-Torn African Societies.* (South Africa: Institute for Security Studies, 1999).

Clapham, Christopher, *Private Patronage and Public Power: Political Clientelism in the Modern State* (London: Pinter, 1986).

Africa and the International System: the Politics of State Survival (Cambridge: Cambridge University Press, 1996).

"African Security Systems: Privatization and the Scope for Mercenary Activity," in *The Privatization of Security in Africa* (Johannesburg: SAIIA Press, 1999).

Clark, Ann Marie, "Non-Governmental Organizations and their Influence on International Society," *Journal of International Affairs* Vol. 48, No. 2 (1995), 507–25.

Diplomacy of Conscience: Amnesty International and Changing Human Rights Norms (Princeton: Princeton University Press, 2001).

Clark, John, "Petro-Politics in Congo," *Journal of Democracy* Vol. 8, No. 3 (July 1997), 62–77.

Clark, Wesley, *Waging Modern War: Bosnia, Kosovo, and the Future of Conflict* (New York: Public Affairs, 2001).

Clarke, S. J. G., *The Congo Mercenary* (Johannesburg: SAIIA Press, 1968).

Clynes, Tom, "Heart Shaped Bullets," *Observer Magazine* (24 November 2002), 34.

Coase, Ronald, "The Regulated Industries: Discussion," *American Economic Review* Vol. 54 (May 1964), 192–197.

Coase, R. H., "The Nature of the Firm," *Economica* Vol. 4, No. 16 (November 1937), 386–405.

Cobb, Charles, Jr., "Chad–Cameroon Pipeline Considered by Congressional Subcommittee," allAfrica.com NEWS (18 April 2002) (available at http://allafrica.com/stories/printable/200204180864.html).

Cock, Jacklyn and Peggie Mckenzie, *From Defense to Development: Redirecting Military Resources in South Africa*, (Ottowa: International Development Research Centre, 1998).

Cock, Jacklyn and Laurie Nathan, *Society at War: the Militarization of South Africa* (New York: St. Martins Press, 1989).

Cohen, Eliot, *Citizens and Soldiers: the Dilemmas of Military Service* (Ithaca: Cornell University Press, 1985).

"A Revolution in Warfare," *Foreign Affairs* (March/April 1996), 37–54.

"Defending America in the Twenty-First Century," *Foreign Affairs* (November/December 2000), 40–56.

"History and the Hyperpower," *Foreign Affairs* (July/August 2004), 49–63.

Cohen, Leonard, *Broken Bonds: the Disintegration of Yugoslavia* (Boulder: Westview, 1993).

Cohen, Rachelle, "Potato Peeling Out, Peacekeeping In," *The Boston Herald* (20 October 1999), 31.

Cohen, Roger, "US Cooling Ties with Croatia after Winking at its Buildup," *New York Times* (28 October 95), A1.

Collier, Paul, "Doing Well out of War: an Economic Perspective," in Mats Berdal and David Malone, eds., *Greed and Grievance* (Boulder: Lynne Rienner, 2000).

Collins, Cindy and Thomas Weiss, *An Overview and Assessment of the 1989–1996 Peace Operations Publications*, Occasional Paper, No. 28 (Providence: Thomas J. Watson Institute, 1997).

Collins, James, Jr., *The Development and Training of the South Vietnamese Army, 1950–1972* (Washington, DC: Department of the Army, 1975).

Conca, Ken, "In the Name of Sustainability: Peace Studies and Environmental Discourse," in Jyrki Kakonen, ed., *Green Security or Militarized Environment* (Brookfield: Dartmouth Publishing Company, 1994).

"International Regimes, State Authority, and Environmental Transformation: the Case of National Parks and Protected Areas," University of Maryland, Harrison Program on the Future Global Agenda, Occasional Paper No. 15 (September 1996).

Cooley, Alexander, "Western Conditions and Domestic Choices: the Influence of External Actors on the Post-Communist Transition," in Adrian Karatnycky, ed., *Nations in Transit 2003: Democratization in East Central Europe and Eurasia* (Lanham, MD: Rowman and Littlefield, 2003), pp. 25–38.

Cooley, Alexander and James Ron, "The NGO Scramble: Organizational Insecurity and the Political Economy of Transnational Action," *International Security* Vol. 27, No. 1 (summer 2002), 5–39.

Cooper, Frederick, "Networks, Moral Discourse, and History," in Thomas Callaghy, Ronald Kassimir, and Robert Latham, eds., *Intervention and Transnationalism in Africa* (Cambridge: Cambridge University Press, 2001).

Cope, John A., *International Military Education and Training: an Assessment*, McNair Paper 44 (Washington, DC: Institute for National Strategic Studies, National Defense University, October 1995).

Cornish, Paul, *Controlling the Arms Trade: the West versus the Rest* (London: Bowerdean, 1996).

CorpWatch, "Guarding the Oil Underworld in Iraq," *CorpWatch* (5 September 2003), available at www.corpwatch.org/issues/PID.jsp?articleid=8328.

Cortell, Andrew and James Davis, Jr., "How Do International Institutions Matter? The Domestic Impact of International Rules and Norms," *International Studies Quarterly* Vol. 40, No. 4 (December 1996), 451–78.

Cowell, Alan, "Conflict in the Balkans," *New York Times* (1 August 1995).

CPA Official Documents, Order No. 17, "Status of the Coalition, Foreign Liaison Missions, their Personnel and Contractors" (available at http://www.cpa-iraq.org/regulations/CPAORD17Status_of_Forces.pdf.

Craig, Gordon, *The Politics of the Prussian Army* (London: Oxford University Press, 1955, 1979).

Crewdson, John, "Contractor Tries to Avert Repeat of Bosnia Woes," *Chicago Tribune* (19 April 2003).

Cudmore, James, "Support Services Contracted by Military," *National Post* (Canada) (9 June 2000).

Cutler, Claire, Virginia Haufler, and Tony Porter, "Private Authority in International Affairs," in Claire Cutler, Virginia Haufler, and Tony Porter, eds., *Private Authority in International Affairs* (Albany: SUNY Press, 1999).

Daalder, Ivo H. and Michael E. O'Hanlon, *Winning Ugly: NATO's War to Save Kosovo* (Washington, DC: Brookings, 2000).

Dahl, Robert, *A Preface to Democratic Theory* (Chicago: University of Chicago Press, 1956).

Daily Star, "Privatizing Peace and Security: a Hobbesian Dilemma," *Daily Star* (28 February 2004).

Danner, Mark, "Endgame in Kosovo," *New York Review of Books* Vol. 44, No. 8 (6 May 1999), 8–12.

"Operation Storm," *New York Review of Books* Vol. 45, No. 16 (22 October 1998), 73–79.

Dao, James, "For Profit, Private Firms Train Iraqi Soldiers, Provide Security, and Much More," *Post Gazette* (28 September 2003).

"Private US Guards Take Big Risks For Right Price," *New York Times* (2 April 2004).

Daragahi, Borzou, "In Iraq, Private Contractors Lighten Load on U.S. troops," *Special to the Post-Gazette* (28 September 2003).

Defense and Foreign Affairs Daily, "Nigerian Sources Deny Probability of New Coup, but Highlights Failure of US Approach to Reshaping Army," *Defense and Foreign Affairs Daily* (12 April 2003).

Desch, Michael, "War and State Strength," *International Organization*, Vol. 50, No. 2 (spring 1996), 237–68.
"Democracy and Victory: Why Regime Type Hardly Matters," *International Security* Vol. 27, No. 2 (fall 2002), 5–47.
Dessler, David, "Constructivism within a Positivist Social Science," *Review of International Studies*, Vol. 25 (1999), 123–37.
Dietrich, C., "Altered Conflict Resolution: EO in Sierra Leone," unpublished thesis, Princeton University, 1997.
DiMaggio, Paul and Walter Powell, "The Iron Cage Revisited: Institutional Isomorphism and Collective Rationality in Organizational Fields," in Paul DiMaggio and Walter Powell, eds., *The New Institutionalism in Organizational Analysis* (Chicago: University of Chicago Press, 1991).
DiMaggio, Paul and Walter Powell, eds., *The New Institutionalism in Organizational Analysis* (Chicago: University of Chicago Press, 1991).
Dinnen, Sinclair, Anthony J. Regan, and Ron May, eds., *Challenging the State: the Sandline Affair in Papua New Guinea* (Canberra: Australian National University, 1997).
Dinstein, Y., "Rules of War," in J. Krieger, ed., *The Oxford Companion to the Politics of the World* (Oxford: Oxford University Press, 1993).
Dogan, Rhys and Michael Pugh, "From Military to Market Imperatives: Peacekeeping and the New Public Policy," paper presented at the British International Studies Association Conference, University of Durham, 17–18 December 1996.
Donahue, John, *The Privatization Decision: Public Ends, Private Means* (New York: Basic Books, 1989).
Dorofeyev, Vladislav and Yelena Artemkina, "Chechnya Opens Trade in Mercenaries," *Moscow Kommersant-Vlast*, No. 9 (17 March 1998).
Douglass, Ian, "Fighting for Diamonds in Sierra Leone," in Jakkie Cilliers and Peggy Mason, eds., *Peace, Profit, or Plunder: the Privatization of Security in War-Torn African Societies* (Pretoria: Institute for Security Studies, 1999).
Downs, Anthony, *An Economic Theory of Democracy* (New York: Harper, 1957).
Inside Bureaucracy (Boston: Little, Brown and Company, 1967).
Doyle, Michael, "Kant, Liberal Legacies, and Foreign Affairs," *Philosophy and Public Affairs* Vol. 12 (summer 1983).
"Liberalism and World Politics," *American Political Science Review* Vol. 80, No. 4 (December 1986): 1151–69.
Doyle, Michael, Ian Johnstone, and Robert Orr, eds., *Keeping the Peace: Multidimensional UN Operations in Cambodia and El Salvador* (Cambridge: Cambridge University Press, 1997).
Drogin, Bob, "A Success Story in the Balkans: Croatians Celebrate Mesic's Inauguration," *Gazette* (Montreal) (19 February 2000), A20.
Drucker, Peter, "Trade Lessons from the World Economy," *Foreign Affairs* (January/February 1994), 99–108.
Dublin, Holly and Alison Wilson, "The Fight for Survival: what have we learned?" http://www.panda.org/resources/publications/species/african_rhino/what_learned.htm
Duffield, John, "NATO's Functions after the Cold War," *Political Science Quarterly* Vol. 109, No. 5 (winter 1994–95), 763–87.

Duffield, Mark, *Global Governance and the New Wars: the Merging of Security and Development* (New York: Zed, 2002).

Duke, Lynne, "South Africa's Ex-Soldiers Becoming "Dogs of War": Apartheid Commandos Peddling Skills," *Houston Chronicle* (24 March 1996), A29.

"Africans Use Training in Unexpected Ways," *Washington Post* (14 July 1998), A01.

Durch, William, *The Evolution of UN Peacekeeping* (New York: St. Martins, 1993).

Durch, William, ed., *UN Peacekeeping, American Politics and the Uncivil Wars of the 1990s* (New York: St. Martins, 1996).

Eagar, Charlotte, "Invisible US Army Defeats Serbs," *Observer* (5 November 1995).

Economist, "Croatia: Tudjman's New Model Army," *Economist* (11 November 1995).

"Can Anyone Curb Africa's Dogs of war?" *Economist* (16 January 1999).

Edwards, Michael and David Hulme, eds., *Beyond the Magic Bullet: NGO Performance and Accountability in the Post-Cold War World* (West Hartford: Kumarian Press, 1996).

Elshtain, Jean, *Public Man, Private Woman* (Princeton: Princeton University Press, 1981).

Ember, Carol R., Melvin Ember, and Bruce Russett, "Peace between Participatory Polities: a Cross-Cultural Test of the 'Democracies Rarely Fight Each Other' Hypothesis," *World Politics* Vol. 44, No. 4 (July 1992), 573–99.

Ero, Comfort, "Vigilantes, Civil Defense Forces and Militia Groups: the Other Side of Privatization of Security in Africa," *Conflict Trends* No. 1 (2000).

Evans, Gareth and Mohamed Sahnoun, "The Responsibility to Protect," *Foreign Affairs* Vol. 81, No. 6 (November/December 2002), 99–110.

Fallon, Andrew D. and Theresa A. Keene, "Closing the Loophole? Practical Implications of the Military Extraterritorial Jurisdiction Act of 2000," *Air Force Law Review* (22 March 2001).

Fallows, James, "Whatever Became of the Military–Industrial Complex?" *Foreign Policy* (November/December 2002).

Farrell, Theo "Figuring out our Fighting Organizations: the New Organizational Analysis in Strategic Studies," *Journal of Strategic Studies* Vol. 19, No. 1 (1996), 122–35.

Fearon, James D., "Domestic Political Audiences and the Escalation of International Disputes," *American Political Science Review* Vol. 88, No. 3. (September, 1994), 577–92.

Fearon, James and David Laitin, "Ethnicity, Insurgency, and Civil War," *American Political Science Review* Vol. 97, No. 1 (February 2003), 75–90.

Fearon, James and Alexander Wendt, "Rationalism versus Constructivism: a Skeptical View," in Walter Carlsnaes, Thomas Risse, and Beth Simmons, eds., *Handbook of International Relations* (New York: Sage, 2002), 52–72.

Feaver, Peter, "The Civil–Military Problematique: Huntington, Janowitz, and the Problem of Civilian Control," *Armed Forces and Society* Vol. 23, No. 2 (1996), 149–78.

Armed Servants: Agency, Oversight, and Civil–Military Relations (Harvard: Harvard University Press, 2002).

Feaver, Peter and Richard Kohn, *Soldiers and Civilians: the Civil–Military Gap and American National Security* (Cambridge: MIT Press, 2001).

Feigenbaum, Harvey and Jeffrey Henig, "The Political Underpinnings of Privatization: a Typology," *World Politics* Vol. 46, No. 2 (January 1994), 185–208.

Feigenbaum, Harvey, Jeffrey Henig, and Chris Hamnett, *Shrinking the State: the Political Underpinnings of Privatization* (Cambridge: Cambridge University Press, 1998).

Feil, Scott, *Preventing Genocide: How the Early Use of Force Might Have Succeeded in Rwanda* (New York: Carnegie Commission on Deadly Conflict, 1998).

Fein, Geoff, "Training Iraqi Army is a Wild Card," *National Defense Magazine* (December 2003).

Feinstein, Lee and Anne-Marie Slaughter, "A Duty to Prevent," *Foreign Affairs* (January/February 2004).

Feketekuty, Geza, *International Trade in Services: an Overview and Blueprint for Negotiations* (Cambridge: Ballinger, 1988).

Feldman, Jonathan, *Universities in the Business of Repression: the Academic–Military–Industrial Complex and Central America* (Boston: South End Press, 1989).

Fellers, Gordon, "Coalition Works to Make Iraqi Pipeline Protection a Top Priority," *Pipeline and Gas Journal* Vol. 231, No. 3 (1 March 2004).

Fenning, Richard, "The Iraqi Security Business Urgently Needs Rules," *Financial Times* (27 May 2004).

Feraru, Ann Thomson, "Transnational Political Interests and the Global Environment," *International Organization* Vol. 28, No. 1 (winter 1974), 31–60.

Ferguson, Niall, "A World Without Power," *Foreign Policy* (July/August 2004), 32–9.

Financial Times, "FT Investigation of the Private Military Business: Foreign Office Faces Opposition to Regulation Green Paper, Downing Street Blocks Publication until after Election," *Financial Times* (18 April 2001).

"US Firm to Take Over State Defense Group," *Financial Times* (5 September 2002).

Fineman, Mark, "Defense Dollars Prompt a Rush to Consolidate," *Los Angeles Times* (17 March 2003).

Finer, S. E., *Man on Horseback: the Role of the Military in Politics* (New York: Praeger, 1962).

Finnemore, Martha, "International Organizations as Teachers of Norms," *International Oganizations* Vol. 47, No. 4 (autumn 1993), 545–97.

"Constructing Norms of Humanitarian Intervention," in Peter Katzenstein, ed., *The Culture of National Security: Norms and Identity in World Politics* (New York: Columbia University Press, 1996).

National Interests in International Society (Ithaca: Cornell Unniversity Press, 1996).

Finnemore, Martha and Katherine Sikkink, "International Norm Dynamics and Political Change," *International Organization* Vol. 52, No. 4 (autumn 1998), 909–15.

Flaherty, Mary Pat, "Iraq Work Awarded to Veteran of Civil Wars," *Washington Post* (16 June 2004).

Flaherty, Mary Pat and Dana Priest, "More Limits Sought for Private Security Firms," *Washington Post* (13 April 2004).

Fligstein, Neil, "Theoretical and Comparative Perspectives on Corporate Organization," *Annual Review of Sociology* Vol. 21 (1995), 21–43.

Fligstein, Neil and Robert Freeland, "Theoretical and Comparative Perspectives on Corporate Organization," *Annual Review of Sociology* Vol. 21 (1995), 21–43.

Florini, Ann, "The Evolution of International Norms," *International Studies Quarterly* Vol. 40, No. 3 (September 1996), 363–89.

Florini, Ann, ed., *The Third Force: the Rise of Transnational Civil Society* (Washington, DC: Japan Center for International Exchange and Carnegie Endowment, 2000).

Forsythe, David P., *Humanitarian Politics: the International Committee of the Red Cross* (Baltimore: Johns Hopkins University Press, 1977).

Fort Worth Star-Telegram, "Lawmakers Seek End to Anti-Drug Contractors in Peru, Colombia," *Fort Worth Star-Telegram* (8 May 2001).

Fox, Robert, "Fresh War Clouds Threaten Ceasefire: Secret US Military Advice Helps 'Cocky' Croats Push toward Eastern Slovenia," *Sunday Telegraph* (15 October 1995), 26.

Francis, David, "Mercenary Intervention in Sierra Leone: Providing National Security or International Exploitation?" *Third World Quarterly* Vol. 20, No. 2 (April 1999), 319–38.

Freeman, Bennett, "Drilling for Common Ground," *Foreign Policy* (July/August 2001), 50.

"Managing Risk and Building Trust: the Challenge of Implementing the Voluntary Principles on Security and the Human Rights," remarks at Rules of Engagement: How Business can Be a force for Peace Conference, The Hague, 13 November 2002.

Freeman, Jody, "The Contracting State," *Florida State University Law Review* Vol. 28 (2000), 155.

Friedberg, Aaron, "Why Didn't the US Become a Garrison State," *International Security* Vol. 16, No. 4 (spring 1992), 109–42.

Friedman, Milton, *Capitalism and Freedom* (Chicago: University of Chicago Press, 1962).

Friman, H. Richard and Peter Andreas, *The Illicit Global Economy and State Power* (New York: Roman and Littlefield, 1999).

Frohardt, Mark, Diane Paul, and Larry Minear, "Protecting Human Rights: the Challenge to Humanitarian Organizations," Occasional Paper No. 35, Thomas Watson Institute, Brown University, 1999.

Frynas, Jedrzei George, "Political Instability and Business: Focus on Shell in Nigeria," *Third World Quarterly* Vol. 19, No. 3 (1998), 457–78.

Frynas, Jedrzei and Scott Pegg, *Transnational Corporations and Human Rights* (New York: Palgrave, 2003).

Furber, Holden, *Rival Empires of Trade in the Orient, 1600–1800* (Minnesota: University of Minnesota Press, 1976).

Gans, Jeremy "Privately Paid Public Policing: Law and Practice," *Policing and Society* Vol. 10, No. 2 (August 2000), 183–206.

Gantz, Peter, "The Private Sectors's Role in Peacekeeping and Peace Enforcement," *Refugees International Bulletin* (18 November 2003).

Gary, Ian and Terry Karl, "Bottom of the Barrel: Africa's Oil Boom and the Poor," Catholic Relief Services Report, June 2003.

Gates, Susan and Al Robbert, "Personnel Savings in Competitively Sourced DOD Activities" (Washington, DC: RAND [MR-1117-OSD]).

Gaul, Matt, "Regulating the New Privateers: Private Military Service Contracting and the Modern Marque and Reprisal Clause," *Loyola Law Review* (June 1998).

George, Alexander, "Domestic Constraints on Regime Change in US Foreign Policy: the Need for Policy Legitimacy," in G. John Ikenberry, ed., *American Foreign Policy: Theoretical Essays* (New York: HarperCollins, 1989).

Gerlach, M., *Alliance Capitalism* (Los Angeles: University of California Press, 1992).

Gerth, H. H. and C. Wright Mills, *From Max Weber: Essays in Sociology* (New York: Oxford University Press, 1946).

Giddens, Anthony, *A Contemporary Critique of Historical Materialism: the Nation-State and Violence* (Berkeley: University of California Press, 1985).

Gilbert, Felix, "Machiavelli," in Peter Paret and Gordon Craig, eds., *The Makers of Modern Strategy* (Princeton: Princeton University Press, 1986).

Gilpin, Robert, *The Political Economy of International Relations* (Princeton: Princeton University Press, 1987).

Giragosian, Richard, "Targeting Weak Points: Iraq's Oil Pipelines," *Asia Times* (27 January 2004).

Global Witness, *A Crude Awakening: the Role of Oil and Banking Industries in Angolan Civil War* (London: Global Witness, 1999).

Goldgeier, James and Michael McFaul, "A Tale of Two Worlds: Core and Periphery in the Post-Cold War Era," *International Organization* Vol. 46, No. 2 (spring 1992), 467–91.

Goldman Charles A., Brace R. Orvis, and Rodger Madison, *Staffing Army ROTC at Colleges and Universities: Alternatives for Reducing the Use of Active-Duty Soldiers* (Santa Monica: RAND, 1999).

Goodman, John, Deborah Spar, and David Yoffie, "Foreign Direct Investment and the Demand for Protection in the United States," *International Organization* Vol. 40, No. 4 (autumn 1996), 565–91.

Gormley, William T., Jr., "The Privatization Controversy," in William T. Gormley, Jr., ed., *Privatization and its Alternatives* (Madison: University of Wisconsin Press, 1991).

Gormley, William T., Jr., ed., *Privatization and its Alternatives* (Madison: University of Wisconsin Press, 1991).

Gosline, Melanie, "Pilot Held as Suspected Mercenary," *The Star* (4 February 2004).

Goulet, Yves, "Mixing Business with Bullets," *Jane's Intelligence Review* Vol. 9, No. 9 (September 1997).

"MPRI: Washington's Freelance Advisors," *Jane's Intelligence Review* Vol. 10, No. 7 (July 1998).

"DSL: Serving States and Multinationals," *Jane's Intelligence Review* Vol. 12, No. 6 (June 2000).

Gourevitch, Peter A., "The Macropolitics of Microinstitutional Differences in the Analysis of Comparative Capitalism," in Suzanne Berger and Ronald Dore, eds., *National Diversity and Global Capitalism* (Ithaca: Cornell University Press, 1996).

Gow, James, *Legitimacy and the Military: the Yugoslav Crisis* (New York: St. Martins Press, 1992).

Gowa, Joanne, "Democratic States and International Disputes," *International Organization* Vol. 49, No. 3 (summer 1995), 511–22.

Graham, Bradley, "Consensus is Building to Privatize Defense Functions," *Washington Post* (20 March 1995).

"US Firm Exports Military Expertise: Role in Training Croatian Army Brings Publicity and Suspicions," *Washington Post* (11 August 1995), A1.

Grant, Bruce, "US Military Expertise for Sale: Private Military Consultants as a Tool of Foreign Policy," National Defense University Institute for National Security Studies, Stategy Essay Competition, 1998; available at http://www.ndu.edu/inss/books/essaysch4.html.

Gray, Stephen,"Iraq Targets Private Guards," *Sunday Times* (6 June 2004).

Greenaway, Norma, "Aid Agencies Told to Hire Mercenaries for Protection," *Ottawa Citizen* (28 January 1999).

Grief, Avner, "Self Enforcing Political Systems and Economic Growth: Late Medieval Genoa," in Robert Bates, ed., *Analytic Narratives* (Princeton: Princeton University Press, 1998).

Grigg, William Norman, "Selective 'Justice' Turns a Blind Eye to Croatian Atrocities," *New American* Vol. 13, No. 21 (October 1997).

Grossman, Larry, "The Privatization of Military Training," *Government Executive* (March 1989).

Guardian, "Army to Privatise some Key Units," *Guardian* (14 February 1999).

"Is Big Business Bad for Our Boys?" *Guardian* (2 March 2003).

Guehenno, Jean-Marie, "The Impact of Globalization on Strategy," *Survival* Vol. 40, No. 4 (winter 1998–99), 5–19.

Guenee, B., *States and Rulers in Later Medieval Europe* (Oxford: Oxford University Press, 1985).

Gullison Raymond E., Richard E. Rice, and Gustavo A. B. da Fonseca, Bruner, Aaron G., "Effectiveness of Parks in Protecting Tropical Biodiversity," *Science* Vol. 291, No. 5501 (January 2001), 125–29.

Gullo, Karen, "Peacekeeping Helped Cheney Company," *Associated Press*, (28 August 2000).

Gurr, Ted Robert, Mony G. Marshall, and Deepa Khosla, *Peace and Conflict 2001* (College Park: Center for International Development and Conflict, 2000).

Gutman, Roy, "What did the CIA Know?" *Newsweek* (27 August 2001), p. 30.

Haas, Peter, "Introduction: Epistemic Communities and International Policy Coordination," *International Organization* Vol. 46, No. 1 (winter 1992), 1–35.

Hall, Peter, "Policy Paradigms, Social Learning and the State: the Case of Economic Policymaking in Britain," *Comparative Political Studies* Vol. 25 (April 1993), 275–96.

Hall, Peter A. and Rosemary C. R. Taylor, "Political Science and the Three New Institutionalisms," *Political Studies* Vol. 44 (1996), 936–57.

Hall, Rodney Bruce, *National Collective Identity* (New York: Columbia University Press, 1999).

Hall, Rodney Bruce and Thomas Biersteker, *The Emergence of Private Authority in Global Governance* (Cambridge: Cambridge University Press, 2002).

Hamre, John J. and Gordon R. Sullivan, "Toward Post-Conflict Reconstruction," *Washington Quarterly* Vol. 25, No. 4 (autumn 2002), 85–97.

Hanna, Mark, "Task Force XXI: the Army's Digital Experiment," *Strategic Forum* No. 119 (July 1997).

Hanser, Lawrence, Joyce Davidson, and Cathleen Stasz, *Who Should Train? Substituting Civilian Provided Training for Military Training* (Santa Monica: RAND, 1991).

Harding, Jeremy, "The Mellow Mercenaries," *Guardian* (8 March 1997).

Hartung, William, "Mercenaries, Inc.: How a US Company Props up the House of Saud," *Progressive* Vol. 60 (April 1996).

Harvard Business School, "Royal Dutch/Shell in Nigeria," (Harvard Business School Case 9-399-126, 20 April 2000).

Hatry, Harry P., "Problems," in *Privatization: the Provision of Public Services by the Private Sector* (Jefferson, NC: McFarland and Company, Inc., 1991).

Haufler, Virginia, "Is there a Role for Business in Conflict Prevention?" in Chester Crocker, Fen Osler Hampson, and Pamela Aall, eds., *Turbulent Peace: the Challenges of Managing International Conflict* (Washington, DC: USIP, 2001).

  A Public Role for the Private Sector (Washington: Carnegie Endowment for International Peace, 2001).

Hawley, Chris, "US Military Headquarters in Afghanistan Provides View of the New, Outsourced Army," *Associated Press* (7 October 2002).

Hedges, Chris, "Nationalists in Croatia Turn Away from West," *New York Times* (27 April 1997), A9.

Held, David and Andrew McGrew, *Global Transformation Reader: an Introduction to the Globalization Debate* (Cambridge: Polity Press, 2003).

Held, David, Anthony McGrew, David Goldblatt, and Jonathan Perraton, *Global Transformations: Politics, Economics, and Culture* (Stanford: Stanford University Press, 1999).

Henderson, David, *Misguided Virtue: False Notions of Corporate Social Responsibility* (London: Institute of Economic Affairs, 2001).

Hentz, James, "Privatization in Transnational South Africa," *Journal of Modern African Studies* Vol. 38, No. 2 (2000), 203–23.

Herbst, Jeffrey, "The Regulation of Private Security Forces," in Greg Mills and John Stremlau, eds., *The Privatization of Security in Africa* (Johannesburg: SAIIA Press, 1999).

Herman, Robert, "Identity, Norms, and National Security," in Peter Katzenstein, ed., *The Culture of National Security* (New York: Columbia University Press, 1996).

Hersh, Seymour M., "Torture at Abu Ghraib," *New Yorker* (6 May 2004).

Hibbs, Jon, "Arms to Africa Envoy Stands by his Decision," *The Telegraph* (4 November 1998).

Hillman-Smith, Kes, "Zaire's Rhinos," *The Times* (13 May 1997).

Hillman-Smith, Kes and Fraser Smith, "Conservation Crises and Potential Solutions: Example of Garamba National Park, Democratic Republic of Congo," (paper presented to the Second World Congress of the International Ranger Federation, San José, Costa Rica, 25–29 September 1997).

Hirsh, John L., "War in Sierra Leone," *Survival* Vol. 43, No. 2 (autumn 2001), 145–62.

Hirshman, Albert, *Exit, Voice and Loyalty: Response to Decline in Firms, Organizations, and States* (Cambridge: Harvard University Press 1970).

Hirst, P. and G. Thompson, *Globalization in Question* (Cambridge: Polity Press, 1996).

Hitt, Jack, "The Eco-Mercenaries," *New York Times Magazine* (4 August 2002), 24.

Hobbes, Thomas, *Leviathan* (New York: Penguin, 1983).

Hoffman, Danny, "The Brookfield Hotel Freetown, Sierra Leone," manuscript (2003).

Holbrooke, Richard, *To End a War* (New York: Modern Library, 1999).

Holsti, Kalevi J., *Peace and War: Armed Conflict and International Order, 1648–1989* (Cambridge: Cambridge University Press, 1991).

Hooper, Jim, "Executive Outcomes," *World Air Power Journal* Vol. 28 (Spring 1997), 38–49.

Hopgood, Stephen, "Reading the Small Print in Global Civil Society: the Inexorable Hegemony of the Liberal Self," *Millennium* Vol. 29, No. 1 (2000), 1–25.

Horvatic, Dubravko and Stjepan Seselj, "Croatian Culture and the Croatian Army," *Hrvatsko Slovo* (27 December 1996).

Howard, Sir Michael, *Soldiers and Governments: Nine Studies in Civil–Military Relations* (London: Eyre and Spottiswoode, 1957).

"What's in a Name? How to Fight Terrorism," *Foreign Affairs* (January/February 2002).

Howe, Herbert, "Private Security Forces and African Stability: the Case of Executive Outcomes," *Journal of Modern African Studies* Vol. 36, No. 2 (1998), 307–31.

Ambiguous Order: Military Forces in African States (Boulder: Lynne Rienner, 2001).

Huizinga, Johan, "The Political and Military Significance of Chivalric Ideas in the Late Middle Ages," in Johan Huizinga, *Men and Ideas* (Cleveland, 1959).

Human Rights Watch, *Rwanda/Zaire. Reaming with Impunity: International Support for the Perpetrators of the Rwandan Genocide*, Human Rights Watch Arms Project, Vol. 7, No. 4 (New York: Human Rights Watch, May 1995).

"THE BAKASSI BOYS: the Legitimation of Murder and Torture" (Human Rights Watch Report, May 2002).

"The Warri Crisis: Fuelling Violence" (Human Rights Watch Report, 17 December 2003).

Huntington, Samuel, *Soldier and the State: the Theory and Politics of Civil–Military Relations*, (New York: Vintage 1957).

Political Order in Changing Societies (New Haven: Yale University Press, 1968).
The Third Wave: Democratization in the Late Twentieth Century (Norman: University of Oklahoma Press, 1991).
Hurrell, Andrew and Ngare Woods, "Globalization and Inequality," *Millennium: Journal of International Studies* Vol. 24, No. 3 (1995), 447–70.
Ibeanu, Okechukwu, "Oiling the Friction: Environmental Conflict Management in the Niger Delta, Nigeria," *Environmental Change and Security Project Report* No. 6 (summer 2000).
ICG Report, "Sierra Leone: Time for a New Political and Military Strategy," (11 April 2001).
"Sierra Leone: Managing Uncertainty," International Crisis Group Africa Report, No. 35 (24 October 2001).
"Sierra Leone After Elections: Politics as Usual?" (12 July 2002).
"A Half Hearted Welcome: Refugee Returns to Croatia," 13 December 2002; available at http://int(-crisis-group.org/projects/balkans/balkans region/reports/A40048_13122002.pdf).
"Sierra Leone's Truth and Reconciliation Commission: A Fresh Start?" (20 December 2002); (available at http://www.intl-crisis-group.org/projects/showreport.cfm?reportid=858).
Ihonvbere, Julius O., "A Critical Evaluation of the Failed 1990 Coup in Nigeria," *Journal of Modern African Studies* Vol. 29, No. 1 (1991), 601–26.
Ikenberry, G. John, *After Victory: Institutions, Strategic Restructuring and the Rebuilding of Order after Major War* (Princeton: Princeton University Press, 2001).
America Unrivaled: the Future Balance of Power (Ithaca: Cornell University Press, 2002).
International Alert, "An Assessment of the Mercenary Issue at the Fifty-Fifth Session of the UN Commission on Human Rights" (May 1999).
"The Mercenary Issue at the UN Commission on Human Rights: the Need for a New Approach"(January 2001), 29–30.
International Consortium of Investigative Journalists, "The Business of War: Privatizing Combat, the New World Order" (Washington, DC: The Center for Public Integrity, 2002) (available at http://www.icij.org/dtaweb/ICIJ_BOW.ASP?L1=10&L2=65&L3=0&L4=0&L5=0&State=).
International Special Reports, "A Nation Resolved to Overcome its Tough Heritage," *International Special Reports – Croatia* (10 March 2002) (available at *http://www.internationalspecialreports.com/europe/01/croatia/ anationresolved. html*).
Irish, Jenny, "Policing for Profit: the Future of South Africa's Private Security Industry," Pretoria, Institute for Security Studies Monograph, No. 39 (August 1999).
Irvine, Jill, "Ultranationalist Ideology and State-Building in Croatia, 1990–1996," *Problems of Post-Communism* Vol. 44, No. 4 (July/August 1997), 30–44.
Isenberg, David, *Soldiers of Fortune, Ltd.: a Profile of Today's Private Sector Corporate Mercenary Firms*, Center for Defense Information Monograph (Washington, DC: CDI, 1997).

"Regulated Private Military Firms have a Role," *Defense News* (11–17 March 2002).

"Security for Sale in Afghanistan," *Asia Times Online* (3 January 2003).

Jackson, Robert, *Quasi-States: Sovereignty, International Relations, and the Third World* (New York: Cambridge University Press, 1990).

Jackson, Robert and Carl Rosberg, "Why Africa's Weak States Persist," *World Politics* Vol. 35, No. 1 (October 1982), 1–24.

Jane's Defence Weekly, "UK Outlines Revised Plans to Privatise Defense Research," *Jane's Defence Weekly* (26 March 2000).

Janowitz, Morris, *The Professional Soldier: a Social and Political Portrait* (New York: Free Press 1960).

Jepperson, Ron, Alexander Wendt, and Peter Katzenstein, "Norms, Identity, and National Security," in Peter Katzenstein, ed., *The Culture of National Security* (New York: Columbia University Press, 1996).

Johnson, Chalmers, *The Sorrows of Empire: Militarism, Secrecy, and the End of the Republic* (New York: Metropolitan Books, 2004).

Johnson, Rebecca, "Advocates and Activists: Conflicting Approaches on Nonproliferation and the Test Ban Treaty," in Ann Florini, ed., *The Third Force: the Rise of Transnational Civil Society* (Washington, DC: Japan Center for International Exchange and Carnegie Endowment, 2000).

Jones, Bruce, *Peacemaking in Rwanda: the Dynamics of Failure* (Boulder: Lynne Rienner, 2001).

Jupille, Joseph, James Caporaso, and Jeffrey Checkel, "Integrating Institutions: Rationalism, Constructivism, and the Study of the European Union," *Comparative Political Studies* Vol. 36, No. 1 (2003), 7–40.

Kaeuper, Richard W., *War, Justice and the Public Order* (Oxford: Clarendon Press, 1988).

Kahler, Miles, "The State of the State in World Politics," in Ira Katznelson and Helen Milner, *Political Science: the State of the Discipline* (New York: W. W. Norton, 2002).

Kakonen, Jyrki, *Green Security or Militarized Environment?* (Dartmouth: Aldershot, Brookfield, 1994).

Kaldor, Mary, *New and Old Wars: Organized Violence in a Global Era* (Stanford: Stanford University Press, 1999).

Kamerman, Sheila B. and Alfred J. Kahn, *Privatization and the Welfare State* (Princeton: Princeton University Press, 1989).

Kant, Immanuel, *Perpetual Peace* (New York: Columbia, 1939).

Kaplan, Robert, "The Coming Anarchy," *Atlantic Monthly* (February 1994), 44–66.

Kapstein, Ethan, "The Corporate Ethics Crusade," *Foreign Affairs* Vol. 80, No. 5 (September/October 2001), 105–20.

Karl, Terry Lynn, *The Paradox of Plenty: Oil Booms and Petro States* (Berkeley: University of California Press, 1997).

"The Perils of the Petro-State: Reflections on the Politics of Plenty," *Journal of International Affairs* Vol. 53, No. 1 (fall 1999), 31–49.

Katzenstein, Peter, ed., *Between Power and Plenty* (Madison: University of Wisconsin Press, 1978).

The Culture of National Security (New York: Columbia University Press, 1996).

Keck, Margaret and Katherine Sikkink, *Activists Beyond Borders: Advocacy Networks in International Politics* (Ithaca: Cornell University Press, 1998).

Keegan, John, *A History of Warfare* (New York: Knopf, 1993).

Keller, William, *Arm in Arm: the Political Economy of the Global Arms Trade* (New York: Basic Books, 1995).

Kelly, Jack, "Safety at a Price: Security is a Booming, Sophisticated, Global Business," *Pittsburgh Post Gazette* 13 (February 2000).

Kelly, Patricia O'Meara, "Broken Wings," *Insight Magazine* (29 April 2002).

Kemp, K. W. and Charles Hudlin, "Civil Supremacy Over the Military: Its Nature and its Limits," *Armed Forces and Society* Vol. 19, No. 1 (1992), 7–26.

Keohane, Robert, "The Demand for International Regimes," *International Organization* Vol. 36, No. 2 (Spring 1982), 325–55.

Keohane, Robert and Joseph Nye, *Power and Interdependence* (Boston: Little, Brown, 1977).

Khan, Sarah Ahmad, *Nigeria: the Political Economy of Oil* (Oxford: Oxford University Press, 1994).

Kier, Elizabeth, *Imagining War* (Princeton: Princeton University Press, 1997).

Kilburn, M. Rebecca, Rachel Louie, and Dana Goldman, *Patterns of Enlisted Compensation* (Washington, DC: RAND, 2001).

Kiley, Sam, "Sudanese Poachers Threaten the Last of the White Rhinos," *The Times* (15 February 1996).

Kinder, Hermann and Werner Hilgeman, *The Anchor Atlas of World History* (New York: Anchor, 1974) Vol. 1.

King, Gary, Robert Keohane, and Sidney Verba, *Designing Social Inquiry: Scientific Inference in Qualitative Research* (Princeton: Princeton University Press, 1994).

Kirshner, Jonathan, *Globalization and National Security* (New York: Routledge, 2006).

Klein, Benjamin and Keith B. Leffler, "The Role of Market Forces in Assuring Contractual Performance," *Journal of Political Economy* Vol. 89, No. 4 (1981), 615–41.

Klotz, Audie, *Norms in International Relations: the Struggle Against Apartheid* (Ithaca: Cornell University Press, 1995).

Kohn, Richard, "Out of Control: the Crisis in Civil–Military Relations," *The National Interest* Vol. 35 (Spring 1994).

"How Democracies Control the Military," *Journal of Democracy* Vol. 8, No. 4 (1997), 140–53.

Soldiers and Civilians: the Civil–Military Gap and American National Security (Cambridge: MIT Press, 2001).

Kolodziej, Edward, "Renaissance of Security Studies? Caveat Lector!" *International Studies Quarterly* Vol. 36 (December 1992), 421–38.

Kostecki, Michel, *Marketing Strategies for Services* (Oxford: Pergamon Press, 1994).

Krasner, Stephen, *Sovereignty: Organized Hypocrisy* (Princeton: Princeton University Press, 1999).

Kratochwil, Friedrich, *Rules, Norms, and Decisions: on the Conditions of Practical and Legal Reasoning in International Relations and Domestic Affairs* (New York: Cambridge University Press, 1989).

Krause, Keith, *Arms and the State: Patterns of Military Production and Trade* (Cambridge: Cambridge University Press, 1992).

Krepinevich, Andrew, "Cavalry to Computer," *The National Interest* (fall 1994), 30–42.

Kuhner, Jeffrey Thomas, "Croatia at Crossroads: Tudjman has Choice of Embracing Pro-Democracy Movement or Trying to Crush it," *Gazette* (Montreal) op-ed (19 August 1999), B3.

Kuperman, Alan J., *The Limits of Humanitarian Intervention: Genocide in Rwanda* (Washington, DC: Brookings, 2001).

LA Times, "Chechens Falling Prey to Russian Soldiers of Fortune," *Los Angeles Times* (25 October 2000).

Lagerquist, Peter and Jonathan Steele, "Company Acts after *Guardian* Investigation," *Guardian* (9 October 2002).

Lake, David, "Powerful Pacifists: Democratic States and War," *American Political Science Review* Vol. 86, No. 1 (March 1992), 24–38.

"Fair Fights: Evaluating Theories of Democracy and Victory," *International Security* Vol. 28, No. 1 (summer 2003), 154–67.

Lancaster, John, "House Kills Training Funds for School of the Americas, Army Facility Accused of Fostering Human Rights Abuses," *Washington Post* (31 July 1999), A03.

Lashman, Paul, "Spicer's Security Firm in Battle with DynCorp over $290m Deal," *Independent* (4 July 2004).

Lee, Dwight R., "Public Goods, Politics, and Two Cheers for the Military Industrial Complex," in R. Higgs, ed., *Arms, Politics, and the Economy: Historical and Contemporary Perspectives* (New York: Homes and Meier, 1990).

Legro, Jeffrey, *Cooperation Under Fire* (Ithaca: Cornell University Press, 1995).

Lens, Sidney, *The Military Industrial Complex* (Philadelphia: Pilgrim Press, 1970).

Leppard, David and Nicholas Rufford, "Arms to Africa: 'no prosecution'" *Sunday Times* (17 May 98).

Levi, Margaret *Of Rule and Revenue* (University of California Press, 1989).

"The State of the Study of the State," in Ira Katznelson and Helen Milner, *Political Science: the State of the Discipline* (New York: W. W. Norton, 2002).

Lieberman, Robert, "Ideas, Institutions, and Political Order: Explaining Political Change," *American Political Science Review* Vol. 96, No. 4 (December 2002), 697–712.

Lipschultz, Ronnie, "Reconstructing World Politics: the Emergence of Global Civil Society," *Millennium: Journal of International Studies* Vol. 21, No. 3 (1992), 389–420.

Lipson, Charles, "International Cooperation in Economic and Security Affairs," *World Politics* Vol. 37 (1984), 31–63.

Reliable Partners: How Democracies Have Made a Separate Peace (Princeton: Princeton University Press, 2003).

Litfin, Karen, *Ozone Discourses* (New York: Columbia University Press, 1994).

Lock, Peter, "Africa, Military Downsizing and the Growth in the Security Industry," in Jakkie Cilliers and Peggy Mason, eds., *Peace, Profit, or Plunder?* (Pretoria: Institute for International Studies, 1999).

Locke, John, *Two Treatises of Government* (New York: Cambridge University Press, 1963).

Lowi, Theodore, "Making Democracy Safe for the World: on Fighting the Next War," in G. John Ikenberry, ed., *American Foreign Policy: Theoretical Essays* (New York: HarperCollins, 1989).

Luckham, Robin, *The Nigerian Military* (Cambridge: Cambridge University Press, 1973).

Lumpe, Lora, "US Foreign Military Training: Global Reach, Global Power, and Oversight Issues," *Foreign Policy In Focus* Special Report (May 2002).

Lyne, Mona and Michael Tierney, "Variation in the Structure of Principals: Conceptual Clarifications," Paper presented at the Conference on Delegation to International Organizations, Park City, Utah, May 2002.

Mabry, Marcus, "Soldiers of Misfortune," *Newsweek* (February 24, 1997).

Machiavelli, Niccolò, *The Prince*, eds. Quentin Skinner and Russell Price (New York: Cambridge University Press, 1988).

Maier, Karl, "Shell May Have to Quit Nigeria," *Bloomberg News* (11 June 2004).

Malan, Mark, "The Crisis in External Response," in Jakkie Cilliers and Peggy Mason, eds., *Peace Profit or Plunder?* (Pretoria: Institute for International Studies, 1999).

Malan, Mark and Jakkie Cilliers, "Mercenaries and Mischief: the Regulation of Foreign Military Assistance Bill," Institute for Security Studies, Occasional Paper No. 25 (September 1997).

Malan, Mark, Sarah Meek, Thokozani Thusi, Jeremy Ginifer, and Patrick Coker, *Sierra Leone: Building the Road To Recovery*, ISS Monograph 80 (Pretoria: ISS, 2003).

Mallaby, Sebastian, "Paid to Make Peace," *Washington Post* (4 June 2001), A19. "Think Again: Renouncing Use of Mercenaries Can Be Lethal," *Washington Post* (5 June 2001).

Mallett, Michael, *Mercenaries and their Masters: Warfare in Renaissance Italy* (London: Military Book Society, 1974).

Mallett, M. E. and J. R. Hale, *The Military Organization of a Renaissance State* (Cambridge: Cambridge University Press, 1984).

Manby, Bronwen, *The Price of Oil: Corporate Responsibility and Human Rights Violations in Nigeria's Oil Producing Communities* (New York: Human Rights Watch, 1999).

Marano, Lou, "The Perils of Privatization," *Washington Post* (27 May 1997), A15.

March, James and Johan P. Olsen, "The New Institutionalism: Organizational Factors in Political Life," *American Political Science Review* Vol. 78, No. 3 (September 1984), 734–49. "The Institutional Dynamics of International Political Orders," *International Organization* Vol. 52, No. 4 (autumn, 1998), 943–69.

Markusen Ann and Sean Costigan, eds., *Arming the Future: a Defense Industry for the Twenty-First Century* (New York: Council on Foreign Relations, 1999).

Marten, Kimberly, *Enforcing the Peace: Learning from the Imperial Past* (New York: Columbia University Press, 2004).

Mathews, Jessica Tuchman, "Redefining Security," *Foreign Affairs* Vol. 68, No. 2 (spring 1989), 162–77.

Mattli, Walter and Anne-Marie Slaughter, "Law and Politics in the European Union," *International Organization* Vol. 49, No. 1 (winter 1995), 183–90.

Maupas, Stephanie, "War Crimes Trial Opens," *LeMonde* 11–17 June 2004.

Mayer, Jane, "Contract Sport," *New Yorker* (February 2004), 80–89.

Mayer, Kenneth, *The Political Economy of Defense Contracting* (New Haven: Yale University Press, 1991).

McNallen, Steve, "South African Headhunters," *Soldier of Fortune* (May 1995).

McNamara, Kathleen, *The Currency of Ideas: Monetary Politics in the European Union* (Ithaca: Cornell University Press, 1998).

McNaugher, Thomas, "The Army and Operations Other than War," in Don Snider and Gayle Watkins, eds., *The Future of the Army Profession* (New York: McGraw Hill, 2002).

McNeil, Donald G., Jr., "Pocketing the Wages of War," *New York Times* (16 February 1997).

McNeill, William, *The Pursuit of Power: Technology, Armed Force, and Society since AD 1000* (Chicago: University of Chicago Press, 1982).

McQuaid, John, "Citizens Not Soldiers," *New Orleans Times Picayune* (11 November 2003).

"US Hostages in Colombia Make One Year," *New Orleans Times Picayune* (13 February 2004).

Mekata, Motoko, "Building Partnerships toward a Common Goal," in Ann Florini, ed., *The Third Force: the Rise of Transnational Civil Society* (Washington, DC: Japan Center for International Exchange and Carnegie Endowment, 2000).

Merle, Renae, "Contractor Investigated by Justice," *Washington Post* (22 May 2004).

Metz, Steven, "Pretoria's "Total Strategy" and Low-Intensity Warfare in Southern Africa," *Comparative Strategy* Vol. 6, No. 4 (1987).

Meyer, Carrie A., "Environmental NGOs in Ecuador: an Economic Analysis of Institutional Change," *Journal of Developing Areas* Vol. 27 (January 1993), 191–210.

Meyer, J. and B. Rowan, "Institutionalized Organizations: Formal Structure as Myth and Ceremony," *American Journal of Sociology* Vol. 83, 340–63.

Meyer, John, David John Frank, Ann Hironaka, Evan Schofer, and Nancy Brandon Tuma, "A World Environmental Regime, 1870–1990," *International Organization* Vol. 51, No. 4 (autumn 1997).

Meyer John W., "The World Polity and the Nation State," in Albert Bergesen, ed., *Studies of the Modern World System* (New York: Academic Press, 1980).

"The Changing Cultural Content of the Nation State: A World Society Perspective," in George Steinmetz, ed., *New Approaches to the State in the Social Sciences* (Ithaca: Cornell University Press, 1996).

Migdal, Joel, *Weak States and Strong Societies* (Princeton: Princeton University Press, 1988).

Milgrom, Paul, Douglass North, and Barry Weingast, "The Role of Institutions in the Revival of Trade: the Law Merchant, Private Judges, and the Champagne Fairs," *Economics and Politics* Vol. 2 (1990), 1–23.

Mill, John Stuart, *On Liberty* (Indianapolis: Hackett Publishing Co., 1984).

Millar, Stuart, "Soldiers of Misfortune," *Guardian* (27 March 1997), T2.

Miller, Gary, *Managerial Dilemmas: the Political Economy of Hierarchy* (Cambridge: Cambridge University Press, 1992).

Miller, John and Christopher Tufts, "A Means to Achieve More with Less," in *Privatization: the Provision of Public Services by the Private Sector* (Jefferson, NC: McFarland and Company, Inc., 1991).

Miller, Laura, "From Adversaries to Allies: Relief Workers' Attitudes Toward the US Military," *Qualitative Sociology* Vol. 22, No. 3 (1999), 181–97.

Millet, Alan, Williamson Murray, and Kenneth Watman, "The Effectiveness of Military Organizations," in Alan Millet and Williamson Murray, eds., *Military Effectiveness: Vol. I: the First World War* (Boston, MA: Houghton Mifflin, 1988), pp. 1–30.

Mills, Greg and John Stremlau, "The Privatization of Security in Africa: an Introduction," in Greg Mills and John Stremlau, eds., *The Privatization of Security in Africa* (Johannesburg: SAIIA Press, 1999).

Milstein, Mark H., "GIs in Gym Suits," *Soldier of Fortune* Vol. 23, No. 5 (May 1998).

Minc, Alain, *Le Nouveau Moyen Age* (Paris: Gallimard, 1993).

Minear, Larry, *The Humanitarian Enterprise* (Bloomfield, CT: Kumarian Press, 2002).

Minow, Martha, *Partners, not Rivals: Privatization and the Public Good* (Boston: Beacon Press, 2002).

Mintz, John, "Outsourcing Goes Right to the Front: Brown and Root's Bosnia Presence Reflects Pentagon Effort to Privatize Military Support," *Washington Post* (21 December 1995), B13.

Misser, François and Anver Versi, "Soldier of Fortune," *African Business* (December 1997).

Mockler, Anthony, *Mercenaries* (London: Macdonald, 1969).

The New Mercenaries (London: Garden City Press, 1985).

Moller, Bjorn "Raising Armies in a Rough Neighborhood: Soldiers, Guerillas and Mercenaries in Southern Africa," CIAO Working Paper, August 2001.

"Private Military Companies and Peace Operation in Africa," paper presented at the seminar on Private Military Companies in Africa: to Ban or Regulate, Department of Political Science, University of Pretoria, 8 February 2002.

Moskos, Charles, John Allen Williams, and David Segal, *The Postmodern Military: Armed Forces after the Cold War* (New York: Oxford University Press, 2000).

Moskos, Charles and Frank Woods, eds., *The Military: More than Just a Job?* (McLean, VA: Pergamon-Brassey's, 1988).

Mukherjee, R., *The Rise and Fall of the East India Company* (New York: Monthly Review Press, 1974).

Munnion, Christopher, "Banks May Use Mercenaries to Fight Robbers," *Daily Telegraph* (26 January 1998).

Muradian, Vago, "DOD Can Save Billions By Outsourcing Work, DSB Says," *Defense Daily* Vol. 193, No. 1 (1 October 1996).

Murphy, James, "DOD Outsources $500m in Spare Parts Work," *PlanetGov. com* (29 September 2000).

Murray, Carla Tighe, "Transformation of In-Kind Compensation and Benefits," in Cindy Williams, ed., *Filling the Ranks* (Boston: MIT Press, 2004), 189–212.

Musah, Abdel-Fatau, "'A Country Under Siege': State Decay and Corporate Military Intervention in Sierra Leone," in Abdel-Fatau Musah and J. Kayode Fayemi, *Mercenaries: an African Security Dilemma* (London: Pluto Press, 2000).

Musah, Abdel-Fatau and J. Kayode Fayemi, *Mercenaries: an African Security Dilemma* (London: Pluto, 2000).

Nagle, James, *A History of Government Contracting* (Washington, DC: George Washington University, 1992).

Nakashima, Ellen, "Pentagon Hires Out more than In," *Washington Post* (3 April 2001), A19.

"Defense Balks at Contract Goals," *Washington Post* (30 January 2002), A21.

Nation, "ExxonMobile-Sponsored Terrorism?" *Nation* (14 June 2002).

NATO, "Partnership for Peace: Framework Document" (January 1994) (available at http://www.nato.int/docu/comm/49–95/c940110b.htm).

Natsios, Andrew, "NGOs and the UN System in Complex Humanitarian Emergencies: Conflict or Cooperation?" *Third World Quarterly* Vol. 16, No. 3 (1995), 405–19.

Naylor, Sean D., "Civilians could Save Troop 'Spaces' at Training Center," *Army Times* (3 August 1998).

Nduru, Moyiga, "Environment: Poachers Return to Zaire's Garamba Park," *Inter Press Service* (8 April 1996).

Nelson, Jane, *The Business of Peace* (London: Prince of Wales Business Leaders' Forum, 2000).

Newman, Cathy, "UN to Hire Mercernaries for Policing Peace," *Financial Times* (13 February 2003).

Nicoll, Alexander, "Cultural Change Sweeps through the RAF," *Financial Times* (29 November 2000), 4.

Nielson, Dan and Michael Tierney, "Delegation to International Organizations: Agency Theory and the World Bank," *International Organization*, Vol. 57, No. 2 (spring 2003), 241–76.

Nielson, Daniel, Michael Tierney, and Catherine Weaver, "The Argument is the Incentive: Agency, Organizational Culture and the World Bank's Strategic Compact," paper prepared for the Conference on Theoretical Synthesis in the Study of International Organizations, Washington, DC, 6–7 February 2004.

North, Douglass, *Structure and Change in Economic History* (New York: W. W. Norton, 1981).

Institutions, Institutional Change and Economic Performance (Cambridge: Cambridge University Press, 1990).

Norton-Taylor, Richard, "Let Mercenaries be Licensed, says Foreign Office," *Guardian* (13 February 2002).

Nye, Joseph and Sean Lynn Jones, "International Security Studies: Report of a Conference on the State of the Field," *International Security* Vol. 12, No. 4 (spring 1998), 5–27.

Nye, Joseph and William Owens, "America's Information Edge," *Foreign Affairs* (March/April 1996), 20–36.

Obradovic, Stojan, "Indictment not only against Generals," *NIJ Weekly Service* Issue 231 (20 July 2001).

O'Brien, Kevin, "Freelance Forces: Exploiters of Old or New-Age Peace-brokers?" *Jane's Intelligence Review* (August 1998), 42–46.

"Private Military Companies and African Security 1990–1998," in Abdel-Fatau Musah and J. Kayode Fayemi, eds., *Mercenaries: an African Security Dilemma* (London: Pluto Press, 2000).

"PSCs, Myths, and Mercenaries," *Royal United Service Institute Journal* (February 2000).

Olson, Mancur, *The Logic of Collective Action* (Cambridge: Harvard University Press, 1971).

"Dictatorship, Democracy, and Development," *American Political Science Review* Vol. 87, No. 3 (September 1993), 567–76.

Oman, Charles, *History of the Art of War in the Middle Ages*, 2nd edition (London, 1924).

O'Prey, Kevin, *The Arms Export Challenge* (Washington, DC: Brookings, 1995).

Orr, Robert, "Governing When Chaos Rules: Enhancing Governance and Participation," *Washington Quarterly* Vol. 25, No. 4 (autumn 2002), 139–53.

Ottoway, Marina, "Reluctant Missionaries," *Foreign Policy* (July/August 2001), 44–55.

Oxfam, "Out of Control: the Loopholes in UK Controls of the Arms Trade," Oxfam GB Policy Paper (December 1998).

Oye, Kenneth, Robert J. Lieber, and Donald Rothchild, eds., *Eagle in a New World: American Grand Strategy in the Post-Cold War Era* (New York: Harper Collins, 1992).

Pagliano, Gary, "Privatizing DOD Functions through Outsourcing: a Framework for Discussions," CRS Report 96-700F (6 August 1996).

Palan, Ronan and Jason Abbott, *State Strategies in the Global Political Economy* (London: Pinter, 1996).

Paris, Roland, "Human Security: Paradigm Shift or Hot Air?" *International Security* Vol. 26, No. 2 (fall 2001), 87–102.

At War's End: Building Peace after Civil Conflict (Cambridge: Cambridge University Press, 2004).

Parker, Geoffrey and Simon Adams, eds., *The Thirty Years War* (London: Routledge, 1997).

Parsons, Talcott, "On the Concept of Political Power," Proceedings of the American Philosophical Society, Vol. 107 (1963).

Pauly, Louis, *Who Elected the Bankers?* (Ithaca: Cornell University Press, 1997).

Pauly, Louis and Simon Reich, "National Structures and International Corporate Behavior: Enduring Differences in an Age of Globalization," *International Organization* Vol. 51, No. 1 (winter 1997), 1–30.

Pearson, Frederic S., "The Question of Control in British Defense Sales Policy," *International Affairs* Vol. 59, No. 2 (spring 1983), 211–39.

Pech, Khareen, "Executive Outcomes – a Corporate Conquest," in Jakkie Cilliers and Peggy Mason, eds., *Peace, Profit, or Plunder: the Privatization of Security in War-Torn African Societies* (Pretoria: Institute for Security Studies, 1999).

"The Hand of War," in Abdel-Fatau Musah and J. Kayode Fayemi, eds., *Mercenaries: an African Security Dilemma* (London: Pluto, 2000).

Pegg, Scott, "The Cost of Doing Business: Transnational Corporations and Violence in Nigeria," *Security Dialogue* Vol. 30, No. 4 (December 1999), 473–84.

"Corporate Armies for States and State Armies for Corporations," paper presented to the annual meeting of the American Political Science Association, Washington, DC, 2001.

Peluso, Nancy, "Coercing Conservation," in Ronnie D. Lipschutz and Ken Conca, eds., *The State and Social Power in Global Environmental Politics* (New York: Columbia University Press, 1993).

Perito, Robert, *The American Experience with Police in Peacekeeping Operations* (Clementsport, Canadian Peacekeeping Press, 2002).

Where is the Lone Ranger When You Need Him? America's Search for a Post-Conflict Stability Force (Washington, DC: United States Institute for Peace Press, 2004).

Peters, Terry, "Public Services and the Private Sector," in *Privatization: the Provision of Public Services by the Private Sector* (Jefferson, NC: McFarland and Company, Inc., 1991).

Peterson, M. J. "Transnational Activity, International Society, and World Politics," *Millennium: Journal of International Studies* Vol. 21, No. 3 (1992), 371–88.

Pevehouse, Jon, "With a Little Help from my Friends? Regional Organizations and the Consolidation of Democracy," *American Journal of Political Science* Vol. 46, No. 3 (July 2002), 611–22.

Pfeffer, J. and G. Salancik, *The External Control of Organizations* (New York: Harper and Row, 1978).

Pham, Alex, "Federal Contracts Help CSC Post Solid Net Income Gain," *Los Angeles Times* (18 May 2004).

Pictet, Jean, *The Fundamental Principles of the Red Cross* (Geneva: Henry Dunant Institute, 1979).

Pierson, Paul, "When Effect Becomes Cause: Policy Feedback and Political Change," *World Politics* Vol. 45 (July 1993), 595–628.

Dismantling the Welfare State? Reagan, Thatcher and the Politics of Retrenchment (Cambridge: Cambridge University Press, 1994).

"Increasing Returns, Path Dependence, and the Study of Politics," *American Political Science Review* Vol. 94, No. 2 (June 2000), 251–67.

Pirie, Madsen, *Dismantling the State* (Dallas: National Center for Policy Analysis, 1985).

Poggi, Gianfranco, *The Development of the Modern State: a Sociological Introduction* (Stanford: Stanford University Press, 1978).

Porter, Michael, *The Competitive Advantage of Nations* (New York: Free Press, 1990).

Posen, Barry, "Command of the Commons: the Military Foundations of US Hegemony," *International Security* Vol. 28, No. 1 (summer 2003).

Powell, Walter, "Neither Market nor Hierarchy: Network Forms of Organizations," in L. L. Cumings and B. Staw, eds., *Research in Organizational Behavior* (Greenwich, CJ: JAI, 1990).

Powell, Walter W. and Paul J. DiMaggio, eds., *The New Institutionalism in Organizational Analysis* (Chicago: University of Chicago Press, 1991).

Powell, Walter and L. Smith-Doerr, "Networks and Economic Life," in Neil Smelser and Richard Swedberg, eds., *The Handbook of Economic Sociology* (New York: Russell Sage, 1994).

Power, Samantha, Robin Knight, Douglas Pasternak, and Alan Cooperman, "The Croatian Army's Friends," *US News and World Report*, 21 August 1995.

Pratt, John and Richard Zeckhauser, *Principals and Agents: the Structure of Business* (Harvard: Harvard Business School Press, 1985).

Press, Daryl, "Lessons from Ground Conflict in the Gulf: the Impact of Training and Technology," *International Security* Vol. 22, No. 2 (autumn 1997), 137–46.

Preston, Richard A. and Sydney F. Wise, *Men in Arms: a History of Warfare and its Interrelationships with Western Society* (New York: Praeger Publishers, 1970).

Price, Richard, "Transnational Society Targets Land Mines," *International Organization* Vol. 52, No. 3 (summer 1998) 413–44.

Priest, Dana, "Special Alliances: the Pentagon's New Global Engagements," *Washington Post* (12 July 1998), A01.

"Private Guards Repel Attack on US Headquarters," *Washington Post* (6 April 2004), A1.

PRNewswire, "DynCorp Joint Venture, NEWTEC, Wins $376 Million Contract," *PRNewswire* (28 August 2000).

Proxmire, William, *Report From the Wasteland* (New York: Praeger, 1970).

Prunier, Gerard, *The Rwandan Crisis: History of a Genocide* (New York: Columbia University Press, 1995).

"The Great Lakes Crisis," *Current History* Vol. 96, No. 610 (May 1997), 193–99.

Radio Free Europe, "FSB Says British NGO Trained Chechens as Terrorists," *Radio Free Europe/Radio Liberty* (11 August 2000).

Ragin, Charles, *Fuzzy Set Social Science* (Chicago: University of Chicago Press, 2000).

Reddy, Anitha and Ellen McCarthy, "CACI in the Dark on Reports of Abuse," *Washington Post* (6 May 2004).

Redlich, Fritz, *The German Military Enterpriser and his Workforce: a Study in European Economic and Social History* (Wiesbaden: Franz Steiner Verlag, 1964).

Reed, Laura and Carl Kayson, *Emerging Norms of Justified Intervention* (Cambridge, MA: Committee on International Security Studies, American Academy of Arts and Sciences, 1993).

Reiff, David, "Humanitarianism in Crisis," *Foreign Affairs*, Vol. 81, No. 6 (November/December 2002), 111–21.

Reiter, Dan and Allan Stam, *Democracies at War* (Princeton: Princeton University Press, 2002).

"Understanding Victory: Why Political Institutions Matter," *International Security*, Vol. 28, No. 1 (summer 2003), 168–79.

Reno, William, "Privatizing War in Sierra Leone," *Current History* Vol. 96, No. 610 (May 1997), 227–31.

Warlord Politics and African States (Boulder: Lynne Rienner, 1998).

"Clandestine Economies, Violence and States in Africa," *Journal of International Affairs* Vol. 53, No. 2 (spring 2000), 577–601.

"Foreign Firms, National Resources, and Violent Political Economies," *Social Science Forum* (21 March 2000).

"Shadow States and the Political Economy of Civil-War," in Mats Berdal and David Malone, eds., *Greed and Grievance: Economic Agendas in Civil Wars* (Boulder: Lynne Rienner, 2000).

"How Sovereignty Matters; International Economics and Local Politics," in Thomas Callaghy, Ronald Kassimir, and Robert Latham, *Intervention and Transnationalism in Africa* (Cambridge: Cambridge University Press, 2001).

Reuters, "South African Security Consultant in Angola Murdered for Food," *Reuters* (10 August 2000).

"Straw Seeks to Rein in Mercenaries," *Reuters* (12 February 2002).

Ripley, Tim, *Mercenaries: Soldiers of Fortune* (London: Paragon Publishing, 1997).

Risch, Erna, *The Quartermaster Corp: Organization, Supply, and Services* (Washington, DC: GPO, 1995).

Risse, Thomas, "The Power of Norms versus the Norms of Power: Transnational Civil Society and Human Rights," in Ann M. Florini, ed., *The Third Force: the Rise of Transnational Civil Society* (Washington, DC: Japan Center for International Exchange and Carnegie Endowment, 2000).

Risse-Kappen, Thomas, "Collective Identities in a Democratic Community," in Peter Katzenstein, ed., *The Culture of National Security* (New York: Columbia University Press, 1996).

Robertson, Lord, "Perspectives on Democratic Civil–Military Relations and Reform," Speech at the Centre for European Security Studies Conference, Taking Stock on Civil–Military Relations, The Hague, 9 May 2001.

Robinson, Linda, "Where Angels Fear to Tread: Colombia and Latin America's Tier of Turmoil," *World Policy Journal*, Vol. 16, No. 4 (winter 1999/2000), 63–72.

Rogers, Charles and Brian Sytsma, *World Vision Security Manual: Safety Awareness for Aid Workers* (Geneva: World Vision, 1999).

Rose, Alexander, "Hurray for Soldiers of Fortune," *National Post* (Canada) (30 August 2000).

Rosen, Stephen Peter, *Societies and Military Power* (Ithaca: Cornell University Press, 1996).

Ross, Michael, "Does Oil Hinder Democracy?" *World Politics* Vol. 53, No. 3 (April 2001), 325–61.

Royce, Knut, "Start Up Company with Connections," *Newsday* (15 February 2004).

Rubin, Elizabeth, "An Army of One's Own," *Harper's Magazine* (February 1997), 44–66.

"Saving Sierra Leone, at a Price," *New York Times* (4 February 1999), A27.

Rufford, Nicholas, "Diamond Dogs of War," *The Times* (10 May 1998).

Ruggie, John, "Territoriality and Beyond: Problematizing Modernity in International Relations," *International Organization* Vol. 47, No. 1 (1993), 139–74.

Constructing the World Polity (London: Routledge, 1998).

"What Makes the World Hang Together? Neo-Utilitarianism and the Social Constructivist Challenge," *International Organization* Vol. 52, No. 4 (autumn 1998), 855–85.

Ruggie, John, ed., *Multilateralism Matters* (New York: Columbia University Press, 1993).

Rumsfeld, Donald, Secretary of Defense, letter to Ike Skelton, ranking Minority Member, Committee on Armed Services, US House of Representatives, attachment "Discussion Paper on Private Security Companies Operating in Iraq" (4 May 2004).

Russell, Frederick H., *The Just War in the Middle Ages* (London: Cambridge University Press, 1975).

SABC News, "SA ex-Air Force Officer in Hot Water in Swellendam," *SABC News* (4 February 2004) (available at www.sabcnews.com/southafrica/crimejustice/0,2172,73352,00.html).

Saint, Steven, "NORAD Outsources," *Colorado Springs Gazette* (1 September 2000).

Sapolsky, Harvey M. and Eugene Gholtz, "Restructuring the US Defense Industry," *International Security* Vol. 24, No. 3 (winter 1999/2000), 5–51.

Saracen, "Concept Proposal for Garamba National Park: Zaire," prepared by Saracen International, Ltd. (17 January 1998).

Savas, E. S., *Privatizing the Public Sector* (Chatham, NJ: Chatham Publishing, 1982).

Schatz, Sayre P., "Pirate Capitalism and the Inert Economy of Nigeria," *Journal of Modern African Studies* Vol. 22, No. 1 (March 1984), 45–57.

Schatzki, Theodore R., Karin Knorr Cetina, and Eike von Savigny, *The Practice Turn in Contemporary Theory* (New York: Routledge, 2001).

Schmitt, Glenn, "Closing the Gap in Criminal Jurisdiction Over Civilians Accompanying the Armed Forces Abroad – a First Person Account of the Creation of the Military Extraterritorial Jurisdiction Act of 2000," *Catholic University Law Review* Vol. 51, No. 1 (fall 2001), 55–134.

Schneider, Gerald and Mark Aspinwall, eds., *Rules of Integration: Institutionalist Approaches to the Study of Europe* (Manchester: Manchester University Press, 2001).

Schrage, Elliot, "A Long Way to Find Justice: What are Burmese Villagers Doing in a California Court?" *Washington Post* (14 July 2002), B2.

"Judging Corporate Accountability in the Global Economy," *Columbia Journal of Transnational Law* Vol. 42 (2003).

Schulhofer-Wohl, Johan, "Peacekeeping in Sierra Leone Could be Privatized," *International Herald Tribune* (15 May 2000).

Scott, W. Richard and John Meyer, *Institutional Environment and Organizations: Structural Complexity and Individualism* (Thousand Oaks, CA: Sage, 1994).

Sen, S. P., *The French in India, 1763–1816* (Calcutta: Frima K. L. Mukhopadhyay, 1958).

Sharp, Jane M. O., "Bosnia: Begin Again," *Bulletin of the Atomic Scientists* Vol. 53, No. 2 (March/April 1997), 17–20.

Shaw, M., *Post Military Society* (Cambridge: Polity Press, 1991).

Shearer, David, *Private Armies and Military Intervention* (Adelphi Paper 316, Oxford University Press, 1998).

"Outsourcing War," *Foreign Policy* (Fall 1998), 68–82.

Sheppard, Simon, "Foot Soldiers of the New World Order: the Rise of the Corporate Military," *New Left Review* Vol. 228 (March/April 1998).

Shiff, Rebecca, "Civil–Military Relations Reconsidered: a Theory of Concordance," *Armed Forces and Society* Vol. 22, No. 1 (fall 1995), 7-24.

Shumpeter, Joseph, *Capitalism, Socialism and Democracy* (New York: Harper, 1942).

Silverberg, D., "Global Trends in Military Production and Conversion," *Annals of the American Academy of Political and Social Sciences* (1994).

Silverstein, Ken, "Privatizing War: How Affairs of State are Outsourced to Corporations Beyond Public Control," *The Nation* (28 July 1997), 11–17.

Private Warriors (New York: Verso, 2000).

"US Oil Politics in the 'Kuwait of Africa,'" *Nation* (22 April 2002).

Simon, Herbert, "Notes on the Observation and Measurement of Power," *Journal of Politics* Vol. 15 (November 1953).

Simon, H. A., *Administrative Behavior* (New York: Macmillan 1961).

Singer, Peter F., "Corporate Warriors: the Rise of the Privatized Military Industry and its Ramifications for International Security," *International Security* Vol. 26, No. 3 (winter 2001/02), 186–220.

Corporate Warriors: the Rise of the Privatized Military Industry (Ithaca: Cornell University Press, 2003).

"Peacekeepers, Inc.," *Policy Review* (June 2003), 59–61.

"War, Profits, and the Vacuum of Law: Privatized Military Firms and International Law," *Columbia Journal of International Law* Vol. 42 (2003), 521.

Sirak, Michael "ICRC Calls for Contractor Accountability in War," *Jane's Defence Weekly* (19 May 2004).

Skocpol, Theda, "Rentier State and Shi'a Islam in the Iranian Revolution," *Theory and Society* Vol. 11 (April 1982).

Skons, E., "The Internationalization of the Arms Industry," *Annals of the American Academy of Political and Social Sciences* (1994).

Sky News, "Peace Role for Mercenaries," *Sky News* (13 February 2002).

Slaughter, Anne-Marie, "Law and Politics in the European Union," *International Organization* Vol. 49, No. 1 (Winter 1995), 185-90.

Smith, Adam, *An Enquiry into the True Nature and Causes of the Wealth of Nations* (New York: Modern Library, 1937).

Snidal, Duncan, "Rational Choice and International Relations," in Michael Brecher and Frank Harvey, eds., *Millennial Reflections on International Studies* (Ann Arbor: University of Michigan Press, 2002).

Snider, Don, Robert Priest, and Felisa Lewis, "The Civilian–Military Gap and Professional Military Education at the Precommissioning Level," *Armed Forces and Society* Vol. 27, No. 2 (winter 2001), 249–72.

Snyder, Jack, "Anarchy and Culture," *International Organization* Vol. 56, No. 1 (winter 2002), 7–46.

Snyder, Jack and Edward Mansfield, "Democratization and the Danger of War," *International Security* Vol. 20, No. 1 (summer 1995), 5–38.

Spear, Joanna, "Britain and Conventional Arms Restraint," in Mark Hoffman, ed., *UK Arms Control in the 1990s* (Manchester: Manchester University Press, 1990).

"The Security Sector: The Political Economy of Private Military Security," Fafo Project on *Economies of Conflict: Private Sector Actors in Civil Conflict and War* (2003).

Spearin, Christopher, "Executive Outcomes in Sierra Leone: a Human Security Assessment," paper prepared for presentation at the 2001 annual meeting of the American Political Science Association, San Francisco, CA, 29 August–2 September, p. 12.

"Private Security Companies and Humanitarians: a Corporate Solution to Securing Humanitarian Spaces?" *International Peacekeeping* Vol. 8, No. 1 (spring 2001), 22–44.

Spegelj, Martin, *Sijecanja vojnika* (*Memories of a Soldier*) (Zagreb: Znanje, 2001).

Spruyt, Hendrik, *The Sovereign State and its Competitors* (Princeton: Princeton University Press, 1994).

Stanley-Mitchell, Elizabeth, "The Military Profession and Intangible Rewards," in Cindy Williams, ed., *Filling the Ranks: Transforming the US Military Personnel System* (Boston: MIT Press, 2004), pp. 93–118.

Starr, Harvey, "Cumulation, Synthesis, and Research Design for the Post-Fourth Wave," in Michael Brecher and Frank Harvey, eds., *Millennial Reflections on International Studies* (Ann Arbor: University of Michigan Press, 2002).

Starr, Paul, "The Case for Skepticism," in William T. Gormley, Jr., ed., *Privatization and Its Alternatives* (Madison: University of Wisconsin Press, 1991).

Steinmetz, George, "The State of Emergency and the Revival of American Imperialism: toward an Authoritarian Post-Fordism," *Public Culture* Vol. 15, No. 2 (2003).

Stephen, Chris, "Doing it for Love," *New Statesman and Society* Vol. 5 (10 January 1992), 184.

Stern, Seth, "Contractors Hover in Gray Area Regarding Legal Liability," *Congressional Quarterly Weekly Report* (8 May 2004).

Stetz, Michael, "Private Bodyguards are Essential in Iraq," *Union Tribune* (3 June 2004).

Stiehm, Judith Hicks, "Civil–Military Relations in War College Curricula," *Armed Forces and Society* Vol. 27, No. 2 (winter 2001), 273–94.

Stiglitz, Joseph, "Post Walrasian Economics and Post Marxian Economics," *Journal of Economic Perspectives* Vol. 7, No. 1 (1993), 109–14.

Strange, Susan, *Retreat of the State: the Diffusion of Power in the World Economy* (Cambridge: Cambridge University Press, 1996).

Sugden, Robert, *The Economics of Rights, Cooperation, and Welfare* (Oxford: Blackwell, 1986).

Sunday Times, "FO Muddle Leaves Boss in Firing Line," *Sunday Times* (17 May 1998).

Swidler, Ann, "Culture in Action: Symbols and Strategies," *American Sociological Review* Vol. 51 (1986).

Tadelis, Steven, "What's in a Name? Reputation as a Tradable Asset," *American Economic Review* Vol. 89, No. 3 (1999), 548–63.

Taguba, Major General Antonio M., "Article 15-6 Investigation of the 800th Military Police Brigade," report to US Central Command (March 2004).

Tatalovic, Sinisa, "Military and Political Aspects of the Croato-Serbian Conflict," *Politicka Misao* Vol. 33, No. 5 (1996).

Taylor, Scott, *Inat: Images of Serbia and the Kosovo Conflict* (Ottawa: Esprit de Corps Books, 2000).

Terry, Fiona, *Condemned to Repeat: the Paradox of Humanitarian Action* (Ithaca: Cornell University Press, 2002).

Teson, Fernando, *Humanitarian Intervention: an Inquiry into Law and Morality* (Dobbs Ferry, NY: Transaction Publishers, 1988).

The Nation, "ExxonMobile-Sponsored Terrorism?" *The Nation* (14 June 2002).

The Star, "Are We Fighting Foreign Wars?" *The Star* (10 February 2004).

Thom, William, "Congo-Zaire's 1996–1997 Civil War in the Context of Evolving Patterns of Military Conflict in Africa in the Era of Independence," *Journal of Conflict Studies* Vol. 19, No. 2 (fall 1999).

Thomas, George, John Meyer, Francisco O. Ramirez, and John Boli, eds., *Institutional Structure: Constituting State, Society, and the Individual* (Newbury Park, CA: Sage, 1987).

Thompson, Mark, "Generals For Hire," *Time* (15 January 1996), 34–36.

Thomson, Janice, *Mercenaries, Pirates and Sovereigns: State Building and Extraterritorial Violence in Early Modern Europe* (Princeton: Princeton University Press, 1994).

Tierney, Michael and Catherine Weaver, "Principles and Principals? The Possibilities for Theoretical Synthesis and Scientific Progress in the Study of International Organizations," paper prepared for the Conference on Theoretical Synthesis in the Study of International Organizations, Washington, DC, 6–7 February 2004.

Tilly, Charles, ed., *The Formation of National States in Western Europe* (Princeton: Princeton University Press, 1975).

Tornquist, Olle, "Rent Capitalism, State, and Democracy: a Theoretical Proposition," in Arief Budiman, ed., *State and Civil Society in Indonesia* (Monash Papers on Southeast Asia, No. 22, 1990).

Toronto Sun, "3.7B Oil Pipeline Official," *Toronto Sun* (13 June 2004).

Trease, Geoffrey *The Condottieri* (New York: Holt, Rinehart, and Winston, 1971).

Tribunal Update 68, 16–21 March 1998, "Blaskic Trial: Paddy Ashdown's Testimony," available at ⟨http://www.bosnet.org/archive/bosnet.w3archive/9803/msg00152.html⟩.

Tromp, Beauregard, "Hired Guns from SA Flood Iraq," *Cape Times* (4 February 2004).

Trubowitz, Peter, *Defining the National Interest: Conflict and Change in American Foreign Policy* (Chicago: University of Chicago Press, 1998).

Trunkey, R. Derek, Robert P. Trost, and Christopher Snyder, "Analysis of DOD's Commercial Activities Program," Center for Naval Analyses, CRM 96-63, December 1996.

UK Ministry of Defence, "Strategic Defence Review," MOD White Paper, July 1998.

UK Parliament, "Sierra Leone: Second Report," Foreign Affairs Committee, House of Commons, Session 1998–99, Vol. 1, p. vi.

Select Committee on Defense, Ninth Report, "The Future of DERA," June 2000 (available at http://www.publications,parliament.uk/pa/cm199900/cmselect/cmdfence/462/46203.htm).

Private Military Companies: Options for Regulation (London: Stationary Office, 12 February 2002, HC 577).

Ulrich, Marybeth, *Democratizing Communist Militaries: the Cases of the Czech and Russian Militaries* (Ann Arbor: University of Michigan Press, 1999).

UN, *The Abidjan Peace Accord* (30 November 1996).

"International Convention Against the Recruitment, Use, Financing, and Training of Mercenaries," A/Res/44/34, 72nd Plenary Meeting, 4 December 1989.

UNDP, "Human Development Report 2002: Deepening Democracy in a Fragmented World" (July 2002).

UN General Assembly, Fifty-Sixth General Assembly, A/SCH/3600, 3rd Committee, 31 October 2001, 26th Meeting. Discussion of Document A/56/224.

UN General Assembly Resolution, "International Convention Against the Recruitment, Use, Financing, and Training of Mercenaries," UN General Assembly Resolution 44/34 (4 December 1989).

UNHCR, *Refugee Camp Security in the Great Lakes Region*, EVAL/01/97, Inspection and Evaluation Service (Geneva: UNHCR, April 1997).

UN IRIN, "South Africa: Authorities Target Alleged Mercenaries," (UN IRIN-SA 4 February 2004).

UN OCHA, "Use of Military or Armed Escorts for Humanitarian Convoys" (OCHA Discussion Paper, the United Nations, New York, 2001).

US Central Intelligence Agency, *The World Factbook, 2001* (Washington, DC: CIA, 2001).

US Congress, "Arms Export Control Act" (P.L. 90-629) *Legislation in Foreign Relations Through 1999*, Vol. I-A (Washington, DC: Government Printing Office, 2000).

US Department of Defense, "Improving the Combat Edge through Outsourcing," DOD Report, March 1996.

Report of the Ninth Quadrennial Review of Military Compensation (Washington: DC: US DOD, March 2002).

US Department of Justice, "CIA Contractor Indicted for Assaulting Detainee Held at US Base in Afghanistan" (Press Release, US Department of Justice, 17 June 2004).

"International Criminal Investigative Training Assistance Program (ICI-TAP): Nigeria," http://www.usdoj.gov/criminal/icitap/nigeria.html.

US Department of State, "End Use Monitoring Report for FY 2001" (available at http://pmdtc.org/docs/End_Use_FY2001.pdf as of October 2002).

"Foreign Military Training and DOD Engagement Activities of Interest," Joint Report to Congress, Department of State, Bureau of Political Military Affairs (available at http://www.state.gov/t/pm/rls/rpt/fmtrpt/).

"International Traffic in Arms Regulations" (22 CFR 120–130) as of 1 April 2001 (United States Department of State, Bureau of Political–Military Affairs, Office of Defense Trade Controls).

"Testimony of Colin Powell before the House Appropriations Subcommittee on Foreign Operations, Export Financing and Related Programs," 13 February 2002.

"Voluntary Principles on Security and Human Rights" (US Department of State, Democracy, Human Rights, and Labor, January 2001).

US General Accounting Office, "Contingency Operations: Army Should Do More to Control Contract Cost in the Balkans" (GAO/NSIAD-00-225, September 2000).

USIP Special Report, "Dayton Implementation: the Train and Equip Program" (September 1997) (available at wysiwyg://261/http://www.usip.org/oc/sr/dayton_imp/train_equip.html).

US News and World Report, "Private US Companies Train Around the World," *US News and World Report*, 8 February 1997.

US White House, *"A National Security Strategy of Engagement and Enlargement"* (Washington, DC: The White House, February 1995).

Uttley, Matthew R. H., "Private Contractors on United Kingdom Deployed Military Operations: Issues and Prospects," paper presented at the International Security Studies Section (ISSS) Meeting of the International Studies Association, US Army War College, Carlisle, PA, 1 November 2003.

Vallette, Jim and Pratap Chatterjee, "Guarding the Oil Underworld in Iraq," *CorpWatch* (5 September 2003).

Van Brabant, Koenrad, *Operational Security Management in Violent Environments*, (Washington, DC: Overseas Development Institute, 2000).

Van Creveld, Martin, *The Transformation of War* (New York: Free Press, 1991).

Vandergriff, David, *Path to Victory: a Critical Analysis of the Military Personnel System and how it Undermines Readiness* (Novato: Presido Press, 2002).

Vankovska, Biljana, "Privatization of Security and Security Sector Reform in Croatia" (draft manuscript 2002).

Vaux, Tony, Chris Seiple, Greg Nakano, and Koenrad Van Brabant, *Humanitarian Action and Private Security Companies* (London: International Alert, March 2002).

Velkke, Bernard H. M., *Evolution of the Dutch Nation* (New York: Roy Publishers, 1945).

Venter, A. J., "Soldiers, Inc." *Jane's Defence Weekly* (22 May 2002).

"Sierra Leone's Mercenary War for the Diamond Fields," *Jane's International Defence Review*, Vol. 28, No. 11 (November 1995), 65.

"Gunships for Hire," *Flight International* (21 August 1996).

Vickers, John and George Yarrow, "Economic Perspectives on Privatization," *Journal of Economic Perspectives* Vol. 5, No. 2 (spring 1992), 111–32.

Vincent, J., "Modernity and Universal Human Rights," in A. G. McGrew and P. G. Lewis, eds., *Global Politics* (Cambridge: Polity Press, 1992).

Vines, Alex, "Gurkhas and the Private Security Business in Africa," in Jakkie
    Cilliers and Peggy Mason, eds., *Peace, Profit, or Plunder: the Privatisation of
    Security in War-Torn African Societies* (Pretoria: Institute for International
    Studies, 1999), 123–40.
    "Mercenaries and the Privatization of Security in Africa in the 1990s," in Greg
    Mills and John Stremlau, eds., *The Privatization of Security in Africa*
    (Johannesburg: SAIIA Press, 1999), 47–80.
Volkov, Vladim, *Violent Entrepreneurs: the Use of Force in the Making of Russian
    Capitalism* (Ithaca: Cornell University Press, 2002).
Vukadinovic, Rudovan and Lidija Cehulic, "Development of Civil–Military
    Relations in Croatia," in Plaman Panter, ed., *Civil–Military Relations in
    South Eastern Europe* (Zurich: Partnership for Peace, ISN, 2001).
Wallender, Celeste, "NATO after Cold War," *International Organization* Vol. 54,
    No. 4 (autumn 2000), 705–36.
Walt, Stephen, "The Renaissance of Security Studies," *International Studies
    Quarterly* Vol. 35, No. 2 (June 1991), 211–40.
Waltz, Kenneth, *Theory of International Politics* (New York: Random House,
    1979).
    "The Emerging Structure of International Politics," *International Security* Vol.
    18, No. 2 (fall 1993), 44–79.
Walzer, Michael, *Just and Unjust Wars* (New York: Basic Books, 1977).
Wapner, Paul, "Politics Beyond the State: Environmental Activism and World
    Civic Politics," *World Politics* Vol. 47, No. 3 (1995), 311–40.
Waugh, Peter and Nigel Morris, "Mercenaries as Peacekeepers Plan under
    Fire," *Independent* (14 February 2002).
Wax, Emily, "Bottom of the Barrel," *Washington Post* (21 March 2004).
Weber, Max, *The Theory of Social and Economic Organization* (New York: Free
    Press, 1964).
Weigley, Russell, *History of the US Army* (Bloomington: Indiana University
    Press, 1984).
Welch, Claude E., Jr., "Civil–Military Agonies in Nigeria," *Armed Forces and
    Society* Vol. 21, No. 4 (summer, 1995), 593–614.
Whitelaw, Kevin, "Have Gun, Will Prop up Regime," *US News and World Report*
    (20 January 1997).
    "The Risky Task of Doing Good," *US News and World Report* (21 August
    2000).
Willenson, Kim with Nicholas Proffitt, "Persian Gulf: this Gun for Hire,"
    Newsweek (24 February 1975).
Willetts, Peter, *"The Conscience of the World": the Influence of Non-Governmental
    Organization on the UN System* (Washington, DC: Brookings, 1996).
Williams, Cindy, ed., *Filling the Ranks: Transforming the US Military Personnel
    System* (Boston: MIT Press, 2004).
Williamson, Oliver, *Markets and Hierarchies: Analysis and Anti-Trust Implications*
    (New York: Free Press, 1975).
    "Comparative Economic Organisation: the Analysis of Discrete Structural
    Alternatives," *Administrative Studies Quarterly* Vol. 36 (1991), 269–96.
    "Public and Private Bureaucracies: a Transaction Cost Economic Perspective,"
    Journal of Law, Economics, and Organization Vol. 15, No. 1 (1999), 306–42.

Wilson, Jamie, "Private Security Firms Call for More Firepower in Combat Zone," *Guardian* (17 April 2004).

Wilson, J. Q., *Bureaucracy* (New York: Basic Books, 1989).

Woodward, Susan, *Balkan Tragedy: Chaos and Dissolution after the Cold War* (Washington, DC: Brookings, 1995).

World Bank Group, "IFC Participants Meeting: Oil and Gas" (Washington, 4–5 June 2002) (available at http://www.ifc.org/syndications/pdfs/Kaldany.pdf).

"The Chad–Cameroon Petroleum Development and Pipeline Project," available at http://www.worldbank.org/afr/ccproj/project/pro_overview.htm.

World Commission on Environment and Development, *Our Common Future* (Oxford: Oxford University Press, 1987).

Wulf, Herbert, ed., *Arms Industry Limited* (Oxford: Oxford University Press, 1993).

WWF, "Garamba National Park" (http://www.panda.org/resources/factsheet/general/temp/garamba.htm).

"New Congo in Great Need of Help to Save Endangered Species" (25 July 1997) (wysiwyg://18/http://www.panda.org/news/press/news_140.htm).

"The Fight for Survival" (http://www.panda.org/resources/publications/species/african_rhino/box_2.htm).

Wynn, Colonel Donald T., "Managing the Logistics-Support Contract in the Balkans Theater," *Engineer* (July 2000).

Yates, Douglas, *The Rentier State in Africa: Oil Rent Dependency and Neocolonialism in the Republic of Gabon* (Trenton, NJ: Africa World Press, 1996).

Zamparelli, Col. Steven J., "What Have We Signed Up For?" in "Issues and Strategies 2000: Contractors in the Battlefield," *Air Force Journal of Logistics*, December 1999.

Zarate, Juan Carlos, "The Emergence of a New Dog of War: Private International Security Companies, International Law, and the New World Disorder," *Stanford Journal of International Law* Vol. 34 (1998), 75–162.

Zunec, Ozren, "Civil–Military Relations in Croatia," in Constantine P. Danopoulos and Daniel Zirker, eds., *Civil–Military Relations in the Soviet and Yugoslav Successor States* (Boulder: Westview, 1996).

Index